Stacey

GW01403115

SECRET SELF

FINDING THE POWER OF YOU

Kisses

By Paul Chaplin

Ted
xxxx

❦ **G2** entertainment

ISBN: 978-1-78281-473-3

PREFACE

Just be your Self. It's not like You have a choice.

The Path to Power

This book has its twin in *Matrixial Logic: Forms of Inequality*.[1]

You can think of this book as being Matrixial Logic applied to the realm of Emotion, and completing an understanding of the Self.

Secret Self follows the journey opened by the pathways of *Matrixial Logic*. Through the ideas, arguments and particularly the *Experiences* presented there and here, the Reader can come to perceive a new state of *connection* between the Self and the world.

What I hope the Reader will take away from this book, and its predecessor, is a sense of *liberation*.

> *To understand how we are is*
> *to comprehend who we are.*

It is the combination of that understanding and comprehension which vests the Self with real power. That's the power I would like this book to help You to find.

This is a power which enables You:[2]

---

[1] The Author (2020)

[2] providing a non-exhaustive list

- to use the architecture of your mind to achieve otherwise impossible things
- to revolutionise your ways of communicating with others
- to heal "emotional" traumas
- to banish stress, fear, and phobias
- to achieve meditative states instantly[3]
- to cure disorders in sleep, digestion and other functions
- permanently to "wipe" traumatic memories.

These powers are already within you: whatever your age,[4] whatever your education.

The groves of academe jealously guard their chambers of secrets. So it's necessary to some degree to couch what's written in this book in the obscurantist language of grove guardians. In my Vlog and YouTube videos, I provide a more user-friendly interface for these ideas.

Origins and Outcomes
You can watch lots of videos about Matrixial Logic, CBT theory and practice, and other matters, on my Vlog.[5] And on my YouTube Channel.[6]

In working with people, I came to notice that the *Experiences* which I show in my CBT videos, and discuss

---

[3] that is, in around 1 minute
[4] of such age as able to understand the ideas communicated, that is
[5] www.paulchaplin.life
[6] https://www.youtube.com/channel/UC2h9wOLXwNNwHU9XAHhlN3w/

in *I Want To Love But: Realising The Power Of You,*[7] really do change how people are able to feel their own power. All these *Experiences* are based on the insights and analysis which I first presented in *I Want To Love But*.

Investigating the scientific basis of these *Experiences* and the analysis and insights which created them, resulted in a surprising conclusion:

The architecture of the way that we think and feel
about ourselves and the world
mirrors
the architecture of the world, of reality, itself.

The book, *Matrixial Logic: Forms of* Inequality, analyses that mirroring process. I show there how the way that we think about matters is not an open landscape. There is an architecture to that landscape. However hard we try, we just can't operate outside that architecture.

The way that we can think governs what we can think.

This is a conclusion which, for many, is deeply counter-intuitive. It appears to contradict that view of the Self, which has become the cultural inheritance of the Enlightenment: the idea that our thoughts are both sovereign and limitless in principle.

These presumed attributes of human thought are then

----

[7] The Author (2019)

considered to be the foundations of free will: because our capacity to think is in principle limitless,[8] this is the ultimate domain of freedom.

There have been arguments counter to free will, for as long as free will has had currency as an idea. Usually, such arguments rely on reasoning from Determinism: exclusionary arguments which rebut the sovereignty element of the free will foundation.

In Chapter 9 of *Matrixial Logic*, I demonstrated the attributes of circularity and arbitrariness which inform the deterministic rejection of free will. I explained how these attributes arise from the Singularity of determinism.

I argue that it is a mistake to seek justification for the idea of free will in a presumed state where the mind has distance, or alienation, from reality. We need not be bound in a nutshell of mentative exclusivity in order to count ourselves sovereigns of infinite space.

Instead, we can come to understand the modes of our connection to the world. We can comprehend the way that our Mentation mirrors the architecture of the world, of reality, itself. To be a mirror of limitless reality is to enjoy truly liberated power: both in ourselves and in the world. It is not for me, or this book, to dictate to You how such

---

[8] contingent only on accidents of culture, knowledge and circumstance

power should be exercised. Still, you come to see how that power is vested in You, as a process, not an event. Any process in infinity is always bounded by an arising of being. Thus power in process generates its own consequences: what we like to call morals or ethics.

Out mentative interaction with the world, of course, a two-way process: our mental architecture is a product of our being in the world, and we change the world in its becoming by application of the products of our mental architecture.

Cause and effect is not a useful way of analysing symbiosis. It's not that the world causes us, and we cause it back: like some anthropomorphic snowball fight. We are entangled in the world. It is that very entanglement which fuels the power of You.

The twin book, *Matrixial Logic*, had as its principal concern, analysis of how we think: our *Mentation*. This book is more concerned with how we feel: our *Emotion*.

This book will have things to say about Emotion which may be surprising. The element of surprise gives way to intuition, as the relationship between Emotion and Mentation becomes clarified.

Just as our thinking, our Mentation, has an architecture, so does our feeling: our Emotion. Our Emotive architecture generates the opposite rule to Mentation:

Mentation
The way that we can think governs what we can think

Emotion
What we emote governs how we can emote

We will be spending a significant part of *Secret Self* in examining developmental issues in early life. Although interesting in itself, these issues provide key foundations for all of life.

The architectures which govern Mentation and Emotion are products of genetics and neurobiology, interacting with early years socialisation. It is these together which produce personality homeostasis by around the age of 7. That is the time when the core You, who will be your Self, is fixed. For the rest of your life.

Matrixial Logic explained principles of human engineering. The architectural logic of all human minds.

This book is the engineering manual for the Self. A Manual for understanding how the Self operates. The wiring diagrams which provide that understanding which allows finding the power of You.

A manual for the Self only explains how the Self operates. It doesn't dictate where to go. That's always a matter for You.

If you've picked this volume off a CBT, or self-help bookshelf, then the central message goes: the Power of You is found in understanding your engagement with your Self, in reality.

The central message from a philosophy or logic bookshelf is that: conscious existence is the reality of the world in human Selfs.

On a psychology turntable,[9] the take-home message would be: there are no states,[10] only functions.

In a video library, attention would inevitably turn to *The Matrix* sci-fi trilogy.[11] In that Matrix, the model is of two life forms sharing the same reality: human Zion (with its exploration vehicles), and the machine Source.

Then, there is the matrix, a digital unreality which interfaces between these two antithetical life forms. The A.I. machines created the matrix, but humans can "jack in". The gist is that, while the matrix is not real, it has real influences and effects.

It may or may not [12] help in grounding your view of ML, to try and locate ML analogously in that martrix. So, we

---

[9] we always have to be different
[10] conscious, unconscious, memory
[11] https://en.wikipedia.org/wiki/The_Matrix_(franchise)
[12] especially if you've never seen *The Matrix*

could say that the computer matrix is similar in function (though not operation) to human consciousness. That conscious awareness is an interface between our organic selves (the community of Zion) and the rest of reality.

The take-home from that analogy is that the matrix, in that analogy, is real. It is the architecture of reality.

A Secret
I called this book *Secret Self*, because understanding our Selfs has always seemed to be the biggest mystery of all.

In one perspective: viewing the whole of our human history, our civilisation, religion and science. They all seem to grow out of the collective efforts of Selfs to understand the Self, to direct and shape it in the world.

Philosophy is the history of seeking to understand how the Self understands the world: a world in which there are Selfs. Psychology is the world's attempt to understand what a Self is and how it works, and malfunctions.

Yet, in all the undoubted progress that these disciplines have made, it seems that the essential problems of understanding are reborn with each new human life that enters the world.

Each new Self emerges from the collective history of Selfs, yet is individually different.

The analytic light with which all these disciplines of thought have illuminated collective humanity, yet appears to dim, the moment it turns individually inwards.

Even neuroscience, which can observe the brain's electrical activity and oxygen use, during actual brain functions, can only give us an aggregate observer view.

The Self retains its mystery. It seems that we each live out our lives in the world as the sole bearer of a secret which none of us can understand.

Using Matrixial Logic

You don't have to read *Matrixial Logic: Forms of Inequality*, in order to read and understand most of *Secret Self*.

Matrixial Logic is sophisticated and complicated, because it is dealing with the interface between the whole of reality, and our mental architecture.

In *Secret Self*, you will get more out of the text if you're familiar with Matrixial Logic ("ML") analysis: the equations, the rules of thinking.

In much of *Secret Self*, you'll be presented with analyses and explanations, but without rigorous logical proofs by means of equations and so on. At some points, there will be cross-references.

Also, some parts of *Secret Self* do deploy ML equations. This is so that you can fit the jigsaw pieces together, to make a logically consistent matrix. But you don't have to do that. You can, if you prefer, skip the equations-based text and just take the explanations at face value.

Experiences

All the way through the book, you'll find *Experiences* that I ask you to undertake. It is really important that you follow them.

Through the *Experiences*, you will gain an understanding of the ideas, not just in your intellect, but in your emotion. You also get to remember those ideas, in a way that no amount of blackboard repetition would.

These are experiments, in the ordinary scientific sense:

- we have a theory
- we invent tests of that theory: operations with pre-defined outcomes, derived from the theory
- we test the outcomes against the theory

By doing the experiments, you the reader gain important knowledge. The way you look at the world will change. Sometimes a little: sometimes a lot.

Lines of arguments in this book are challenging to many precepts: in logic, philosophy, psychology and science. Sceptical response is understandable.

The *Experiences* provoke significant difficulties for scepticism. As we say, following an *Experience*:

    whatever is going on here, something is going on.

Matrixial Logic provides an explanation. Now, you can seek to refuse the explanation. But you can't deny the *Experience*. Refuting the ML explanation poses some difficulty: because you only got to do the *Experience* by reason of the practical operation of ML.

If there were only *Experiences* limited in some dimension, then they might be capable of being disregarded as just an artefact of something odd. But you will undergo *Experiences* in many different areas of your interaction with yourself, and the world.

The *Experiences* are not "tricks": you can see every element of them. There are no hidden wires. You just get a simple set of written instructions: you follow them, and you decide what the result is.

The *Experiences* do not operate under hypnosis. There is no induction such as would precipitate a hypnotic state. There's just a few lines of written instructions. Indeed, you will find that you experience a widening of awareness.

Some of the *Experiences* from *Matrixial Logic* are repeated or varied here. That's either because the *Experience* usefully gets a technical point of ML across, without the underlying pages of explanation; or because the *Experience* illuminates some aspect of the Matrix, which is relevant to Emotion, and its interactions in the Self.

The Matrixial Logic Experiments
In conjunction with the publication of Matrixial Logic, the *Experiences* were digested into 3 Sets. The Sets were distributed to 90 volunteer Subjects, selected at random from a data base compiled by an independent research company.

The results are spectacular in their significance.

It's one thing for subjects to self report subjective experiences: they could be mistaken, or inaccurately reporting.

The Experiments *I-Pen* and *Noming*, involve objectively verifiable interactions between the Subject and the world.

These Experiments demonstrated a +50% to +70% positive result. This is undeniable empirical validation.

As the Matrixial saying goes:
  whatever is going on here, something is going on.

It's difficult to assign probabilities to the novel. If even 5% of Subjects reported a positive change interaction in these Experiments, that would be significant.

This book explores and explains the secret Systems

Architecture and Processes of the Self: using Matrixial Logic methods.

That understanding has generated ways of communicating simple directions, which have effect radically to change motor and time functions of individuals: which we can measure against the objective world.

Results from +50% to +70% constitute compelling empirical evidence that this understanding of the Matrixial Self has firm scientific foundation in observable reality.

Matrixial Logic works: and we can prove it.

The experiments will be fully written up, with commentary, in *The Matrixial Experiments.*

Matrixial Healing

Unlike *Matrixial Logic*, this book is not merely a tool for understanding. *Experiences* in this book can be used therapeutically.

Matrixial Healing: the therapeutic uses of the scientific principles of ML, have acquired the labels *Psychotectics* and *Biomorphics.*

The name *Psychotectics* derives from the psychological architecture of the Self. It concerns techniques for using that architecture to effect alterations in Self Systems dynamics.

The name Biomorphics derives from the elements of the discipline:

(1)   human biology: its functions and malfunctions, essentially the landscape of traditional medicine;

(2)   the forms of biological interaction with Mentation and Emotion.

There is a logic to the forms of interaction between our biological processes and how we think and feel about them.

In *Secret Self*, you'll be introduced to Psychotectic and Biomorphic *Experiences*. You'll learn how you can overcome stress.[13] To deal with panic attacks and phobias. To overcome traumatic memories. To en-tune with others in ways that provide you with entire new insights on human relationships.

These *Experiences* are not practices: as in, do X a day for Y days and you may achieve Z. Each *Experience* takes a few minutes. Once your Self has learned from that process, it doesn't need to be repeated.

That's because the learning realised by the Self automatically becomes integrated into the Matrix of the Self.

These short words can't really convey the largeness of the

---

[13] what is often mistakenly referred to as "anxiety"

responses you can have to these *Experiences*. So, turn the following pages, and see for your Self.

These *Experiences* will show you that logic is not the opposite of Emotion. They reveal the logic of Emotion. The most logical process in our Self.

Reading this book is an inverted iceberg experience. The vast majority of the book is taken up with explanation of the components of the secret Architecture of Self, and the Systems which that Architecture reveals. We then deal with Processes under those Systems.

The remaining elements of the book are quite short. That's because once we understand the Self Systems Architecture and Processes, there are revealed many paradoxes, but nothing is secret any longer.

So, we don't labour over long analyses of relationships or the Self in life.

The task here is to set out the architectural and engineering manual of the Self. The journey You each undertake: well that's entirely yours. But at least You can travel with understanding of the vehicle which allows your journey.

Paul Chaplin
2020

PART (1)
THE MAP IS NOT THE JOURNEY

CHAPTER 1

COMPASS

The book, *Matrixial Logic*, provided a new explanation of how our mental life is naturally organised in an architecture.

That architecture is what allows our mental life to occur at all. It shapes the dynamic of our thinking. It is the architecture which both mirrors reality and allows each of us to commune with reality.

- The Matrixial architecture of our mind is what makes reality of our mentation.
- The methods of Matrixial Logic now seek to explain Emotion.

That may seem counter-intuitive. Surely logic and emotion are opposites. Or at least so different to each other, that one can't shine any light on the other.

It's understandable how this view has come about. We consider that we can "see" one thought with another thought. That we can hold our thoughts up to a mirror or structure of instropection. Which allows us to gain insights and to order our thoughts.

It seems, by contrast, that we can't use one emotion to "think" about another. Our emotions just happen. We can try to think about the causes and about the effects, but what happens in between is a landscape which is thoughtless.

The take home message of this book, is that these things seems like they are, just because they aren't. What seems to each of us to be how our Selfs work, is real. But that reality is available to us only because of the *Systems Architecture* of Self.

The Matrixial Logic Compass
So as to avoid the Reader having to trog through 600 pages of *Matrixial Logic,* we do need to cover a basic summary of that ground.

We are not going to present the Reader with a repetition of the rules-based learning of how ML equations work. For that, the Reader should consult Chapters 2-4 of *Matrixial Logic.*

The Fundamental ML Equations
There are 2 key equations in ML:
1.   (A) $\neq$ (nA) = [E]: the equation of Being
2.   (A) $\neq$ (-A) = [I]: the equation of Becoming

There exists a third category, that of Chaos. The equations

of being and becoming are equations of order: which contrast with the inequations of Chaos.

That category of Chaos [C] is important to understand in itself. It also has a derivative significance: [C] produces bridges of Singularity [Si]. Those [Si] bridges are critical in understanding how we, as Self, come from birth to understand the world. But to keep prelimary exposition as uncluttered as possible, we'll reserve detailed discussion to a later Chapter.

The first is the equation of being: [E]:
$$(A) \neq (nA) = [E]$$

This [E] is a frame of reference ("FoR"). It shows how we are looking at something.

The [E] FoR concerns things which exist in spacetime. To exist is to be "extended" in spacetime. That is, we could in principle assign a set of 4 dimensional spacetime co-ordinates to the thing.

We denote that thing as (A). The brackets don't have a function: they are simply there to keep matters tidy.

The second is the equation of becoming: [I]
$$(A) \neq (-A) = [I]$$
This [I] is a frame of reference ("FoR"). It shows how we are looking at something.

The [I] FoR concerns things which are becoming: the water flow in a river; the growth of a tree. An equivalent way of stating:

$$(A) \neq (-A) = [I]$$

is to write:

$$\Delta^n \sum \infty$$

by which we mean: moments aggregated in infinity.

Technically, $[\Delta^n \sum \infty]$ is the *Nodal form* of the [I] equation. That's something we will certainly get to later.

Let's undertake our first *Experiences* in *Secret Self*, so we can gain more prespective on these concepts.

Experience: Suspended
Setup:
Open your eyes and visualise in your room
A ball (about basketball size)
Suspended from the ceiling by a stiff rod (say about 6 feet long).
Something like this:

Step 1:

Now:

• move the ball (vertically) up and down the rod

Discussion:

(1)   Easy.

Step 2:

Do not use the picture for this: use your visualisation in your room.

Now, without moving the rod:

• move the ball (horizontally) off the rod sideways

Discussion:

(1)   The ball just won't move.

To use the catchphrase of ML *Experiences*:

Whatever is going on here, Something is going on

The ball is Substance in an FoR. The ball is defined by and so captivated by, its form of inequality [E].

$$(A) \neq (nA) = [E]$$
$$>$$
$$(Ball\ on\ Rod) \neq (nBall) = Rod\ [E]$$
$$>$$
$$(Ball\ on\ Rod) \neq (Space\ on\ Rod) = Rod\ [E]$$

That is why the ball won't move off the rod. In the

architecture of your Mentation, you have created an inequality equation: a relationship of things in which the contents [(Ball on Rod) ≠ (Space on Rod)] cannot exist for you, in your mind, without the form = Rod [E].

This is the first, and fundamental rubric of the Self:
>*How we can think governs what we can think.*

Experience: Rods
Setup:
As in Suspended:

> Open your eyes and visualise in your room
> A ball (about basketball size)
> Suspended from the ceiling by a stiff rod (say about 6 feet long).

And now:
Visualise another rod suspended vertically from the ceiling (say about 6 feet long)
About 6 feet away from the 1st rod.
Something like this:

Step 1:

Now:

- move the ball (horizontally) from one rod to another
- and back again

Discussion:

(1)   Easy.

Step 2:

Now, without moving the rod:

- move the ball in any direction away from both the rods

Discussion:

(1)   The ball can move a little.

(2)   But it's like there's a magnetic attraction, pulling the balls back to one of the rods.

The ball is Substance in an FoR. The ball is defined by and so captivated by, its form of inequality [E].

If you think about the relationships created here, the Rods have been defined as Ball carriers, and the Ball as that which "activates" a Rod: but has no existence apart from a Rod.

$$(A) \neq (nA) = [E]$$
$$>$$
$$(\text{Rod } 1) \neq (\text{Rod } 2) = [E]$$
$$>$$
$$(\text{Rod } 1) \neq (\text{Rod } 2) = \text{Ball } [E]$$

That is why the ball feesl stuck to the rods. In the architecture of your Mentation, you have created an inequality equation: a relationship of things in which the contents [(Rod 1) ≠ (Rod 2)] cannot exist for you, in your mind, without the form = Ball [E].

Later in this Chapter, we're going to see how the same "thing" can function in different Plenums, as Substance, and then as Form, depending upon the context.

But, that alteration of FoR completely changes the nature of the "thing". It's something we may not notice. After all, the Ball image looks exactly the same in the *Experiences of Suspension*, and *Rods*. It just looks like, well, a ball.

Yet the function of that entity in the architecture fo your mind is completely different in those two *Experiences*: you've just felt it.

> *How we can think governs what we can think.*

This is the Aristotelian problem of changing a Subject into a Predicate:

- In *Suspension*, the Ball functions as a Substance: a Subject.

$$(Ball\ on\ Rod) \neq (Space\ on\ Rod) = Rod\ [E]$$

- In *Rods*, the Ball functions completely differently, as a Form: a Predicate.

$$(Rod\ 1) \neq (Rod\ 2) = Ball\ [E]$$

These are not the same function. The architecture of your mind treats them completely differently. Yet the Ball appears as exactly the same:

- graphically: as an image
- in vocabulary.

We all know that looks can be deceiving. Matrixial Logic tells us that:

Appearance is not equivalent to Form

This is a useful rule in thinking about thought. It's a vital rule in thinking about Emotion.

We've run a couple of *Experiences* to demonstrate the reality, in the architecture of your mind, of:

1. $(A) \neq (nA) = [E]$: the equation of Being

Now, let's visit the other realm of Order:

2. $(A) \neq (-A) = [I]$: the equation of Becoming

Experience: Droplet
Setup:
With your eyes open or closed -
    Visualise a single droplet of water
    Dripping down a tile

Something like this:

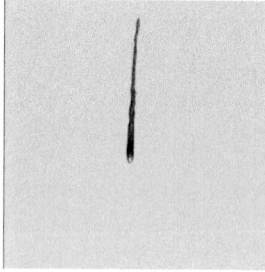

You need to make sure that you see the droplet as having movement; that it's dripping, and moving; not static.

Do not use the picture for this: use your visualisation.

Step 1:

Now:

• make the droplet change course

Discussion:

(1)   Perhaps after a brief hesitation, you can change the course of the droplet, so it starts to run left, or right

Step 2:

Again: do not use the picture for this: use your visualisation.

Now:

• make the droplet create loops

<u>Discussion</u>:

(1)   Now that you've taken control of the droplet in the architecture of your mind, you can move the droplet freely.

You can do this because the [I] FoR concerns things which are becoming: the water flow in a river; the growth of a tree.

Following the [I] equation:
$$(A) \neq (-A) = [I]$$
$$>$$
$$(\text{Droplet Place}) \neq (\text{Droplet Place}^n) = \text{Tile [I]}$$

Remember that the function of the operator (-A) is to denote change in (A).

An equivalent way of stating:
$$(A) \neq (-A) = [I]$$
is to write:
$$\Delta^n \sum \infty$$
by which we mean: moments aggregated in infinity.

If the tile was infinite, we could say:
$$(\Delta \text{Droplet Places}^n) \sum \text{Tile} \infty$$

You will have felt that Infinity ∞ function. In Step 2, when you started manipulating the dropley freely, you will have felt that notion: this could go on forever.

Experience: Pane

Setup:

With your eyes open or closed -

> Visualise a single droplet of water
> Dripping down a tile

Something like this:

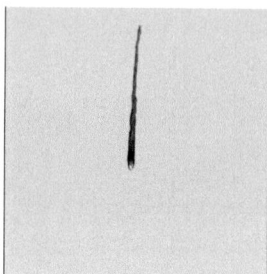

You need to make sure that you see the droplet as having movement; that it's dripping, and moving; not static.

Do not use the picture for this: use your visualisation.

Step 1:

> <u>Take the tile away. Disappear it. Make it gone.</u>

Now:

• move the droplet

<u>Discussion</u>:

(1)   The droplet won't move

(2)   It's like the droplet is suddenly frozen

(3)   It won't even run like it did at the start of *Droplet Experience*.

Here we go again, with ML *Experiences*:[14]
   Whatever is going on here, Something is going on

You created the droplet and tile. You disappeared the tile. It's all in your head. Surely, you control the contents of your own head, at least those which you deliberately create?

What's going on is you experiencing, for yourself, in your own reality:
   How we can think governs what we can think.

Following the [I] equation:
$$(A) \neq (-A) = [I]$$
$$>$$
$$(\text{Droplet Place}) \neq (\text{Droplet Place }^n) = \text{Tile } [I]$$

But we removed: = Tile [I]

$$(A) \neq (-A) = [I]:$$
$$><$$
$$\textbf{(Droplet Place)} \neq \cancel{(\text{Droplet Place }^n)} = \cancel{\text{Tile } [I]}$$

Without a context of tile Infinity ∞, the droplet lost its quality as Δ^n. The droplet became an isolate, suspended

---

[14] we won't keep repeating after this: promise

and frozen in its being. It could no longer participate in a process of becoming.

Yet the Droplet appears as exactly the same:
- graphically: as an image
- in vocabulary.

As Matrixial Logic tells us:

Appearance is not equivalent to Form

This may seem crazily complicated. That thinking just about one ball, or one drop of water, can be so multi-layered, so complicated. How do we ever get any productive thinking done?

The short answer to that is: by taking short-cuts. By abstracting so that the different architectural functions of Ball (as a Substance, or as Form) don't matter to the reasoning computation.

That's achieved by the Theta Θ axis field. We'll come to that later.

Our Emotion is also very good at taking short-cuts. It has to be, otherwise we'd never make it through a minute of the waking day. How that all works is what much of *Secret Self* is about.

Nodes in Matrixial Logic

We said earlier:

An equivalent way of stating:

$$(A) \neq (-A) = [I]$$

is to write:

$$\Delta^n \sum \infty$$

by which we mean: moments aggregated in infinity. Technically, $[\Delta^n \sum \infty]$ is the *Nodal form* of the [I] equation.

Chapters 4 and 5 of *Matrixial Logic* provide detailed explanation of Nodes.

For the purposes of this summary here, let's confine ourselves to this:

A Chi ⅏ Node occurs when an Event $<\sum E>$, which is a combination of [E] Forms of Substance contents, interacts with a course Δ^n of Infinity ∞.

A Phi Φ Node occurs when one <set of Moments Δ^n in Infinity ∞> meets another.

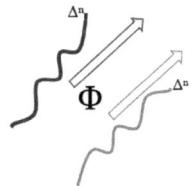

This creates an Interference Node, rather than a Point Node.

Let's use some Experiences to meet the differences between Chi ⅏ Node[15] and Phi Φ Node.

---

[15] this "Chi" has nothing to do with the body-energy concept: it's just an accident of nomenclature

Let's start with the Chi 市 Node, by doing a simple thought experiment:

> Imagine you tap your fingers to a beat, which you run in your head, at about 1 beat per second.
> *Where is the most reality in this scene?*

Most responses would say: on the beat. That makes sense. It's where you're actively interacting with reality. So let's test that:

Experience: Chi
Setup:
Take the two largest fingers
of the hand you usually write with
Get them ready to tap
On your table top, or your thigh

Step 1:
Now:
- Give yourself a slow rhythm (about 1 tap per second)
- Tap once each beat

Discussion:
(1)   Just notice how you set up an expectancy.
(2)   You created a framework with a *potential* [∠].[16]
(3)   That potential was active as expectancy in the gaps between the beats.

_____
[16] we will be explaining this in a few pages

Where was the most reality in this Experience?
Outside of this Experience, there was an obvious answer. Yet inside it, you understand a very different answer. Why is there such a difference?

It's because you engaged your Emotional | E | *potential* [∠].[17]

A Chi 丽 Node occurs when an Event <∑E>, which is a combination of [E] Forms of Substance contents, interacts with a course Δ^n of Infinity ∞.

You created a "river" of [∠] potential finger-tap Moments Δ^n in Infinity ∞:

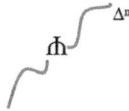

This manifested a Frame of Expectancy ("FoE"). Visualise you, right now, looking at this graphic: that's an analogue of your FoE in this experience.

The tap is the Chi 丽 point. It manifests the Expectancy, and realises the [∠] potential.

Now, let's look at the Phi Φ Node.

---

[17] which is stating without explaining; we'll explain in a few pages

Experience: Phi

Setup:

Read the directions then do the simple actions.

Just close your eyes and allow yourselkf a bit of calm space

Imagine just lying on your sofa, or a sun lounger

Step 1:

Now:

- Just be there, calmly, for a few moments

Discussion:

(1)   Review the history of your head.

(2)   As you replay the *Experience*, notice that you were breathing.

(3)   Just regular, calm, breaths

Step 2:

Back to just lying on your sofa, or a sun lounger

Now:

- Just be there, calmly, for a few moments
- Focus on your breathing, where you are, right now

Discussion:

(1)   Compare your process to that in the *Chi Experience*.

(2)   You can see that in this *Phi Experience*, you had no FoE.

(3)   There was no interaction with a "river" of [∠] potential.

(4)   Instead, your braething just happens, you notice it. That's all.

Why is this like this? It's because your finger-tapping is an arificially manufactured event. You're not born with an organic need to tap your fingers.

By contrast, your breathing is autonomic. You're definitely born with an organic need to breathe. So, you don't need to manufacture an FoE in which breaths will happen. They'll happen automatically.

So:
- finger-tapping creates an FoE
- breathing does not create an FoE

As we said:

A Phi Φ Node occurs when one <set of Moments Δ^n in Infinity ∞> meets another. This creates an Interference Node, rather than a Point Node.

In the graphic, the amber river is your autonomic breathing: $<\Delta^n \sum B>$.

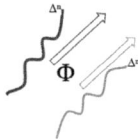

The blue river is your directed awareness: $<\Delta^n \sum A>$.

Together, these create an Interference. This doesn't means something harmful. It just means that one dynamic interacts with another.

Those two arrows indivcate that another process is also going on:

$$<\Delta^n \sum B> \neq <\Delta^n \sum A> = [x]$$

We'll come to that later.

For now, we've introduced the ML concept of the Chi ᛘ Node and Phi Φ Node, and shown you difference between them.

What Time?
Due to currently vexed questions in quantum field theory, we cannot simply say "becoming in space time".

Indeed, there are fundamental issues with the concept of spacetime. We will encounter some of these later. For the groundwork, please see Chapter 7 of *Matrixial Logic*.

ML Fundamental Principles
These are the principles which will inform everything we do in *Secret Self*. We will use them explicitly. And we'll find them coming back at us in places we didn't expect: emerging out of the landscape of Mentation and Emotion.

The fundamental principles of ML are:

- no thing has existence in isolation
- no thing is identical to any other thing.

That nothing solitary exists, is the ML *Law of Plurality*.

That there is never identity between things, is the *ML Law of Inequivalence*. This is the function in equations of the inequality ≠ sign.

We think that we are doing our reasoning under the rubric of identity: (A) = (A). This is an inheritance from Aristotle, through the medieval Scholastics and through into the Modern.[18]

Matrixial Logic showed that we don't actually think like that. Indeed, if you pause for a moment, and consider, it becomes very difficult to envisage how we could ever really think like that. Thorny questions arise from such an idea: such as some of the following.

(i) On what basis are we supposed to determine whether one (A) is identical to another (A)?
(1) Just by looking: but how could that be a reliable metric?
(2) By some inherent a priori knowledge: in which case we couldn't know that we know.[19]
(3) By reference to some external metric: in which case we are denying any independent reality to any (A), and

---

[18] see Chapter 3 *Matrixial Logic*
[19] all a priori reasoning is an infinite regress to some Singularity, express or disguised

making it merely a manifestation of that metric.

(ii) Even if we could determine, by some mystical process, that one (A) is identical to another (A), where exactly would that get us?

We can't derive originality, novelty or indeed change from a a tautology: and that's all an identity consists of.

In fact, as Chapters 4 and 5 of *Matrixial Logic* show, version (3) is exactly how we go about parts of our Mentative process: the Theta Θ operations.

As we do so, we are not following a law of identity: we are abstracting attributes and placing those under a computation. We transform things in the world, as represented in our /S/ubjective mind, in to the equivalent of logical operators.

That transforming happens through our Scalar /S/ thinking process. In /S/ thought, we use rules of similarity, not identity. We recognise, categorise, and analyse through analogy. We use inductive reasoning to arrive at premises, then build on those premises through deductive reasoning.

So: no thing in the world, is identical to any other thing:

$$(A) \neq \text{anything else}$$

The world is a reality of inequalities $\neq$.

We think of the world in *Forms of Inequality.*

We should also mention a third ML Law: the *Law of Plenum.* This states that the concept of existence can be applied to any things (in plurality) only as extensions of a Form of existence.

The Law of Plenum can also be stated as: any Form is the form of its contents. This is the *hylopmorphic principle.*[20]

Mentation and Emotion

Now that we are in the landscape of the Self, we need to denote two fundamental categories:

| M | Mentation
| E | Emotion

| M | is the realm of thought. That is thought which operates in /S/ axis fields and Theta Θ axis fields.[21]

| E | is the realm of Emotion. The | E | realm uses a different form of equation to the equations of Order:

1. $(A) \neq (nA) = [E]$: the equation of Being
2. $(A) \neq (-A) = [I]$: the equation of Becoming

---

[20] it differs fundamentally from the hylomorphic arguments of Aristotle: in ML, it is a law about the architecture of how we perceive, not the attributes of what is perceived

[21] see Chapters 5 and onwards in *Matrixial Logic*

The equation used in | E | is:

$$(\epsilon) \neq (\partial) \sum \Omega^{22}$$

This is a very different mode of equation to those of Order: [E] and [I]. That's because Mentation | M | works differently to Emotion | E |.

We will be examining the Ohm equation in much more detail later. At this stage, let's just note some aspects.

The symbol (ϵ) denotes an <emote>. An <emote> is not a thing, nor is it a moment. It is a *potential* [∠]. That potential ∠ may be constrained or amplified by its antigone [≠(∂)].

The aggregate function $\sum$ then represents the cumulation of those potentials in dynamic differentiation: [(ϵ) ≠(∂)].

Finally Ohm Ω itself represents not a quantity, but a *registration*. In order to understand what this means, let's take a simple example:

(1)   an <emote> (ϵ) has a potential ∠(x)
(2)   an <emote> (∂) has a potential ∠(y)
(3)   the imbalance, or inequality ≠ between those
         potentials signifies $\sum$ a registration Ω.

Some Readers may notice a broad analogy between the Ohm equation and the equations in electricity and electro-magnetism.

---

[22] spoken as "Ohm"

That's an interesting analogy. We developed the equations and concepts for $|E|$ out of applied Matrixial Logic. It then became apparent that the concepts do bear analogy to, for example, the behaviour of electrical circuits.

So, we can take a simple classic circuit diagram, and the formulas of Ohm's Law:

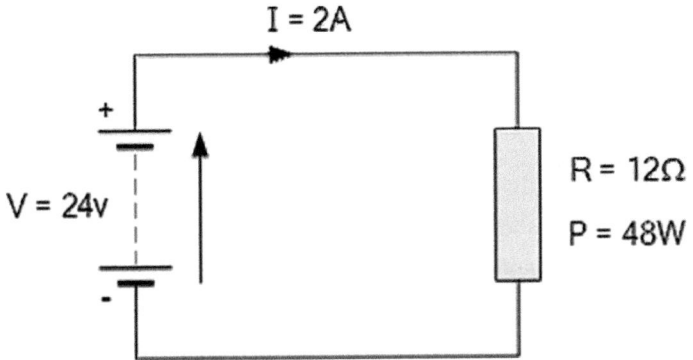

I = 2A

+

V = 24v

R = 12Ω

P = 48W

-

Voltage $[V = I \times R] = 2 \times 12Ω = 24V$
Current $[I = V \div R] = 24 \div 12Ω = 2A$
Resistance $[R = V \div I] = 24 \div 2 = 12 \ Ω$
Power $[P = V \times I] = 24 \times 2 = 48W$

The Ohm $Ω$ equation "plugs" in at each stage of the circuit. Thus you could analogise the voltage gap as:

$[(\epsilon) \text{ potential } \angle(2)] \neq [(\ni)) \text{ potential } \angle(12)] \sum_{24} Ω$

An electrical circuit is a classic reaction/action dynamic. There exists a dynamic potential. When an event occurs, the potential reacts, realising action: with an electrical crcuit in the mode of power.

Revisiting the *registration* concept, we see a positive registration in $[\sum_{24} \Omega]$ in the voltage example. But suppose that the potentials $\angle^n$ were differently oriented, or differently affected. That could result in a smaller, greater, or nil registration.

As we uncover more of *Secret Self*, we will discover that:
   | E | is a reaction/action dynamic across potentials.

We then will see:
- how that dynamic can be activated
- what results from the activated dynamic
- why it matters

in understanding our Selfs.

Directions to Nowhere
Modern psychology and philosophy both set their foundations in the secrecy of the Self.

There is your internal self-life: something which is in part knowable only to you, and yet much of which you can't really know.

Viewed like that, these are sciences of the unknowable. We can study behaviours and assign cause-effect relationships to behaviour patterns.

We can then reason by similarity, and say: You behave like (x), as do other people and therefore [diagnosis]. But it's not a diagnosis as in medicine. A knee or a spine or a kidney has its function. The same function for everyone. But the whole point of recognising that there are selves, is that no thought or feeling has the same function for everyone.

Indeed, we don't analyse in these sciences in terms of functions, but in experiences. And our starting point is that each individual has one thing in common: that the experiences of each Self are unique.

We can reason in aggregates. We say: because (X) number of people are observed to behave (Y) way under (Z) stimulation, this tells us something.

We can then generate principles, and apply ideas which we reason from those principles, to individuals:

Observed Micro-Population

(Z)	(X)	(Y)	[C]
Stimulation	Observed People	Response	Psychological Conclusion

Individual Self

[C]	(Z)	(Y)	Self
Psychological Analysis	Stimulation	Response	As if Observed Person

This is the approach of science since the Enlightenment. By

induction, we generalise rules derived from experiments. We then apply those general rules to particular cases, so as to make predictions.

So long as we appreciate what it is we're doing and the means by which we are doing it: great advances in knowledge can be made.

But there is a trap. It's as old as formal reasoning. Until Matrixial Logic revealed it, we didn't even realise the trap was there.

This inductive approach to thinking about anything relies upon two key assumptions:
(1)   That the law of identity (A=A) is valid
(2)   That syllogistic reasoning is valid.

While we were limited by those two assumptions we could never get deeper than artificial and arbitrary superficiality. In the disciplines of mathematics, physics and chemistry, we don't need to go deeper, in order to realise profound consequences.

We have changed the world with a logically constructed set of empirically validated understandings of substances and processes in nature.

We have never found a need to understand the internal "life" of a molecule, or a quark: because we do not for a moment suppose that they have one.[23]

We thus need to understand these atomic process only at the superficial level of how the elements of one atom (in process as energy) relate to another. Then build up from there.

We are not saying thyis is a trivial exercise. It's way beyond the pay-grade of the Author. But the exercise is predicated upon the eminently sensible proposition that no atom has any individual opinion about the matter.

Indeed, the bedrock assumption of the material sciences is that one atom[24] is exactly the same as another. One electron, one photon, one gluon or meson (etc): each is identical in its properties and functions as another. That is also a conclusion derived from exhaustive experimental data.[25]

We can call this the axiom of *functional identity*. Nothing in this book is intended to cast the slightest doubt upon that assumption or conclusion. The axiom of functional identity is secure in the physical sciences.

But the idea of identity also assumes another guise. That

---

[23] proponents of panpsychism aside

[24] of one element

[25] with the interesting anomalies of entanglement, quantum foam, point density matter, and so on

the attributes of something in thought are the same as the attributes of something else: the axiom of *attributive identity*.

Matrixial Logic shows that the axiom of attributive identity does not operate in the realm of human thought. It is absolutely not the case that A=A. Indeed, (A) never attributively equals anything else in the universe conceived in human thought.

Upon that realisation, the categorical syllogism also fails:
• All men are mortal
• Socrates is a man
∴ Socrates is mortal.

Summarising what is set out in intricate detail in Chapter 3 of Matrixial Logic: this most elementary Barbara form of categorical syllogism, is false.

We can see that immediately from Table 3.6 in Chapter 3 of Matrixial Logic:

Ackrill/Aristotle Categorical Sentence Transitions to ML

	C S	ML Equation	Type
A	Every A is B	$(A) \neq (-A) = B[I]$	Categorical Universal
E	No A is B	$(A) \neq (B) = N[E]$	Reflexive Universal
I	Some A is B	$(A^n) \neq (nA^n) = B[E]$	Reflexive Opposition
O	Not Every A is B	$(A^n) \neq (-A^n) = B[I]$	Reflexive Negation

Table 3.6

That is because the term "men", which is used as a subject in the first premise, then as a predicate in the second premise, is not the same term at all.

The change from uiversal subject to particular predicate seems to be an application of the Universal Affirmative (A) categorical sentence: *All men are mortal.*

But it really isn't. The Universal Affirmative operates under the form of [I]: as iterations of a process, an infinity:
$$(A) \neq (-A) = [I]$$

But the statement <Socrates is a man> operates under the [E] form, as a substance in opposition:
$$(A) \neq (^{NOT}A) = [E]$$

Conjoining these two forms [I] and [E] involves *crossing the matrix*. That crossing is disguised by the linguistic manifestation of the concepts. But they are very different concepts.

Another way of making the same point, although perhaps a less accessible way,[26] is that the words "are" and "is" do not merely constitute singular and plural conjugations of the verb "to be". They are synthetically different concepts, in these contexts.

To return to the *Suspended* and *Rods Experiences*, concerning that ball. You remember how, when the Ball was in relationship to a rod, the ball could move up and

---

[26] unless the Reader has ploughed through Chapter 3 of *Matrixial Logic*

down the rod. And then between rods. But the ball could not just move anywhere off the rods.

All because the ball was an entity operating under two completely different functions: in one case as Substance; in the other case as Form.

Having reached this stage in exposition, we can now sophisticate the analysis of those *Experiences*.

In Suspended, we saw the fulfilment of the equation:

$$(A) \neq (nA) = [E]$$
$$>$$
$$(Ball\ on\ Rod) \neq (nBall) = Rod\ [E]$$
$$>$$
$$(Ball\ on\ Rod) \neq (Space\ on\ Rod) = Rod\ [E]$$

This is, of course, a typical (O) form of Categorical Syllogism: Some A is B. Sometimes the ball is <here> on the rod and sometimes <here^n>.

Now, to help understanding at that stage, we posed the Rods equation as:

$$(A) \neq (nA) = [E]$$
$$>$$
$$(Rod\ 1) \neq (Rod\ 2) = [E]$$
$$>$$
$$(Rod\ 1) \neq (Rod\ 2) = Ball\ [E]$$

But, as you may have guessed in retrospect (having done the *Droplet* and *Pane Experiences*), the *Rods Experience* is not really about [E] at all:

$$(A) \neq (-A) = [I]$$
$$>$$
$$(Rod\ 1) \neq (Rod\ 2) = [I]$$
$$>$$
$$(Rod\ 1) \neq (Rod\ 2) = Ball\ [I]$$

In your mental architecture, the function of the ball is to provide a form for the rods, in terms of movement of the ball. It is change of position Δ^n of the ball with respect to the rods, which comprises the mode of existence of the ball.

Because we truncated the *Rods Experience*, the implications of an equation in [I] was not obvious:

Experience: Rodness
Setup:
As in Rods:

> Open your eyes and visualise in your room
> A ball (about basketball size)
> Suspended from the ceiling by a stiff rod (say about 6 feet long).

And now:
Visualise another rod suspended vertically from the ceiling (say about 6 feet long)

And now:

Visualise a whole population of rods suspended vertically from the ceiling (say about 6 feet long)

Something like this:

Step 1:

Now:

- move the ball (horizontally) from one rod to another
- and back again

Discussion:

(1)   Easy.

Step 2:

Add many more rods

Now:

- move the ball in any direction from rod to rod
- if you want to move where there isn't a rod: add a rod, then move to it

<u>Discussion</u>:

(1)   Now that you can just add a rod anywhere that
       you want to the ball to be, it's easy to move.

Clearly, you could create a sea of rods, each coming into
existence so that the ball can move. And as the ball moves
from $<\text{rod}_1>$, you can allow that $<\text{rod}_1>$, to disappear as
$<\text{rod}_2>$ appears; and so on:

       It is change of position Δ^n of the ball with respect
       to the rods, which comprises the mode of existence
       of the ball

We have granted the ball an infinity ∞ of spatial movement
in Δ^n <rods>. We have created ball-space.

So, we see that the *Rods Experience* was really an illustration
of (A) form of Categorical Syllogism: Every A is B.

In the (A) form of Categorical Syllogism, <Ball> operates
as a Predicate. In the (O) form of Categorical Syllogism,
<Ball> operates as a subject.

And the "so what" of all this is that you can't just swap out
<Ball> as Predicate and <Ball> as Subject without *crossing
the Matrix*. Not, that is, without violating the architecture
of your mind. A mode of logic which relies upon doing
exactly that can't really support a claim to being useful.
Yet, for 2,500 years: exactoy that claim has been made.

Let's test the utility, for your mental architecture of the idea that the mere descriptive properties of the ball (spherical, yellow and so on) and its functional identity (of the class of balls which can move on poles), completely determine its Attributive Identity.

Experience: Sine
Setup:
As in Rods:

> Open your eyes and visualise in your room
> A ball (about basketball size)
> Suspended from the ceiling by a stiff rod (say about 6 feet long)
> and
> Visualise a whole population of rods suspended vertically from the ceiling (say about 6 feet long)

Something like this:

Step 1:
Do not use the picture for this: use your visualisation.

And:

- move the ball from one rod to another

Now:

- pull the ball away from the rods, towards you

Discussion:

(1)   Moving the ball between rods is easy.

(2)   Pulling the ball towards you, is not easy.

The ball feels "stuck" to the rods. The ball has been created in your mental architecture as the form of the rods:

> It is change of position Δ^n of the ball with respect to the rods, which comprises the mode of existence of the ball

You are trying to take a ball, which in your mind exists as a Form :

$$(\text{Rod } 1) \neq (\text{Rod}^n) = \text{Ball [I]}$$

and to use that Ball [I] as if it had a spatial relationship to in Substance you:

$$[\text{Ball}] \neq [\text{nBall <you>}] = \text{Spatial Distance [E]}$$

You see the attempted transition here:

$$(\text{Rod 1}) \neq (\text{Rod}^n) = \text{Ball [I]}$$

$$[\text{Ball}] \neq [\text{nBall <you>}] = \text{Spatial Distance [E]}$$

Experience: Rounds

Setup:

As in *Sine*:

> Open your eyes and visualise in your room
> A ball (about basketball size)
> Suspended from the ceiling by a stiff rod (say about 6 feet long)
> and
> Visualise a whole population of rods suspended vertically from the ceiling (say about 6 feet long)

And:

Visualise a second ball

levitate it so that

Ball2 floats in the room an arm's length away from you

just above head hight

Something like this:

Step 1:

Do not use the picture for this: use your visualisation.

And:

- focus on Ball2
- allow otherBall and rods to fade away
- move Ball2 up/down and sideways a little
- pull Ball2 towards you and away from you

Then:

- bring otherBall and Rods back into focus

Now:

- Put Ball2 onto a rod

Discussion:

(1)   Ball2 will move towards a rod

(2)   You can even get Ball2 to almost touch a rod

(3)   But then it's like a force is repulsing Ball2 from the rod.

But these two balls are identical. You visualised them so. They are completely identical in their properties. Yet they will not function in attributive identity.

OtherBall has become, in the architecture of your mind, a Form [E]. You made Ball2, in the architecture of your mind, Substance, in realtion to <you> and Spatial Distance [E].

You just experienced that you can't get either ball to cross the matrix: to assume attributive identity.

We will see more about this in Chapter 7 *Shadows*.

So: the fundamental logical form of reasoning expressed in the Barbara mode of Categorical Syllogism, is wrong:

> The change from uiversal subject to particular predicate seems to be an application of the Universal Affirmative (A) categorical sentence: *All men are mortal*.

> But it really isn't. The Universal Affirmative operates under the form of [I]: as iterations of a process, an infinity: $(A) \neq (-A) = [I]$

> But the statement <Socrates is a man> operates under the [E] form, as a substance in opposition: $(A) \neq (^{NOT}A) = [E]$

> Conjoining these two forms [I] and [E] involves *crossing the matrix*. That crossing is disguised by the linguistic manifestation of the concepts. But they are very different concepts.

For any reader even slightly versed in classical logic, or its modern first-order iterations, this all seems so bizarre, that it can't possibly be true.

The logical Reader has felt the impact of these Experiences.

Whatever is going on, something is going on. But surely, the logical Reader protests, it can't be that there's something wrong with a form of reasoning which is 2.5 millenia old: and which forms the basis of logical reasoning?

Perhaps the notion of a Universal Class provides a solution. Let's just "solve" these *Experiences* in Categorical Sentence mode (A): <Every (A) is (B)>.

Experience: Uni

Setup:

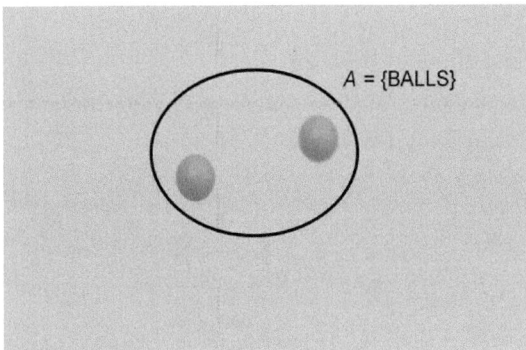

Let's clear a space in our mental architecture.

> Here's the set of all yellow balls.
>
> They are all identical: so A=A.
>
> So: <Every (A) is (B)>.

These are the UniBalls we are going to work with.

As in *Rounds*:

> Open your eyes and visualise in your room

A UniBall (about basketball size)

Suspended from the ceiling by a stiff rod (say about 6 feet long)

and

Visualise a whole population of rods suspended vertically from the ceiling (say about 6 feet long)

And:

Visualise a second ball

levitate it so that

UniBall2 floats in the room an arm's length away from you

just above head hight

Something like this:

See the Universal Set connecting the UniBalls.

Feel their connectedness: that they are the same, identical, in the framework of that Universal Set.

You know that Universal Set is true.

Step 1:

Do not use the picture for this: use your visualisation.

Now:

• Swap the UniBalls

Discussion:

(1)   Both are stuck.

Step 2:

Do not use the picture for this: use your visualisation.

Repeat the logical truth to yourself:

A=A.

So: <Every (A) is (B)>.

See the Universal Set connecting the UniBalls.
Feel their connectedness: that they are the same,
identical, in the framework of that Universal Set.
You know that Universal Set is true

Now:

• Move one UniBall from one rod to another

Discussion:

(1)   It won't move.

You can, with effort, get the rod-held UniBall to move.

But, review the history of your head. You achieved that

63

only by breaking the Universal Set connection. You had to treat the UniBall which you want to move as being different from the other UniBall. *You had to violate the law of identity in order to allow dynamic.*

As we said earlier:

> Indeed, the bedrock assumption of the material sciences is that one atom is exactly the same as another. One electron, one photon, one gluon or meson: each is identical in its properties and functions as another. That is also a conclusion derived from exhaustive experimental data.

> We can call this the axiom of *functional identity*. Nothing in this book is intended to cast the slightest doubt upon that assumption or conclusion. The axiom of functional identity is secure in the physical sciences.

> But the idea of identity also assumes another guise. That the attributes of something in thought are the same as the attributes of something else: the axiom of *attributive identity*.

The UniBalls do not even have functional identity. That's because they are not like atoms, which exist in nature. They are manifestations of a manufactured (Si).

So, now you can see why Matrixial Logic takes the view

that the attributive law of identity, and its function in syllogistic reasoning, are not the compass needles which can usefully map a geography of the Self.

These twin concepts:

$$A=A.$$

And:

$$<Every\ (A)\ is\ (B)>$$
$$<Some\ (x)\ is\ (A)>$$
$$\therefore\ <Some\ (x)\ is\ (B)$$

have proven to be barriers to uncovering of the Self. The concepts have functioned, by deductive reasoning, to ever greater abstractions from the reality of Self.

In the same way that, once you abstracted any reality ball, into a "Universal Set" (all balls are round and yellow), that abstraction just could not be plugged back into reality.

What's more, these twin concepts are ultimately derivatives of Singularity. The Universal Set is an artificial (Si). We can derive content relationship for reality from naturally occurring (Si): we do it all the time, as later Chapters will show.

But a manufactured (Si) is a non-dynamic, a "dead" abstraction. It is neither Substance, Moment, nor Form. It can't function in reality, because it is not part of reality.

We will see that we manufacture (Si) all the time. It's what we call *Shadow Slices*.[27] It's a significant way that we try to control our interface between Mentation and Emotion.

The short story on that[28] is:
- it doesn't work
- it creates huge problems in efficient function of the Self
- it is significantly implicated in addiction behaviours.

The idea of Singularity and the conception of god overlap. Deistic thinking is the anthropomorphic analogue of thinking in Singularity.[29]

It is only by positing a universal, which is outside reality, that any part of reality can be conceived of as an iteration Δ^n of an "ultimate" truth.

It is only under a Universal form that iterations can be conceived of as having identity: not in relation to each other, but in relation to the Universal.

Thus (A) relates to [I] as an iteration Δ^n of [I]; and what ML would denotes as (-A) also relates to [I] as an iteration Δ^n of [I]; and those iterations have attributive identity (or equality). Thus A=A in [I].

————————————

[27] see Chapter 7

[28] just to let you know that there are these "real people problems" discussions to look forward to in later Chapters

[29] there will be more on this in later Chapters too.

That all looks perfectly reaonable. But the reality of the matter is that, in this Singularity-based logic (A) has no independent attribute of Existence [E]. Which is why the second premise of Barbara is wrong: no such thing as "a man" exists, such that Socrates can be it.

Indeed, all that "exists" is [I] in its iterations [Δ^i]. But to self-iterate is not to exist. Becoming is not the same as being.

Your Uniballs could function only as iterations of the Set of Uniballs. That Set is outside reality: you made it so when you chose to think that A=A.

So, the axiom of *attributive identity* leads inevitably to abstraction, not merely from the Self, but from existence: from any thing in being. From that hypothetical point of Singualrity, whatever path we tread back is arbitrary, and can only navigate in the superficial.

Which almost amounts simply to saying that we cannot treat Selfs like atoms. The same method which is used in the material sciences, can't be applied to the Self.

This doesn't mean that the methods we use in discovering the Self are any less scientific. Rather, it's an acknowledgement that, whereas material sciences can use a functional identity shortcut (without which material science really couldn't be done at all), Self sciences can't use an attributive identity shortcut.

When Self sciences do use an attributive identity shortcut, it's the wrong direction to nowhere. You end up with useless UniBalls.

All Points Everywhere
In this Chapter, we have started understanding, through the analysis and *Experiences*, a compass for the Self.

A compass which follows the rules of Matrixial Logic. The equations show us how to orient the instrument.

We've explored how any orientation device which relies on the law of identity <A=A> can't guide us anywhere in the domain of the Self.

The Experiences have also shown us that we are not creating a compass. We are discovering the orientation mechanisms that are built into our mental architecture.

We are born with this architecture. It is our genetic and biological inheritance. Yet it still seems shocking to suggest that:

How we can think governs what we can think.

This rubric appears to run counter to our deepest Enlightenment convictions about the sovereignty of the Self, free will, and foundations of ethics.

It looks to have more in common with religious creationism, than the blind evolution of the human Self.

We will go on to discover that these deeply held beliefs are in fact the vestiges of millenia-old superstitious thought. It comes as something of a shock to realise that what we consider to be an utterly modern scientific and materialistic conception of self: isn't.

It is the progress of material science and technology, which has long left behind our thinking about the Self. We've created a shadow show, in which the way we do material science has become utterly divorced from the way we like to think we're doing it.

That very progress has in turn become part of the process by which the reality of the Self starts to become uncovered. The frontiers of quantum physics, cosmology, biology, chemistry and computing,[30] have smashed the law of identity in the material sciences.

It's a strange vestigal idea that A=A could survive the theories of relativity. QM entanglement, missing particles, the inability to form a grand unified field theory. The mystery of human interactiuon with the material world. All these problematics have moved material science away even from the assumtion of *functional identity*.

---

[30] amongst others

How counter-intuitive does it really need to be that:

Mentation
How we can think governs what we can think

Emotion
What we can emote governs how we emote

We can only see and hear parts of the electromagnetic and audio spectrum. We need a heart and lungs and a circulatory system. These essentials are part of what being a human Self is.

We have these brain structures which in their gross formation and attributes are alike for every human ever born.[31]

Why then should it be so odd that the architecture of these systems of Mentation and Edmotion should be fixed?

Fixed architecture does not imply, or require, limitations upon freedom. That architecture is active in Nodes of infinity ∞. No spacescape of any other conception could provide boundless multiples of infinity.

The supposed disconnect between the Self and material reality is what poses limitations: the exact opposite of the sovereign self agenda.

---

[31] save for exceptional defects

Suppose that a photon or an electron[32] were a sovereign self, demarcated from all that it is not. That would make for a poor universe. Indeed, there could be no cosmological reality at all.

The architecture of the Self is neuro-biologically fixed. Yet it is that very fixing, which allows human kind to participate in reality, such as to create the conditions of technological civilisation.

Our highest dreams, our deepest thoughts, our churning emotions, our very senses, are able to interact with reality, and to shape it to our designs, because that architecture exists.

Some may never wish to move beyond the fantasy that a god exists,[33] and that we are the equal manifestations of that Singularity, granted sovereignty in our selves. As a fantasy, it's inherently contradictory. As a model of reality, it's useless. But you're the boss of You.

We have begun to discover the Matrixial Logic compass of the Self. Now let's go look at the map.

---

[32] or their respective constutuent quarks
[33] by whatever name such Singularity may be called, from era to era

CHAPTER 2

GLOBE

This is the map.

$$(\epsilon)$$
$$\text{ᚦ} \quad /S/\{E\}$$
$$\sum \Omega \quad (T) \neq (nT) \quad = \Theta \approx >$$
$$\Phi \quad /S/\{I\}$$
$$(\partial)$$
$$<\sum \maltese^{*}> \Leftrightarrow (\supset^{n}) \neq (-\supset^{n}) | \maltese^{n} \Leftrightarrow <\sum \maltese^{*}>$$

With the primary equations for the map dynamics: the equations which provide the compass.

Matrixial Logic explained part of the architecture of these elements of the Self map:

72

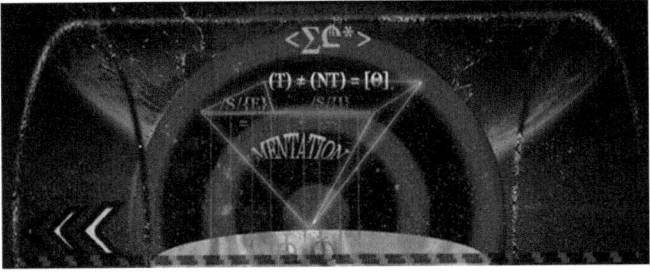

Secret Self explains the architecture of this part of the Self map:

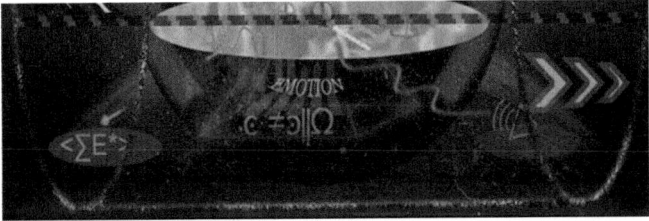

and then puts the whole Globe together.

We then apply what we have discovered, in practical therapeutic methods: *Psychotectics* and *Biomorphics*.

The map is not like an atlas. The Self is a globe. A spinning entity: indeed an entity that spins one way in its top half and the other way in its bottom half.

That's what the striped equator line represents. All of this needs explaining: we will.

This Chapter is almost an entire book in itself. Referencing this Globe, we need to travel inwards and outwards, inside, and upwards and downwards.

So, unusually as a matter of our usual editorial style, we are providing Section break headings, and numbered sectors. These are map markers, to allow the reader to see where we have reached in these journeys.

SECTION A: |M| ENTATION

1.   *Connecting Views*

In the rest of this Part 1, we will build out the wirework for:

- |M| entation
- |E| motion
- |T| ime.

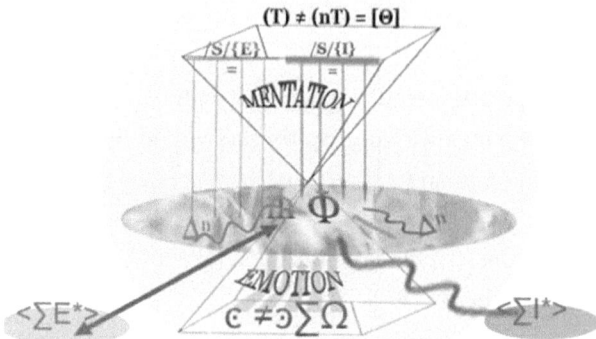

We need to state something now. As we layer up the Matrix of the Self, these statements will become more meaningful, and more evidenced:

The Matrixial Self Trilogism

(I)   Self is Reality.

(II)   Self is a constant dynamic of Becoming, which at every moment of Time is in Being.

(III)   Self is the reality of the world in its process in human entities.

The immediate important implications of the Matrixial Self Trilogism ("MST") are:

(1)   Each model of Mentation and Emotion, is not a representation of static elements.

(2)   The models show dynamics: elemental processes.

(3)   When we speak of "architecture" we don't actually mean a fixed structure, like a building.

(4)   This "architecture" describes the self-limiting nature of those processes.

(5)   The Mentation | Emotion model is not like a biochemical model, or the dissection of a frog, or the pattern of a snowflake, or a building plan.

(6)   It's not that Mentation is "above" and "Emotion" is below.

(7)   These are dynamic, interactive processes, in and of the human body and brain: but not in any par-

ticular organic place.[34]

(8)   The interaction of the Self with the external world is always, that is: at every moment, fixed in place and time.

(9)   The Self is thus always in Being: which is an *absolute*.

(10) Yet, the Self is also in Becoming, in each Chronal Gap (see *Time* Chapter), and each Becoming is *relative* to every other.

It may help to give an example of how Matrixial modelling works. Suppose we were creating a material sciences model of <rainwater>.

We would want the chemical elements of <water>, being H_2O. Ultimately, that can take us into modelling the energy quotients in those atoms, right down to the sub-atomic quark level. And modelling the forces involved.

With those elements of the model, we will be able to define the "architecture" of the process of those elements. That process is self-defining, and self-limiting as <water>. Those elements, in that atomic combination, can't make anything else.

---

[34] Neuroscience has been able to specify places in brain architecture which relate to certain states: but always with the caveat (if stated regorously) that it is always the entire neural network that is ultimately implicated.

We will then put that <water> model in context, in material reality. We will analyse that <water> may assume the properties of liquid, gas, or solid. So, we define the conditions in which it is liquid.

Then we turn to atmospheric systems, which brings us to chaos theory, and gravitation.

And throughout these model lattices, we will be folding them into a cylinder of Time.[35]

Finally, we get a dynamic model of <rainwater>.

Now, we can't easily assign by way of analogy, elements of the ML model of Self, to this rainwater example. Obviously, the droplets don't have the choice of thinking about whether to rain or not.

Still, what this analogy should demonstrate is that, when we model in the material sciences, we create lattices of elements, and then layer them into a dynamic matrix. As the lattice elements become part of the whole dynamic, we more closely approach reality.

So it is with Matrixial modelling. There is a matter of caution. Models can be very powerful in their explanatory force. They can come to be our reality for that which is

---

[35] which, given the problematics of Time in quantum mechanics, is not easy: and not easily reconcilable with Einsteinian spacetime

being explained, rather than the real world thing itself.

Science itself has had to cope with these "paradigm shifts"[36] again and again. Where a model takes such a hold over thought, that enquirers end up being excommunicated. By way of examples: from civil society: Socrates; from religious society: Galileo; from scientific society: endless examples, right up to 2020.

But surely you, the reader, are more sophisticated than that. Such paradigm-stickers must have a defect of reason or culture.

Surely, we can choose our perspectives freely, if we choose to. Let's test that:

Experience: Lens
Setup:
Find a Landscape to look at
Could be a park, or garden
The bigger the vista, the better this *Experience* will work

You can use the image provided if you really have to: but please click the link and bring up the biggest size of it you can.

---

[36] *The Structure of Scientific Revolutions.* Thomas Kuhn (1962)

LANDSCAPE IMAGE

Step 1:
Relax your gaze upon the image
Notice whatever you notice

Next:

Visualise in your head a Lens
You look through the lens with both eyes.
The lens is clear: it does not distort in any way

It help to form your forefinger and thumb into a circle,

hold that half an arm's length away and look through that: to give you the sense of the lens visual.

Now:
- put that Lens over one part of the Landscape view (not the whole Landscape)
- focus your visual attention through the Lens

Stop

Discussion:
(2)   You notice that the non-Lens Landscape fades out of view.
(3)   This will be something familiar to anyone who has used spectacles, or binoculars.

So, what does that tell us about paradigm views? Not very much that we didn't already know. Obviously, we can choose not to look through the Lens, and just view the Landscape as we did before the Lens was introduced. Can't we?

Step 2:
Enact the same Setup, with Landscape and Lens.

Next:
Leave the Lens floating there, looking at the Landscape

In your mind's eye,

You take position so that you are viewing the Landscape and Lens, like this:

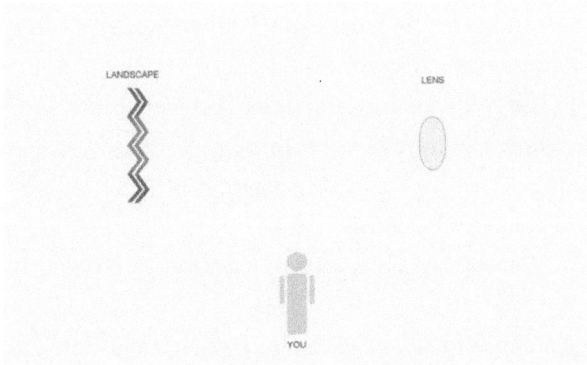

Do it with your own view: don't use this graphic.

Now:
• try viewing through the lens from where you are

Stop
<u>Discussion</u>:
(2)   Now you find that you can't see through the Lens

Step 3:
Continue with Setup as per Step 2

And: while holding the presence of Lens in your attention

Now:
• try to view the Landscape
Stop

Discussion:
(1)   You can't really see the Landscape
(2)   You know the Landscape is there, but you can't focus a view on it
(3)   The more you try, the more you feel stuck
(4)   Now you can't see anything

We meet again the rubric:

> *How we can think governs what we can think.*

Being unable to see at all, seems worse than only being able to see from a limited perspective. Perhaps the elders of Athens, in their scarred psyche after losing the Peloponnesian war, had a point.

This Mentative *Experience* had, for you, an Emotional quality. The *Matrixial Logic* book looks, from the outside, like it would be an unemotional passage through intellectual courses. Yet the *Experiences* in that book, although designed to articulate explanation of the ideas, were also (and deliberately) constructed so as to engage Emotions.

But this is deeply counter-intuitive: how can just thinking about a Landscape and Lens get emotional?

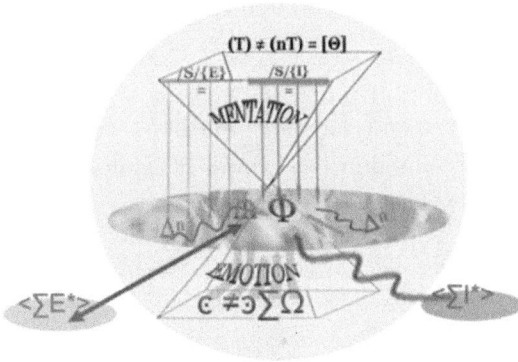

Our Mentation does engage our Emotions. The connection between our Mentation and our Emotions is the core of Self.

Mentation-Emotion synergy is the fusion of diffusion.

We will unwrap this rubric over the pages to come.

Within Matrixial Logic, and its application to the Self, such paradigm shifts occur deliberately. We change the viewing Lens for the Landscape, in such a way that you don't become stuck: you become more liberated.

Using ML is a heuristic process. You learn by doing learning. During that process, your understanding of what something, or some relationship, or some equation "means", becomes changed.

That's why the equations are so important. They are the

paths which we travel through the architecture of all the paradigms.

We want to spend most of this book discussing the working of Emotion |E|, and its interaction with Mentation |M| and reality.

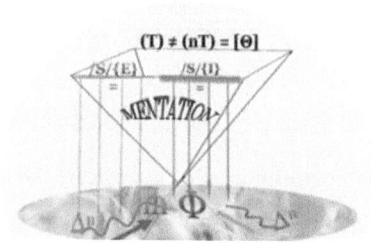

So, we first need to provide the ML working model of Mentation |M|. We did that in *Matrixial Logic*.[37] So, here, we are just going to summarise the "top half" of the Self globe.

This will be a series of assertions, not explanations. The explanations and *Experiences* to support them can be found in *Matrixial Logic*.

---

[37] especially Chapters 4 and 5

2.   *<Node>s and Reality*

We want to reach a jumping-off stage in the Matrix of the Scalar /S/ axis fields.

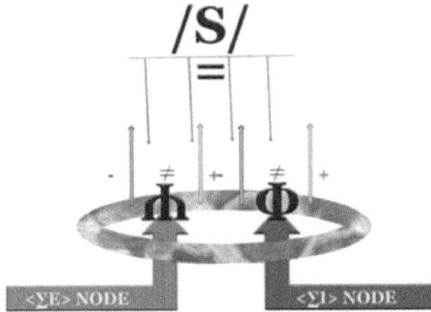

How this process works is explained in detail in Chapters 4 and 5 of *Matrixial Logic*.

Let's begin with <Node>s. To summarise:

(1)   A <Node> <∑E> is created when 2 Forms of [E] (or[I]) interact.

(2)   Such a <Node> is inherently unstable.

(3)   A form of a Form does not exist in itself in reality.

(4)   It is the way that the existence of actual things in reality is transmitted to us (and indeed through out the world).

That sounds odd, at first. Don't we, for example, just look at things, see them, and so know them. It certainly seems like that: because we have no reason to notice the architecture of observation.

Yet, just as there is an architecture of Mentation: that which constrains your thinking about balls and rods, and landscapes and lenses; so there is an architecture which limits our observational interaction with reality.

We need <Node>s to interact with reality, even though we don't realise it. Let's experience this.

Experience: Cap
Setup:
Recreate this simple Scene on your desktop, or coffee table:

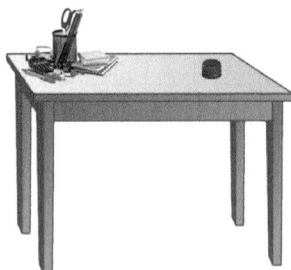

The Scene elements are: desk; various objects; and the cap from a water bottle.

Please use the actual Scene in your room, not the guidance graphic.

Step 1:
Relax your gaze upon the image
Notice whatever you notice

Now:

- Think of moving the Cap around the desk

Stop

<u>Discussion</u>:

(1)   This is easy.

(2)   It perhaps takes a little concentration, but once you're relaxed into it, no problem.

Step 2:

Clear the table, so there is only the Cap on the table top:

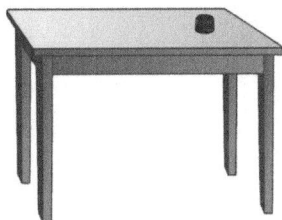

Please use the actual Scene in your room, not the guidance graphic.

Now:

- Think of moving the Cap around the desk

Stop

<u>Discussion</u>:

(1)   This is easy.

In both these Scenes, you are visualising with <Node>.

At Step 1:

(1)   There are Substance relationships between the Cap; the desk stuff; and the desk in 3D space (although obviously represented in 2D in the graphic).

(2)   The inequalities combine to produce a combination of Content inequalities:[38]

$$(Cap) \neq (Table) = TableCap \; [[E]$$
$$\neq$$
$$(Table) \neq (Stuff) = TableStuff \; [E]$$
$$\text{and so on} =>$$
$$<\textstyle\sum CapSpace>$$

(3)   There are multiple <Node>s here.

(4)   This <∑CapSpace> <Node> allows you to create Scalar /S/ relationships of +/- movement in a plane.

At Step 2:

(1)   There are fewer <Node>s.

(2)   But the table in 3D space, in the room, is sufficient to create a <Node>:

$$(Cap) \neq (Table) = TableCap \; [[E]$$
$$\neq$$
$$(Table) \neq (Legs) = TableStuff \; [E]$$
$$\text{and so on} =>$$
$$<\textstyle\sum CapSpace>$$

---

[38] we are not being rigorous with the equation formulations here. For more detailed workings of <Node>s, see Chapters 4 and 5 of Matrixial Logic

(3)   Again, this <∑CapSpace> <Node> allows you to create Scalar /S/ relationships of +/- movement in a plane.

Since we don't usually think about what is allowing us to see, or otherwise experience, the outside world, we don't spend much time thinking about it.

Material science has a full explanation of the physics, biology and neurology of vision. But what that leaves out, is the architecture of that process, for |M| Mentation and Emotion |E|.

Your experience of everything is context dependent. Stated in a "weak" way, that is an iteration of the obvious. Of course, what we experience and how we experience it, depends on context.

The concept of <Node>s transforms that weak dependency into a structural limit of architecture. The architecture of the human mind is such that experiences of outside objects and events can only come to us through <Node>.

This point is of such importance that it's being stressed here, because what matters for our |M| Mentation matters in like manner for our Emotion |E|.

It's understandable to think that no such architecture exists. Because it's invisible: until we can see it. So let's see it now.

Experience: Flick
Setup:

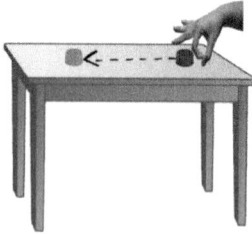

This is similar to *Cap*.

Please arrange your table top so there is only the water bottle Cap on it.

Please use the actual Scene in your room, not the guidance graphic.

Next:
Flick the Cap with your finger.

Step 1:

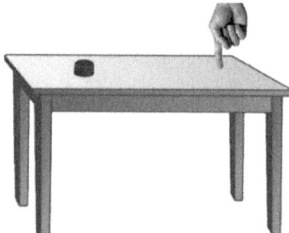

Hold your finger down in the table, at the point you flicked the Cap

Now:
Look at the Cap on the bare desktop, and

• Think of moving the Cap back to your finger

Stop
<u>Discussion</u>:
(1)   It's stuck

You just can't visualise the Cap moving at all. The more you focus, the worse it gets. You can think the abstract thought about moving the Cap: but you can't realise that thought in the architecture of your Mentation |M|.

If you have been trying really hard to realise that "move" thought, you |E| will have become engaged. Feelings of frustration, puzzlement.

Why are we suddenly in this position? What's changed as a matter of <Node>s to make our |M architecture unable to process movement visualisation?

The answer is that, by holding that finger on place, You are placed as part of the scene. If you recall the *Lens Experience*, the finger is acting like the Lens. It is fixing our Frame of Reference.

Our |M| architecture is seeing the Cap "through" its relationship to our finger. We are designed to behave like this. It's the architecture which would allow us to catch that Cap if it were thrown towards us.

Let's put this into ML equations:
$$(Cap) \neq (nCap) = ?[E]$$
$$>$$
Let's say that the table top functions as (nCap) here:
$$(Cap) \neq (Tabletop) = Exists\ (place)\ [E]$$

We are not able to get a movement relationship out of that inequality.

We don't get to apply a Scalar /S/ [+ / -] ordination of space in which the Cap can move:

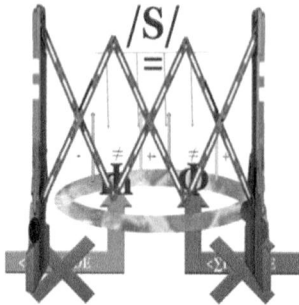

Because there is no <Node>. All we have to work with is this:

It's like the classic *Soloclip Experience*, which we worked through, in various iterations, in *Matrixial Logic*.

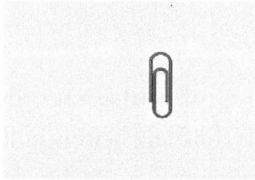

Why is that Cap dimension of existence so limited? Because our finger has created and is maintaining a fixed spatial framework in which there is no <Cap Exists> substance:

Remember that <Substance is that which is extended in spacetime>.[39]

The fixed index finger is creating a spacetime FoR, in relation to that Cap. The ≠ inequality as a form of extension which is limited by the fixed index finger:

(Cap) ≠ (Tabletop) = Exists (place) [E <finger space>]

---

[39] *Matrixial Logic*. Chapter 2 and Appendix

Without the <finger>, the <Cap> does not exist. But with the <finger>, the <cap> has no extension in spacetime other than <finger>.

So: <cap> cannot move. And you're shortly going to to discover an even more extraordinary consequence for the absence of <Node>.

This paradigm does, of course raise deep issues about how we function as thinking beings in the world:

(1)   One index finger has effect to so limit the function of our mental architecture, such that what ought to be a trivial exercise in Mentation |M| becomes impossible.

(2)   Is that a truth about our entire Mentative existence in the world?

(3)   Does a similar architecture subtend our Emotional |E| experience?

These are large questions. Much of this book is concerned with answering them.

Our |M| depends upon being able to assign co-ordinate axis values within a field.[40]

So, our |M| architecture is more than merely context dependent, in a weak or trivial sense. In order to function,

---

[40] we're going to unwrap this proposition in a few pages.

our |M| architecture needs reality to present itself to us in <Node>.

In *Flick,* we created a Scene in which there was no <Node> which allowed thinking under a form of movement. Now, we're going to vary that Scene, to allow that thinking, within the architecture of your Mentation |M|.

Experience: Allow
Setup:

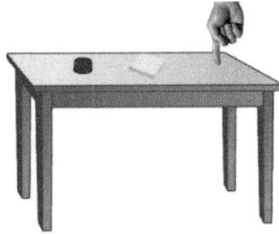

This is similar to Flick.

Please arrange your table top so there is the water bottle Cap on it.

And also now place a pack of post-it notes, or some other small object, between finger and Cap.

Please use the actual Scene in your room, not the guidance graphic.

Step 1:

Now:
Look at the Cap, and

- Think of moving the Cap back to your finger

Stop
Discussion:
(1)   Now, you can move the Cap

It's as though the pad creates a 3d Sphere of movement possibilities.

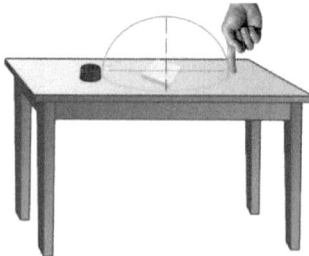

So you can:
- "jump" the Cap over the pad
- circle the Cap around the pad.

As we explained in Chapter 4 of Matrixial Logic:
$$A <Node> <\textstyle\sum ...] \; is$$
any convergence of two Forms in the same domain.

This is a <Node>: $(\square 1) \neq (\square 2)$ [~] $<\sum E>$

In ML, we do say "form of forms" because it has a nice ring. But it is, strictly, an oxymoron. That is why there is no aequalis = joining the two sides but instead a Nodal [~].[41]

Let's put the *Allow Experience* into ML equations:
$$(Cap) \neq (nCap) = ?[E]$$
$$>$$
$$(Cap) \neq (Pad) = 3d \; Space_1 \, [E] \approx (\square Cap_1)$$
$$>$$
$$(Cap) \neq (Pad) = 3d \; Space_2 \, [E] \approx (\square Cap_2)$$
$$>$$
$$(\square Cap_1) \neq (\square Cap_2) \, [\sim] <\sum CapMove>$$

So, now we have a <Node> $<\sum CapMove^n>$.

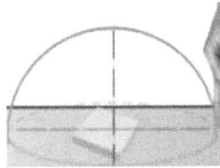

This is not merely theoretical, or abstract. You have seen that you actually cannot think the thought of the Cap moving, without this <Node>: the Cap is stuck. That is your reality. Suppose that:

---

[41] we often just do without the [~]

- "stuck" Cap position was closer to you, and the Cap were a searing fire. That matters
- the Cap were a speeding car on a trajectory through its static point (orthagonal to you), and it was going to hit someone. That matters.
- the Cap represented any reality of opportunity or danger: it all matters.
-

So, now we have a <Node> <$\sum CapMove^n$>. The Cap can move. But what type of <Node> is it? You are still stuck in the Scene:

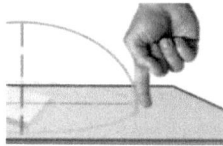

This is not a <Node> of free movement Δn in [I] Infinity ∞. The <Node> point is Chi m̅, not Phi Φ:

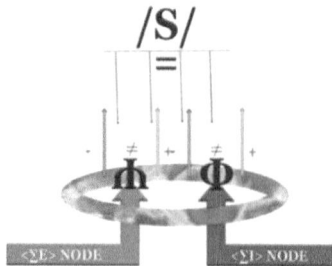

The Cap can move, but you are stuck.

As you can see, this is a strange situation for the operation of your Scalar /S/ axis:

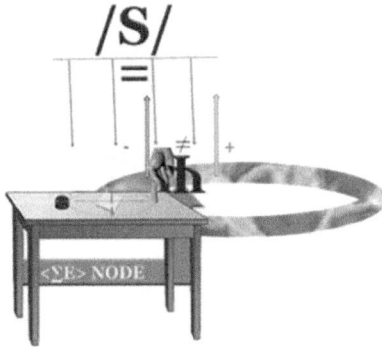

You are trying to apply /S/ logic to a Scene which you are part of.

Essentially, you are trying to look at reality from the point of view of your own fingertip. Your Frame of reference for reality is not whatever can be seen to exist before your eyes, but what can exist as a <Node> <$\sum$CapMove^n>.

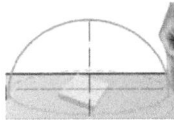

That <Node> can be realised by lots of different movements of the Cap [Move^n]. But all movements are limited to your strange /S/ FoR.

Let's see the difference between this artificially restricted

FoR and the one you're used to in daily reality.

Experience: Allow 2

Setup:

Visualise this Scene, as in *Allow*:

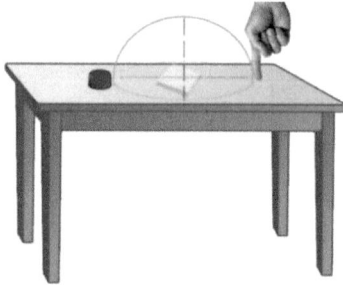

Step 1:

Look at where your finger tip is on the table

Mark that point in your head

Take your finger away from the table.

Now:

• Think of moving the Cap back to where your finger tip was

Stop

Discussion:

(1)   Now the Cap moves freely again

By taking yourself out of the scene, you've made a radical change in the FoR:

You as part of Scene   You not in Scene

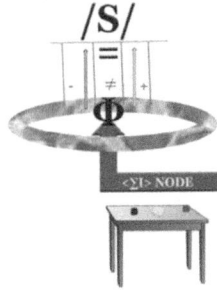

This is why the Cap now has complete freedom of movement. It can move to where your fingertip was, or anywhere else.

It may be useful to restate the ML Rules laid out in Chapter 4 of *Matrixial Logic*:

> Hopefully, it is self-evident from all that has been written before, that:
>> *an Event <$\sum E$> and an Interference <$\sum I$>,*
>> *cannot possibly be the same sort of phenomenon:*
>> *whether in the world, or in perception.*[42]

---

[42] here intended to be a vacuous catch-all word for whatever one might term as "subjective", or occuring inside human beings, their minds, their feelings

Tabulating the essential differences between [I] and <∑I>

Form and <Node> in [I]

Form [I]	<Node> <∑I>
• in Potential	• of Potential
• mediated by ≠ with	• interacting [~] with
• Moment (A), (-A)	• Form $\Delta\,\Delta$
• stable	• unstable
• dynamic	• static
• self-actualising	• externally actualised
• deductive	• inductive

<Node> relates to the Contents of its constituent Forms, only indirectly.

When we simplified:

(1.1) $([(A^1) \neq (-A^1) = [I^1]]) \neq ([(A^2) \neq (-A^2) = [I^2]])$ [~] $\sum(FoR_2)$

$$\approx$$

(2.1) $(\Delta 1) \neq (\Delta 2)$ [~] $\sum(FoR_2)$

$$>$$

(2.2) $(\Delta 1) \neq (\Delta 2)$ [~] <∑I>

the underlying cross-dynamics at (1.1)
are present in the <Node> as the function of its
Potential in Infinity, but present differently:

[I] Form is   in Potential.
<∑I><Node> is   of   Potential.

Again, this is not saying that we cannot "map" <∑I> <Node>s onto the real world. We can.

Interference, Infinity and Potential

Moment (A), (-A) is a Potential Δ^n in Infinity ∞.

It is tempting to give examples from the "real world". But any example we give at this time will serve only to detract from the explanation.

Interference Φ

We have seen that Interference between Potentials $\Delta\,\Delta$, can create <∑I> <Node>s.

Potentials may *interfere* with each other, producing a simulacrum of an Event <∑E>.

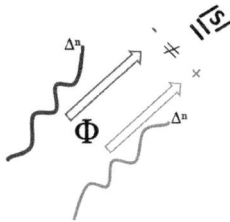

Interference does not prompt or effect Collapse $\square$ of any Potential.

And, as we stated in *Compass*:

A Chi ሐ <Node> occurs when an Event <∑E>, which is a combination of [E] Forms of Substance contents, interacts with a course Δ^n of Infinity ∞.

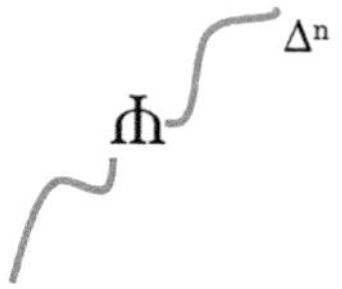

A Phi Φ <Node> occurs when one <set of Moments Δ^n in Infinity ∞> meets another.
This creates an Interference <Node>, rather than a Point <Node>.

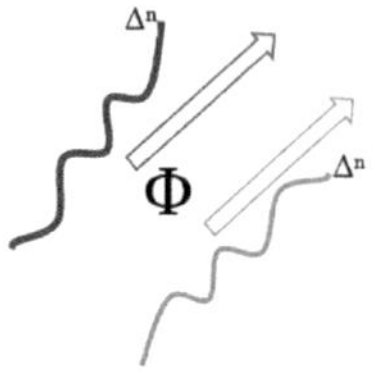

So, we now have, with the fingertip out of the way, and free space for the Cap to move in:

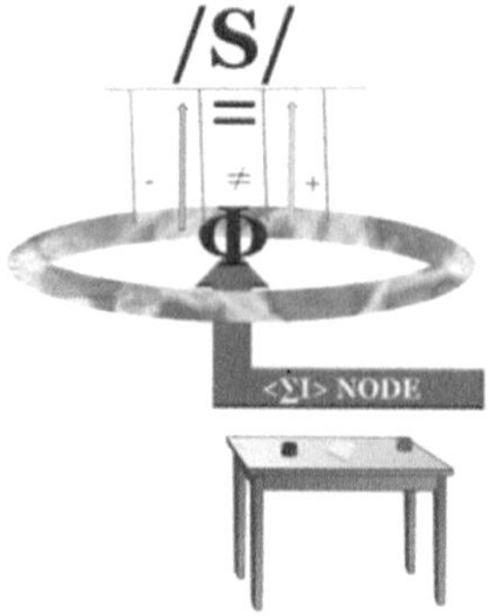

$(\Delta\text{CapMoving}_1) \neq (\Delta\text{CapMoving}_2)$ [~] <∑CapMove> [I]

Our /S/ measurement can provide co-ordinate points and for all such movements, in accordance with vector geometry.

Here, we want to zoom in on this Φ Phi Interference <Node>:

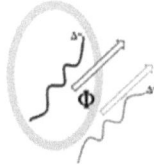

In *Matrixial Logic*, Chapter 5, we showed how the sound of a dog bark produces a Φ Phi Interference <Node> in out auditory system. It is known that we have auditory sense systems running from our ears to our brain: that we have an architecture for receiving, and transmitting, sound.

Neuroscience plainly demonstrates[43] that we have an architecture for tracking external movements. We use |M| measurement estimates of speed and time to predict movement. Thus we are able to interact with moving objects (to capture or avoid).

The blue river in the graphic represents our sensory input structure within that architecture. This sense input overlaps with the viewing of static objects, of course. We use the same eyes.

The crucial distinction is that the Δ^n river is connected to our /S/{I} architecture. Our brain processes which are "wired" to scale movement.

---

[43] https://news.mit.edu/2018/study-reveals-how-brain-tracks-objects-motion-0306

Why, then, is there such a shift in FoR by removing the fingertip? Or, to state that differently, why is there a change from $\hbar$ to Φ ?

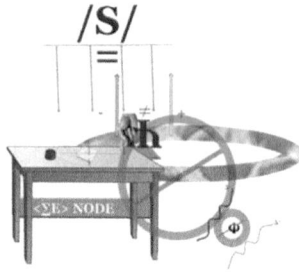

In this Scene, as denoted by the red "no entry" signs", there is no freedom of movement such as would allow an Infinity ∞ of Δ^n to be present within our Mentation

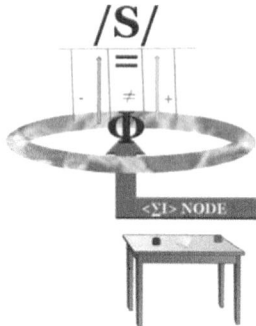

But in this Scene, there complete freedom of movement such as would allow an Infinity ∞ of Δ^n to be present within our Mentation

What we deliberately did in these *Experiences*, was to channel your visual sensory input into one <Node>, rather than another.

- Where your fingertip was on the table, your FoR was limited to a Chi 𝝘 <Node>. The movement architecture of your brain was not activated. So, you were unable to access the features of that architecture. Result: stuck.
- In the contrasting Scene, your FoR included the Phi Φ <Node>. This did activate the movement architecture of your brain. Result: being able to think of movement.

Before we proceed further with this analysis, let's just consider the question: why are we doing it? The answer is that: analogous rules apply in the realm of Emotion |E| and all of our thinking about |E|.

If we cannot understand the rules of our mental architecture, in the matter of a simple bottle Cap and its movement, how may we possibly understand the rules which apply to happiness, sadness, heartbreak and joy? And all the other categories and dynamics of |E| life.

We restate a core proposition of *Secret Self*:

Mentation

How we can think governs what we can think

Emotion

What we can emote governs how we emote

This is because our |M| and |E| share a parallel architecture. It is the architecture of each part of the Self globe, which constrains:

• what we can think
• how we we emote.

These ideas do run counter to what we are encultured to believe. But this is a modern, post-Enlightenment, belief.

In the medieval and before, we did not believe ourselves to be unconditioned emperors of our own thoughts and feelings. We believed them to be dependent upon, and subject to, other powerful forces: both in society, and in the relationship of humankind to the worlds of gods and nature.

We may think that it serves us to hold this belief in the sovereign self. But the fundamental problems of modern philosophy, classic issues in psychology, and societal issues, are all founded in this belief. Yet, we can so easily show this belief to be unfounded.

Let's use a variation of the *Cap Experience* to demonstrate. By now, you're very familiar with this Scene. Yet it still holds important lessons.

Experience: Finger
Setup:

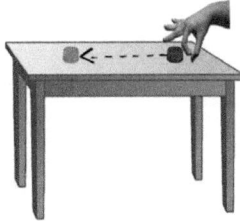

This is similar to *Cap*.

Please arrange your table top so there is only the water bottle Cap on it.

Next:
Flick the Cap with your finger.

Step 1:
Hold your finger down in the table, at the point you flicked the Cap

Next, you will need to use some strong visualisation.
Please really try and focus, under the following directions.

And:

Look at the Cap on the bare desktop, and

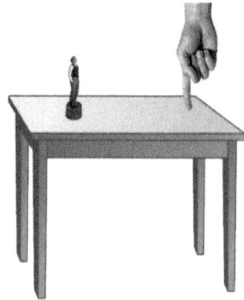

Imagine a miniature You, standing on the Cap

Miniature You is standing on the Cap and Miniature You is looking up at the finger

Please use the actual Scene in your room, not the guidance graphic.

Look at the finger through the eyes and vision of Miniature You

Now: ask Miniature You to
• tell your finger to move

Stop
Discussion:
(1)   It's stuck.
(2)   No matter how hard you focus, you can't lift your finger.

Why? Because there is no <Node> for movement here. You are now in the FoR of miniature You. The finger is like the Cap, when you were in the FoR of your fingertip.

Please consider the following extraordinary matter:
That is your finger and it is stuck in the real world.
In reality.

Your finger is as stuck, in reality, as if it had been superglued to the table top. Yet, you're not hypnotised. You are experiencing reality, the only way that this Scene allows you to experience it.

Your fingertip is extended in spacetime:
(Fingertip) ≠ (Table) = Gap [E]

But there's no "second layer" of landscape to allow the creation of a movement <Node>.
(Fingertip) ≠ (Table) = Gap [E]
|
~~(Fingertip) ≠ (///) = /// [E]~~ ≈ (□///)
|
~~(□///) ≠ (□///) [~] <∑///>~~

That's technical. What about Emotion | E | ? Let's explore:

Experience: Heat
Same Setup with miniature You.

Step 1:

Look at the Cap on the
bare desktop, and

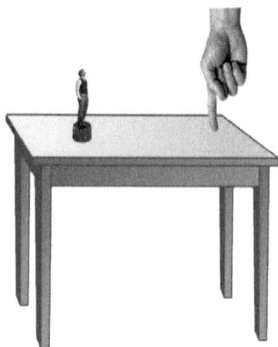

Imagine a miniature You,
standing on the Cap

Miniature You is standing
on the Cap and looking
up at the finger

Please use the actual Scene in your room, not the guidance
graphic.

Step 2:

And now:

Miniature You is standing
on the Cap and looking up
at the finger

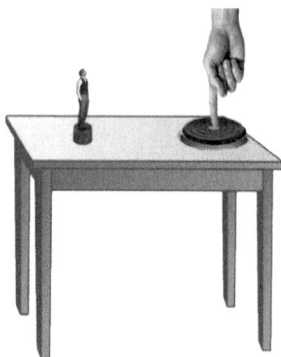

There is a hotplate under
the finger

The plate is getting hotter
and hotter

Now:

• Try to lift your finger

Stop

Discussion:

(1) It's still stuck.

(2) No matter how hard you focus, you can't lift your finger.

(3) You can feel the discomfort of the heat.

(4) As you focus on trying to lift the finger, it gets to the point of being painful.

As we said, there's no "second layer" of landscape to allow the creation of a movement <Node>. That's technical.

As we asked: what about Emotion | E | :

Mentation

How we can think governs what we can think

Emotion

What we can emote governs how we emote

If you really allowed yourself to follow this *Heat Experience*, then you found something even more disturbing than the *Finger Experience*:

• You couldn't move your finger: in the real world

• Even when that non-movement was causing you discomfort, on the border of actual pain.

113

What's the | E | relevance of this in real life? Suppose that, instead of that hot plate causing you discomfort leading to pain, it were:

- a relationship
- a lifestyle
- an addiction.

You can become stuck, just on your own table top. A Scene in which you should be in complete and constant control. But: you're not.

> *The architecture of your Mentation and Emotion*
> *limits what you can think, and how you can feel.*

This is why understanding the Matrixial Logic of <Node>s is so important. It matters to your stuck finger, in the real world. It matters even more to your potentially painful emotional condition, in the same real world.

The Scalar Axis Field

In the last few pages, we have worked through how sensory inputs get channelled to different architectures in our Mentation.

Now let's briefly consider the internal structure of these architectures. We will be considering these matters in much more detail later, as we look at the interfaces with | E.

A useful way to view the Scalar axis field /S/ is as an

infinite set of co-ordinating vectors:

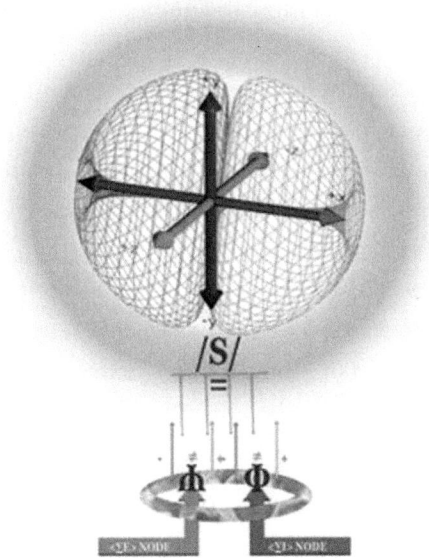

We receive an input. We then categorise, classify, and apply + / - criteria.

This is the realm of subjective estimation. It's the crucial active element in what makes you You: as a personality.

There are no rules here, save any you choose to enact. It's not scientific: this is the realm of estimation, of guesswork. There's no mandate for consistency: you can apply a + rating to a thought content and change your mind to make it a − rating.

Indeed, a thought content may by + rated in one context and simultaneously – rated in another.

Once you actually have a thought content, you are sovereign over it. But, as the previous Experiences have shown, the architecture of our Mentation determines how we can form thought contents, in the first place. *How we can think governs what we can think.*

In order to allow effective use of our /S/ architectures, we develop habits of thought ("/S/ Patterns"). These are not fixed, and they can change. But we tend not to change our /S/ Patterns unless we really need to.

Our /S/ Patterns become interconnected: one set of thoughts becomes triggering for another, and so on. Establishing new interconnections takes effort. It can lead to us losing a sense of place, and that can be uncomfortable.

Further, our /S/ Patterns are encouraged by our surrounding culture. By sharing /S/ Patterns in a culture, we again save much time and energy.

So, /S/ Patterns are efficient: until they aren't.

3.   *The Theta Θ Axis Field*

In *Matrixial Logic*, Chapters 5 and 7 we explain and analyse the Theta axis field Θ in great detail.

Here, we'll replay key *Experiences* from *Matrixial Logic*. Better than any amount of narrative, these show you the nature and reality of the Theta axis field Θ.

Experience: Extract

Please click the link, if it helps to see a bigger version of the picture:

https://hips.hearstapps.com/hmg-prod.s3.amazonaws.com/images/blue-velvet-sofa-living-room-1534263798.png

Step 1:

Look at this simple picture. Lots of ordinary things in here, from a perfectly ordinary part of the real world Just look at the picture, with your eyes open Focus on some object in the room.

Now:
- lift that object out of its background
- turn it in the air
- pull it into your head

Stop

Discussion:

(1)   It won't move.

Step 2:

Repeat Step 1, but this time looking at something (at least 6 feet away), in your actual room

Now:
- lift that object out of its background
- turn it in the air
- pull it into your head

Stop

Discussion:

(1)   You still can't do it. The object is stuck.

Try this out in your own room view as well.

Now, try this version:

Experience: YouTwo

Preparation:

This is really important
You need to focus and really try here

Imagine a second you. A perfect replica copy of you.
This is secondYou: You$_2$

For this *Experience*:
- imagine you're on a tennis court
- with the room at the other end
- and You$_2$ where the umpire would be
- on your right-hand side[44]

Step 1:
Just look at the picture again, with your eyes open
Pick a Thing

---

[44] your left-hand side, if you're left-handed

Now:

imagine You$_2$ looking at You seeing the room
You$_2$ can see You
You$_2$ can see the space between You and the room
You$_2$ can see You looking at the room

And **with You$_2$ watching you**

Now:

- You$_1$
- lift that object out of its background
- turn it in the air
- pull it into your head

Stop

Discussion:

(1)   Now it's easy.

Step 2:

Now, look at your actual room

Pick a Thing

Now:

imagine You$_2$ looking at You seeing the room
You$_2$ can see You
You$_2$ can see the space between You and the room
You$_2$ can see You looking at the room

And **with You$_2$ watching you**

Now:

- You$_1$
- lift that object out of its background
- turn it in the air
- pull it into your head

Stop

Discussion:

(1)   Now it's just as easy in reality.
       Notice how you didn't need to keep thinking of
       You$_2$ You just needed to perform the projection
       once: and You$_2$ stayed there. Occasionally you
       popped the You$_2$ reference thought into your head.

But *so long as you knew You$_2$ was there*, you could pull
objects freely into your head.

It's like the room became "yours": completely under your
control. That relationship, inside your head, with You$_2$
"other you" changed everything.

Drawing from Chapter 5 of *Matrixial Logic*:

{Θ} Theta Axis Field
$$(T) \neq (nT) = \Theta$$

This is the realm of the Objective. Or, as we more
functionally and glamorously say, the Theta Axis
is:

Universal Television (1985-1989)

The Θ Theta Axis takes Subjective states, which are Scalar /S/ modified from the original disparate subjective sea inputs, and *equalises* them.

We can't of course show you this function going on, in real time, in the brain: in its chemistry or anatomy. But then, we can't do any of these things with most of what we over-generously refer to as scientific inspection of reality.[45]

However, we are aware, by induction from the observed facts, that this *equalising* function occurs. Otherwise human kind would not still be here. For all human civilisation is due to it.

---

[45] see *Complete Reality* Chapter

We can actually prove the existence and operation of the *equalising* function of the Θ Theta Axis. In fact, we have already done so repeatedly in the *Experiences*. The ones which required You$_2$ to solve them. We'll say more about this, shortly.

The *equalising* function of the Θ Theta Axis needs to be childishly simple. Otherwise infant brains would be unable to get to grips with it in the first 18 months of life.

So, now we can start to see how You$_2$ works, as an imaginative personalisation of the Θ Theta axis field.

In the *Extract Experience*, like in *Cap*, we have a limited landscape.

There was an <Object> which you were trying to lift out of the landscape.:

$$(\text{Object}) \neq (\text{Landscape}) = \text{Exists (place) [E]}$$

We are not able to get a movement relationship out of that inequality. There is no <Node> for movement.

When we subject the <Object> and the ,Landscape> to the Θ Theta axis field, we automatically effect equalisation:

$$(\text{T}) \neq (\text{nT}) = \Theta$$
$$>$$
$$(\text{Object}) \neq (\text{Landscape}) = \text{Dimension } \Theta$$

The <Object> is not really "moving", like the Cap did here:

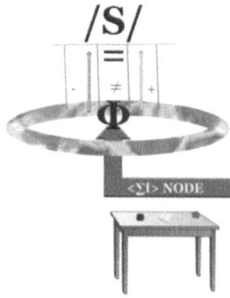

> But in this Scene, there complete freedom of movement such as would allow an Infinity ∞ of Δ^n to be present within our Mentation

The Θ Theta axis field *equalises*: it treats everything in its field of axes as being *unidimensional*:[46]

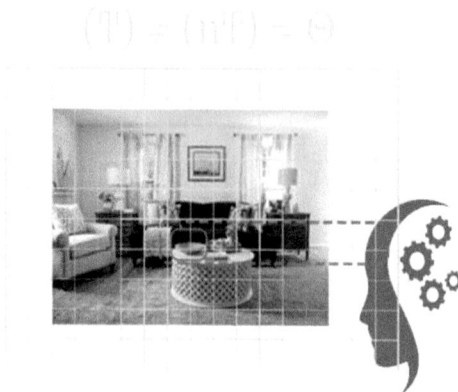

---

[46] we will sophisticate and amend this idea later

Everything in the Θ Theta axis field exists simultaneously in Θ Theta time and space.[47] It's not that the <Object> moves: it does not need to move because it is held in unidimensional stasis.

This may seem difficult to follow, and if followed, bizarre.

Experience: Since

Setup:
Look at this simple picture. Lots of ordinary things in here, from a perfectly ordinary part of the real world
Just look at the picture, with your eyes open

Step 1:
Focus on some Object in the room
Take *the whole picture of the Object and Landscape into your head*
Close your eyes

---

[47] we will discuss Time in Chapter 3

If you need to refresh your memory by looking a few times, that's fine

And: when you're sure you have the Object and Landscape in your head

With your eyes closed:

Now:
- lift that Object out of its background
- turn it in the air
- move the Object out of the Landscape

and
- move the Object somewhere else in your head

Stop

Discussion:
(1)   This is easy

Here, you can see how this is working in your Scalar /S/ axis:

You probably didn't remember the whole picture: just the parts you needed. You took a "snapshot" and held that image in your head.

Then, of course, you can play around with that image however you wish. As we said earlier:

> We receive an input. We then categorise, classify, and apply + / - criteria.

> This is the realm of subjective estimation. It's the crucial active element in what makes you You: as a personality.

> There are no rules here, save any you choose to enact. It's not scientific: this is the realm of estimation, of guesswork. There's no mandate for consistency: you can apply a + rating to a thought content and change your mind to make it a – rating.

Your subjective /S/ scalar domain can do almost anything. But there are limits.

Firstly, you can't bring the Object into your head, separate from the Landscape, *because both are already there*. So there is a parallel to the Theta Θ axis field, in that the components of Mentation are already present, in that field.

But there is a crucial difference.

- Your /S/ field relies upon the functions: categorise; classify.

- /S/ reasons by comparison and analogy. /S/ makes judgments about everything which becomes a component of its field.
- If /S/ cannot recognise the data *by reference to what is already in /S/*, then /S/ rejects it as an input.

Theta Θ does not function like that. Θ accepts all inputs as valid, without judgment or discrimination. It then equalises them and provides equalised or "normalised"[48] output.

Experience: Already
Setup:
Look at this simple picture. Lots of ordinary things in here, from a perfectly ordinary part of the real world

And a non-ordinary thing.

Just look at the picture, with your eyes open:

---

[48] the analogy here is being set to a 0 threshhold, as in audio normalisation

Step 1:

Take the whole picture of the Landscape into your head

Close your eyes

If you need to refresh your memory by looking a few times, that's fine

And: when you're sure you have the Landscape in your head

With your eyes closed:

Now:

• Look around the Landscape in your head

Stop

Discussion:

(1) Static imaging the Landscape, behind closed eyes, in your head, is easy

(2) But the strange Symbol:

just won't reast easy in your head.

(3) It's like your head keeps being pulled back to look at the picture, and Symbol, to try and resolve the conflict.

We have the explanation as to why this is happening:

- If /S/ cannot recognise the data *by reference to what is already in /S/*, then /S/ rejects it as an input.

The Symbol was deliberately designed as an abstract with no obvious reference to anything in our experience.

As we said:

> Your subjective /S/ scalar domain can do almost anything. But there are limits.

If you review the history of your head, you'll see that your Mentation held the Symbol apart from the Landscape. Your /S/ axis field "parked" the Symbol in a "to be determined" box, separate from the familiar room landscape.

Let's try again:

Experience: Thrope
Setup:
Look at this simple picture. Lots of ordinary things in

here, from a perfectly ordinary part of the real world

And a non-ordinary thing.

Just look at the picture, with your eyes open

Now:
imagine You$_2$ looking at You seeing the room
You$_2$ can see You
You$_2$ can see the space between You and the room
You$_2$ can see You looking at the room

And **with You$_2$ watching you**

Step 1:
Take the whole picture of the Landscape into your head
Close your eyes

If you need to refresh your memory by looking a few times, that's fine

And: when you're sure you have the Landscape in your head

With your eyes closed:

And **with You$_2$ watching you**

Now:

* Look around the Landscape in your head

Stop

Discussion:

(1)   Now the strange Symbol:

sits in your Theta Θ axis field.

(2)   You don't feel like your head keeps being pulled back to look at the picture, and Symbol.

(3)   It does not feel that there is any conflict to try and resolve.

Theta Θ equalises, without judgment or discrimination. Θ is an entirely value-neutral axis field. The only criteria for Θ operation is that an item of data <exists> in your /S/ function.

Now, without assuming anything at this stage, suppose that Theta Θ is implicated in your | E | emotive processes.

- This would obviously be a big deal. We think of | E | as being entirely a value-driven realm: good / bad, love / hate, like / fear, and so on.
- To see that our /S/ function operates by value recognition is friendly and familiar. But to find part of our Mentation which simply runs an <exists> program, is unsettling.
- Which then is in charge? Our cuddly value driven vortices of | E | and /S/? Or, our neutralist Θ function? And how can one relate to the other?

Put like this, we can see the importance of these last pages. *Whatever is going on here, something is going on.* We are having successive Experiences showing to us that: *the way that we can think determines what we can think.*

There appears to be an indefeasible architecture of our Mentation. We are accustomed to not noticing it's there. But clearly, it's always present in every moment of our Mentation.

The Author did not insert those architectures, as part of some hypnotic experience. It's quite the opposite. The *Experiences* are revealing explicitly to the reader the mental architecture by which you realise your daily moments in Mentation.

The Theta Θ axis field starts to look like a kind of superpower. Θ is undoubtedly powerful. Using it can enable you to achieve things which otherwise your /S/ can't.

But, to use the power of Θ, you have to be able to engage it. Let's meet some Kryptonite:[49]

https://www.cyberark.com/resources/threat-research-blog/krypton-stealer-kryptonite-for-credentials

Experience: Twist
Setup:

---

[49] https://en.wikipedia.org/wiki/Kryptonite

Recall the *Cap Experience.*

Please arrange your table top so there is only the water bottle Cap on it.

Next:

Flick the Cap with your finger.

Step 1:

Hold your finger down in the table, at the point you flicked the Cap

Please use the actual Scene in your room, not the guidance graphic.

Now:

• Try to move the Cap, in your head

Stop

<u>Discussion</u>:

(1)   It's stuck.

Step 2:

Hold your finger down in the table, at the point you flicked the Cap

Please use the actual Scene in your room, not the guidance graphic.

Now:

imagine You$_2$ looking at You seeing the room

You$_2$ can see You

You$_2$ can see the space between You and the room

You$_2$ can see You looking at the room

And **with You$_2$ watching you**

Now:

- Try to engage You$_2$

and

- Try to move the Cap, in your head

Stop

Discussion:

(1)   You$_2$ won't engage.

(2)   You are stuck, in your reality, in the Scene.

We have now met a scenario where you You$_2$ will not engage. You are completely stuck:

- there is no <Node> for movement to allow /S/ movement perception

- your Θ won't engage.

Now, suppose that someone is stuck in:

- a relationship
- an obsession
- an addiction.

Could it be that it is the involvement of that individual in the Scene, as participant and not merely observer, which is creating that immobility: that inability to break free?

Yet, if there is mileage in that notion, how can it assist us in life? Isn't each of us a direct participant in all the life that we live? How could we possibly disengage from the life in which we participate, so as to access the Theta Θ superpowers?

These are big questions. The discussion of Mentation in this Chapter, so far has allowed us to ask them. That's what Matrixial Self analysis is for: to allow us to ask new questions, which may provoke helpful answers.

But, we must postpone that culminating exercise until we have made more progress in these discussions.

We need to track back to Matrixial Logic, Chapter 5 again:
    The first action your Theta axis = Θ takes is to decide the existence value ("EV") of the Scalar information.

That existence value is (T), in:
$$(T) \neq (nT) = \Theta$$

Now, we must tread carefully here. Theta is not deciding whether anything exists out there in the world: whether there is an external reference point for the Scalar data. That is not Theta's mission statement.

Consider the matter: why should it be otherwise? It is the job of your senses and your Scalar translation of <Node> $\hat{m}$ and Wave Φ interfaces, to detect whether something exists or not. Although that task is already done by the world "out there". Either a thing exists, whether perceptible by any of the 5 senses, or it doesn't.

Of course, there's a whole world of things which exist, and of which we are not perceptibly aware. But until we do become aware of any it as information in perception, it cannot be in our heads. Whether you are a rampant subjectivist, or objectivist, that necessary relationship is a fact of the matter.

Once we do become aware of that information, then it exists for us, whether we like it or not. That's a commonplace: information is presented to us, and we may say "I really didn't want to know that". This involuntary information idea is, after all, at the core of the Woke phenomenon.

In like manner, you may fill your Scalar domains, being purely subjective, with unicorns, bald present kings of France, honest politicians, and any manner of fantasies.

You may manufacture whatever fancies you wish out of the raw stuff of your perception information: and you do. That is all you do.

You don't process reality in your thoughts. You process information about reality. That "about" can vary from distance (in time) of a microsecond, to multiple millienia of years, and trillions of miles.

Look how we had you in the *Experiences*, interacting with photographs, with imagined landscapes and sounds, with imaginary paperclips, with words and sentences. *They are all just made up in your Subjective head.* But they are really real.

They are really real to the Axis which counts reality: your Theta Θ Axis.

Theta Θ is the supermarket cashier. It is not Theta's job to determine how the goods got in your basket or from which shelf you got them, nor indeed whether any such shelf "exists".

What is in your basket is what the Theta cashier

sees. To which Theta then (metaphorically) applies the rule-based tasks of:

- categorising[50]
- adding up
- deducing a total

There must be a framework for such a rule-based system, and an underpinning, immoveable, unprovable premise.

The premise is: Exists.

To Exist in Θ, means that (T) is extended in objective internal spacetime.

Let's take some more Experiences from *Matrixial Logic*:

Experience: Sheeted
Step 1:
See this blank sheet:

---

[50] not in the sense of qualities, but in the sense of ordering of equivalent data

There is nothing else to see.

If you can look at this sheet, here in the book, without your eye catching any words, so that you can focus on only this sheet, that's fine.

Or, you can hold this sheet in your head.
Ready?

Now:
- Imagine on the sheet a paperclip:
- which you know is not there

- Keep trying

Stop

Take a breath. Look around you. Relax.

Discussion:
(1)   You can't do it
(2)   The harder you try, the worse it gets. You actually feel stress, and some emotional distress.

How is this possible? All through this Book, we've had you imagining all sorts of things. Manipulating them, encountering difficulties. But never have you experiences an inability to make your mind just think of something.

Something very powerful is limiting the operation of your mentation. That something, that process, or function, is so powerful that your emotions become aroused, to deal with the stress which you are encountering.

Step 2:

• See the same blank sheet:

There is nothing else to see.

If you can look at this sheet, here in the book, without your eye catching any words, so that you can focus on only this sheet, that's fine.

Or, you can hold this sheet in your head.
Ready?

Now:

• Imagine on the sheet Two paperclips:

> *both of which you know is not there*

• Keep trying

Stop

Take a breath. Look around you. Relax.

Discussion:

(1)   You can't do it

(2)   It becomes like some insane cartoon: one paper-
      clip sort of emerges onto the sheet, and it's like the
      sheet rejects it; then the other paperclip tries, and
      is rejected.

(3)   The harder you try, the worse it gets. The *trying to
      exist clips* just seem to spiral in and out of reality.
      bit like a spin up / spin down quark.

(4)   You actually feel stress, and some emotional dis-
      tress.

You did the *Cap* and *Flick Experiences*, just a few pages
back in this Chapter. There you were, getting stuck with
one bottle Cap, then become gloriously free with a Cap
and a Post It Note.

But now, the other thing doesn't come to the rescue. It
make matters worse.

We are encultured to believe that anyone can make up
anything. That children, from around 3 onwards, make up
both small and increasingly intricate fantasies. It's what
we pay poets, and novelists and Hollywood scriptwriters
billions of dollars for.

It's what Professor Jordan Peterson, following Jung, calls our "Maps of Meaning".[51] The idea that we have a-historical cultural archetypes, stories and meta-truths which are, yes, just "made up": but which we did make up.

Experience: Mote
Setup:
Look around you at the room you are in.
Take a few relaxed normal breaths.
Relax.
Step 1:
Ready?

Now:

• Imagine, there in the room, a paperclip:
> *which you know is not there*

Stop

<u>Discussion</u>:
(1)   The non-existent paperclip appeared.
(2)   It was automatic.
(3)   It was as if, something reached over your shoulder, through your head, and stuck that paperclip right there in the room.

Step 2:

---

[51] Jordan Peterson (1999)

Look around you at the room you are in.

Take a few relaxed normal breaths.

Relax.

Ready?

Now: you're going to repeat what you just did

- Imagine, there in the room, paperclip:

    which you know is not there

and Now:

- move that non-existent paperclip around the room
- whatever colour it isn't, change that to some other colour it isn't
- whatever size it isn't, change the size:
    - larger
    - smaller
    - wider
    - narrower
- make it move

and Now:

- Make it disappear

Stop

Discussion:

(1) The non-existent paperclip appeared, of course. Easy

(2) As you worked with it, you became used to it

(3) You could perform all the manipulations

(4) ***Yet all the time you knew that the paperclip did not exist.***

> *To Exist in Θ, means that (T) is extended*
> *in objective internal spacetime.*

Your Θ does not care whether what you mentate in /S/ has any existence in reality:

> The first action your Theta axis = Θ takes is to decide the existence value ("EV") of the Scalar information.

> That existence value is (T), in:
> $$(T) \neq (nT) = \Theta$$

> Now, we must tread carefully here. Theta is not deciding whether anything exists out there in the world: whether there is an external reference point for the Scalar data. That is not Theta's mission statement.

Once a data item (T) is in the Θ "shopping basket" the cashier will not let you take it out again. Let's demonstrate.

Experience: Whovering
Look around you at the room you are in.
Take a few relaxed normal breaths.
Relax.

Ready?

Step 1:
You're going to repeat what you just did

Imagine, there in the room, paperclip:
>   *which you know is not there*

And:
Just allow the paperclip to be there
Relax with it
If you feel it wants to move, that's fine

Now:
- Think to yourself: *This paperclip does not exist*
- Keep the non-existent paperclip there in the room
- Keep repeating that phrase: *This paperclip does not exist*

Stop

Discussion:
(1)   The paperclip appeared, of course. Easy
(2)   Look into the history of your head: as you repeated *This paperclip does not exist*: what word or idea came into your head?
(3)   If you're not sure, go back into the paperclip room, in your head and repeat the *Experience*.

As you repeated that phrase, a totally true statement of

the state of affairs, what else did come come to think?

You thought:

<I>

Saying that phrase repeatedly was pushing you to say:

But I <u>do</u> exist

I exist

I

You were challenging your Theta Θ Axis Field function. You were trying to tell the cashier it doesn't know how to add up the Existence Value (EV) of the items in the shopping basket.

And the Theta Θ cashier was insisting that, yes, it does know very well. And nothing that you have to say will persuade it otherwise.[52]

That is why the Theta Axis Field function is:
= Θ
I Am

We will have much more to say about <I> and <Me> in Part 2.

Restating, for convenience from Chapter 5 of Matrixial Logic:

---

[52] Think about that one, and its consequences for opinion and belief

Just as:

=[E] is the existence of Substance (A), in

opposition

[≠(nA)], extended in objective external spacetime.

So as:

=[Θ] is the existence of information (T), in

opposition

[≠(nT)], extended in objective internal spacetime

To mix philosophical metaphors: =[Θ] is the cash value for <I> of information (T). It is the existential register of such information as exists (T) in the objective world that is <I>.[53]

You were challenging your Theta Θ Axis Field function. Telling yourself that the imagined paperclip:

does not exist

Your Theta Θ Axis Field function insisted:

But I do exist

I exist

<I>

We have recreated the Experience which Descartes recorded, almost 400 years ago.

[53] we are trying to avoid using the "me " word: that is a completely different concept

Cogito ergo sum:
I am thinking, therefore I am existing.[54]

And, despite Descartes's best idealist intent, it was a triumphant recording of objective materialism.[55]

That observation was clearly correct: since you have just experienced it yourself. As does every adult human being over the age of 3, who undergoes the experience.

Which happens every moment of the waking day. You are using your Theta Θ Axis Field function in every waking moment of your life. The Theta Θ cashier is ever busy, summing the differentiated totals of existential information $[(T) \neq (nT) =]$ into language forms.

If Theta Θ is so busy in me all the time, you might say, why don't I notice it? We answer: for much the same reason that you don't notice your heart beating, or your circulation pumping: until you choose to notice.

But also for another reason: your life and mental

---

[54] *Principles of Philosophy.* Part 1, At 7 (1644) Published originally in French *Discourse on Method* (1637)
[55] Although there is an argument that Descartes was actually trying to unite reality and consciousness, not sever them

health significantly depend upon you not noticing. As we will see in *Secret Self*, one of the operative elements of Mentive dysfunction, is dis-ordering of the relationship between /S/ and Theta Θ.

In whichever human individual the joy of purely subjective shopping (ℏ, Φ) is being done, the Theta Θ cashier uses the same rules of accounting. The Theta Θ rules are universal. Across every culture, society, and community. Across historical time. That which is universal in every sphere of human existence is objective.

To be a universal phenomenon is what "objective" means. We might say that universality is a necessary, but not sufficient criteria for being denoted as "objective".

Do you recall the scene from *1984*,[56] in the Ministry of Love:

'How many fingers, Winston?' 'Four! Stop it, stop it! How can you go on? Four! Four!' 'How many fingers, Winston?' 'Five! Five! Five!' 'No, Winston, that is no use. You are lying. You still think there are four. How many fingers, please?' 'Four! five! Four! Anything you like. Only stop it, stop the pain!'

O'Brien was working to make Winston deny his Theta Θ function. To do that, Winston had to give up his sense of <I>. With Winston's emotional

---

[56] George Orwell (1949) p221

sacrifice of Julia to the rat, in Room 101, Winston finally became free: of himself.

With the non-existent paperclip, you have just had a taste of Winston's agony. Would you like some more?

Experience: MinLove
Setup:
Look around your room
Find an object: let's say a chair
Focus on the chair
Keep your eyes open

Step 1:

Now, say to yourself:
* *That chair does not exist… does not exist… not exist*
* Sat it over and over again
* Try to make it so
* Try to lift the chair out of its landscape
* Try hard
* Keep repeating to yourself … *not exist*

Stop

Step 2:
Now: look at the chair
* Say to yourself *I exist*
Stop

Discussion:

(1)   It started off with you having feelings of *so what*

(2)   As you intensified the pressure, it became increasingly uncomfortable

(3)   The words ... *not exist*, were getting an echo in
your head: *I exist...I...I*

(4)   That's why we stopped you, then did a reset.

(5)   When you affirmed your <I>, you felt OK again

Theta Θ expresses the <I>, of you as a Self in Being.

You were challenging your Theta Θ cashier. You
were arguing that some (T) which, for Theta Θ, is
in the basket, does not exist in the basket.

We can appreciate the amazing insight of Orwell.
The whole of *1984*, is filled with these astonishing
insights into relationships between the workings of
our Mentation, and the world.

We said:

To be a universal phenomenon is what "objective"
means. We might say that universality is a
necessary, but not sufficient criteria for being
denoted as "objective".

Fair enough. What then is the necessary criteria?
That it be necessary; inescapable; unavoidable;
incapable of evasion.

Well, you've just tried, with all your mentative strength to evade the shopping basket filed with things which exist and a clip which does not exist: and you didn't succeed. You've just tried to tip an object in your room, which certainly does exist, out of the basket. You failed.

Once a (T) is in the Θ basket, you can't get it out again, before the Theta Θ cashier does the accounting.

Next, we are going to move through the Self globe, to | E | Emotion. But first, we need to instil a deep understanding of how Theta Θ affects not just Mentation, but action in the world.

Experience: I-Pen

Prologue:

You must use whatever is your non-ordinary writing hand, in this experience.

- If you are right-handed, use your left. Your You$_2$ will come from your right.
- If you are left-handed, use your right. Your You$_2$ will come from your left.

Materials:

Get a pad of paper, limed or unlined

Get a ballpoint pen (because it writes most clearly and easily)

Start

Step 1:

- With your normal writing hand: write A B C on the pad
- Do it with reasonable care and concentration. Not slapdash

Stop

Step 2:

- With your Other hand: write A B C on the pad
- Do it best you can. Take your time

Stop

Step 3:

You$_2$

Imagine You$_2$

Connect

Feel the connection

Get used to maintaining the connection

Now:

- With your Other hand: write A B C on the pad
- **Keep your You$_2$ connection going all the time**
- Do it best you can. Take your time

Stop

Rest. Let the You$_2$ connection drop.

Step 4:

You$_2$

Reconnect with You$_2$

- With your Other hand: write a b c , on the pad
- **Keep your You₂ connection going all the time**
- Do it best you can. Take your time

Stop

Rest. Let the You₂ connection drop.

Here is a sample:[57]

Normal Hand   Unassisted   You²
                       Other Hand   Other Hand

and, in a second round of practice, a few moments later:

Normal Hand   You²
                                                  Other Hand

Another sample from a different individual:

---

[57] by a friend of the Author

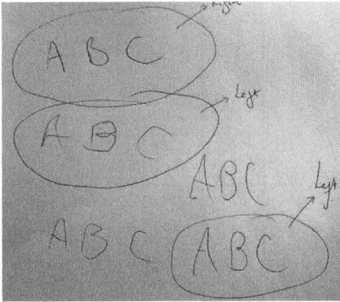

1. Normal Hand

2. Left:
without You$_2$

3. Left:
with You$_2$

The 3rd writing was performed moments after the 2nd writing.

More samples:

(3)

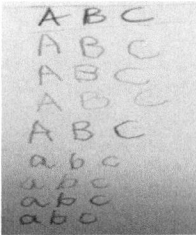

1. Normal hand

2. Left: without You2

3.1 Left: without You2

3.3 Left: with You2

(4)

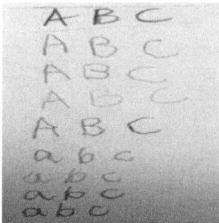

1. Left: without You2

1.1 Left: without You2

2. Left: with You2

2.1 Left: with You2

In the *Matrixial Logic* version of the I-Pen *Experience*, we left the scene, without much explanation. We simply confined ourselves, in Chapter 10, to noting that I-Pen completely repudiates both existing camps of Western philosophy: materialism and dualism.

Whilst it's useful to correct 400 years of error in philosophy, that's somewhat trivial compared to the importance of I-Pen in understanding your *Secret Self*.
We will return to this in Part 2.

The Matrixial Experiments
We have seen above some graphic examples of the change in writing effected by use of the You$_2$ Avatar for the Θ function.

In October to November 2020, an independent research company sent Sets of Matrixial Experiments out to cohorts of volunteers, selected from a database of random samples.

We used close questioning with 3 alternatives answers to capture the experiences of the Subjects:

Step 1: Response (1)		12.1
PROPOSITION:		MARK
At Part 2, the quality of my other hand writing,		
compared to normal hand was below 30%		
A	Agree	

B	Disagree	
C	Not Sure	

Step 1: Response (2)		12.2
PROPOSITION:		MARK
With You$_2$ the quality of my other hand writing,		
compared to normal hand was 80% or above		
A	Agree	
B	Disagree	
C	Not Sure	

Step 2: Response (1)		12.3
PROPOSITION:		MARK
At Part 2, the quality of my other hand writing,		
compared to normal hand was below 30%		
A	Agree	
B	Disagree	
C	Not Sure	

Step 2: Response (2)		12.4
PROPOSITION:		MARK
With You$_2$ the quality of my other hand writing,		
compared to normal hand was 80% or above		
A	Agree	
B	Disagree	
C	Not Sure	

If the Θ function was ineffective, we would see a zero or near zero result for application of the *I-Pen Experience.* Instead, averaged across 3 Set groups,[58] we saw these results:

	I-Pen Step 1	I-Pen Step 1 cont	I-Pen Step 2	I-Pen Step 2 cont
AVERAGES	40	33	40	23
	73%	62%	71%	45%
	54	54	54	54

The results are clear and paradigm-shattering.

> *62% of Subjects reported success in altering their other-handed writing by a factor of 80%.*

There is no prior probability of being able to do something that you can't do. Or perhaps one might say that the prior probability is ≈0: which amounts to the same thing.

If only 5% of Subjects reported an effect then, we could say: *whatever is going on here, something is going on.*

To see a positive effect of anything over 33%, is well above whatever could rationally be ascribed to chance, or inaccurate self-reporting.

The lower case writing is graphically more challenging that upper case writing. So we should expect to see a

---

[58] and normalised for inconsistent answers to the Control questions

smaller success percentage at Step 2 Response (2).

- that is generally what we see

but, within the detailed Results data

- we also see Subjects getting better at using the Θ Avatar function, as they progress in the Tests over time.

We will be publishing the full Tests, data Sets and Analyses, with commentary in *The Matrixial Experiments*.

What we can with certainty conclude at this point is that the Θ Avatar function, supplied with simple communicative instruction, has significant observable effect in the world: an effect which is empirically verifiable.

The Θ function is emanant and observable in reality. For those versed in Classical Accounts of neuroscience, philosophy and psychology: this is a profound change. The paradigms which found the theoretical frameworks of those disciplines can no longer stand.

Instead, we have new paradigm: the Systems Architecture of Self, transparent in its processes. In the next Sections, we will analyse the detail of these elements.

4.　　Summarising |*M*| *entation*

In this Section A, we have recapitulated essential architectural analysis, which is fully developed in *Matrixial Logic*.

The take-home points, in preparation for the next Sections are:

- the architecture of |M| is unique
- the assertion (which we need to evidence in later Sections) that |E| has a completely different architecture, and functions completely differently
- that |M| architecture is a gestalt, comprising:
- /S/: what we in classical accounts and folk wisdom refer to as the "subjective"
- Θ: which has no equivalent in classical accounts and folk wisdom
- /S/ works by equivalence (hence its inherent subjectivity)
- Θ works by equalisation (hence its inherent objectivity)
- /S/ is an infinite continuum of possibility; yet bounded by its place in |M| architecture:

We have tried, therefore to explain the |M| rubric:
The way that we can think determines what we can think

Section B, coming next, explains the Systems and Consequences of the |E| rubric:
　　　What we can emote governs how we emote

Section C then examines the Interaction of the machinery of |M| and |E|, and provides the composite architecture of the Self.

SECTION B: | E | MOTION

(1) INTRODUCTORY

Now, after that important preceding Section, we turn to discuss the realm of Emotion | E |. Its sub-Architecture and Systems within the Self.

1. *Sectoring the Globe*

It's obviously important to essay a definition of | E |. To do so in terms of qualities, attributes and functions, is not helpful at this stage.

With reference to the globe of Self, we can distinguish the reality of | E | in this way:

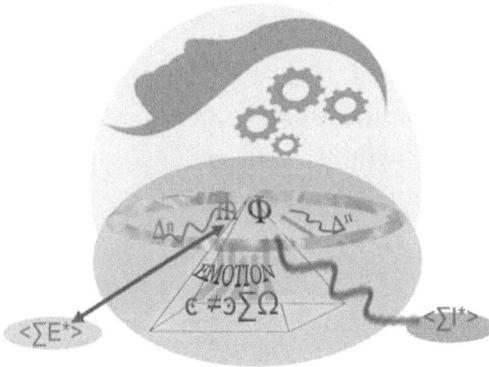

We can draw out immediate elements:

* sensory inputs
  - from the world | W |

- from physiognomy | P |
- quasi-sensory inputs from | M | entation
- <Node>s corresponding to inputs.

In this and the next secti0ons, we are going to discuss each of these dynamic elements of | E |, and their interaction.

Sometimes, the notation that we use will run slightly ahead of explanation. That's simply because it becomes too unwieldy to write out three of four words in full, when a combination of symbols expresses the composite idea.

If you do come across a symbol and aren't sure what it means, the explanation of its use will always follow in a few pages: so please come back.

We also want to add that this Chapter is intended to be re-read. It's in the nature of any analysis of a gestalt phenomenon, that the parts are best understood from the entire perspective of the whole.

2.   *Functional Locus*

What we will be explaining is the machinery underlying this familiar conceptual graphic:

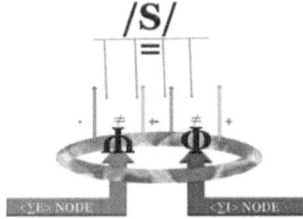

We will focus initially on one type of <Node> interaction:

The like explanation[59] obtains for a <Node> in <E>.

In *Matrixial Logic*, we didn't vouch this explanation, because it was not necessary. We explained <Nodes> in the world, and their interaction with our Scalar /S/ subjective domain.

Editorially, it would have added another 300 pages to a book already pushing 700 pages. Thematically, we wanted to focus in *Matrixial Logic* on |M|entation. In *Secret Self*, our focus is on |E|motion and its interaction with |M|entation; and deriving theoretical and practical methodologies from that interaction.

---

[59] *mutandis mutatis*

So, we need in this *Globe* Chapter to unwrap the meeting of the <Node> and You:

3.   *The Classical Account*

We are generally in this Chapter going to use <T> and <F> as shorthand for <thoughts> and <feelings>. Our use of these symbols will get "tighter" as the analysis progresses.

Traditional neuroscience, philosophy and psychology take as a premise of all theories, that there is some distinction between <T> and <F>.

There are then still wholly unresolved questions as to:

- which "comes first"
- which influences what
- how
- whether control of <F> is possible, or desirable
- the inter-relation of <T> and <F> and human physiology
- how to understand animal "psychology".

Yet all classical accounts depend upon a paradigm:

(1)   that we derive emotional stimulus directly from our interaction with |W|.

(2)   that our senses are just a fishing net which delivers |W| interactions direct to our |E|.

(3)   that such delivery is unmediated.[60]

(4)   That such so stimulated |E| then produces "drives", which produce changes in states of consciousness.

(5)   That we can thereby analytically reverse engineer such processes: but only to an extent.

(6)   We can analyse some of \<T\> and less of \<F\>, and some of their interactions.

(7)   This is the domain of cognitive behavioural psychology: the use of observed, and theoretically inducted, aggregates of behaviours; then reasoning backwards to individual consciousness states.

(8)   The ultimate concatenation of stimulus to |E|, resulting in "drives" is ultimately unknowable.

This is indeed the psychology of a secret \<self\>. Like Churchill's aphorism on Soviet Russa:[61]

a riddle, wrapped in a mystery, inside an enigma

The new discussions of interoception do abandon the \<T\> and \<F\> disticntion paradigm. However, these create their own problems, as we will see.

---

[60] save as for deformations or dysfunctions in our |P|
[61] Radio Broadcast (1 October 1939)

4.   *The Matrixial Analysis*

We deny that the <self> is a secret. We will provide analyses which lead to the conclusion that much about Self is a paradox.

We do say that there are some things about the process which is Self, that we can't even in principle know. But these are the same sort of things we can't know about lots of phenomena: such as exactly how many atoms or sub-atomic particles comprise this book. Or how exactly how many cells there are in your body at this moment. Or all the decimal numbers of Pi.

But these quantitative uncertainties do not dissuade us from the scientific view or common sense view that we know all that can be needed to know, about such matters.

With the techniques of analysis made possible by Matrixial Logic, we can make the entirety of the processes transparent. Moreover, we can use that understanding to effect immediate and lasting effects in the "psyche" of an individual.

We can succeed, where traditional neuroscience, philosophy and psychology cannot. Yes, that is grandstanding. But so said in order to highlight the dramatic break with traditional thought, and the consequences of that break.

There is no intelligent reasoning, in any subjective sense, in the mechanical interaction of the world and our emotional system: $|W| => |c| => \sum \Omega$.[62]

No more than our autonomic circulatory or breathing systems act "intelligently". They are biological functions. They have the same intelligence quotient as a paramecium.

In passing, this accounts for the power of the Hameroff and Penrose thesis: *Consciousness in the universe: A review of the 'Orch OR' theory* (2014). [63]

We don't agree with the cumulative conclusions of the thesis, but we appreciate elements of it in assisting the technical explanation of sensory mechanics.

Ohm Ω stands in the spot lit place, which the classical account reserves for "emotions" and "feelings". But Ω:

- is not a set of "emotions" or "feelings" at all. It is the biomechanical aggregate of sensory input transformations
- does not "drive" anything, anywhere. Ω refers transformed information to $|P|$ and $/S/$
- is not a reservoir. It is not a puddling collection of sensory raindrops.

Ω is an in-out *distributed referral system*. Sensory information arrives, is transformed, and referred. All as a

---

[62] we will fully explain these symbolic usages during this Chapter
[63] see *https://doi.org/10.1016/j.plrev.2013.08.002*

matter of biomechanics.

Once the referral has occurred, that sensory transformation is gone. And you will never, ever , in the life of the universe, get to replay exactly that interaction again.

Once we have explained the Ω information transformation and referral system, that conclusion will become obvious. We will see that Heraclitus was, in that sense, right.

Experience: Fog
Just sit back and relax.
Close your eyes if you like

Now:
• Just allow yourself to sense whatever you sense

Discussion:
(1)   Nothing to see here.
(2)   Just vague clouds, shapes, fog.
(3)   None of it "means" anything.

Experience: Bulb
Sit back and relax
Close your eyes if you like

Just allow yourself to sense whatever you sense

Now:

- Find 3 words which match what you're sensing.

<u>Discussion</u>:
(1)   This was easy to do.
(2)   We do it all the time, incessantly.

Congratulations! You just created some <feelings>.

The vague clouds, shapes, fog: that is the raw stuff which we use to generate <F>.

We will explain how that generation occurs, unceasing moment after moment. We will see how the process of generation results in an aggregate: $\sum\Omega$. This is why the Ω formula joins with a $\sum$ not a =. It is this unidimensional, formless stuff from which <feelings> are made.

We could get Copenhagen quantum about it and suggest that $\sum\Omega$ is a field of potential, like the spin and momentum of an elementary wave-like particle. It could be in any state under a mathematics of probability expressed in imaginary numbers. But,[64] the moment you apply <thought> to the elements of $\sum\Omega$, you create <feeling>.

In the *Fog Experience*, that is not "emotions" or "feelings" which you are witnessing. You are observing, without <T>, the process of Ω information transformation and referral.

---

[64] Copenhagen or not

You are noticing sensory processes connected to your autonomic physiognomy. Your |P| needs that information referral constantly: whether you're awake or asleep; conscious or anaesthetised or in a coma.

Your /S/ is welcome to tune in and watch. But nothing thoughtful will you learn in it. No emotional experience will you have within it.

The process of Ω information transformation and referral is not "driving" any part of your |M|. Neither (more obviously) is it "driving" any part of your |P|.

Your |P| processes that information, with adequate or clinically inadequate function. Whatever you might want, subjectively, to imagine you think or feel about that.

This interaction between Ω and /S/ will be the terrain of Part 2. In the following Sections of this Part, we will explore how the dynamics of Ω itself come to become.

5.   *Allostasis and | E | motion*

The classical account has been modulated in recent decades by theories of Allostasis.

We appreciate that new empirical analyses undertaken under the expanding banner of Allostasis. But, we see the new theories falling subject to the same inherent contradictions, as the paradigms they are meant to displace.

Allostasis may be an unfamiliar term to the lay reader. Allostasis means "achieving stability through change"; it was introduced by P. Sterling and J. Eyer in 1988.[65]

The first usage of the term was limited. Like so much in biological psychology, the notion then assumed wings took off into the stratosphere and beyond. As Ramsay and Woods wrote in 2014:[66]

> Homeostasis, the dominant explanatory framework for physiological regulation, has undergone significant revision in recent years, with contemporary models differing significantly from the original formulation.

> Allostasis, an alternative view of physiological regulation, goes beyond its homeostatic roots, offering novel insights relevant to our understanding and treatment of several chronic health conditions.

---

[65] Sterling, P., & Eyer, J. (1988). Allostasis: A new paradigm to explain arousal pathology. In S. Fisher, & J. Reason (Eds.), Handbook of life stress, cognition and health (pp. 629-649). New York: John Wiley & Sons.

[66] Ramsay DS, Woods SC. Clarifying the roles of homeostasis and allostasis in physiological regulation. *Psychol Rev.* 2014;121(2):225-247. doi:10.1037/a0035942

Despite growing enthusiasm for allostasis, the concept remains diffuse, due in part to ambiguity as to how the term is understood and used, impeding meaningful translational and clinical research on allostasis.
...
Over the last fifty or more years, a number of physiologically plausible models have been proposed that operationalize wise homeostatic control via a central command center, and in so doing, most of these models relied upon constructs taken from engineering control theory such as centrally regulated variables, set points, comparators and/or error signals or their equivalent. *Cannon (1945)* himself acknowledged that his advocation of purposeful coordination of responses to serve an animal's best interest by defending critical regulated variables rendered homeostasis teleological, but the intuitive appeal of this tenet undoubtedly contributed to the enormous success of his model in generating hypotheses, stimulating research and interpreting experimental findings. However, limitations resulting from this perspective, how they have been considered by others, and how new data have resulted in novel insights about regulation, conspired to foster dissatisfaction with Cannon's original view of homeostatic regulation.

The point is that in spite of the widespread influence of the homeostatic model, both theorizing as well as empirical research on physiological regulation have identified situations that appear inconsistent with its basic tenets. These seeming inconsistencies have spawned numerous alternative explanatory models (and a plethora of new terms) in an effort to address apparent gaps in homeostatic thinking.

Hence, the literature on physiological regulation has become sprinkled with terms such as predictive homeostasis (*Moore-Ede, 1986*), reactive homeostasis (*Moore-Ede, 1986*), homeorhesis (*Bauman, 2000; Bauman & Currie, 1980; Waddington, 1957, 1968*), homeorheusis (*Nicolaidis, 2011*), homeokinetics (*Soodak & Iberall, 1978*), rheostasis (*Mrosovsky, 1990*), homeodynamics (*Yates, 1982, 1994, 2008*), teleophoresis (*Chilliard, 1986; Chilliard et al., 2000*), poikilostasis (*Kuenzel, Beck, & Teruyama, 1999*), heterostasis (*Selye, 1973*), allodynamic regulation (*Berntson & Cacioppo, 2000, 2007*) and allostasis (*Sterling, 2004, 2012; Sterling & Eyer, 1988*).

174

Overview of Allostasis

By far the most influential of these alternative models has been Sterling and Eyer's (1988) allostasis, a term they defined as achieving stability through change.

More specifically, Sterling and Eyer coined the term allostasis to reflect the process whereby in order to be adaptive, organisms must be able to change the defended levels of one or more regulated parameters as needed to adjust to new or changing environments.

For example, in an especially stressful environment an individual might maintain, and defend, an elevated level of blood pressure relative to the level maintained in a less-stressful environment. Sterling and Eyer argued that a strict interpretation of homeostasis disallowed an organism's defending a different level, as it went against the necessity of constancy of the internal environment maintained by an invariant set point. Sterling and Eyer explicitly incorporated learning and anticipatory responding in their description of allostasis, thus incorporating a second major departure from canonical views of homeostasis.

To summarize, the originally stated basic tenets of allostasis are that (1) the most efficient regulation is anticipatory, relying upon experience or learning from past events, (2) rather than regulated variables having invariant set points, the defended level of a regulated value can and should change to optimally cope with the demands presented by environmental changes, and (3) optimal regulation is achieved by a central command center (in the brain) that directs the activation/ deactivation of the multiple responses that influence one or more regulated variables in order to arrive at the most cost-beneficial compromises. As discussed below, this might include activating a hormonal stress response that, while facilitating an animal's overall ability to respond to a challenge to one regulated variable, may also lead to concurrent activation of responses that have opposite and competing effects on a different regulated variable.

Allostasis has quickly grown in popularity, with numerous scholars moving it in directions not included in its original description. Perhaps most importantly, whereas Sterling and Eyer (1988) viewed allostatic regulation as achieving optimal and efficient operation of key systems in the body with minimal energy expenditure, others have redefined allostasis as the process that occurs when maintenance of key variables comes at a considerable underlying cost, and allostasis is consequently associated with pathophysiological regulation by many (Power, 2004). McEwen and Stellar (1993) suggested the term "allostatic load" to account for the cost to the response system for maintaining a regulated variable at a value chronically displaced from its previous level by prolonged activation of compensatory effectors. Day (2005) posed the reasonable question as to whether the cost of regulation is already inherent within the model of homeostasis (i.e., homeostatic load) without requiring allostasis, the point being that while the cost of responding is important, it does not necessarily differentiate between homeostasis and allostasis.

The legitimate question has been raised as to whether the concept of allostasis provides any new value in understanding regulatory physiology (Power, 2004; Woods & Ramsay, 2007). Carpenter (2004) stated that allostasis provides no added value because it is a vaguely characterized cluster of concepts that have always been part of the ordinary conceptual basis of homeostasis. Cabanac (2006) asserted that allostasis actually blurs the understanding of the regulatory process.

A complicating factor in evaluating the potential value of allostasis is the lack of a common understanding of the concept; i.e., there is as yet no general consensus as to what the model actually is other than it goes beyond homeostasis in some specific ways. In the concluding commentary of an edited volume about allostasis, Power (2004) noted that the contributors differed considerably in their conception of allostasis. Berridge (2004) makes the similar point that because allostasis is a relatively new term it is difficult to predict which of its meanings will become most accepted. The point is that there is still considerable variability in how the term is being used, and this may partially explain why the translation of allostatic principles into clinical research and practice is only just beginning (Peters & McEwen, 2012).

Thus, the field is now confronted with two competing models of regulation that are not easily integrated. For example, Sterling (2004) suggested that allostasis should replace homeostasis (see also Le

Moal, 2007) while Power and Schulkin (2012) contend that allostasis and homeostasis are compatible and complementary components of physiological regulation. At the same time, new insights based on empirical studies of regulation have challenged key assumptions of both models. Thus, a critical analysis and comparison of homeostasis and allostasis, as well as physiological regulation per se, is warranted.

We have provided such a lengthy quotation, because it so usefully illustrates the dead end of the allostasis notion: a free-floating diagnostic, without architecture. Change so as to facilitate interfaces: that is not an explanation. It's a tautology.

As stated in Kim Armstrong's 2019 report:[67]

The core task of a brain working in service to the body is allostasis: regulating the body's internal systems by anticipating needs and preparing to satisfy them before they arise.

Interoception - your brain's representation of sensations from your own body - is the sensory consequence of this activity, Barrett says, and is central to everything from thought, to emotion, to decision making, and our sense of self.

This, while well-intentioned, is a also tautological road to nowhere. It has disutility: reliance upon the allostasis concept as having independent explanatory effect, results in adding layers of confusion, not clarity.

---

[67]https://www.psychologicalscience.org/observer/interoception-how-we-understand-our-bodys-inner-sensations. A length quotation, because it covers much useful ground

6. Introduction Survey

We have provided a brief overview. Without the systems analysis, some of what we just said will have appeared obscure, or even just plain wrong: steeped as we are in the classical account.

The long Chapter ahead now follows this structure:

(1)   Introductory: as above.

(2)   Systems: in which we set out processes. Analysis of these processes allows us to understand what exactly are the phenomena which the classical account conceives of as "emotions" and "feelings.

(3)   Consequences: the new lessons that we can draw from this systems analysis.

(4)   Construction: exploring the architecture of interactions between |M| entation and |E| emotion.

(5)   Realisation: exploring the interaction of the Self in consciousness, and the rest of reality.

Throughout this Chapter, we will be twisting the Rubik's Cube of Self: from its internal connections, through to its architecture, and back again.

To achieve this, we have need to be clear about the outline the architecture:

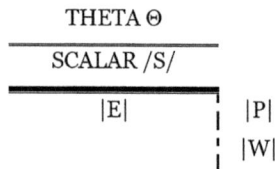

THETA ⊖

SCALAR /S/

|E| |P|

|W|

We have already seen this matrix in the Globe graphics. In the following sections, we're going to chart a course through this matrix as follows:

➢ analysing the outside world |W|, as it interacts with whatever is going on in |E|, the realm of "emotion".

➢ analysing the internal mechanics of |E|.

➢ seeing how |E| interacts with |P|hysiology: both by transmission, and receiving stimulation.

➢ seeing then how |E| transmits to /S/.

➢ then how /S/ stimulates |E|.

➢ analysing the interaction of <feelings>, <thoughts> and the Theta Θ equalisation function.

Finally:

➢ returning to our starting point on the "cube", to see how we can understand "outward" interactions of this Matrixial Self architecture, with the |W|orld.

So, we have a plan. Let's get started.

(2) SYSTEMS

7.   *The Sensation Machine*

Exclusion Function

$(\geq\varsigma^*) \neq (\leq \Theta^*) = \int[x]$

Let's now focus on a sensory input:

- producing a sensation
- being noticed as something like "feeling".

Take a sound. That's an acoustic wave $<\sum I^*>$, arriving in our senses:

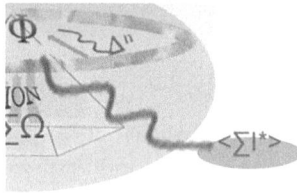

The next part of the process is the *Exclusion Function*. Here we meet a new equation:

$(\geq\varsigma\ ^*) \neq (\leq \Theta^*) = \int[x]$

Breaking this one down:

$(\geq\varsigma\ ^*)$	$\neq$	$(\leq \Theta^*)$		$\int[x]$
Input	<resistor>	Internal	=	Exclusion
<signal>		<signal>		Function

Now, let's explain the new terms, with reference to the EF graphic:

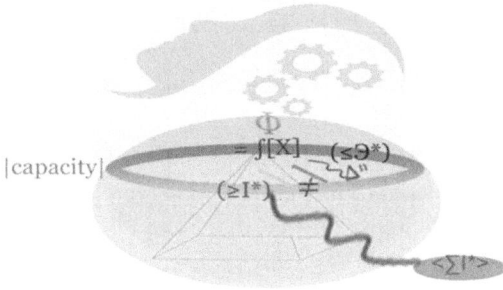

Exclusion Function Definitions

(1)   <Node>

We have established above, and in *Matrixial Logic*, Chapters 4 and 5, how it's necessary that there be a <Node>, in order for there to be mode of interaction between Self and │W│.

(2)   │capacity│

Our <Senses> are *Capacities* for acknowledging sensory data. The acoustic architecture, from our ears, through our neurological structures, and beyond, is a capacity. It is reactive. It awaits auditory input data.

(3)   <resistor>

Our <Senses> are reactive capacities and act as a <resistor>. A <resistor> is the [≠] in the *Exclusion* Function equation.

(4)   <signal>

In coming into contact with a ∣capacity∣, which is active through a <resistor>, a <Node> becomes coherent as a <signal>, symbolised as (≥ς *).

(5)   <potential>

It is well established that we have (≤Ɔ*) Internal Signals running through us every microsecond of our lives. the Self is constanttly modelling estimations and approximations of of expected input:

>   Our (≤Ɔ*) Internal Signals are *Potentials*:

(6)   Exclusion Function

The interaction between <signals^n> under <resistance> produces = ∫[x] a quantity of <Node> Output.

<u>Exclusion Function Operations</u>

With these definitions, we now need to explain the operations.

(1)   <Node>

From Matrixial Logic:

>   Tabulating the essential differences between [I] and
>   <∑I>:

Form and <Node> in [I]

Form [I]	<Node> <∑I>
• in Potential	• of Potential
• mediated by ≠ with	• interacting [~] with

- Moment (A), (-A)
- stable
- dynamic
- self-actualising
- deductive

- Form $\Delta \Delta$
- unstable
- static
- externally actualised
- inductive

Any <Node> is inherently unstable. If we were being quantum theory about it, we could say that a <Node> is in a state of superposition. That "suspended reality" collapses upon meeting an interference medium.[68]

A dog bark is a sound <Node>. We saw how the origination of that all works, in Chapter 5 of Matrixial Logic.

This graphics a sound <Node>. A sound wave propagates such that it meets your body: specifically your ear.[69]

All that is interesting in this domain is well-established by the material sciences (as to the wave origination and properties) and in biology (as to your sense receptors). *Matrixial Self* can simply take these as data.

---

[68] we don't mean to imply here that you are any kind of "observer" as in the Copenhagen interpretation: none of this has anything to do with Consciousness
[69] although you can of course sense sound vibrations at any part of your body

(2) | capacity |

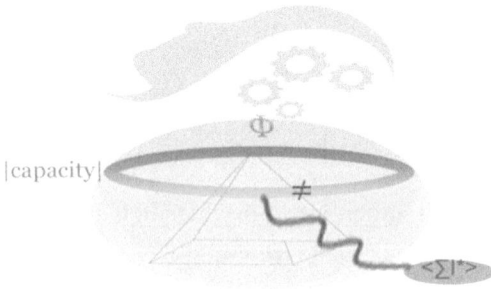

We denote this term between | |. As readers will know from Chapter 7 of *Matrixial Logic*, this notation signifies <gap>.

So, what's the significance of a | gap |. Surely that's just a nothing. Let's see:

Experience: Gaps
Step 1:
See this image:

Now:

• Just see what you can see. Think whatever you think.

Stop

Step 2:
See this image:

Now:

- Just see what you can see. Think whatever you think.

Stop

Discussion:

(1)   You see the Line.

(2)   It doesn't seem to "do" anything.

(3)   After a while you just "tune out" the Line.

Remember back to the *Already Experience*:

How you "parked" that unfamiliar sigil, because it made
no /S/ sense in the Landscape.

185

This is similar. The Line seems to have no connection to the Landscape of | capacity | .

Step 3:
See this image:

Now:
- Just see what you can see. Think whatever you think.

Stop

<u>Discussion</u>:
(1)   You see the Lines.
(2)   Now, they suddenly create a new definition for the Landscape.
(3)   They become their own distinct LineScape.

Question:
- are you now seeing the Landscape first, with the LineScape just there as something separate;

or

• are you now seeing the Landscape through the prism of the LineScape?

Let's see a comparison graphic to check:

It really is different in your reality, isn't it? In fact, these parallel images now have you creating a | | | relationship: a tri-line structure, which is becoming more "real" than the Landscapes.

This is of course well-known as "pattern recognition". Our minds, and our senses are tuned by nature to discern patterns: visual, visual-movement, auditory, sensory, and so on.

We asked:

> So, what's the significance of a | gap |. Surely that's just a nothing.

Now we have an answer. A | gap | is a *Form of Differences*. To make a | gap | requires more than just one difference. It requires a plurality of differences, which together create a *Form of Differences*.

Yes, this is an inequality ≠. But, a ⎮gap⎮ is a passive Form. It's a difference, but does not activate anything else. It's a precursor, not a catalyst.

Let's just test this, with a Question:
• does the LineScape bring any thought or feeling to you; or
• is the LineScape just "there", doing nothing.

You can see how the LineScape is a ⎮gap⎮. It's simply passive. It has changed your relationship to the Landscape, to create a new ⎮gap⎮ layer.

The ⎮gap⎮ has also done something else. We chose a graphic above that somewhat concealed it. Now let's reveal.

Experience: Shards
Step 1:
See this image:

Now:

• Allow that sea to flow, in your mind's eye.

Stop

<u>Discussion</u>:

(1)   Easy.

Step 2:

See this image:

Now:

• Again: allow that sea to flow, in your mind's eye.

Stop

<u>Discussion</u>:

(1)   You see the Line.

(2)   It doesn't stop the water flow at all.

(3)   You don't feel like the Line has to "be" in the water. The Line can just hover and the water flows as at Step 1.

Step 3:

See this image:

Now:

• Again: allow that sea to flow, in your mind's eye.

Stop

Discussion:

(1) You see the Lines.

(2) Now, the water just won't flow.

(3) You may be able to get the water to flow with this arrow:

(4)   or this arrow:

(5)   But, as soon as you really focus on the | gap |, the
        water becomes frozen.

So now we see that a | gap | is a *Form of Differences*:
*   which creates its own reality dimension (the LineScape)
*   which "freezes" movement, defining that new stasis by
    reference to the | gap |.

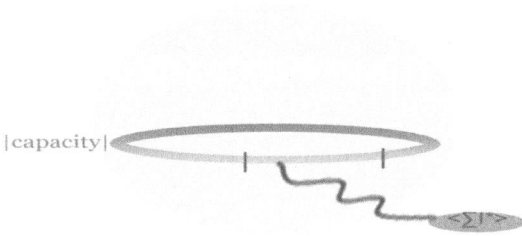

Here, with the bare wirework, we can see | capacity | in
its gapping operation.

The sound <Node> arrives:
*   Perhaps its at a frequency outside the human hearing
    range. Then, no | capacity | is engaged. We don't sense it.
or
*   it's within the human auditory frequencies. We hear.
    | capacity | is engaged.

Then, with a <Node> having arrived, we move to the next
part of the process.

(3)   <resistor>
        Our <Senses> are reactive capacities and act as a

<resistor>. A <resistor> is the [≠] in the *Exclusion Function* equation.

It might be more helpful, by analogy, to think of the <resistor> as part of a <potentiometer>. The analogy is that an electrical resistor has a set resistance. 4.7k Ω.[70] Whereas a potentiometer, like a volume pot, has a variable resistance.

The other part of this element is the Exclusion Function: = ∫[x]. It's probably most helpful to explain the <resistor> together with the EF.

(4)   <signal>: (≥ς*)
     In coming into contact with a |capacity|, which is active through a <resistor>, a <Node> becomes coherent as a <signal>, symbolised as (≥ς*).

Process:
- A <Node> is unstable. Upon meeting a |capacity|, a <Node> "collapses".
- The interaction of <Node> and |capacity| can produce a <signal>.

A <signal> is:
- reflexive of (a "mirror" of) the original <Node>, arriving from outside[71]
- a quantity.

---

[70] the definition of 1Ω is the resistance between two points where 1 volt (1V) of applied potential energy will push 1 ampere (1A) of current
[71] we will modify this later, to include internal meta-<<Node>s>

This latter point requires some reflection. Throughout *Matrixial Logic* to date, we have almost exclusively dealt with intrinsically unquantified phenomena:

- in [E] an (A) or (nA) is a thing, a "1" thing. But that is not a quantity. It is "that" thing extended in spacetime. Any application of a quantitative attribute (being part of a number series) occurs at the level of Form, not Substance.
- in [I], Moments Δ^n are quasi-quantitative. But they are in unbounded infinity ∞. Any number series places a boundary on infinity.[72]

Now, insofar as the latter proposition gave you any difficulty in Chapters 2-7 of *Matrixial Logic*, or indeed here, let's just take a dive into that ∞ concept.

Let's just reference some terminology:[73]

Natural numbers : The counting numbers {1, 2, 3, ...} are commonly called natural numbers; however, other definitions include 0, so that the non-negative integers {0, 1, 2, 3, ...} are also called natural numbers. Natural numbers including 0 are also called **whole numbers**.

Integers : Positive and negative counting numbers, as well as zero: {..., −3, −2, −1, 0, 1, 2, 3, ...}.

Rational numbers : Numbers that can be expressed as a ratio of an integer to a non-zero integer. All integers are rational, but the converse is not true; there are rational numbers that are not integers.

Real numbers : Numbers that can represent a distance along a line. They can be positive, negative, or zero. All rational numbers are real, but the converse is not true.

Irrational numbers: Real numbers that are not rational.

---

[72] if you want proof of that, open any book on calculus

[73] https://en.wikipedia.org/wiki/List_of_types_of_numbers

Imaginary numbers: Numbers that equal the product of a real number and the square root of −1. The number 0 is both real and imaginary.

Complex numbers :Includes real numbers, imaginary numbers, and sums and differences of real and imaginary numbers.

You might want to state that any of these number sets constitutes an Infinity ∞. That's fine if you're doing mathematics, and that idea works for your number system.

But it does not work for logic. In logic, the statement of any number imposes a boundary upon Infinity ∞, which boundary is expressed by the "distance" from any other number in that series. Distance there must be, otherwise the concept of number loses its essential meaning. Any such distance is intrinsically bounded: and thus is not Infinity ∞.

Putting that all back together as a rubric in Matrixial Logic:

Quantification is a function of Form, not Number

Form can be expressed in number, but such number is a derivation from Form: it is not Form itself.

A <Node> is Infinity ∞ represented in an unstable derivation of Form.

Now the definition makes sense:

In coming into contact with a | capacity |, which is active through a <resistor>, a <Node> becomes coherent as a <signal>, symbolised as (≥ς*).

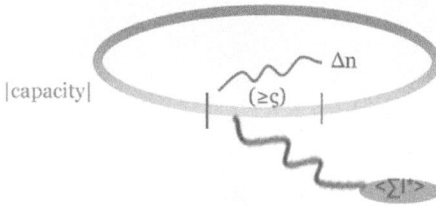

It's because the <signal> is a quantity that it is, unusually in ML, symbolised as (≥ς*). The ≥ symbol indicates a quantity greater than zero.[74]

Mathematically, we would designate <ς*> as being a quantity which is a positive real number greater than zero.

It's difficult to think of a negative, or zero sound wave, as a matter of common sense. As a matter of logic: since any Form (and derivation of Form) is hylomorphically reflexive of its contents, there cannot be a Form acting with effect in the material world, which has a zero content.

We can of course invent arithmetic forms of zero and negative, and imaginary numbers and so on. But these are

---

[74] the symbol does not perform the same role, were it being used as a mathematical operator

constructs in the Scalar /S/ domain of mentation. They are not things in the world.[75]

The strength of a <signal> obviously depends upon:

- the attributes of the <Node>
- the attributes of |capacity| in relation to that Node.

So, now a complex <Node>, comprised of unstable derivation of Form, has been *transformed* by |capacity| into a <signal>.

This transformation is what alters an "outer" (or external world) manifestation of reality into an "internal" psycho-physical manifestation of reality.

That signal $(\geqslant\varsigma^*)$ can now act as Moments Δ^n in Infinity ∞. To pull a concept from *Matrixial Logic*, there is created a Heraclitan "river".

On its own, of course, the signal $(\geqslant\varsigma)$ cannot do anything. It needs an antipode. There needs to be the creation of a Form.

(5)   <potential>: $(\leqslant\Theta^*)$

It is well established that we have $(\leqslant\Theta^*)$ Internal Signals running through us every microsecond of our lives. the Self is constantly modelling estimations and approximations of of expected input. Our $(\leqslant\Theta^*)$ Internal Signals are *Potentials*.

---

[75] even if they accurately reflect quantum processes of things in the world

That form arises through the opposition:

$$(\geq\varsigma^*) \neq (\leq \Im^*) =$$

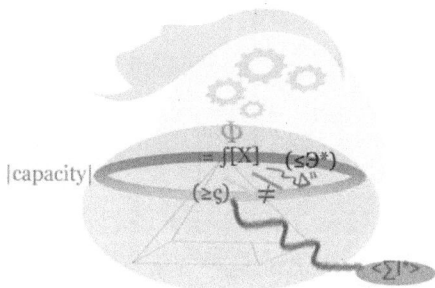

A human being is, self-evidently as a matter of biology and material sciences a complex network of signals. Those signals move between the structures of our body: anatomical, neurological.

We take the developing data of anatomy, physiology and neurology as givens, for the purposes of the *Matrixial Self*. There is always more to be discovered, but it should be uncontentious that we now have a good understanding of the material processes by which human beings function as organic entities.

Our senses self-evidently work through nerve signals: electro-chemical discharges. Our neurons works through synaptic electro-chemical signalling, and ephaptic electrical timing coherence.

We can therefore take all of this as a given. And draw from that body of material science the elementary conclusion that we have (≤Ɛ*) running through us every millisecond of our lives.

Our (≤Ɛ*) Internal Signals are *Potentials*. By which we mean that our nervous system is ready to receive an external <signal> relating to heat, or cold, or light, or dark, or sound: and so on.

Obviously, those Potentials are being activated within ourselves every millisecond in our ordinary life processes. You could be in a soundproof room, but your auditory <potential> would remain in state.

We use the like notation (≤ Ɛ*) to a transformed <Node>. We said of <ς*>:

> Mathematically, we would designate < ς*> as being a quantity which is a positive real number greater than zero. It's difficult to think of a negative, or zero sound wave, as a matter of common sense. As a matter of logic: since any Form (and derivation of Form) is hylomorphically reflexive of its contents, there cannot be a Form acting with effect in the material world, which has a zero content.

The <signal> potential of (≤ Ɛ*) internal states is obviously different. There can be (≤ Ɛ*) internal states:
- at a low or nil "firing", until disturbed
- with a constant "firing", which is subject to change up or down.

In any of these cases, the <signal> potential of ($\leq \Theta^*$) internal states provides the necessary antigone to external <Nodes> transformed by |capacity| resistance into <signals> of <ς^*>.

At this point in the analysis, we are treating ($\leq \Theta^*$) as if they were autonomous. Some Potentials are. Some are subject to interaction with /S/. Some are subject to indirect interaction with Θ. We will deal later with the complexities of these interactions.

(6)   Exclusion Function: = $\int[x]$

The interaction between <signal> and <potential> under [<resistance> $\neq$] produces = $\int[x]$, which is a quantity of Output.

Now, we're ready to pull the whole equation together:

Exclusion Function

$$(\geq \varsigma^*) \neq (\leq \Theta^*) = \int[x]$$

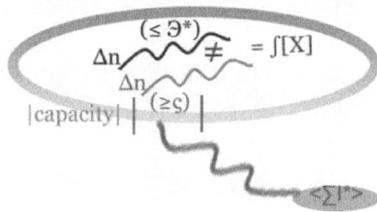

The final term of the EF equation: $\int[x]$ is unusual in *Matrixial Logic*. It is the first time we have seen the use of a $\int$ operator.

This is because $\int$ is dealing with quantities $\geq$ / $\leq$. We could write the EF equation as:

$$(\varsigma^*) \neq (\ni^*) = [x]$$

But when we do that, we can see immediately that the $[x]$ term looks odd. Is it in $[E]$ or $[I]$, or something else? Is it a Form, or some other hylomorphic term?

The EF equation as properly written answers these questions:

- $\int[x]$ is hylomorphic to the qualities and quantities of the <signal> $\neq$ <potential> interaction
- $\int[x]$ is not a <Node>
- but it is unstable, not being a Form of Contents.

We thus attain the understanding that $\int[x]$ is not something in itself, or for itself: $\int[x]$ *is a bridge, which transforms*.

8. The $\int[x]$ Transformation Bridge

A bridge to what? $\int[x]$ is a bridge to the Ohm function Ω.

Obviously, there is no bridge if $= \int[0]$. There is only a bridge if $= \int[x]$ is a non-zero output.

This is all more obvious that it might seem. Take your galvanic skin response:

(a)   There's your body, in the world, interacting with it: W=>.

(b)   Your senses, what we and the classical account, envisage as your "fishing nets" catch bits of | W |. They interact with | W |.

(c)   We know from physiology and neurology, that your sensory systems have to translate that material nexus into nerve signals.

(d)   Those nerve signals then get assembled and distributed.

(e)   The relevant nerves then activate to make your hair stand on end or give you goose bumps.

So, for example, when you see something accompanied by its sound: a dog barking; your visual cortex assembles that sense input separately to your auditory cortex. These different signal batches are then brought together, to render the impression of: dog bark.

The Exclusion Function equation reflects part of these processes:

* a <Node> is transformed by (variable) resistance in meeting | capacity |
* transformation effects[76] a state change in <signal>
* which interacts with <potential>
* producing a function of that quantitative interaction in $\int[x]$.

---

[76] or fails to effect

In the (a) to (e) narrative above, the Exclusion Function gets us part way through (c).

So, we need to map the architecture of Ohm Ω. That requires us to pause, and consider a vital primary function of Ω.

9. The Sanity Barrier

Foetal You is in a protected state. You are developing the systems which will allow you, at the end of 9 months, to exist in an autonomous state.

Not autonomous, in the sense that you can look after yourself, but so that you can cope with exposure to the world of sense experiences.

It's important to begin here. Because we have hundreds of years of philosophy premised on the notion that it's our brains which do the sorting of experience: which effect an exclusion function.

This sort of reasoning implies a mature, reasoning, autonomous individual. Not a newborn baby. The neonate architecture is surprisingly powerful, as studies over the last decade are increasingly showing.[77]

———————

[77] *The Newborn Infant: A Missing Stage in Developmental Psychology.* Emese Nagy. Infant and Child Development. Inf. Child. Dev. 20: 3–19 (2011) Published online 14 May 2010 in Wiley Online Library (wileyonlinelibrary.com). DOI: 10.1002/icd.683

Here, we simply recognise the obvious reality of the neonate: the immature /S/ continuum brain is too underdeveloped to guide the Exclusion Function.

The neonate is subject to the same cacophony of interaction with the world, as you are, sitting reading this.

If there were no sorting mechanism for potential sensory data, you would go insane in a few minutes. Your adult brain could not possibly process the trillions of interactions, from the sub-atomic level right up to social interactions.

That sorting mechanism is grown in the intrauterine stage of development. The trauma of birth itself seems to activate it: which makes sense.

We thus discover the primary role of the Exclusion Function: to act as your sanity barrier, from the first moments of your newborn experience.

sensory over-responsivity (SOR):[78]
Temperamental negative affect and fear were moderately correlated with auditory and tactile SOR symptoms.

Prenatal complications significantly predicted tactile symptoms after controlling for child characteristics. Additionally, females with a male co-twin showed greater SOR at age two than same-sex female dizygotic twins, suggesting a possible risk associated with *in utero*

[78] Keuler MM, Schmidt NL, Van Hulle CA, Lemery-Chalfant K, Goldsmith HH. Sensory overresponsivity: prenatal risk factors and temperamental contributions. *J Dev Behav Pediatr.* 2011;32(7):533-541. doi:10.1097/DBP.0b013e3182245c05

testosterone exposure. Both auditory and tactile SOR domains were heritable. Bivariate genetic analyses showed that each SOR domain had a similar genetic relationship with fear and negative affect.

A small subset of both children and adults report unusually intense, even painful, responses to everyday sensory stimuli that most individuals experience as innocuous. The reactivity of senses to external stimuli appears to vary widely. For instance, most individuals experience no auditory sensation from long florescent light bulbs, but a few find the hum of these lights so uncomfortable that they cannot work in a room with florescent lighting. Clinicians observe this sensory over-responsivity, sometimes called sensory defensiveness, in children with a range of diagnoses, including attention-deficit hyperactivity disorder (ADHD), autism, and Fragile X Syndrome, but sensory over-responsivity, importantly, also occurs in children without any apparent medical condition.

Over-responsivity can occur in response to tactile, visual, auditory, or other modalities of stimuli. Some individuals experience a broad range of sensitivities that are chronic and severe; these sensitivities often begin very early in life and may impact mastering key developmental milestones. Although these sensitivities may not always elicit strong concern from clinicians, parents and teachers have viewed multiple, severe symptoms of sensory over-responsivity as adversely affecting social interactions, peer and family relationships, and school performance of the child.

In fact, the new diagnostic entity called Sensory Processing Disorder (SPD) has already been acknowledged in some diagnostic classification schemes and proposed for inclusion in the next installment of the *Diagnostic and Statistical Manual of Mental Disorders*.

The incidence of Sensory Processing Disorder ("SPD") has been studied in children, with therapeutic interventions being established:[79]

---

[79] https://childmind.org/article/treating-sensory-processing-issues/

Both the description and treatment of SPD are based on the work of Dr. A. Jean Ayres, an OT[80] who added to the traditional five senses two "internal" senses:
- body awareness (proprioception); and
- movement (vestibular).

Proprioceptive receptors, found in the joints and ligaments, facilitate motor control and posture;

Vestibular receptors, located in the inner ear, tell the brain the body's position and where it is in space, key to balance and coordination, among other things.

Meanwhile, leading SPD researcher and advocate Lucy Jane Miller adds an eighth sense,
- interoception,

to the mix.

The founder of the SPD Foundation and author of Sensational Kids: Hope and Help for Children With Sensory Processing Disorder, who was trained by Ayers, explains that this internal sense relays sensations that come from the organs.

When the brain is connecting the dots, these seven (or eight) senses afford a clear understanding of what's happening both inside and outside the body. But when it isn't, the mangled messages can become impairing or overwhelming, leading to a wide variety of defensive or compensatory behaviours.

Those with SPD can be over-reactive (hypersensitive), under-reactive (hyposensitive), or both, which can lead to meltdowns and tantrums, as well as behaviours from picky eating to hitting and hugging too tightly.

Dr Ayres used a systems model of sense experience organisation:[81]

---

[80] (1920-1988); "OT" means Occupational Therapist

[81] Lane SJ, Mailloux Z, Schoen S, et al. Neural Foundations of Ayres Sensory Integration®. *Brain Sci.* 2019;9(7):153. Published 2019 Jun 28. doi:10.3390/brainsci9070153

Based on her research and clinical experience, she developed the theory and practice of sensory integration which describes how the nervous system translates sensory information into action and posits that adequate sensory integration is an important foundation for adaptive behavior.

Sensory integration theory emphasizes the active, dynamic sensory–motor processes that support movement as well as interaction within social and physical environments and that act as a catalyst for development. Ayres' theory and practice emanated from a decades-long program of research.

Today this body of work is recognized as Ayres Sensory Integration® (ASI) and includes theory, postulates about the mechanisms of sensory integration's effects, assessment strategies to identify challenges in sensory integration, intervention principles, a manualized intervention to guide treatment, and a measure of fidelity that is used to support research and practice.

Acting only with knowledge of neuroscience at the time in which she lived, Ayres was prescient in her thinking. Much of her work remains supported by current literature.

Ayres was guided by two important principles: "the brain is a self-organizing system" and "intersensory integration is foundational to function". Typically, she began papers or lectures with simple hypotheses reflecting these principles. An example:

> "The brain, under normal circumstances, is a self-organizing system. When it is unsuccessful in accomplishing its integrative task, the behavior directed by the brain fails to fall within 'normal' expectations", [10] (p. 41).

Ayres then continued, eloquently, supporting her hypotheses with neuroscience. For example:

> "Intersensory integration can occur within a single neuron, a nucleus or the diencephalon, an entire hemisphere or even between hemispheres. One of the methods by which the CNS [Central Nervous System] integrates sensory information from several different sources is by directing it to a common neuron called a convergent

206

neuron. Whenever there is multiplicity of input all related to a single
sensorimotor process, there is probably convergence of input."

What the studies in Sensory Processing Disorder show is
that:

(1)   we are born with a set of sensing mechanisms,
        which also act as sensation limiters
(2)   in the weeks and months that follow, we become
        more adept at forming mental constructs to match
        what we sense
(3)   if our limitation function is unbalanced, we suffer
        sensory and mental disfunction.

This is necessarily a learning process: a heuristic. Each
of us as babies learns what sensations to let through and
which to block. We learn what messages to pass on and
to where.

Hebb formulated brain plasticity theories 70 years ago.[82]
As we pass sensation messages to our brain, we develop
synaptic connections:[83]

> The idea that the brain can change in response to experience is
> supported by neuroscience research that shows that experience-
> dependent learning shapes both brain function and behavior.
>
> Experience-dependent learning is the ongoing process of creation

[82] Hebb D.O. The Organization of Behavior: A Neuropsychological
Theory. Wiley; New York, NY: USA; 1949
[83] Lane SJ, Mailloux Z, Schoen S, et al. Neural Foundations of Ayres
Sensory Integration®. *Brain Sci.* 2019;9(7):153. Published 2019 Jun 28.
doi:10.3390/brainsci9070153

and organization of neuronal connections that occur as a result of experiences. An understanding of experience-dependent learning emerged from early experiments by Donald Hebb who showed, in simple organisms, that synaptic efficacy improves when presynaptic cells repeatedly and persistently stimulate the postsynaptic cell.

In other words, neurons that fire together, wire together, a statement that reflects Hebbian learning.

We now understand the Exclusion Function as one of the critical elements of |E|, performing two vital roles:

- to act as a sensory sieve: preventing us from becoming overwhelmed by our continual sensory interaction with the world
- to act as an information processor: to pass on information from our senses, after sensory sieving.

We now need to look at the ∫[x]=>Ω nexus. This is a concept which seldom appears explicitly in classical accounts. Yet all of them depend upon it.

10.   *Exclusion Function to Ω*
In Chapter 8 of Matrixial Logic, we introduced the Ohm equation:

$$(\epsilon) \neq (\ni) \sum \Omega$$

We said in that Chapter:

Emotional interactions give an unusual form of inequality equation. We sometimes use | | in place of ∑: the dipoles effect the equivalent operation to the summing.

The antipoles (ɛ) ≠ (ɔ) are neither opposites nor negations of each other. Thus, they do not produce a form, but sum over $\sum$ as Ohm Ω.

We can immediately notice the similarities with Chaos [C]. But what is also immediately different, is that Ohm Ω is not producing Singularities (Si).

We will set out some further assertive rules, before proceeding:

- Ohm Ω is directly mediated by /S/
- Ohm Ω is not directly mediated by Theta Θ
- Ohm Ω is accessed by Theta Θ only indirectly via /S/.

The implications of these rules fall to be addressed later in this Chapter, and more comprehensively in *Secret Self*.

So, now it's time to make good on that promise.

The Exclusion Function:

$$(\geq\varsigma^*) \neq (\leq \Theta^*) = \int[x]$$

reflects the process by which <Nodes> are transformed into differential interaction between <signal> and <potential>.

This brings us to a very recognisable set of ML equation types:

$$(\geq\varsigma_1) \neq (\leq \Im_1) = \int[x_1] \qquad\qquad (\geq\varsigma_2) \neq (\leq \Im_2) = \int[x_2]$$

$$> \qquad\qquad\qquad\qquad\qquad >$$

$$(\epsilon) \qquad\qquad \neq \qquad\qquad (\ni) \qquad\qquad\qquad =$$

$$\Sigma\Omega$$

This is obviously a modified form of a Nodal equation set:

(1.1) $\quad ((A^1) \neq (nA^1) = [E^1]) \neq ((A^2) \neq (nA^2) = [E^2])\ [\sim]$ $\Sigma(FoR_2)$

$$\approx$$

(2.1) $\qquad\qquad\qquad (\Box 1) \neq (\Box 2)\ [\sim]\ \Sigma(FoR_2)$

$$>$$

(2.2) $\qquad\qquad\qquad (\Box 1) \neq (\Box 2)\ [\sim] <\Sigma E>$

The difference between a <Node> in the external world and <emote> $(\epsilon)/(\ni)$ in $\Sigma\Omega$ is probably obvious. The external world is unbounded, save as a precinct of universality. The Self is a bounded part of the world. That boundary limits universality.

Thus:

- the Exclusion Function expresses a *quantitative* inequality: $[(\geq\varsigma^*) \neq (\leq \Im^*)]$
- the Ohm aggregate $\Sigma\Omega$ expresses a *qualitative* inequality: $(\epsilon) \neq (\ni)$.

The question then naturally arises: is activation of the Ohm aggregate $\Sigma\Omega$ dependent upon an interaction of more than one Exclusion Function?

Putting the matter another way: why does a <Node> not simply transform into <signal> / <potential> and then directly engage the Ohm aggregate $\sum\Omega$?

Possibly, if our | E | process did operate like a computer, we could envisage a state of affairs in which one <Node> transformation could directly affect us "emotionally": such that the effect is unilinear, and affects no other element of | E |.

Even under that imaginative hypothesis, it would obviously have to be a very simple computing function.

The reality of Selfs places such an idea in the realm of impossibility. We are active process systems. We have <potentials> running through us constantly.

There is no biological possibility of a single <Node> having effect within us, without concomitant effect in other parts of the holistic entity:[84]

> When I am looking at my coffee machine that makes funny noises, this is an instance of multisensory perception - I perceive this event by means of both vision and audition. But very often we only receive sensory stimulation from a multisensory event by means of one sense modality, for example, when I hear the noisy coffee machine in the next room, that is, without seeing it.
>
> The aim of this paper is to bring together empirical findings about multimodal perception and empirical findings about (visual, auditory,

---

[84] Nanay B. Multimodal mental imagery. *Cortex*. 2018;105:125-134. doi:10.1016/j.cortex.2017.07.006

tactile) mental imagery and argue that on occasions like this, we have multimodal mental imagery: perceptual processing in one sense modality (here: vision) that is triggered by sensory stimulation in another sense modality (here: audition).

Multimodal mental imagery is not a rare and obscure phenomenon. The vast majority of what we perceive are multisensory events: events that can be perceived in more than one sense modality - like the noisy coffee machine. And most of the time we are only acquainted with these multisensory events via a subset of the sense modalities involved - all the other aspects of these multisensory events are represented by means of multisensory mental imagery. This means that multisensory mental imagery is a crucial element of almost all instances of everyday perception.

and, also by Nanay:[85]

Many philosophers use findings about sensory substitution devices in the grand debate about how we should individuate the senses. The big question is this: Is "vision" assisted by (tactile) sensory substitution really vision? Or is it tactile perception? Or some sui generis novel form of perception?

My claim is that sensory substitution assisted "vision" is neither vision nor tactile perception, because it is not perception at all. It is mental imagery: visual mental imagery triggered by tactile sensory stimulation. But it is a special form of mental imagery that is triggered by corresponding sensory stimulation in a different sense modality, which I call "multimodal mental imagery."

This is the logic of the scientific, empirical studies of these phenomena. The literature is vast, running across: biology, biochemistry, physiology, psychology, quantum biology, and beyond.

---

[85] Nanay B. Sensory Substitution and Multimodal Mental Imagery. *Perception*. 2017;46(9):1014-1026. doi:10.1177/0301006617699225

The question which we have been addressing arises (not unfairly) from the trap of thinking that this second equation: $(\geq\varsigma_2) \neq (\leq \Theta_2) = \int[x_2]$, must represent an external <Node> transformation.

That is not what we are saying at all. Rather, the $[_2]$ in that second equation is equally capable of representing an internal <Node>.

That leads on to the next question: how do we specify or identify particular internal Nodes? The answer is: we don't try to. It's pointless. The complexity of the human organism makes such enquiry redundant, save as aggregate reverse engineering for the purposes of clinical medicine.

And saying this, is to make a brave assumption of the possibility of knowledge:

- You breathed in and out at least once reading that sentence
- Breathing in required $|W| <Node>=>\int[x]$ transformation
- then further transition in Ω
- then referral to $|P|$

Trying to work out the $|E|$ effects of that throughout your whole Self entity, would self-evidently be absurd, and impossible.

Now, saying that we can't know something sounds terrible. But it's only bad if we have a need to know that something. We really don't need to know how the literally trillions of overlapping <Nodal> physical interactions are affecting our |E|, milliseconds at a time.

We can see these aggregates in function in this pictographic:

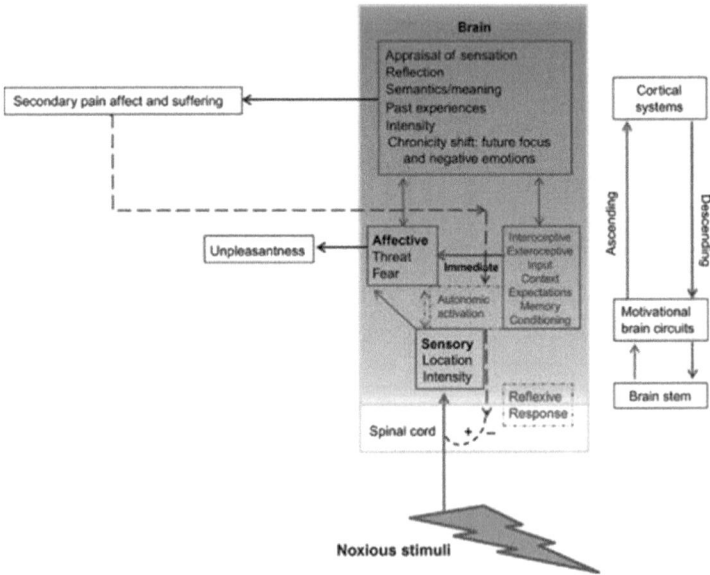

from: *Stress: Concepts, Cognition, Emotion, and Behavior.*
Handbook of Stress Series Volume 1. Ed. G Fink (2016)

Now we see why the Ω equation uses the term $\sum$ and not =. All we can ever do is analyse in terms of aggregates.

Those aggregates are powerful: analytically and as a matter of Self process.

- we can usefully analyse aggregates of Exclusion Function => Ω processes
- it is those aggregates which interact with Mentation.

Matthew Fulkerson[86] makes a useful case for sensory pluralism:

Start with two seemingly true statements: (i) We have many senses; (ii) They often interact.

These statements are now widely acknowledged and incorporated into recent work on perception, but they are also in deep tension with one another. Once we allow that the sensory modalities interact, and do so pervasively at multiple levels of sensory processing, with effects at all levels of our psychology (subpersonal, behavioral, and phenomenal), then it becomes difficult to make sense of what, exactly, these individual senses might be. Vision is less a single coherent modality than a complex collection of interacting subsystems. And that collection has features different in kind from those found in the auditory, vestibular, and nociceptive systems (of course, there are many similarities too). Indeed, it can become difficult to maintain the idea that we can have anything like a unified conception of sensory modalities and their interactions.

I start with a detailed discussion of human thermoreception, using it as a case study for the sort of tensions I describe above. I then discuss the general implications of this example, and propose a robust theoretical framework for addressing this tension.

My claim is that we should abandon any single theoretical account of sensory interaction, and adopt a view according to which sensory systems and their interactions are classified in part by our explanatory purposes.

---

[86] Fulkerson M. Rethinking the senses and their interactions: the case for sensory pluralism. *Front Psychol.* 2014;5:1426. Published 2014 Dec 10. doi:10.3389/fpsyg.2014.01426

> The upshot of this proposal is that it allows us to fully acknowledge the deep interactions between sensory subsystems without thereby giving up entirely on the very idea of separate sensory modalities.
>
> The main target of my view is any form of sensory monism that assumes there will be a single, authoritative, and context free account of what it is to be a sensory modality and for an interaction between them to be "multisensory" or "multimodal." On such a monist view, there should be a single determinate answer to the question of whether vestibular awareness or pain or any other putative sense counts as a sensory modality. I believe such a view is implausible and deeply problematic, and in what follows I offer a substantive alternative account.

We endorse Fukerson's opposition to sensory monism. That is an artefact of Decartian thinking, as it underwent transformation into mechanical monism during the machine age (late 18th to late 19th century).

However, there is an Architecture within which these Systems function and by which they function as dynamics of the Self.

It may surprise the general reader that, after a century of experimentation and exploration in clinical psychology, we still have no consensus on how we feel something as simple as heat: much less vision.

The Matrixial Self does not require to enter into that debate. What we can usefully take from it, is that the Self model we have described is reflected by the science: as are the express limits of our knowledge within that model.

Having contextualised the matter, it's important to restate the possible derivations of Ω:

Externals}		
=> from |W| External}		=> from |W| External}
$(\geq\varsigma_1) \neq (\leq \vartheta_1) = \int[x_1]$		$(\geq\varsigma_2) \neq (\leq \vartheta_2) = \int[x_2]$
$>$		$>$
(ε)	$\neq$	$(\backepsilon)$ $= \Sigma\Omega$

Mixed}		
=> from |W| External}		=> from |P| or |S| Internal}
$(\geq\varsigma_1) \neq (\leq \vartheta_1) = \int[x_1]$		$(\geq\varsigma_2) \neq (\leq \vartheta_2) = \int[x_2]$
$>$		$>$
(ε)	$\neq$	$(\backepsilon)$ $= \Sigma\Omega$

Internals}		
=> from |P| or |S| Internal}		=> from |P| or |S| Internal}
$(\geq\varsigma_1) \neq (\leq \vartheta_1) = \int[x_1]$		$(\geq\varsigma_2) \neq (\leq \vartheta_2) = \int[x_2]$
$>$		$>$
(ε)	$\neq$	$(\backepsilon)$ $= \Sigma\Omega$

If the Exclusion Function only ever transformed External} <Nodes>, then tracing the derivation of Emotes $(\varepsilon)\neq(\backepsilon)$ would be a simple matter of clinical materialism.

That might be so, even if Internal} <Nodes> were limited to $|P|$. We approach such a case in examples of coma, or more clearly vegetative brain death.

In the latter condition, an external machine is replicating the generation of Internal} $|P|$ <Nodes>. Here, we can see that the machine is:

- stimulating EF response to External}<Nodes>
- cross-stimulating EF response to Internal}<Nodes>

These 3 paradigms of the EF also correspond to changing life conditions:

- a neonate moves from a "greener" state to a "bluer" state
- significant (for any particular individual) changes in circumstances create a new "greener" state, which then needs to be internalised by moving to a "bluer" state

Blue Internal}|S|<Nodes> can deliberately try to replicate the effect in Ω of External}|W|<Nodes>. This can only be intuitive: a matter of trial and error. It's a talent, which improves with experience. Let's see an example of this talent:

Experience: Temp
Hold both your hands in the air in front of you

Step 1:
- Imagine a warm plate under your right hand
- Allow yourself to feel the heat effect
Stop

Step 2:
Now
- Imagine a cold plate under your left hand
- Allow yourself to feel the cold effect
Stop

Step 3:

Now

- Imagine a warm plate under your right hand
- Allow yourself to feel the heat effect

and, at the same time

- Imagine a cold plate under your left hand
- Allow yourself to feel the cold effect

Stop

Discussion:

(1)   Steps 1 and 2 work fine.

(2)   But Step 3 just doesn't work.

You'll be familiar from grade school science class with the experiment where you put either hand in warm and cold water.

Under the varied stimulus of | W | <Nodes> for hot and cold, your EF works and produces the relevant <Affect> in Ω.

But, when you try to stimulate Blue Internal} | S | <Nodes> to replicate the effect in Ω of hot and cold External} | W | <Nodes>: that's a limited talent.

In this *Experience*, we also touched on the Narcissus problem: which we'll come to in detail in Section C, Segment} (4) *Unfaithful Reflections*.

The *Temp Experience* also illustrates an example of:

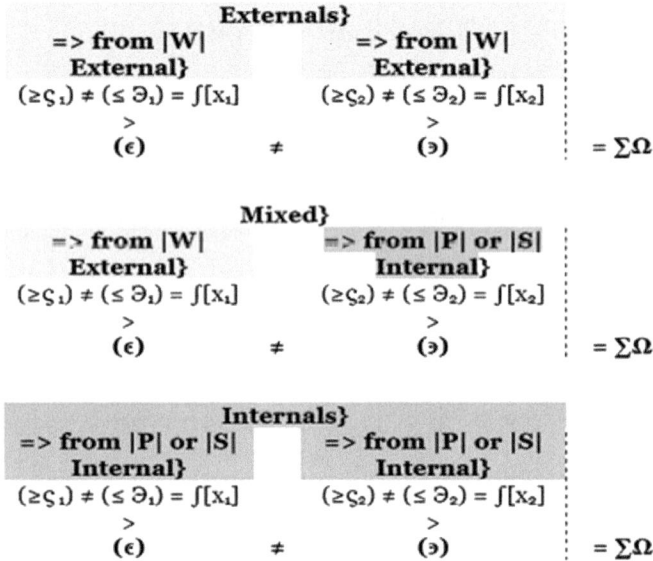

Externals}

=> **from |W|**		=> **from |W|**
External}		**External}**
$(\geq\varsigma_1) \neq (\leq \ni_1) = \int[x_1]$		$(\geq\varsigma_2) \neq (\leq \ni_2) = \int[x_2]$
>		>
(ε)	**≠**	**(ɘ)**	= $\Sigma\Omega$

Mixed}

=> **from |W|**		=> **from |P| or |S|**
External}		**Internal}**
$(\geq\varsigma_1) \neq (\leq \ni_1) = \int[x_1]$		$(\geq\varsigma_2) \neq (\leq \ni_2) = \int[x_2]$
>		>
(ε)	**≠**	**(ɘ)**	= $\Sigma\Omega$

Internals}

=> **from |P| or |S|**		=> **from |P| or |S|**
Internal}		**Internal}**
$(\geq\varsigma_1) \neq (\leq \ni_1) = \int[x_1]$		$(\geq\varsigma_2) \neq (\leq \ni_2) = \int[x_2]$
>		>
(ε)	**≠**	**(ɘ)**	= $\Sigma\Omega$

You used Internal}<Nodes> to generate $\int[x]$ outputs in $\Sigma\Omega$. This is a deeply important and interesting dynamic under the $/S/\Leftrightarrow|E|$ architecture. We'll consider this at length, at the end of this Section B, *(2) Systems.*

This *Experience* also illustrates operation of the *Sanity Barrier*:

- Your |P|hysiology is, via its own <Nodes> providing a <potential>. This is meeting with the <signal> transformed from your $/S/$=><Node> for hot, and the one for cold.
- Your $\int[x]$ is running its function. The output is not zero, but certainly nothing like the output from a real |W|=><Node> for hot or cold.

11. |E| *Systems Context*

We can now define terms, with a meaningful content:

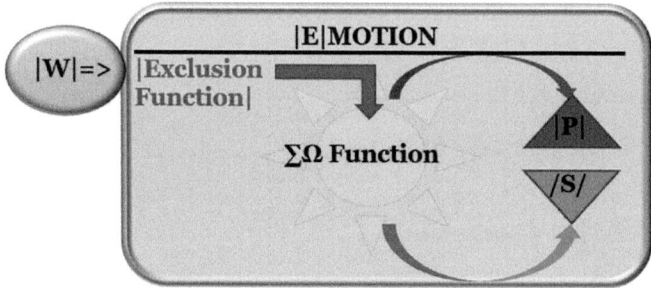

(1) Ω *is the domain where the output of the Exclusion Function engages with* |P| *and* |M| *in Self*

This definition arises simply from the architecture of |E|. However, it corresponds to an architecture which shatters the classical account.

(2) |E|*motion is a gestalt of different functions*
       From this we can determine the following rubrics:

(a) |E| is mechanical, not meaningful

(b) |E| receives and refers, but does not store or "remember"

(c) |E| develops changing EF |capacity|, which alters the effect and <Affect>of <signals>

We will discuss (2)(a) in detail later. Just to note here, that this rubric stands in complete opposition to the fundamental tenets of cognitive therapy.

12.   *Behavioural Memory Theory*

The implications of (2)(b) and (2)(c) are also very significant. They completely contradict the classical account of effect and affect, which looks like some variation of this:

Classical "Emotion"

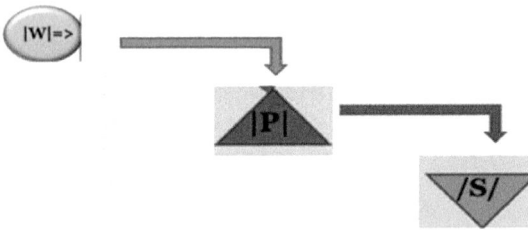

(1)   The classical account relies much on be-haviourism: Pavlov, Skinner et al.

(2)   This account merges the very different functions within |E| into a melange: a fictitious {e}.

(3)   This fictitious {e} is "plastic". That idea is harm-less, although useless, in itself.

(4)   But the idea of plasticity, under the gravity of behaviourism, leads theorists to treat the <signals> themselves as being the unilinear carriers of <Affect>information.

(5)   Under the classic account, we "remember" <signal> affects.

(6)   That "memory" is treated as being a function of cognition, in /S/.

This is a failure of architectural reasoning. It leaves us in a position where, frankly, therapeutic intervention can be no better than guesswork.

If you formulate a theoretical belief that the <Affect>of <signals> is behaviourally "remembered" in the brain, then you logically end up:
(a)   using electric shock therapy
(b)   fiddling around with surgical intervention in the physical brain
(c)   seeking pharmaceutical interventions.

Chemicals become seen as the nicer alternative methods to (a) and (b). They are just as misguided.

Let's just compare graphically, the matrixial architecture of |E| and the classical un-structured process narrative:

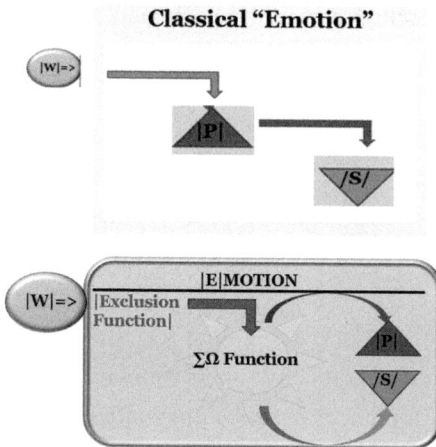

223

There is a learned response function within |E|. The conclusion by induction of behaviourists that somehow animals and humans do learn response patterns, is indisputable. Feed or kick a dog a few times and the conclusion is obvious.

The classical account proceeds in reversal of reality: it treats process as a thing, and things as processes.

The problem arose at the start of the 20th century when behaviourists attempted to locate the "memory centre" for that learned response: without an architecture. The result was a century of theories of response process, terminating in mysterious subjective cognitive states.
The matrixial Self has already identified the architectural locus of learned response.

It is the |capacity| gap in the Exclusion Function, which serves as the "memory". The primary effect of |capacity| is to act as our sanity barrier.

The development of |capacity| is a matter of trial and error. The neonate begins with an elementary, although sophisticated, |capacity|. That is then modified over time.

The variation of |capacity| over time and experience is not a "set" of memories. It is a physiological response to experience. You are already utterly familiar with this idea.

It's just that we are not used to applying it in the right places.

If we say that a baby develops the use of its eye physiology by looking, its hand physiology by gripping, and later its motor physiology by crawling, then walking: you reply *well of course that's obvious.*

If we say that a baby develops the use of its gastric physiology by eating: you reply *well of course that's obvious too.*

And we say it's utterly obvious that our |capacity| undergoes physiological development, according to all these growing needs and uses for the baby.

The |capacity| function can thus be seen just like the eyes, limbs, and stomach of the baby. It adapts to service the needs of its "end user" Self.

So, we can approximately think of |capacity| like a muscle. It alters with use by the user: You. That is obvious, not mysterious.

You can poetically say that the muscle has acquired a "memory". And of course that's a phrase in popular parlance. But we know we don't really mean the word "memory".

What we mean is that repeated experience of a type has induced alteration in muscular function, such that the muscle will now react differently to its reaction prior to the repeated stimulus. A better word is "reflex".

In like manner, life experience from birth involves the experience of stimulus repetition, which naturally induces alteration in |capacity| function. We learn |capacity| reflexes.

Again, we want to emphasise that this is nothing to do with what we classically conceptualise as "memory". Organic nature is filled with reflexes: how a flower head reacts to light, a fly to air movement and so on. We do not tend to think that such reflexes are memorial.

Indeed, we are used to thinking of much of our own reactions as being reflexes: to being touched, to noise, to seeing something.

We apply the development of such reflexes as a metric of neonate development: both in paediatric medicine, and common sense.

Indeed, because |capacity| is more like a volume potentiometer, than a mere "on/off" switch, that conceptualisation becomes more powerful: and more like a muscle.

Then you ask: *OK, but what has that to do with our subjective thinking*? And we reply: in itself, absolutely nothing. The young growth, and senescent withering, of our musculature, has nothing in itself to do with our subjective thinking either: and the classical account takes no issue with that.

We can of course, through thoughts translated into action, change the environment in which muscular change happens: but that plainly has nothing to do with the architecture of | E | motion.

We can also by / S / interaction with the Exclusion Function, alter its <signals> operation. We will come to that at the end of this *Systems* Segment.

13. Why is the EF Bridge Necessary?

Classical accounts treat | E | as being, in effect, a functionality defined by exclusion: that which is not in conscious awareness, or is not rational,[87] is what constitutes <emotion>.

We say that the same failure of classical accounts of mind to recognise the divided architecture of | M | entation, suffer the same absence of architecture in dealing with | E | motion.

---

[87] classical accounts differentiate themselves on this axis

In the brief survey *Behavioural Memory Theory*, we have adverted to some of the terrible consequences which have ensued from a theory which treats process as a thing, and things as processes.

That's all description, comment and assertion. We are required under the argumentative burden of proof:

- to establish the necessity of the EF Bridge to Ω
- to explain why <signals> and <potentials> cannot have effect on Ω directly.

It may be apparent that, in stating the matter in the second of these ways, the question evaporates. Because, if we do indeed have <potentials> ($\leq\ni$), then:

- they must have effect somewhere, and
- such that they can meet <signals>($\geq\varsigma$) as inequalities, and
- there must be a function which transforms them, as inequalities, and
- the function must have effect or affect.

All of which requires the Exclusion Function, operating through |capacity|. However, we would not wish to demonstrate an argument by recourse to an unjustified exogenous premise. Moreover, it is fundamental to understanding the architecture of |E| that the <signals> process is fully explored, and accepted.

Let's suppose a counterfactual: that there is no EF; and that what we call the Ohm Ω function is just a strange

228

way of talking about processes which effect <emotional> affect.

(1) Under the Counterfactual, if | capacity | is just "emotion", this makes it impossible to account for different modes of <potentials> (≤Ɔ) and <signals>(≥ϛ), depending upon whether the source is: | W |, | P |, or / S /.

> Empirical evidence, and common sense, both as demonstrated simply in the *Temp Experience*, show that these different modes do indeed act differently in the Self.

(2) The Counterfactual has to account for these differences, somehow.

> So, the Counterfactual has to assert that different sources originate different "types" of <emotion>. Yet the empirical evidence is that they just don't.

(3) What's more, the Counterfactual has to account for self-stimulated <emotion>, under the empirically validated fact that some self-stimulated <emotion> has like effect to other-originating processes which effect <emotional> affect.

> That returns us to the conundrum at (1), which is contradicted by the escape route at (2).

Without an architecture that includes the Exclusion Function, any account of | E | tends to circularity and self-contradiction.

Matrixial analysis proposes that the Exclusion Function operates autonomously from our /S/ubjectivity, whilst being an essential part of the gestalt Self architecture. This entails that:

- while our /S/ can have effect in the EF
- the EF operates whether or not our /S/ becomes involved in its function.

This conception of the interface between /S/ and |P|hysiological affect is not radical. The classical account, and common sense, are both perfectly happy to accept the biological facts of autonomic functions, and their effects.

Whilst we may appeal to "instinct" in relation to walking, reaching, holding and the like, we don't even need that appeal in relation to breathing, blood circulation, digestion and so on.

From this common ground, matrixial analysis draws the conclusion that there must exist a |capacity| function to regulate |P|hysiological interaction with the |W|orld. Papers cited in this Chapter exemplify a vast body of medical and biological enquiry which evidences empirically this proposition.

The |capacity| intermediation between |W| and |P| can therefore be taken as a datum. We then ask how it could be imagined that the subjective <self> could access sensory information other than via such |capacity| intermediation.

The classical account does not seek to proffer some exogenous explanation. Acceptance that $|W| => |P|$ comes prior to any subjective experience, is indeed the fundament of the "Hard Problem of Consciousness". [88]

In *Matrixial Logic*,[89] we evidenced, through *Experiences* and analysis, that we cannot derive data directly from $|W|$. That which is present as Substance or Moment in $|W|$ must present itself to us in <Nodes>, so that we may access its data, as subjective experience.

(1)   This then requires that there be within us some "receiver" of <Node> information. Some function which transforms external <Nodes> into usable synaptic signals.

(2)   In the classical account, this important stage in the processing of external information, tends to be taken for granted.

(3)   Now, it can be proposed that we are operating as a "radar" station: sending out transmissions to $|W|$ and interpreting bounce-back transmissions. Whilst animals which use echo-location do work like that, it does not appear to be how our sensory systems work.

(4)   But, even if they did work like that, such an idea requires a radar "station", or set of stations. And they need to be operating a transmissions interpretation system: which would be exactly what we call $|$ capacity $|$.

---

[88] as to which see *Matrixial Logic*, Chapter 10
[89] especially Chapter 5

So, whichever path of enquiry we choose, we end up in the necessity of some function which translates exogenous |W| information into endogenous synaptic, neural transmissions.

Now, if that role is to be played by a classical account of <emotion> we meet this further difficulty. The essence of <emotion> is that it.

- is diffuse
- is undefinable, except by exclusion from rationality
- is always subjectively affective.

As to this latter point, under the classical account, <emotion> occurs and has to have affect somewhere. So it must smokily loiter in the back rooms of our unconscious, storing itself up.

The idea of an <emotional> "state" which has zero effect is, under the classical account, an oxymoron.

So, we end up being pictured as sea-faring vessels of subjectivity, bobbing on an ocean of <emotion>, borne by current-shaping waves over which we have no control, because we have limited awareness.

Such phantom <emotion> is a concept alien to the physiological processes which manifestly keep us alive moment by moment in interaction with |W|:

- it is a remarkably non-materialist account; yet

- it is the bedrock assumption of most materialist and behaviourist theory.

Although it is frontier science, empirical studies are now evidencing that the wave interactions Exclusion Function model of the Self, is well founded in reality:

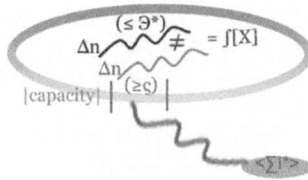

Kim Armstrong (2019) reports the new general theory:[90]

> It's common to conceive of the brain as an organ designed to react to stimuli from the outside world. A heavy book falls off a table next to you, and your brain allows you to see, hear, and feel the impact. Watch a muted *video* of a book falling off a table, however, and your brain may still generate a version of these sensations - causing you to jump at the illusory slam of the book hitting the ground even though the signals we would normally process as sound or vibration are absent.

> This is because our brains didn't evolve to react to the world around us, but rather to predict what's going to happen to us next,[91] APS President Lisa Feldman Barrett of Northeastern University explains.
>> "Brains didn't evolve for rationality," said Barrett. "They did not evolve for you to think or to perceive the world accurately. They didn't even really evolve for you to see or hear or feel. Brains

---

[90]https://www.psychologicalscience.org/observer/interoception-how-we-understand-our-bodys-inner-sensations. A lengthy quotation, because it covers much useful ground.

[91] with this, we don't agree

evolved to regulate a body so that it could move around the world efficiently."

The core task of a brain working in service to the body is Allostasis: regulating the body's internal systems by anticipating needs and preparing to satisfy them before they arise. Interoception - your brain's representation of sensations from your own body - is the sensory consequence of this activity, Barrett says, and is central to everything from thought, to emotion, to decision making, and our sense of self.

> "Your body is part of your mind, not in some gauzy mystical way, but in a very real biological way," she said during an Integrative Science Symposium at the 2019 International Convention of Psychological Science (ICPS) in Paris. "This means there is a piece of your body in every concept that you make, even in states that we think of as cold cognition."

To maintain allostasis, Barrett continued, the brain must continually construct concepts that guide the body by integrating scraps of sensory input with memories of similar experiences from the past. Creating this internal model of your body in the world allows the brain to infer the causes of the sense data that it receives through the retina and other sensory organs.

"This predictive process is the way your brain navigates the world, guides your actions, and constructs your experiences," she said.

Barrett's work with functional MRI (fMRI) has also shed light on the role of the brain's default mode network, which helps to initiate prediction signals, and the salience network, which helps to determine which unexpected sense data are important to learn in a given moment. Barrett's research shows that both networks, working in concert, contribute to allostasis and its interoceptive consequences.

Ironically, Barrett notes, these regions' limbic cortices, once derided as the brain's reactively emotional "inner beast," may be closely tied to the anticipatory processes that construct our perception of the world.

Listen to Your Heart
In the absence of input from the outside world, the brain might

generate its own spontaneous activity, but it's also possible that such activity reflects the brain processing visceral input from our internal organs, said Catherine Tallon-Baudry, who studies cognitive neuroscience at École Normale Supérieure in France. The heart and the gastrointestinal tract both generate their own electrical activity (this is what allows a donor heart kept in cold-storage to continue beating on its own) and, during fetal development, these organs begin contracting before the brain becomes fully active. This suggests that the brain develops in response to these organs.

This sensory interplay may be about more than just allostatic regulation, however - Tallon-Baudry's research suggests that it may also support first-person perspective taking, a foundational building block for our sense of self.

To be conscious, you need to have a subject of consciousness, she explains, and interoception of signals from our organs may help our brains unite incoming information - including sight, body placement, and cognitive categories - into a singular point of view.

Discussions of consciousness can easily veer into philosophical territory, Tallon-Baudry said, but her work focuses mainly on the mechanical aspects of this phenomenon.

"We know there is a lot of unconscious information processing in the brain, so having first-person perspective is not necessarily a default mode. We need a mechanism to account for it," she said.

In a *Journal of Neuroscience* study probing the link between the heart and first-person perspective, Tallon-Baudry and colleagues Mariana Babo-Rebelo and Craig G. Richter (École Normale Supérieure) monitored 16 individuals' heart and brain activity using magnetoencephalography (MEG) as their minds wandered. The participants were periodically interrupted by a visual stimulus, at which point they reported the content of their thoughts. During thoughts that participants later reported being about themselves, individuals demonstrated a greater neural response to their own heartbeat in the default mode network than during thoughts about someone or something else.

"How the brain responds to heartbeats distinguishes between self and other," Tallon-Baudry said.

As we stated earlier:

> It is not thought to require any proof here that we have (≤Ͽ*) Internal Signals running through us every microsecond of our lives. Our (≤Ͽ*) Internal Signals are *Potentials*.

Although we would take issue with theese new general theory interpretations of the experimental data, the base level evidence is clear:

(1)   the Exclusion Function operates initially as a sieve of sensory experiences[92]

(2)   we have Mentative and Physiological expectations: what we called above "standing waves"

(3)   these interact with the outputs of our Exclusion Function

We have been arguing around the necessity of of the EF bridge, by demonstrating negatively the difficulties encountered by not having one. We can now state the rubric:
The EF bridge is necessary to translate into endogenous <emotes> :

1.   *exogenous <Nodes>*

2.   *endogenous <Nodes>*

such as to be

(i)   *capable of having like affect in | E | , but*

(ii)   *not necessitating like affect in | E | .*

---

[92] which sieve can clinically malfunction, as can any of our organic capacities. Such malfunctions are evidence din Sensory Processing Disorder.

We said under this (2) *Systems*, Segments (7) and (8):

Now, we're ready to pull the whole equation together:

Exclusion Function

$$(\geq\varsigma^*) \neq (\leq \Im^*) = \int[x]$$

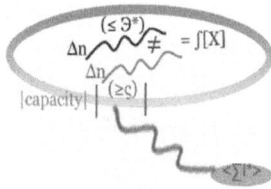

We thus attain the understanding that $\int[x]$ is not something in itself, or for itself: *$\int[x]$ is a bridge, which transforms.*

A bridge to what? $\int[x]$ is a bridge to the Ohm function Ω.

Obviously, there is no bridge if $= \int[0]$. There is only a bridge if $= \int[x]$ is a non-zero output.

The interaction between <signal> and <potential> under [<resistance> $\neq$] produces $= \int[x]$, which is a quantity of Output.

The Exclusion Function operates so that it is capable of returning a $= \int[x]$ zero output. The natural genius of such a system is that diversity of input origin, whether exogenous and/or endogenous, interacts so as to produce a quantum output.

Suddenly, we are returned to the foundational elements of matrixial logic, as set out in Chapter 2 of *Matrixial Logic*, and elaborated in Chapters 4 and 5.

The Exclusion Function is operating a wave interference model. The |capacity| potentiometer transforms all incoming <Nodes> into wave functions:

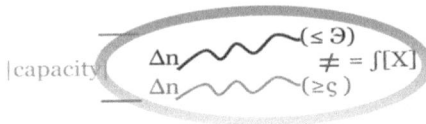

Waves interfere: $\geq \neq \leq$. The output is a modification function $\int(+ \ / - \ / \ 0)$.

Clearly, operation of the wave interference function is indifferent to the origin of <Nodes> which are transformed by |capacity| into the waves of <signal> / <potential>.

- Any <signal> ($\geq\varsigma$) performs the same function as any other ($\geq\varsigma$), irrespective of source.
- Any ($\leq\ni$) performs the same function as any other ($\geq\varsigma$), irrespective of source

The cumulative effect of wave interactions is a scale of infinity. $\int[x]$ may be anything from 0 to anything under ∞.

Thus, the entirety of our Self interactions with |W|, and our endogenous self-stimulated interactions, are expressed in multiple applications of the simple wave function equation: $(\geq\varsigma^*) \neq (\leq \ni^*) = \int[x]$.

14. *Why is the Ohm Function Necessary?*
This raises the proximate question: why do $\int(x)$ quantitative outputs have to undergo a further level of processing?

Why, in the functional graphic, can't the EF simply stand in place of the Ohm $\sum\Omega$ function?

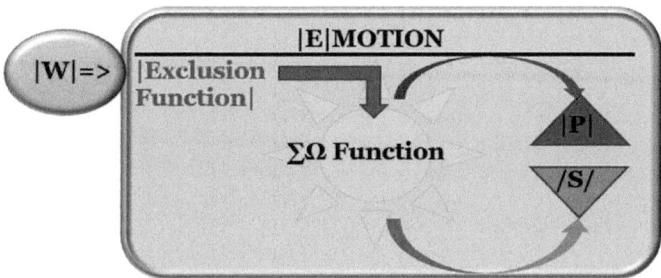

The Classical Account
Under both the classical and common sense account of <emotion> it is common ground that <emotions> have qualities. That's how we tell them apart: sad / happy; calm / angry.

These qualities can have a vague comparative metric: more sad; less happy. But it is nevertheless a metric of some distinguishable quality.

We agree that │E│ exhibits qualities. The classical account then needs to explain how qualities can emerge directly from interactions with the world.

This is the notorious problem of *qualia*: is blue something in the object, or something in perception only? That problem is magnified exponentially by the scientific reality of our multi-model processing of sense interactions with the world.

The *qualia* problematic arises because the end point of transmission from │W│ needs to be a quality: blue, hot, cold; and matching qualitative "states": sad / happy, and so on.

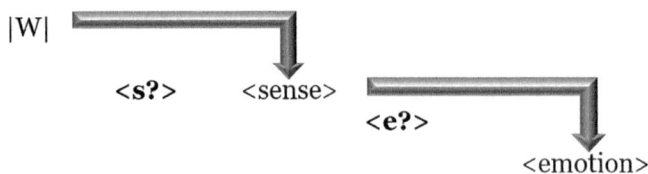

│W│

<s?>   <sense>

<e?>

<emotion>

Neuroscience gives us lots of useful accounts of <s?>: how the visual, auditory and somatic cortexes function.

But there's an odd ellipsis in explanation:
- an <object> exists in │W│
- photons transmit information about <object> to retinal cones ands rods
- neural information is conveyed by electrochemical synapse function
- we experience seeing <object>.

240

But we don't see a collection or stream of photons. We see an actual <object>. To use the cinematic paradigm:

We see This   Not This

   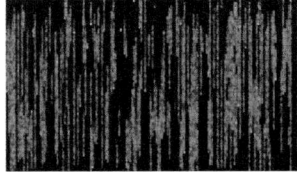

https://www.digitalspy.com/movies/a29498105/the-matrix-4-cast-release-date-plot-trailer-keanu-reeves-news/

What's more, upon seeing the qualitative <object> image, we have a supra-qualitative <emotion> response.

So, the classical account entirely fails to offer any explanation of how:

- qualities in |W| become qualities in <sense>:
- qualities in <sense>, working as neural signals (manifestly quantities) become qualities in <emotions>:

In summary, the basic problem of *qualia* is the inability to explain how quality transforms through quantity, and back into quality again: but of a different kind.

What is usually not stated in classical *qualia* explanations, is the presumption that <s?> (whatever it is, and however it works) is something different to <e?> (whatever it is, and however it works).

241

This is useful, because we can partly resolve the question <why is Ohm Ω necessary?> by answering that the classical account requires a distinction between <s?> and <e?> .

The Matrixial Self in |E|

Under this (2) *Systems*, Segment (10), we've already provided an answer:

- the Exclusion Function expresses a quantitative inequality: $[(\geq\varsigma^*) \neq (\leq \Theta^*)]$
- the Ohm aggregate $\sum\Omega$ expresses a qualitative inequality: $(\epsilon) \neq (\Theta)$.

We also said:

> There is no biological possibility of a single <Node> having effect within us, without concomitant effect in other parts of the holistic entity…

> This is the logic of the scientific, empirical studies of these phenomena. The literature is vast, running across: biology, biochemistry, physiology, psychology, quantum biology, and beyond.

> The question which we have been addressing arises (not unfairly) from the trap of thinking that this second equation: $(\geq\varsigma_2) \neq (\leq \Theta_2) = \int[x_2]$, must represent an external <Node> transformation.

Let's apply this rubric to a simple example. We know from science and common sense and by example of the

Temp Experience, that:
- we can self-stimulate: the endogenous creation of hot/cold affect; which
- can mimic exogenous creation of hot/cold affect; but
- such mimicry is limited in its qualitative experience.

So, we know that there must be some function which can operate on exogenous and endogenous transmissions, without regard to origin: but that there must be a further "sorting" function.

We can go further and say that such sorting function is an application of the Sanity Barrier. Otherwise we could imagine ourselves into conditions which mimic, say, hypothermia. Without the matrixial architecture of Self, we would need to hypothesise some novel control function, and then explain where such operates: in the 'mind', in 'emotion' or wherever.

The EF formula provides its own elegant answer to the problematic of self-stimulation:

Internals}		
=> from |P| or |S| Internal}	=> from |P| or |S| Internal}	
$(\geq \varsigma_1) \neq (\leq \Theta_1) = \int[x_1]$	$(\geq \varsigma_2) \neq (\leq \Theta_2) = \int[x_2]$	
$>$	$>$	
(ϵ) $\neq$	$(\ni)$	$= \Sigma\Omega$

When we are trying, for example, to mimic hot or cold sensations, we are trying to recapitulate this:

243

$$\text{Mixed}\}$$

$$\begin{array}{ccc}
\Rightarrow \text{ from } |W| & & \Rightarrow \text{ from } |P| \text{ or } |S| \\
\text{External}\} & & \text{Internal}\} \\
(\geq\varsigma_1) \neq (\leq \eth_1) = \int[x_1] & & (\geq\varsigma_2) \neq (\leq \eth_2) = \int[x_2] \\
> & & > \\
(\epsilon) & \neq & (\ni) & = \Sigma\Omega
\end{array}$$

but without any exogenous <signal>.

In any of this, we are trying to create a Form out of inequalities. The foundation rules of matrixial logic tell us that, to derive a [Form], we must state in inequality $\neq$ which can function in that [Form]:

$$\begin{array}{ccc}
\textbf{External}\} & \neq & \textbf{Internal}\} & =[F]? \\
(\geq\varsigma_1) \neq (\leq \eth_1) = \int[x_1] & & (\geq\varsigma_2) \neq (\leq \eth_2) = \int[x_2]
\end{array}$$

It is elementary that any Form is hylomorphic to its contents. It is also elementary that a [f]]orm of Forms can only function as a <Node>.

Matrixial logic thus provides us with an inexorable emergent <Nodes> interaction:

- We don't have to impose a necessity for Ohm Ω at all.
- Ohm Ω simply emerges as the necessary result of <Nodes> interacting with each other.

Without getting all quantum physics about it, and just observing a classical water wave interference pattern, we can use this graphic, to illustrate as follows:

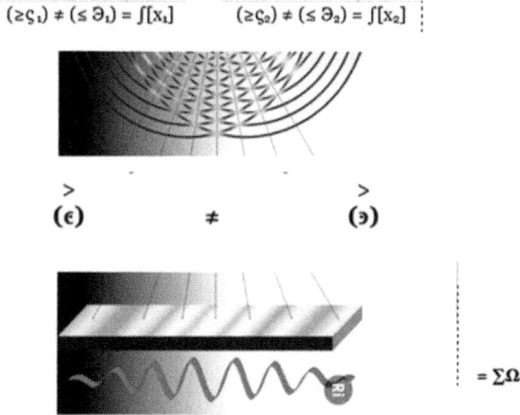

$$(\geq\varsigma_1) \neq (\leq \ni_1) = \int[x_1] \qquad (\geq\varsigma_2) \neq (\leq \ni_2) = \int[x_2]$$

$$\overset{>}{(\epsilon)} \qquad \neq \qquad \overset{>}{(\ni)}$$

$$= \Sigma\Omega$$

The bars on the screen are the transformed results of the wave interferences: quantity transforms into quality.

That quality is, in itself, a modulation. The bars resulting from classical, and quantum, wave interference appear like this:

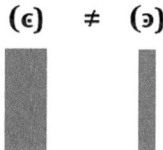

$$(\epsilon) \quad \neq \quad (\ni)$$

That's a difference in quality, not merely quantity.

We have stated the EF rubric:
The EF bridge is necessary to translate into endogenous

<emotes> :

1. exogenous <Nodes>
2. endogenous <Nodes>

such as to be

(i)   capable of having like <Affect> in | E |, but
(ii) not necessitating like <Affect> in | E |.

We can now state the Ohm Ω rubric:

The Ohm Ω function is the emergent necessity of <Nodes> meeting as wave functions.

Putting these together, we arrive at the conjoined proposition that:

FX transforms <Nodes> of Qualities into Quantities
Ohm Ω is the representation of Quantities as Qualities.

There never was a *qualia* problem. It was simply the emergent insoluble problematic of the classical account's failure to construct a Self systems architecture.

15.   Locating Functions

We then ask: where in the body and brain is all this happening?

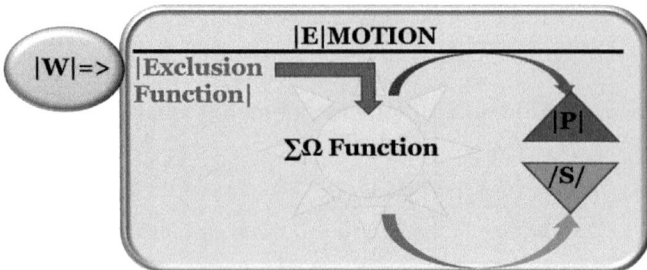

The answer is: everywhere in the body and brain, all the time, moment by moment.

Biology and neurology have been able to locate specific areas of body and brain which are implicated in specific functions, for example:
- motor cortex
- visual cortex
- auditory cortex
- somatic areas.

This is interesting fact-based knowledge. But it's of limited use in multi-modal interactions of Self with the world: which amounts for almost everything we experience.

Moreover, flip this graphic so that it lies like a pancake on a table.
- Now add piles of pancakes all the way to the ceiling
- Now get a second such pile
- Now interleave both piles.

This more approaches the reality in life experience of this logical architecture.

When we ask: where is the Ohm Ω modulation (quantity to quality) happening, that's another (legitimate) way of asking: how does it work?

We used this graphical metaphor in the previous Segment:

$$(\geq \varsigma_1) \neq (\leq \partial_1) = \int[x_1] \qquad (\geq \varsigma_2) \neq (\leq \partial_2) = \int[x_2]$$

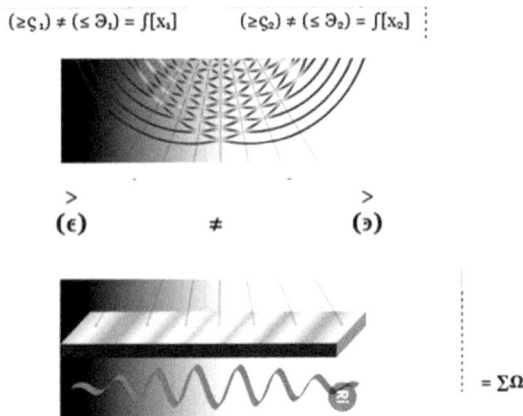

$$\overset{>}{(\epsilon)} \qquad \neq \qquad \overset{>}{(\ni)}$$

$$= \Sigma\Omega$$

Now, we would add to it, by saying that the Ω qualitative representation of the EF interactions, autonomically acts as a *distribution mechanism*.

We are at the half-way point in setting out the architectural components of $|E|$.

We have looked at how <Node> input becomes subject to transformation transformation in Exclusion Function, as the bridge to Ω, and thus available:

- for $|P|$ interaction
- for $/S/$ interaction.

We now need to examine how Ω functions to effect such distributions.

16. *The Ω Distribution System*

We can use the very useful 6th to 8th senses noted previously, to illuminate the Ω Ohm emotional distribution system:

6th	proprioception	Our bodies' receptors relating to movement
7th	vestibular	Our sense of ourselves in space
8th	interoception	Relays between organs and the brain

In this Segment, we are focusing on this element of the whole |E| picture:

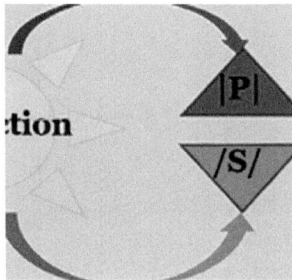

Let's recall this rubric from Segment (14):

FX transforms <Nodes> of Qualities into Quantities
Ohm Ω is the representation of Quantities as Qualities.

We talk of an Ω distribution system. We don't suppose that Ω engages some kind of mysterious "intelligence". Nor that it runs some kind of computer program guiding decision making.

So, it's legitimate to ask:

how does Ω effect discrimination in its referral?

Experience: Slide
Setup:

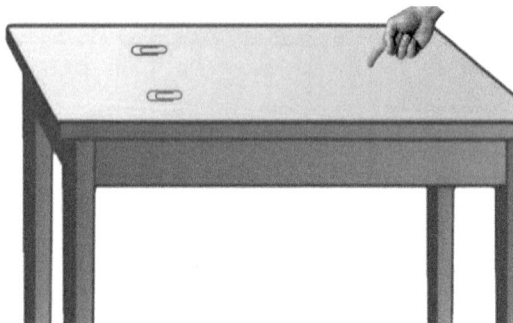

Make space on your table top.
Get 2 paperclips, and place them 6 inches or so apart, parallel to each other, as in the graphic.

Place your finger on the table, around twice as far away, as they are apart.

Hold your finger on the table top.

Now:
• try and choose to move your finger along the table top, towards one clip, or the other

Stop

Discussion:

(1)   You can't move your finger.

(2)   There's nothing to allow you to choose.

You have no <feelings> about the matter, nor is there any <thought> which you can coherently have about the matter.

This *Slide Experience* is a rough analogy for a hypothetical situation where:

- your Exclusion Function is working to produce quantitative data
- there is qualitative Ω distribution;
- but no receipt by your | P |, nor your / S /.

Experience: Tilt

Setup:

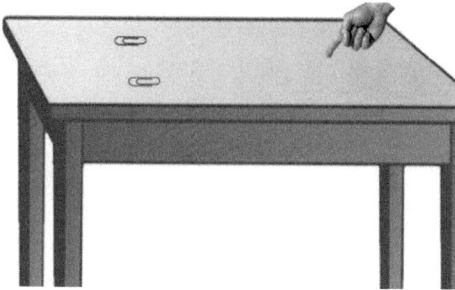

As in *Slide*:

Make space on your table top.

Get 2 paperclips, and place them 6 inches or so apart, parallel to each other, as in the graphic.

But now: add a 3rd paperclip, in between them like so:

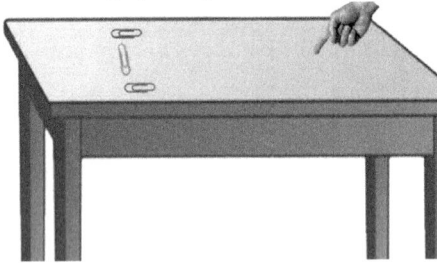

Place your finger on the table, in the same position

Hold your finger on the table top.

Now:

- move your finger along the table top, towards any of the clips

Stop

Discussion:

    (1)   Your finger felt "pulled" towards the middle clip.

As we stated in Section A, Segment (2):

    We restate a core proposition of *Secret Self*:

Mentation

How we can think governs what we can think

Emotion

What we can emote governs how we emote

This is because our | M | and | E | share a parallel architecture. It is the architecture of each part of the

Self globe, which constrains:

- what we can think
- how we we emote.

We were asking:

how does Ω effect discrimination in its referral?

These *Experiences* help to illuminate the answer:

Ω refers in accordance with the receiving potential.

We used an "out there" in | W | Experience Scene, to demonstrate how a simple change in relative positioning makes all the difference between: being stuck; and irresistible attraction.

Thus, our neural | P | hysiology makes available "attraction" points, to which Ω outputs are referred. In the material science of synapse transmission, this is exactly how synapses work.

The same applies for our /S/ <feelings> and <thoughts>. You will recall this much used graphic (from Section A, Segment (1)):

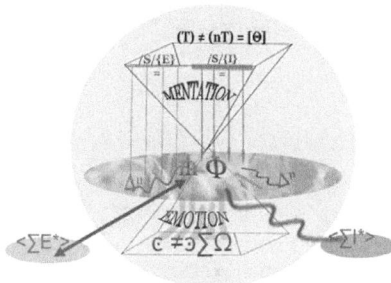

Chapters 4 and 5 of *Matrixial Logic* focused on the equivalence function of /S/{E} and [I]. How |M|entation interacts with Chi and Phi <points>. The interactions being represented by the down brown and blue arrows.

If you analogise the 3 paperclip Scene to (for example) the operation of the blue down arrows, then you can see how they work to create an "attractor" for the Δ^n (+ / -) gaps, either side of the <points>.

So, we arrive at the understanding that Ω is referring universally, like a radio transmitter. But only sets tuned to that frequency[93] receive that signal.

It's a very simple principle:[94]

- close your eyes: no photonic interaction with your visual cortex
- upon your eyes: now there's a "landing zone", so your visual cortex is engaged.

We see this <transmission v exclusion / reception> model throughout nature. There is no need for any mysterious "intelligence", or any kind of computer program, to guide decision making.

In common sense, we recognise that we can't get someone

---

[93] another rough analogy
[94] this an even less directly applicable analogy; but stated just to highlight the concept, which applies in many circumstances

to feel or think something that they are not set up to. If that person doesn't have the "3rd paperclip" for that transmission, then no <feelings> or <thought> about the matter is engaged.

If we want that transmission to be received, then we have to find a collateral way to get something to move such 3rd paperclip into position. Those are skills of psychology and persuasion.

17.   *Neuroscience Evidence*
The architectural logic of the matrixial Self is empirically supported.

The <transmission v exclusion / reception> model, is fundamental to neuroscience.

In this Segment, we will focus on the classical synaptic account of brain functions. Theer is a new ephaptic account, which relies on "brainwaves". The fundamental existence of brainwaves has been known for a century. But only in the last 20 years or so, has there arisen a new account which seeks to equate <consciousness> and ephaptic information transmission.

These matters are so important, that we devote an Annex to them. For now, let's return to the classical account.

It is elementary that Neurons have specialized projections

called **dendrites** and **axons**:
- Dendrites bring information to the cell body
- Axons take information away from the cell body.

Information from one neuron flows to another neuron across a **synapse**. The synapse contains a small gap separating neurons. The synapse consists of a:

(1) presynaptic ending that contains neurotransmitters, mitochondria and other cell organelles

(2) postsynaptic ending that contains receptor sites for neurotransmitters

(3) synaptic cleft or space between the presynaptic and postsynaptic endings.

There is far too much neuroscience literature to even begin to essay a survey. Instead, in this Segment, we want to do two things:
- to provide a micro-guide to the theory and evidence of synaptic transmission
- by way of example, to show how still developing theoretical frameworks interleave with the architectural logic of the matrixial Self .

Let's begin with a summary of synaptic processes:
Overview of transmission at chemical synapses[95]

---

[95] https://www.khanacademy.org/science/biology/human-biology/neuron-nervous-system/a/the-synapse

Chemical transmission involves release of chemical messengers known as **neurotransmitters**. Neurotransmitters carry information from the pre-synaptic (sending) neuron to the post-synaptic (receiving) cell.

As you may remember from the article on neuron structure and function, synapses are usually formed between nerve terminals (axon terminals) on the sending neuron and the cell body (or dendrites) of the receiving neuron.

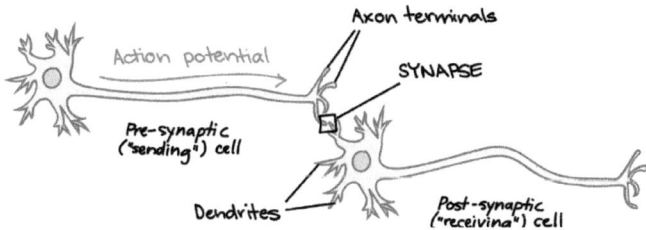

Schematic of synaptic transmission. An action potential travels down the axon of the presynaptic (sending) cell and arrives at multiple axon terminals branching off from the axon. The axon terminal is adjacent to the dendrite of the postsynaptic (receiving) cell. This spot of close connection between axon and dendrite is the synapse.

A single axon can have multiple branches, allowing it to make synapses on various post-synaptic cells. Similarly, a single neuron can receive thousands of synaptic inputs from many different presynaptic (sending) neurons.

Inside the axon terminal of a sending cell are many **synaptic vesicles**. These are membrane-bound spheres filled with neurotransmitter molecules.

There is a small gap between the axon terminal of the presynaptic neuron and the membrane of the postsynaptic cell, and this gap is called the **synaptic cleft**.

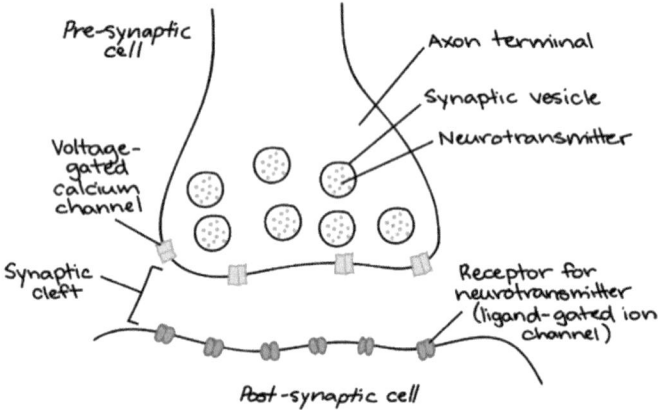

Image showing pre-synaptic cell's axon terminal containing synaptic vesicles with neurotransmitters. Voltage-gated calcium channels are on the outside surface of the axon terminal. Across the synaptic cleft, there is the post-synaptic cell surface covered in receptors (ligand-gated ion channels) for the neurotransmitter.

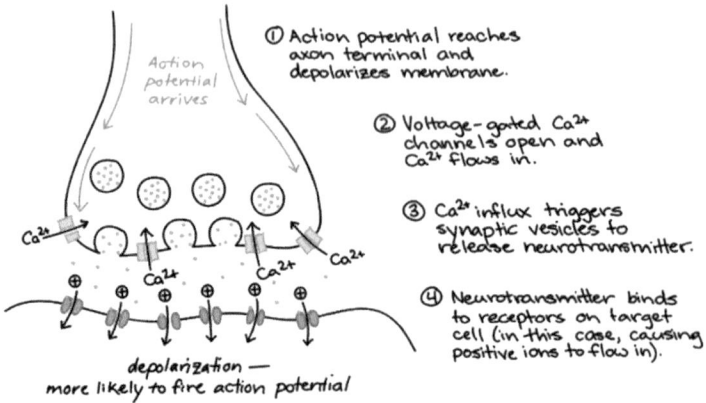

① Action potential reaches axon terminal and depolarizes membrane.

② Voltage-gated Ca²⁺ channels open and Ca²⁺ flows in.

③ Ca²⁺ influx triggers synaptic vesicles to release neurotransmitter.

④ Neurotransmitter binds to receptors on target cell (in this case, causing positive ions to flow in).

Image showing what happens when action potential arrives at axon terminal, causing ion flow and depolarization of target cell. Step by step: 1. Action potential reaches axon terminal and depolarizes membrane. 2. Voltage-gated calcium channels open and calcium ions flow in. 3. Calcium ion influx triggers synaptic vesicles to release neurotransmitter. 4. Neurotransmitter binds to receptors on target cell (in this case, causing positive ions to flow in).

The molecules of neurotransmitter diffuse across the synaptic cleft and bind to receptor proteins on the postsynaptic cell. Activation of postsynaptic receptors leads to the opening or closing of ion channels in the cell membrane. This may be **depolarizing** (make the inside of the cell more positive) or **hyperpolarizing (**make the inside of the cell more negative) depending on the ions involved.

In some cases, these effects on channel behavior are direct: the receptor is a ligand-gated ion channel, as in the diagram above. In other cases, the receptor is not an ion channel itself but activates ion channels through a signaling pathway. See the article on neurotransmitters and receptors for more info.

Excitatory and inhibitory postsynaptic potentials

When a neurotransmitter binds to its receptor on a receiving cell, it causes ion channels to open or close. This can produce a localized change in the membrane potential (voltage across the membrane) of the receiving cell.

- In some cases, the change makes the target cell *more* likely to fire its own action potential. In this case, the shift in membrane potential is called an **excitatory postsynaptic potential**, or **EPSP**.

- In other cases, the change makes the target cell *less* likely to fire an action potential and is called an **inhibitory post-synaptic potential**, or **IPSP**.

An EPSP is depolarizing: it makes the inside of the cell more positive, bringing the membrane potential closer to its threshold for firing an action potential. Sometimes, a single EPSP isn't large enough bring the neuron to threshold, but it can sum together with other EPSPs to trigger an action potential.

IPSPs have the opposite effect. That is, they tend to keep the membrane potential of the postsynaptic neuron below threshold for firing an action potential. IPSPs are important because they can counteract, or cancel out, the excitatory effect of EPSPs.

Spatial and temporal summation

How do EPSPs and IPSPs interact? Basically, a postsynaptic neuron adds together, or integrates, all of the excitatory and inhibitory inputs it receives and "decides" whether to fire an action potential.

- The integration of postsynaptic potentials that occur in different locations - but at about the same time - is known as **spatial summation**.
- The integration of postsynaptic potentials that occur in the same place - but at slightly different times - is called **temporal summation**.

For instance, let's suppose that excitatory synapses are made on two different dendrites of the same postsynaptic neuron, as shown below. Neither synapse can produce an EPSP quite large enough to bring the membrane potential to threshold at the axon hillock—the place where the action potential is triggered, boxed below. If both subthreshold EPSPs occurred at the same time, however, they could sum, or add up, to bring the membrane potential to threshold.

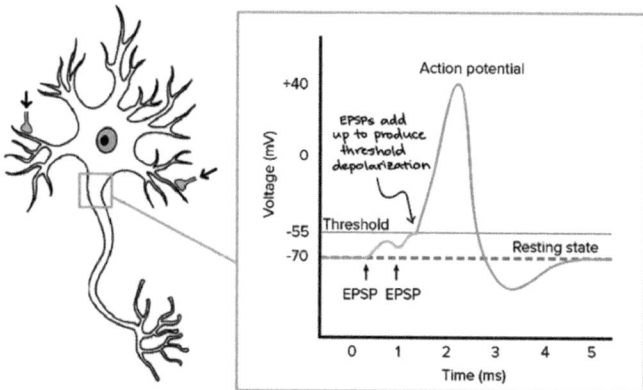

Image credit: modified from Communication between neurons: Figure 2 by OpenStax College, Anatomy & Physiology, *CC BY 3.0* and Action potential by tiZom, *CC BY-SA 3.0*; the modified image is licensed under a *CC BY-SA 3.0* license

Illustration of spatial summation. A neuron has two synapses onto two different dendrites, both of which are excitatory. Neither synapse produces a large enough excitatory postsynaptic potential, EPSP, when it signals to generate an action potential at the hillock— the place where the axon joins the cell body and where the action potential is initiated. However, when the synapses fire at nearly the same time, the EPSPs add up to produce an above-threshold depolarization, triggering an action potential.

This process is shown on a graph of voltage in millivolts vs. time in milliseconds. The graph monitors the membrane potential (voltage) at the axon hillock. Initially, it is at -70 mV, the resting potential. Then, one synapse fires, resulting in a small depolarization to roughly - 60 mV. This is not sufficient to reach the threshold of –55 mV.

However, just a tiny bit later, the other synapse fires, and it "adds on" to the first depolarization, resulting in a total depolarization that reaches -55 mV and triggers an action potential depolarization to +40 mV, followed by a repolarization and hyperpolarization below –90 mV, and then a gradual recovery to -70 mV, the resting membrane potential.

On the other hand, if an IPSP occurred together with the two EPSPs, it might prevent the membrane potential from reaching threshold and keep the neuron from firing an action potential. These are examples of spatial summation.

What about temporal summation? A key point is that postsynaptic potentials aren't instantaneous: instead, they last for a little while before they dissipate. If a presynaptic neuron fires quickly twice in row, causing two EPSPs, the second EPSP may arrive before the first one has dissipated, bumping the membrane potential above threshold. This is an example of temporal summation.

Signal Termination

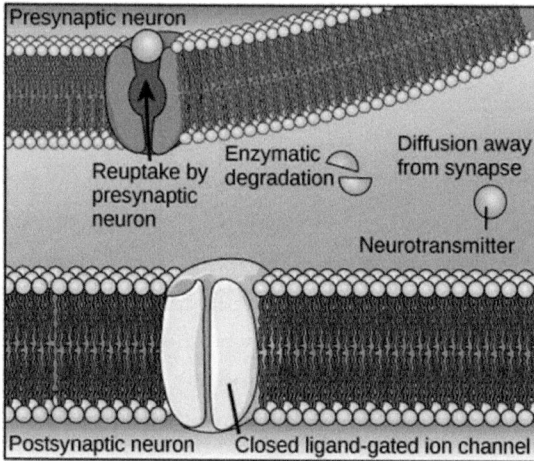

Reuptake by the presynaptic neuron, enzymatic degradation, and diffusion away from the synapse reduce neurotransmitter levels, terminating the signal.

Image credit: modified from *Nervous system: Figure 9* by OpenStax College, Biology, adapted by Robert Bear and David Rintoul, *CC BY 4.0*

A synapse can only function effectively if there is some way to "turn off" the signal once it's been sent. Termination of the signal lets the postsynaptic cell return to its normal resting potential, ready for new signals to arrive.

For the signal to end, the synaptic cleft must be cleared of neurotransmitter. There are a few different ways to get this done.

The neurotransmitter may be broken down by an enzyme,

it may be sucked back up into the presynaptic neuron, or it may simply diffuse away. In some cases, neurotransmitter can also be "mopped up" by nearby glial cells (not shown in the diagram below).

Anything that interferes with the processes that terminate the synaptic signal can have significant physiological effects.

For instance, some insecticides kill insects by inhibiting an enzyme that breaks down the neurotransmitter acetylcholine. On a more positive note, drugs that interfere with reuptake of the neurotransmitter serotonin in the human brain are used as antidepressants, for example, Prozac.

Applying Matrixial Logic

This classical neuroscience "how it works" analysis is very useful. We can see how the architectural logic of the matrixial Self mirrors this empirical analysis.

The *Experience: Tilt,* was designed to show you in an intuitive way, how synapric transmission works. In effect, we presented you with a *synaptic cleft*: the gap between your finger and the clips.

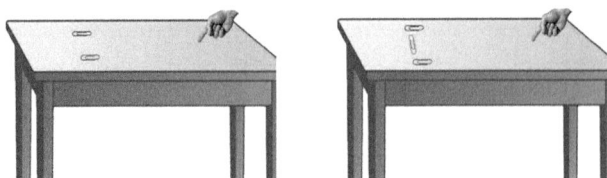

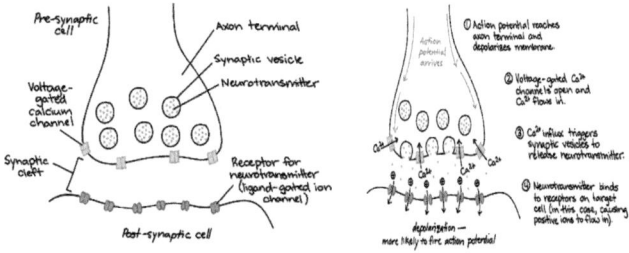

We demonstrated, in the first Scene, that no synaptic firing for movement could take place. Then in the second Scene, how the architecture of Ω compelled movement, in a predictable way.

Now, we must be careful to distinguish between architecture and systems. This whole Chapter is concerned primarily with architecture: with the framework in which systems have effect.

We also provide the wirework of systems:

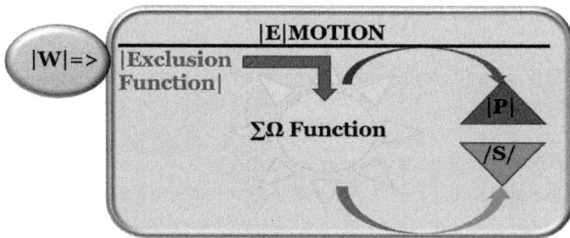

The FX and Ω equations represent that wirework. They effect the logic of the systems, which is not the same as the actual material systems themselves.

To understand how important this all is, below we can see an example of how, at the frontiers of science, investigations are searching for an architecture of neural experience.

Why Neurons Have Thousands of Synapses, a Theory of Sequence Memory in Neocortex.[96]

ABSTRACT Pyramidal neurons represent the majority of excitatory neurons in the neocortex. Each pyramidal neuron receives input from thousands of excitatory synapses that are segregated onto dendritic branches. The dendrites themselves are segregated into apical, basal, and proximal integration zones, which have different properties.

It is a mystery how pyramidal neurons integrate the input from thousands of synapses, what role the different dendrites play in this integration, and what kind of network behavior this enables in cortical tissue.

It has been previously proposed that non-linear properties of dendrites enable cortical neurons to recognize multiple independent patterns.

In this paper we extend this idea in multiple ways. First we show that a neuron with several thousand synapses segregated on active dendrites can recognize hundreds of independent patterns of cellular activity even in the presence of large amounts of noise and pattern variation.

We then propose a neuron model where patterns detected on proximal dendrites lead to action potentials, defining the classic receptive field of the neuron, and patterns detected on basal and apical dendrites act as predictions by slightly depolarizing the neuron without generating an action potential. By this mechanism, a neuron can predict its activation in hundreds of independent contexts.

[96] Hawkins Jeff, Ahmad Subutai. *Frontiers in Neural Circuits.* Volume 10 (2016) https://www.frontiersin.org/article/10.3389/fncir.2016.00023. DOI=10.3389/fncir.2016.00023

We then present a network model based on neurons with these properties that learns time-based sequences. The network relies on fast local inhibition to preferentially activate neurons that are slightly depolarized. Through simulation we show that the network scales well and operates robustly over a wide range of parameters as long as the network uses a sparse distributed code of cellular activations.

We contrast the properties of the new network model with several other neural network models to illustrate the relative capabilities of each.

We conclude that pyramidal neurons with thousands of synapses, active dendrites, and multiple integration zones create a robust and powerful sequence memory.

Given the prevalence and similarity of excitatory neurons throughout the neocortex and the importance of sequence memory in inference and behavior, we propose that this form of sequence memory may be a universal property of neocortical tissue.

This paper adds a dimension to the systems architecture, which we haven't covered so far: the hyper-system of *predictability*. In that, it provides another piece in the jigsaw puzzle of interoceptive prediction.

Suppose that your finger in *Tilt*, could predict that the 3rd clip would be there. Or, that the 3rd clip has always come to fill the gap, so that your finger becomes habituated to moving accordingly.

In our view, these ideas are taking empirically validated (or potentially validated) matters of neurological fact, and pressing them into a theory whih makes these facts irrelevant.

Reversing the Flow

As we stated in *Segment (11) Architecture,* |E| is a gestalt. The $\Omega \Leftrightarrow$ /S/ two-way information processing is pictured by the gold arrows in the graphic:

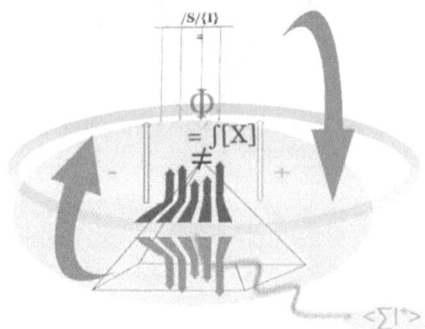

We have been focusing so far on the "up" arrow: and that makes sense: [97]

> "We tend to think that the brain is sitting on top of the pyramid, and it's controlling the body in general - actually, it's probably the other way around," Tallon-Baudry said.

> One indication of this is the way in which information is relayed to and from the brain through the body's sensory pathways: 80% of fibers in the vagus nerve ascend from organs such as the stomach and the heart to the brain, while just 20% descend in the reverse direction.

Now, let's consider that "reverse direction": from /S/=>Ω, via the Exclusion Function.

---

[97]https://www.psychologicalscience.org/observer/interoception-how-we-understand-our-bodys-inner-sensations. A length quotation, because it covers much useful ground

18.   Self-Stimulated Exclusion Function

It is obvious that our subjective mind movements can <Affect> our | E | motional process.

For the purposes of understanding and explaining the architecture of Self, we have so far in this Chapter been looking at external stimulus: from | W |. We have discussed internal stimulus from | P | in passing.

It seems that there are limits on what any of us can do to alter or control interactions between | W | and the Self. But what about within the Self?

Thinking To Our Selfs

Now, we consider how / S / can have effect in Ω. That's probably seen as the most important aspect of Self.

Classical accounts have, in effect, defined <self> as being a personality which has the power to influence, or even control, its own thoughts, feelings and emotions.

Modern materialism denies this idea of <self>, especially in its poster-child incarnation as "no free will". All is claimed to be contingent. Either it is determined in a deterministic universe. Or it is random in a quantum universe.

What both accounts have in common is an acceptance that we can think to our Selfs. That we can transmit internally <thoughts> or <feelings>. That doing so has effects:

- actioning motor movements
- engaging emotional states
- reciprocating in other <thoughts> or <feelings>.

The Descartian battle flag of human consciousness *cogito ergo sum*, is firmly planted in this landscape.

This is certainly *terra firma,* although plainly not *terra cognita.* We believe that just know that we can engage actions, states and subjective mind movements, by engaging relevant thoughts.

The whole of psychotherapy is based on the premise that we have some freedom to choose what thoughts we engage.

In *(2) Systems,* Segment (12), we compared graphically, the matrixial architecture of |E| and the classical un-structured process narrative:

Classical "Emotion"

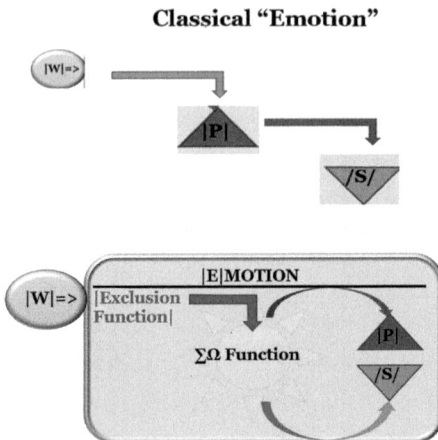

We explained that the classical account has been unable to generate a successful theory of this transmission of | W | information to / S /.

We say that the same problem obtains in reverse: only magnified and distorted. It's bad enough for a goldfish to seek reason in the food which drops into its bowl: it's even worse for the goldfish to work out where the sides of its own bowl are.[98]

In this Segment, we say: once we understand the *Systems* operating within *Architecture*, of our Self-thought, the battle between idealist and materialist accounts simply melts away.

These accounts then appear as what they are: mereological fallacies posited in the absence of matrixial logic analysis of the architectural whole.

We have explored and explained in matrixial logic, the architectural limits of our subjectivity. We restate a core proposition of *Secret Self*:

Mentation

How we can think governs what we can think

Emotion

What we can emote governs how we emote

---

[98] think about it: swim to one side, and you've "lost" the other.

What we can emote depends upon what can be active as <signal> or <potential> under our Exclusion Function (EF).

Elementary Systems Architecture

|E| is the architecture of systems which organise interactions, and generate <Affect>.

We know, from examining |W| => |E| that:

- |W| produces <Nodes>
- <Nodes> interact with |capacity|, being transformed in (≥ς) <signal>
- Under the Exclusion Function, <signal> interacts with <potential> : (≥ς) ≠ (≤Ө)
- the interaction operates like wave interactions: with an output that can be zero, or non-zero: ∫[x]
- this is a quantitative output

and then

- multiples of ∫[x] outputs are automatically registered as qualitative outputs: as <emotes> (ϲ) ≠ (ɔ)
- these aggregate as ∑Ω
- if there exists a "receiver" for an ∑Ω aggregate, there is reception
- if no receiver exists, at that moment, there is no reception.

We'll now show how the architecture of our subjective /S/ transmits information potential to our |E|, using the same systems process as the external world |W|.

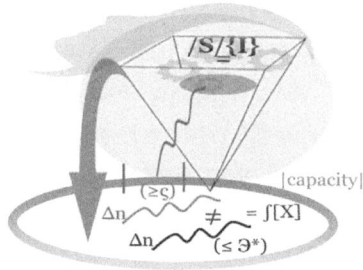

We said in Section B, Segment (10):

The *Temp Experience* also illustrates an example of:

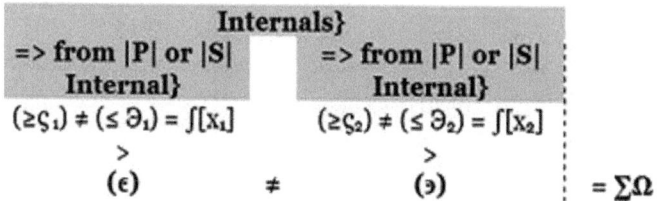

Internals}		
=> from |P| or |S| Internal}		=> from |P| or |S| Internal}
$(\geq \varsigma_1) \neq (\leq \vartheta_1) = \int[x_1]$		$(\geq \varsigma_2) \neq (\leq \vartheta_2) = \int[x_2]$
>		>
(ε)	≠	(ɔ)

$= \sum \Omega$

You used Internal}<Nodes> to generate ∫[x] outputs in $\sum \Omega$. This is a deeply important and interesting dynamic under the /S/ ⇔ | E | architecture. We'll consider this at length, at the end of this Section B, (2) Systems.

We now want to consider the process where /S/ meets FX, stimulating Emotes, and thus effecting change in | E | : the "down" arrow in the above graphic.

We start with this rubric:

/S/ *effects change in* Ω *only through* <signal> *in EF.*

Let's now justify this rubric and its articulations.

We can't analyse in any empirical way, any single neuronal impulses, travelling down the vagal pathway, to our physiology.[99] We can aggregate such processes, for clinical diagnostic purposes. What we can understand though, is the logical matrix of that internal <Node> transmission and reception.

As we established in *Matrixial Logic,* and restated in Section A, above:
- the Theta Θ axis field, is an Equaliser
- the /S/ <{E} / {I}> axis field an an Equivalence function.

Our subjective /S/ axis field operates to compare, qualify and codify. To produce expectations.[100]

That /S/ equivalence function proceeds by negotiation. There are no absolutes, no certainties, no truths. Everything is a negotiated equivalence, the results of which we take, always conditionally, for our reality.

<Nodes> Creation in /S/

As we said earlier (Segment (10) *Exclusion Function to* Ω):

> The question which we have been addressing arises (not unfairly) from the trap of thinking that The question which we have been addressing arises this second equation: $(\geq\varsigma_2) \neq (\leq \Im_2) = \int[x_2]$, must represent an external <Node> transformation.

That is not what we are saying at all. Rather, the

---

[99] we can study single neural excitations *in vitro*
[100] see Section B, Segment (17) *Neuroscience Evidence*

[$_2$] in that second equation is equally capable of representing an internal <Node>.

We know from Section B, Segments (8) and (10) that:

- Ohm $\sum \Omega$ is cumulative, an aggregate of Emotes: $(c) \neq (\jmath)$.
- Emotes are carriers of Exclusion Function output
- Emotes can only be effected by EF outputs: Emotes cannot be directly effected by <signal> or <potential>.

Now, it's time to analyse just how that internal <Node> transmission system works.

In /S/, we derive an "equals" Form $<= [E] / =[I]>$ as the result of negotiated equivalence: $(x) \neq$ (its opposite or antigone).

We create <Node> relations, in that negotiation. The easiest way to conceive of this is that:

- the <Node> transmits to | capacity | in EF
- the contents of the Form of [f]orms [$(x) \neq$ (its opposite or antigone)] stay "at home" in the mind.

If we analogise to our experiences of reality: a barking dog in | W | does not actually, physically, enter our head. That real-world phenomenon stays in the real world. It "sends" a <Node> of itself to us and we process it.

In like manner, when we simply <think> of a dog barking, our /S/ creates the <Node>. The <Node> then transmits to | capacity | in EF. The ideas in our subjective landscape[101] which came together, in forms of inequality, remain in that landscape.

These concepts are novel and admittedly difficult to articulate. Let's provide an analogy:

Experience: Tanner
Setup:

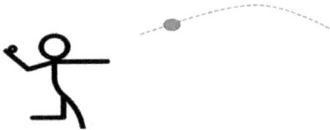

Visualise yourself throwing a ball.

See yourself at side angles like this, around 12 feet from where you're sitting.

So:
see yourself, throwing the ball
see the ball slowly in flight

Now:
- make yourself (the stick figure) disappear
- try to keep the ball in flight

Stop

---

[101] which we will explain later as {idents}

<u>Discussion</u>:

(1)   As soon as Stick-You disappears, the ball disappears as well.

(2)   If you try to keep visualising the ball, the Stick-You keeps coming back.

This is an analogy for how the process of <Node> transmission from /S/ to FX works. The analogy is effective because of the supervening architecture of the mind.

We established back in *Matrixial Logic*, that <movement> is a <Node>. A <Node> is unstable. In the *Experience*, you are cohering the <Node> by constant re-visualisation. It's like you're throwing the ball over and over again, or witnessing it being thrown over and over again.

As soon as you "blank" elements of the Contents which go to make up the <Node>:

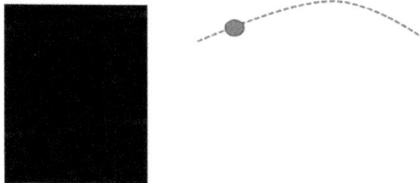

it loses coherence.

Now, you may or may not want to claim that some subjective identity is intending the /S/ <Node> to be sent, and / or watching its transmission. It doesn't matter.

The /S/ <Node> transmission mechanism is the same.

You may wonder quite why we are placing such emphasis on this matter: *"the Contents stay at home in /S/"*. It's because this understanding is really important in therapeutic understanding and practical intervention. That will become apparent in Volume 2.

Transmission Emerges From Plurality

The process of /S/ => ʃ{x} interaction summons a powerful proposition:

> */S/ {idents} transmit only from plurality to EF ʃ{x}.*

We don't mean that we have to transmit multiple thoughts to EF ʃ{x}. This rubric reflects the existential reality of our minds: that we cannot think a <thought> as a Singularity (Si). We demonstrated this repeatedly in *Matrixial Logic*.

We do not just think "x" and transmit "x". We think:

$$<(x) \neq (^{NOT}x) = [E_1]> \neq <(y) \neq (^{NOT}y) = [E_2]> \sum E^*>$$
$$\approx \square_1 \neq \square_2 = \sum E^*>$$

for a <Node> in [E]

or

$$<(x) \neq (-x) = [I_1]> \neq <(y) \neq (-y) = [I_2]> \sum I^*>$$
$$\approx \Delta_1 \neq \Delta_2 = \sum I^*>$$

for a <Node> in [I].

In other words, it's no good trying to match in an isolinear way, single <thoughts> conceived of as being "in a bubble", to <Affect> in | E |. Let's examine this.

Experience: Dish
Setup:
You're going to think of your favourite food: fish and chips, curry, burger, vegan salad: whatever.

This is quite tricky to do, but:
- Just think of the food itself
- not the café, or environment
- not the eating experience

Just picture a picture of the food, on a plate, on a blank surface

Now:
• what Emotions do you register feeling?

<u>Discussion</u>:
(1) You probably don't register any emotional <Affect>
(2) It's like you could be looking at a picture of bland wallpaper: you can see it's there but "so what?"

The reason for this strangeness is that we deliberately stopped you from forming a <Node> for that eating experience.

You don't send a unilinear isolate down to | capacity |.

You can try, but nothing registers. Your |capacity| only registers a <Node>: a complex of forms of inequality. A "bubble idea" has no impact.

Experience: Eats
Setup:
You're going to think of your favourite food: fish and chips, curry, burger, vegan salad: whatever.

This time, think of the experience around the eating: of being hungry and enjoying; of the environment, and so on

Now:
- what Emotions do you register feeling?

Discussion:
(1)   This time, it's what you would expect.
(2)   You probably feel a bit hungry, having been sent these <Nodes>.

So, you see, contrary to intuition, it's not the pictures of the food at the café that stimulate |E|. It's being there, in the eating experience place, and probably with physiological hunger <Nodes> also arriving at |capacity|, which create the registered |E| experience.

It's a mildly useful part of the explanation to say that: *we only think <thoughts> and <feelings> in context.* Because that's a bit vague, we don't usually formulate it in this way.

So:

/S/ transmits only from plurality to EF ʃ{x}.

This innocent rubric produces vast implications for understanding Self, and for producing diagnostic interventions for Self.

Self <signals> and <potentials>

So, here we have the system. /S/ produces <Nodes>, then, just as for <Nodes> originating in |W| :

- <Nodes> interact with |capacity|, being transformed in (≥ς) <signal>
- Under the Exclusion Function, <signal> interacts with <potential> : (≥ς) ≠ (≤Ə)
- the interaction operates like wave interactions: with an output that can be zero, or non-zero: ʃ[x]
- this is a quantitative output

and then

- multiples of ʃ[x] outputs are automatically registered as qualitative outputs: as <emotes> (ε) ≠ (ɔ)
- these aggregate as ∑Ω
- if there exists a "receiver" for an ∑Ω aggregate, there is reception
- if no receiver exists, at that moment, there is no reception.

An /S/<Node> can function under EF ʃ[x] as <signal>, or as <potential> : (≥ς) ≠ (≤Ə).

Now, that is a crucial difference between |W| => |capacity| and /S/ => |capacity|. Obviously, |W| can't provide us with <potential> ($\leq\ni$). That's an internal process: the waves running within ourselves.

The only origins of <potential> ($\leq\ni$) are $|P|$ and $/S/$.

Recall the *Temp Experience*, (in *(2) Systems*, Segment 16). When we are trying, for example, to mimic hot or cold sensations, we are trying to recapitulate this:

Mixed}

=> from $\|W\|$ External}	=> from $\|P\|$ or $\|S\|$ Internal}	
$(\geq\varsigma_1) \neq (\leq\ni_1) = \int[x_1]$	$(\geq\varsigma_2) \neq (\leq\ni_2) = \int[x_2]$	
>	>	
(ϵ) $\neq$	$(\ni)$	$= \sum\Omega$

but without any exogenous <signal>.

Internals}

=> from $\|P\|$ or $\|S\|$ Internal}	=> from $\|P\|$ or $\|S\|$ Internal}	
$(\geq\varsigma_1) \neq (\leq\ni_1) = \int[x_1]$	$(\geq\varsigma_2) \neq (\leq\ni_2) = \int[x_2]$	
>	>	
(ϵ) $\neq$	$(\ni)$	$= \sum\Omega$

We are trying to engage with $|P| => |$ capacity $|$ dynamics. Trying to make $|P|$ react via the exclusion Function, as if the <Nodes> source of <signal> were $|W|$, instead of $/S/$.

As we said in *Exclusion Function to* Ω (under *(2) Systems*, Segment 10):

> This *Experience* also illustrates operation of the *Sanity Barrier*.

Your |P|hysiology is, via its own <Nodes> providing a <potential>. This is meeting with the <signal> transformed from your /S/=><Node> for hot, and the one for cold.

Your ʃ[x] is running its function. The output is not zero, but certainly nothing like the output from a real |W|=><Node> for hot or cold.

We can /S/=> |capacity|, so that we are providing both <signal> and <potential>:

Experience: Cliff
Relax. Close your eyes, or just 'daydream' with your eyes open.
Think of a nice little rabbit.
Hopping and scampering across a field.

Now:
• think of bunny running over a cliff edge

Discussion:
(1)   You may have felt a twinge of sad, or a laugh

Which happy or sad face it was depends on how you were contextualising the rabbit: as a cartoon bunny, or as a Watership Down personality.

What's important here is to see that You made

that "emotional" <Affect> happen. In very crude approximation of the detailed process:

$$\text{Bunny Fall} \qquad\qquad \text{Funny} \mid \text{Sad}$$
$$(\geq\varsigma) \qquad\qquad\qquad (\leq\ni)^n$$

You provided the <potential>$(\leq\ni)^n$ for the self-stimulated experience.

In doing so, you chose which <potential>$(\leq\ni)^n$ to generate. Let's prove that. Run the *Cliff Experience* again. This time, make sure to generate the opposite <potential>$(\leq\ni)$ to the one you spontaneously did the first time around.

$$\text{Bunny Fall}_2 \qquad\qquad \text{Funny}_2 \mid \text{Sad}_2$$
$$(\geq\varsigma) \qquad\qquad\qquad (\leq\ni)^n$$

That was easy enough.

But just think how you might react if the event occurred in the real world. If it were $\mid W \mid =><Nodes>$ for [Bunny Fall]. Can you be sure which <potential>$(\leq\ni)^n$ that would meet in the Exclusion Function? Indeed, can you now be sure which way you'll go if you run the *Fall Experience* once again?

Obviously not. We might like to think it would be <potential>$(\leq\ni)$ which <emotes> as sad. But we can never be sure in advance.

The logic of both *Architecture*, and *Systems* brings us, via different routes to the same fundamental.

Our <thoughts> and <feelings>
depend upon a virtual reality system:
$$[Z] => |EF| \sum \Omega$$
(where [Z] stands for any of $|W|$, $|P|$, $/S/$).
in which we fully participate, but never control

Understanding the systems architecture demystifies the secret of Self. It also grants us therapeutic understanding and remedial power over our Selfs.

Parallel Architecture
Not by accident, we thus arrive at a mirror image result:

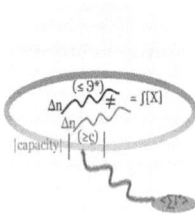

External <Node>	Internal <Node>
transmission to $|capacity|$	transmission to $|capacity|$

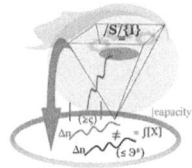

Since decades of experimental data evidences that our $|E|$ cannot easily tell the difference between external source input, and internal source input, this result is inevitable.

However, until we had became able to explain all of these processes through matrixial logic forms of inequality, we had no dynamic model by which to explain them.

Now, we do:

(1)   Our /S/ axis field creates a negotiated equivalence <Node>.

(2)   Which is then submitted as <signal>[102] to our FX |capacity| "resistor".

(3)   whther there is, or isn't an FX ∫[x] output, and what "strength" it is, depends upon the cross-frequencies of "wave" interactions under the FX equation.

(4)   This provides the potential for <emote> formation, aggregating in a ∑Ω output transmission.

(5)   Receipt of that ∑Ω transmission depends upon the "paperclips" state of the receiving system at |P| or /S/, or both.

This all looks straightforward. It's kind of like tearing a playing card in half, with a jagged edge. One part stays in /S/, and the other part goes as <signal> (≥ç) to |capacity|.

But there's no guarantee that what is ultimately by ∑Ω output transmission "matches" the jagged edge of the part which was left behind in /S/. It's a matter for judgment in /S/, using the equivalence function, to work out how closely the jagged edges fit.

---

[102] or <potential>

In Section C, *Unfaithful Reflections,* we consider some of the consequences of this disjunction between effect and <Affect>.

Mirrors

What this explanation leaves out is the how of it. How, exactly, do we create <Nodes> in /S/?

The shorts answer is: by use of Mirrors which are intrinsic to the Architecture on which the /S/ continuum functions.

The explanation of that comes in Part 2 Chapter 6.

19. | *P* | *hysiology and Exclusion Function*

The previous Segments of *(2) Systems,* have already done much of the work for this Segment topic.

So we can jump straight in and state:

- <Nodes> interact with |capacity|, being transformed in (≥ς) <signal>
- Under the Exclusion Function, <signal> interacts with <potential> : (≥ς) ≠ (≤Э)
- the interaction operates like wave interactions: with an output that can be zero, or non-zero: ∫[x]
- this is a quantitative output

and then

- multiples of ∫[x] outputs are automatically registered as qualitative outputs: as <emotes> (ε) ≠ (ə)
- these aggregate as ∑Ω
- if there exists a "receiver" for an ∑Ω aggregate, there is reception
- if no receiver exists, at that moment, there is no reception.

|P| produces <Nodes>, then, just as for <Nodes> originating in |W|:

A |P|<Node> can function under EF ∫[x] as <signal>, or as <potential> : (≥ς) ≠ (≤Ɔ).

That is a crucial difference between |W|=>|capacity| and |P=> |capacity|. Obviously, |W| can't provide us with <potential> (≤Ɔ). That's an internal process: the waves running within ourselves. The only origins of <potential> (≤Ɔ) are |P| and /S/.

We said of /S/=>EF:

> In /S/, we derive an "equals" Form <= [E] / =[I]> as the result of negotiated equivalence: (x) ≠ (its opposite or antigone).

> We create <Node> relations, in that negotiation. The easiest way to conceive of this is that:
> - the <Node> transmits to |capacity| in EF
> - the contents of the Form of [f]orms [(x) ≠ (its opposite or antigone)] stay "at home" in the mind.

Now we need to say something which may[103] surprise you: exactly the same <Node> transmission function operates in |P|.

----

[103] or may not

As a matter of synapse mechanics, that <Node> transmission function is an empirical datum, particularly the stay "at home" part. "Home" here is not of course in /S/, but in |P|.

It's probably reasonably in tune with your intuition for us to say that:

- |P| forms a <Node>
- send <Node> to EF
- resulting a <signal> within EF, and the contents of the <Node> back at origin.

We can well imagine an arm muscle sending our awareness a message: that message reflecting the condition of the organ which sent it.

Similarly, it's well intuitive that we have <potentials> cascading inside us every moment, and that these react to incoming <signals>.

So, the systems architecture of |P| /=>EF, takes little persuading.

It does, however, come with some corollaries, which might not be quite so intuitive:

- not every physiological moment has an expression in thought or feeling
- not every thought or feeling has an expression in physiology

- some physiological moment does have an expression in thought or feeling
- some thought or feeling does have expression in physiology.

Somewhere in these rubrics is an idea, to which you nod and say "Sure, that figures" Elsewhere you're reaction is more "Say what?" It depends on the reader.

However, we don't need to doubt the reality of the matter. We've been though *Experiences* which illustrate each of these rubrics, and there will be more to come.

20.   *Classical Accounts and Beyond*

What you have read in this Book so far, is novel. It is indeed beyond novel. Matrixial Logic proceeds in opposition to the vast library of neuroscience and psychology; and of course philosophy and logic ("the Classical Corpus").

We are in good company, in asserting that all these disciplines have, for the last century, suffered from fundamental conceptual errors.

As neuroscientist M. R. Bennett and philosopher P. M. S. Hacker say in *Philosophical Foundations Of Neuroscience*:[104]

the characteristic form of explanation in contemporary cognitive neuroscience consists in ascribing psychological attributes to the brain and its parts in order to explain the possession of psychological

---

[104] 2003. Malden, MA: Blackwell Publishing

attributes and the exercise (and deficiencies in the exercise) of cognitive powers by human beings. (p. 3)

As Schaal's review puts it:[105]

That this is the form of explanation common in cognitive psychology, with mind (or its hypothetical components) substituted for brain, has been noted by dozens of behavioral scientists and theorists, none more consistently or effectively than Skinner. But despite generations of argumentation to the contrary, cognitive neuroscience is still largely a dualistic, reductionistic enterprise. Well-known facts about the brain, such as the homuncular organization of the sensorimotor cortex, often seem to support such a conception. The continued and often successful mission to localize cognitive function in the brain seems to answer the question "where" (as in "Where is memory stored, where is fear represented, and where is the rat's spatial map?"), and in so doing gives many neuroscientists confidence that they are on the right track.

Bennett and Hacker use conceptual analysis in the tradition of Wittgenstein to argue against these most basic assumptions of neuroscientists. Their arguments are rooted in the history of thought about the brain and mind, in extensive and scholarly reviews of the theoretical language of modern cognitive neuroscientists, and in careful logico-grammatical analyses of psychological concepts.

Although they praise neuroscientists for their accomplishments (Bennett is a neuroscientist) and express confidence that neuroscientists will elucidate the brain activity that makes learning, thinking, remembering, imagining, perceiving, and so forth, possible, they state clearly what neuroscience cannot do:

What it cannot do is replace the wide range of ordinary psychological explanations of human activities in terms of reasons, intentions, purposes, goals, values, rules and conventions by neurological explanations . . . . And it cannot explain how an animal perceives or thinks by reference to the brain's, or some parts of the brain's,

---

perceiving or thinking.

For it makes no sense to ascribe such psychological attributes to anything less than the animal as a whole.

It is the animal that perceives, not parts of its brain, and it is human beings who think and reason, not their brains. The brain and its activities make it possible for us—not for it—to perceive and think, to feel emotions, and to form and pursue projects. (p. 3)

This quotation expresses the theme of the book, that it is usually nonsense to ascribe to the brain psychological concepts that make sense when ascribed to whole humans (and often other animals). This explanatory tendency of neuroscientists (and cognitive psychologists) is called the *mereological fallacy*.

One of the reasons why the Segments of this Chapter have proceeded with such textbook style turgidness, is the necessity to build from ground zero.

That task is made so much harder when there are so many weeds to clear. The Classical Corpus hides many diamonds in much more rough. To extract the gems and use them in the constructions of Matrixial architecture, is always difficult, and sometimes simply impossible.[106]

One of the reasons why we ask you to undertake so many *Experiences*, is that each one provides some antidote to the Classical Corpus. You get to proceed through the construction of systems architecture, without having to use the autistic paradigms of the Classical Corpus.

Another, and not incidental feature of the *Experiences* is

---

106   within the confines of one readable text

that the Classical Corpus contains no diagnostic tools with which to explain them.

As shown in Chapter 10 of Matrixial Logic, both camps – Materialist and Idealist/Dualist – are helpless to explain these phenomena which you know to be real through the *Experiences*.

We achieve all these dramatic consequences without expensive machinery, or endlessly elaborative and utterly counter-intuitive arguments.[107]

Instead, we rely on the creation of more effective Concepts. The use of logic, freed from its 2.5 millenia of error. Matrixial logic, building matrixial systems architecture of the Self.

We don't need to argue that it works. Through the Experiences, you actually know that it works.

Or, if you like the fancies of Thomas Nagel (which as Beckett and Hacker point out, have become de rigeur for the neuroscience community): you know *what it is like to know* that Matrixial Logic works.

Letting Beckett and Hacker speak for themselves:[108]
Conceptual questions antecede matters of truth and falsehood. They

---

[107] none of which are in real life practiced by their proponents
[108] Bennett, Maxwell. Neuroscience and Philosophy (2007) Columbia University Press. p. 4-5.

are questions concerning our forms of representation, not questions concerning the truth or falsehood of empirical statements. These forms are presupposed by true (and false) scientific statements and by correct (and incorrect) scientific theories. They determine not what is empirically true or false, but rather what does and what does not make sense.

Hence conceptual questions are not amenable to scientific investigation and experimentation or to scientific theorizing. For the concepts and conceptual relationships in question are presupposed by any such investigations and theorizings.

Our concern here is not with trade union demarcation lines, but with distinctions between logically different kinds of intellectual inquiry.

Distinguishing conceptual questions from empirical ones is of the first importance. When a conceptual question is confused with a scientific one, it is bound to appear singularly refractory. It seems in such cases as if science should be able to discover the truth of the matter under investigation by theory and experiment - yet it persistently fails to do so.

This passage elegantly distils part of the agenda of Matrixial Logic. Matrixial analysis is conceptual analysis. It provides the systems architecture within which empirical data can best be understood and assimilated.

We would part company from Bennet and Hacker at various points. One being that matrixial analysis is indeed:
amenable to scientific investigation and experimentation or to scientific theorizing

The Experiences and their analyses are exactly that. Matrixial logic is no less an analysis of being and becoming in reality, than physics or chemistry. We simply use different tools of enquiry.

As Beckett and Hacker further say:[109]

3.1 Mereological Confusions In Cognitive Neuroscience

Ascribing psychological attributes to the brain Leading figures of the first two generations of modern brain-neuroscientists were fundamentally Cartesian.

Like Descartes, they distinguished the mind from the brain and ascribed psychological attributes to the mind. The ascription of such predicates to human beings was, accordingly, derivative - as in Cartesian metaphysics.

The third generation of neuroscientists, however, repudiated the dualism of their teachers. In the course of explaining the possession of psychological attributes by human beings, they ascribed such attributes not to the mind but to the brain or parts of the brain.

They produce some rubrics, which deserve careful attention:

- Whether psychological attributes can intelligibly be ascribed to the brain is a philosophical, and therefore a conceptual, question, not a scientific one (p19)
- The misascription of psychological attributes to the brain is a degenerate form of Cartesianism
- The ascription of psychological attributes to the brain is senseless
- Neuroscientists' ascription of psychological attributes to the brain may be termed 'the mereological fallacy' in neuroscience

And, we must include the following:

14.5 Why It Matters

On the question of how it will <Affect> the next experiment, we can imagine a scientist reading our analytical discussions with some bafflement. He might be mildly interested in some of our connective

---

[109] Bennett, Maxwell. Neuroscience and Philosophy (2007) Columbia University Press. p15.

analyses, yet nevertheless puzzled at what seems to be endless logic chopping. 'Does all this really matter?', he might query when he has read our opening discussions. 'After all', he might continue, 'how is this going to <Affect> the next experiment?'

We hope that any reader who has followed us thus far will not be tempted to ask this question. For it displays incomprehension.

Whether our analytic reflections do or do not <Affect> the next experiments is not our concern. They may or may not—that depends on what experiment is in view, and what the neuroscientist's presuppositions are.

It should be obvious, from our foregoing discussions, that, if our arguments are cogent, some experiments might best be abandoned. Others would need to be redesigned. Most may well be un<Affect>ed, although the questions addressed might well need to be rephrased, and the results would need to be described in quite different ways than hitherto.

Our concern is with understanding the last experiment. Our concern has not been with the design of the next experiment, but rather with the understanding of the last experiment.

More generally, conceptual investigations contribute primarily to understanding what is known, and to clarity in the formulation of questions concerning what is not known. It would not matter in the least if our reflections have no effect on the next experiment.

But they do have considerable effect on the interpretation of the results of previous experiments. And they surely have something to contribute to the asking of questions, to the formulation of questions, and to distinguishing between significant and confused questions. (If we are right, then questions about 'the binding problem', understood as the problem of how the brain forms images, are largely expressions of confusion4, and much of the debate about mental imagery is misconceived.)

Does it matter? If understanding matters, then it matters Does all this apparent logic chopping, all this detailed discussion of words and their use, matter? Does neuroscience really need this sort of thing?

If the moving spirit behind the neuroscientific endeavour is the desire to understand neural phenomena and their relation to psychological capacities and their exercise, then it matters greatly.

For irrespective of the brilliance of the neuroscientist's experiments and the refinement of his techniques, if there is conceptual confusion about his questions or conceptual error in the descriptions of the results of his investigations, then he will not have understood what he set out to understand. (p. 45-47).

We also urge attention to the counter-arguments put by Dennett and Searle, in this book, as well as Hacker and Bennett's rebuttals. Both Dennet and Searle land some convincing counter-punches.

They are able to do that because their own stances within the Classical Corpus make them immune from criticism. That's primarily because the foundations of their ideas are self-contradictory: so whichever side of their cognitive dissonances you attack, the other side can ride to the rescue.

To be fair, it's not the job of, for example, Dan Dennet, to derive therapeutic interventions which actually improve the life of any human being. He's just a Classical Corpus philosopher. His cash value in altering interaction between human beings and their world, to the improvement of either: is $nil.[110]

---

[110] we are not seeking to be rude. All of these thinkers exhibit brilliance of thought and argument. Biut in the absence fo systems architecture, it is at best entertainment: not science.

Take that part of Dennett's Rebuttal, where he argues that it's perfectly legitimate to keep reducing from the whole through sub-processes, until you reach a process which could be undertaken by a robot. He seems to say that this is indeed mereological, but it is neither confused, nor in error.

If Dennett wants to think of motor neurology and anatomy as being a process of "little robots", he is as entitled to his fantasy as any child is entitled to believe that fairies put dew on mushroom caps. It's the same order of imagination as used by Cartesian theatre buffs.

But no kind of robot, large of small, has impaired (or sub-optimal) processes which can instantly be improved by engagement of the Theta Θ axis field: such as to change handwriting; synchronise external time; effect anaesthesia: and so on.

Here's a simple challenge for Dennett: utilise all your argumentative skill to fantasise construction of any set of little robots, as follows. That your little robots can, in reality, operate both their own time, and operate in synchronisation with external time.[111]

One can predict how Dennet would shape such an argument. He would assert [XYZ], which *looks like*, they operate both internal and synchronous time, and therefore

---

[111] for more on [T]ime, see *Matrixial Logic* Chapter 7, and the next Chapter

it's just [as if] it were the same.

The course of his thinking is that obvious, because it's the course of all of his thinking. Dennet, like his Classical Colleagues, is stuck in the circularity of a logic which claims that: if A looks like B, then A=B.

It is the analogising method of using the law of identity: A=A. Since that law is wrong, everything built from it, is wrong. Back we come to the foundations of Matrixial Logic.

The endless piling of fantasy bricks, one upon on another, is a task available to the Classical Corpus, because their ideations are not constrained by a systems architecture which needs to work in reality.

We do something completely different. Matrixial Logic assembles a holistic and heuristic systems architecture, the operation of which, even by a 3rd party who is not you, but works through you, has undeniable effects in the material world.

Dennett, and his Classical Corpus colleagues, from both sides of the aisles, are helpless to explain *Biomorphic* and *Psychotectic* techniques and effects, [112] or many of the *Experiences*.

---

[112] see Parts 2 and 3

The Secret Self is neither secret, nor an isolate:

To be a self is to participate, under systems architecture,
in systemic reality, which allows systemic reality to effect
operations in the systems architecture of that self.

Our task, which are part-way through at this point in the book, is to uncover the operating elements of that systemic architecture, in reality: and then to apply these discoveries in effective therapeutic intervention.

Some Useful Experimental Insights

It would be more fair to describe the literature cited from below as being a meta-classical account. We include them only to demonstrate that the concepts of matrixial Self systems architecture are not mere fancies: neuroscience is discovering the working out of exactly these structures in empirically investigated neurobiological processes.

Let's begin with this example:[113]

> Mental imagery is a complex cognitive process that resembles the experience of perceiving an object when this object is not physically present to the senses. It has been shown that, depending on the sensory nature of the object, mental imagery also involves correspondent sensory neural mechanisms.

> However, it remains unclear which areas of the brain subserve supramodal imagery processes that are independent of the object modality, and which brain areas are involved in modality-specific imagery processes. Here, we conducted a functional magnetic resonance imaging study to reveal supramodal and modality-specific networks of

---

[113] Zvyagintsev M, Clemens B, Chechko N, Mathiak KA, Sack AT, Mathiak K. Brain networks underlying mental imagery of auditory and visual information. *Eur J Neurosci.* 2013;37(9):1421-1434. doi:10.1111/ejn.12140

mental imagery for auditory and visual information.

A common supramodal brain network independent of imagery modality, two separate modality-specific networks for imagery of auditory and visual information, and a common deactivation network were identified. The supramodal network included brain areas related to attention, memory retrieval, motor preparation and semantic processing, as well as areas considered to be part of the default-mode network and multisensory integration areas. The modality-specific networks comprised brain areas involved in processing of respective modality-specific sensory information.

Interestingly, we found that imagery of auditory information led to a relative deactivation within the modality-specific areas for visual imagery, and vice versa. In addition, mental imagery of both auditory and visual information widely suppressed the activity of primary sensory and motor areas, for example deactivation network. These findings have important implications for understanding the mechanisms that are involved in generation of mental imagery.

It should not be necessary to evidence psychosomatic induction of the Exclusion Function. This quote from just one of thousands of studies should suffice:[114]

Multisensory interactions are the norm in perception, and an abundance of research on the interaction and integration of the senses has demonstrated the importance of combining sensory information from different modalities on our perception of the external world.

However, although research on mental imagery has revealed a great deal of functional and neuroanatomical overlap between imagery and perception, this line of research has primarily focused on similarities within a particular modality and has yet to address whether imagery is capable of leading to multisensory integration.

---

[114] Berger CC, Ehrsson HH. Mental imagery changes multisensory perception. *Curr Biol.* 2013;23(14):1367-1372. doi:10.1016/j.cub.2013.06.012

Here, we devised novel versions of classic multisensory paradigms to systematically examine whether imagery is capable of integrating with perceptual stimuli to induce multisensory illusions. We found that imagining an auditory stimulus at the moment two moving objects met promoted an illusory bounce percept, as in the classic cross-bounce illusion; an imagined visual stimulus led to the translocation of sound toward the imagined stimulus, as in the classic ventriloquist illusion; and auditory imagery of speech stimuli led to a promotion of an illusory speech percept in a modified version of the McGurk illusion.

Our findings provide support for perceptually based theories of imagery and suggest that neuronal signals produced by imagined stimuli can integrate with signals generated by real stimuli of a different sensory modality to create robust multisensory percepts. These findings advance our understanding of the relationship between imagery and perception and provide new opportunities for investigating how the brain distinguishes between endogenous and exogenous sensory events.

That the collation and curation of Exclusion Function outputs by <signal> referral from (what we call) the /S/ axis field, should again be uncontroversial.

An elegant sudy reveals, for example:[115]

To this day, the study of the substratum of thought and its implied mechanisms is rarely directly addressed. Nowadays, systemic approaches based on introspective methodologies are no longer fashionable and are often overlooked or ignored. Most frequently, reductionist approaches are followed for deciphering the neuronal circuits functionally associated with cognitive processes.

However, we argue that systemic studies of individual thought may still contribute to a useful and complementary description of the multimodal

[115] Letailleur A, Bisesi E, Legrain P. Strategies Used by Musicians to Identify Notes' Pitch: Cognitive Bricks and Mental Representations. *Front Psychol.* 2020;11:1480. Published 2020 Jul 7. doi:10.3389/fpsyg.2020.01480

nature of perception, because they can take into account individual diversity while still identifying the common features of perceptual processes.

We propose to address this question by looking at one possible task for recognition of a "signifying sound", as an example of conceptual grasping of a perceptual response. By adopting a mixed approach combining qualitative analyses of interviews based on introspection with quantitative statistical analyses carried out on the resulting categorization, this study describes a variety of mental strategies used by musicians to identify notes' pitch. Sixty-seven musicians (music students and professionals) were interviewed, revealing that musicians utilize intermediate steps during note identification by selecting or activating cognitive bricks that help construct and reach the correct decision. We named these elements "mental anchorpoints" (MA).

Although the anchorpoints are not universal, and differ between individuals, they can be grouped into categories related to three main sensory modalities - auditory, visual and kinesthetic. Such categorization enabled us to characterize the mental representations (MR) that allow musicians to name notes in relationship to eleven basic typologies of anchorpoints. We propose a conceptual framework which summarizes the process of note identification in five steps, starting from sensory detection and ending with the verbalization of the note pitch, passing through the pivotal role of MAs and MRs.

We found that musicians use multiple strategies and select individual combinations of MAs belonging to these three different sensory modalities, both in isolation and in combination.

In parentheses, we would wish to be able to compile a whole volume of such studies to accompany the analysis of the Matrixial Self. Such studies are endlessly fascinating and thought-provoking in themselves.

Functionally, they provide an empirical warranty of the scientific foundations of the *Matrixial Self*.

Some of what these countless studies reveal accords with our intuition as to the matter. Much does not, or simply shows connections and correlations which lie beyond imagination: in the observed realities of our interactions with the world.

The /S/ axis field is not a domain of truth.[116]

It is well understood that the brain integrates information that is provided to our different senses to generate a coherent multisensory percept of the world around us (Stein and Stanford, 2008), but how does the brain handle concurrent sensory information from our mind and the external world?

Recent behavioral experiments have found that mental imagery - the internal representation of sensory stimuli in one's mind - can also lead to integrated multisensory perception (Berger and Ehrsson, 2013); however, the neural mechanisms of this process have not yet been explored.

Here, using functional magnetic resonance imaging and an adapted version of a well known multisensory illusion (i.e., the ventriloquist illusion; Howard and Templeton, 1966), we investigated the neural basis of mental imagery-induced multisensory perception in humans.

We found that simultaneous visual mental imagery and auditory stimulation led to an illusory translocation of auditory stimuli and was associated with increased activity in the left superior temporal sulcus (L. STS), a key site for the integration of real audiovisual stimuli (Beauchamp et al., 2004a, 2010; Driver and Noesselt, 2008; Ghazanfar et al., 2008; Dahl et al., 2009). This imagery-induced ventriloquist illusion was also associated with increased effective connectivity between the L. STS and the auditory cortex.

---

[116] Berger CC, Ehrsson HH. The fusion of mental imagery and sensation in the temporal association cortex. *J Neurosci*. 2014;34(41):13684-13692. doi:10.1523/JNEUROSCI.0943-14.2014

> These findings suggest an important role of the temporal association cortex in integrating imagined visual stimuli with real auditory stimuli, and further suggest that connectivity between the STS and auditory cortex plays a modulatory role in spatially localizing auditory stimuli in the presence of imagined visual stimuli.

As this study shows (what we call the) /S/ axis field, is a domain of comparative judgment, not truth: but that which we create in /S/ is reality for us.

That's what over 100 Experiences in this book so far, plus *Matrixial Logic*, have shown us.

Those *Experiences* work, because Matrixial Logic gives a unique account of the *Systems Architecture* of cognition. An architecture which mirrors cognate reality: the external world. That is why you can't move the bottle Cap.[117]

However, in the studies cited,[118] there is again an absence of architecture. So, the empirical results of analysis lead to fascinating data. But the information lacks explanatory power.

---

[117] and so on

[118] and many more published

The Barrett Model

A new paradigm has developed over the last decade or so. It concerns the inter-relationship of $[\, |W| \text{ or } |P| \,] => EF => \sum \Omega \Leftrightarrow /S/$: although it is understandably not spoken of in these terms.

It is given brilliant and clear voice by Lisa Feldman Barrett in *How Emotions Are Made: The Secret Life of the Brain:*[119]

> Simple pleasant and unpleasant feelings come from an ongoing process inside you called interoception.
>
> Interoception is your brain's representation of all sensations from your internal organs and tissues, the hormones in your blood, and your immune system.
>
> Think about what's happening within your body right this second. Your insides are in motion. Your heart sends blood rushing through your veins and arteries. Your lungs fill and empty. Your stomach digests food.
>
> This interoceptive activity produces the spectrum of basic feeling from pleasant to unpleasant, from calm to jittery, and even completely neutral. Interoception is in fact one of the core ingredients of emotion, just as flour and water are core ingredients of bread, but these feelings that come from interoception are much simpler than full-blown emotional experiences like joy and sadness. (p56-57)

Barret explains the discontinuity of the new paradigm with the classical model:

> The classical view typifies this mindset: when the snake appears, a "fear circuit" in your brain, which is usually in the "off" position, supposedly flips into the "on" position, causing preset changes in your face and body. Your eyes widen, you scream, and you run away.3

---

[119] (2018)

The stimulus-response view, while intuitive, is misguided. Your brain's 86 billion neurons, which are connected into massive networks, never lie dormant awaiting a jump-start. Your neurons are always stimulating each other, sometimes millions at a time. Given enough oxygen and nutrients, these huge cascades of stimulation, known as intrinsic brain activity, continue from birth until death. This activity is nothing like a reaction triggered by the outside world. It's more like breathing, a process that requires no external catalyst.

The intrinsic activity in your brain is not random; it is structured by collections of neurons that consistently fire together, called intrinsic networks. These networks operate somewhat like sports teams. A team has a pool of players; at any given moment, some players are in the game and others sit on the bench, ready to jump in when needed. Likewise, an intrinsic network has a pool of available neurons. Each time the network does its job, different groupings of its neurons play (fire) in synchrony to fill all the necessary positions on the team.

You might recognize this behavior as degeneracy, because different sets of neurons in the network are producing the same basic function. Intrinsic networks are considered one of neuroscience's great discoveries of the past decade.

You might wonder what this hotbed of continuous, intrinsic activity is accomplishing, besides keeping your heart beating, your lungs breathing, and your other internal functions working smoothly.

In fact, intrinsic brain activity is the origin of dreams, daydreams, imagination, mind wandering, and reveries, which we collectively called simulation in chapter 2.

It also ultimately produces every sensation you experience, including your interoceptive sensations, which are the origins of your most basic pleasant, unpleasant, calm, and jittery feelings.

To understand why this is the case, let's take your brain's perspective for a moment. Like those ancient, mummified Egyptian pharaohs, the brain spends eternity entombed in a dark, silent box. It cannot get out and enjoy the world's marvels directly; it learns what is going on in the world only indirectly via scraps of information from the light, vibrations, and chemicals that become sights, sounds, smells, and so on.

Your brain must figure out the meaning of those flashes and vibrations, and its main clues are your past experiences, which it constructs as simulations within its vast network of neural connections. Your brain has learned that a single sensory cue, such as a loud bang, can have many different causes - a door being slammed, a bursting balloon, a hand clap, a gunshot. It distinguishes which of these different causes is most relevant only by their probability in different contexts.

It asks, Which combination of my past experiences provides the closest match to this sound, given this particular situation with its accompanying sights, smells, and other sensations? And so, trapped within the skull, with only past experiences as a guide, your brain makes predictions. (p57-59)

The is new paradigm combines several features:

- interoception: which we call $|P| => EF \Leftrightarrow /S/$
- intrinsic networks or resting state neural activity
- simulation
- prediction

We accept the *empirical findings* behind these theoretical constructs. Indeed, they are very exciting, as they provide empirical evidence for exactly the systems architecture we have been surveying in this Chapter.

We endorse the concept of *resting state neural activity*, and the principle of *degeneracy* (within external limits)

We like the emphasis on *interoception*. It does much to rebalance the Classical Account which we discussed in earlier Segments.

308

However, there are fundamental problems with the Barret Model:

- The idea that our brains cannot connect directly with | W |.
- that / S / operates by prediction.

(1) The idea that our brains cannot connect directly with | W | is simply wrong, and *Matrixial Experiences* prove the error.

(2) There is a *predictive* system, but that originates in | E | motion, not | M | entation. We will come to this analysis in the next Chapters.

(3) There is *simulation* happening in | M | entation. But it is not a single or unilinear process. Rather, there is an architecture for layers of simulations: those which use the Exclusion Function; and Theta Θ, which doesn't.

(4) It's right that / S / operates by equivalence: evaulation, comparison and judgment. All *subjective*, with no necessary relation to external reality. But / S / is not the only mode of | M | entation we use. The Theta Θ axis field operates in equalisation, synchronised to | W |.

The Barret Model has some systems, but lacks an architecture. Or rather, the fundamental supposition:

the brain spends eternity entombed in a dark, silent box. It cannot get out and enjoy the world's marvels directly

invests in the wrong architecture.

One need not then read further,[120] to appreciate that this half right / half wrong Model must operate in circularity. A tempting target for Dennett-style fantasist reductionism.

As this abstract evidences, neuroscience and psychology suffer from the lack of a systems theory embedded in a dynamic architecture:[121]

> The replication crisis facing the psychological sciences is widely regarded as rooted in methodological or statistical shortcomings.

> We argue that a large part of the problem is the lack of a cumulative theoretical framework or frameworks. Without an overarching theoretical framework that generates hypotheses across diverse domains, empirical programs spawn and grow from personal intuitions and culturally biased folk theories.

> By providing ways to develop clear predictions, including through the use of formal modelling, theoretical frameworks set expectations that determine whether a new finding is confirmatory, nicely integrating with existing lines of research, or surprising, and therefore requiring further replication and scrutiny. Such frameworks also prioritize certain research foci, motivate the use diverse empirical approaches and, often, provide a natural means to integrate across the sciences. Thus, overarching theoretical frameworks pave the way toward a more general theory of human behaviour

This is why we are taking such pains, in these early Chapters, to build the model architecture, process by process.

By understanding process in the logic of the scientific data, we are able to construct an architecture which answers

---

[120] although one should: as it is marvellously informative throughout
[121] Muthukrishna, M., Henrich, J. A problem in theory. *Nat Hum Behav* 3, 221–229 (2019). https://doi.org/10.1038/s41562-018-0522-1

to the reality of the matter. That then allows us to prescribe interventions which are therapeutically helpful. The world is changed by changing how people interact with it.

21.   *Systems Survey*

We can now summarise the systems architecture with this set of graphics:

(1)   The Domains:

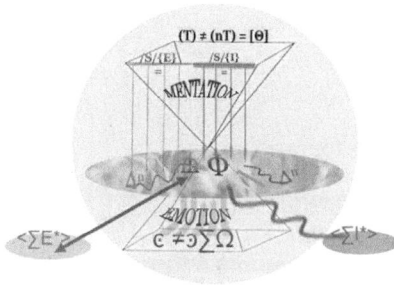

(2)   The Architecture:

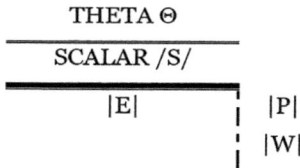

(3)   Systems Example: | W | => | E |

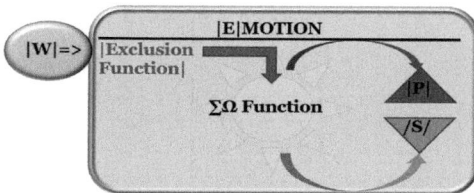

(4)   Systems Configurations (using /S/ as Exemplar);

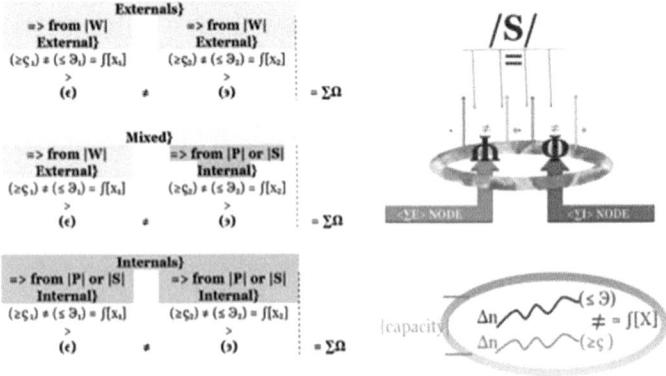

(5)   Systems Operations:

- <Nodes> interact with |capacity|, being transformed in (≥ς) <signal>
- Under the Exclusion Function, <signal> interacts with <potential> : (≥ς) ≠ (≤Ə)
- the interaction operates like wave interactions: with an output that can be zero, or non-zero: ∫[x]
- this is a quantitative output

and then

- multiples of ∫[x] outputs are automatically registered as qualitative outputs: as <emotes> (ε) ≠ (ɔ)
- these aggregate as ΣΩ
- if there exists a "receiver" for an ΣΩ aggregate, there is reception
- if no receiver exists, at that moment, there is no reception.

(6)   The Self Globe:

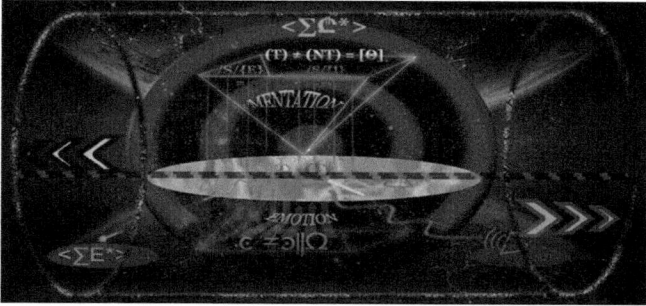

$$\sum\Omega \quad (T) \neq (nT) \quad = \Theta \approx >$$

The missing element, which we have not examined so far in this book,[122] is matrixial | T | ime.

We will see in Chapter 3 how | T | ime is the factor which both correlates and separates. Through which *chronometric synchronisation* has effect so that a Self in *becoming* entrains the universe as a Self in *being*.

We have spent around 200 pages over 2 Sections and some 20 Segments, to build out the systems architecture of Self.

In the next Section C, we discuss:
• Consequences
• wider Implications of the Self systems architecture
• Realisation in reality.

---

[122] although see *Matrixial Logic*, Chapter 7

SECTION C: INTERACTION

(1) CONSEQUENCES

1.   Emotes and Feelings

It would be tempting to think that the output of the Ω equation:

$$(\varepsilon) \neq (\mathfrak{o}) \sum \Omega$$

constitutes <feelings>.

But that's not what <Emotes> and Ohm Ω are. Rather, Ohm Ω is an information distribution system. It distributes quantitative $\int[x]$ as qualitative Ω. The means of distribution are the Emotes $(\varepsilon) \neq (\mathfrak{o})$.

It's an oddity that we do not have a clear working model in western psychology, or neuroscience of how it is that our thoughts can produce feelings.

Search online, and you'll find various types of notion. One is the cognitive behavioural therapy idea, for example:[123]

> a principle that underlies much of contemporary practice in *psychotherapy-* namely that behind every disturbing emotional state lurks a triggering negative thought. *Cognitive-behavioral therapists help people who are struggling with emotional disorders involving anxiety, anger, or depression, by helping them identify the particular thought triggers that underlie their emotional responses and then helping them change how they think in order to change how they feel.*

---

[123]https://www.psychologytoday.com/gb/blog/the-minute-therapist/201512/feeling-your-thoughts

Another is a shuffling around of uninear jigsaw pieces, for example:[124]

> The current study examined 4- to 10-year-olds' and adults' ($N = 280$) tendency to connect people's thoughts, emotions, and decisions into *valence-matched mental state triads* (thought valence = emotion valence = decision valence; such as, anticipate something bad + feel worried + avoid) and *valence-matched mental state dyads* (thought-emotion, thought-decision, and emotion-decision).
>
> Participants heard vignettes about focal characters who re-encountered individuals who had previously harmed them twice, helped them twice, or both harmed and helped them. Baseline trials involved no past experience. Children and adults predicted the focal characters' thoughts (anticipate something good or bad), emotions (feel happy or worried), and decisions (go near or stay away).
>
> Results showed significant increases between 4 and 10 years in the formation of valence-matched mental state triads and dyads, with thoughts and emotions most often aligned by valence. We also documented age-related improvement in awareness that uncertain situations elicit less valence-consistent mental states than more certain situations, with females expecting weaker coherence among characters' thoughts, emotions, and decisions than males. Controlling for age and sex, individuals with stronger executive function (working memory and inhibitory control) predicted more valence-aligned mental states. These findings add to the emerging literature on development and individual differences in children's reasoning about mental states and emotions during middle childhood and beyond.

With Matrixial Logic analysis of the Self, we are now able to understand the transmission mechanism between thoughts and feelings, via the | E | motion distributed referral system.

---

[124] Lagattuta KH, Elrod NM, Kramer HJ. How do thoughts, emotions, and decisions align? A new way to examine theory of mind during middle childhood and beyond. *J Exp Child Psychol*. 2016;149:116-133. doi:10.1016/j.jecp.2016.01.013

We will now tabulate the propositions of classical psychology, and our rebuttals:

Classical Account Proposition	ML Rebuttal
That we derive emotional stimulus directly from our interaction with |W|.	No, we don't.
That our senses are just a fishing net which delivers |W| interactions direct to our |E|.	No. The process is transformation and referral
That such delivery is unmediated.	No. It is mediated by the Exclusion Function, and then further mediated by the $\sum\Omega$ function
That such so stimulated |E| then produces "drives", which produce changes in states of consciousness.	There is no drive, only instantaneous, disappearing data. "Use it or lose it".
That we can analytically reverse engineer such processes: but only to an extent.	We can't analyse what doesn't exist in any version of reality.
We can thereby analyse some of \<T\> and less of \<F\>, and some of their interactions.	Not with Classical Theory. But we can with ML.
This is the domain of cognitive behavioural psychology: the use of observed, and theoretically inducted, aggregates of behaviours; then reasoning backwards to individual consciousness states.	It is. Why is why CBT is at best useless, at worst, harmful.
The ultimate concatenation of stimulus to |E|, resulting in "drives" is ultimately unknowable.	Indeed, because no such "drives" exist.

We are at one with Barrett in saying that our <feelings> are simply <thoughts> which we attach to Ω referrals.[125] That Ω <emotes> are generated from $|W| => |FX|$ and $|P| => |FX|$.

This passage from Barrett is illustrative of that idea:[126]

> Every moment that you are alive, your brain uses concepts to simulate the outside world. Without concepts, you are experientially blind, as you were with the blobby bee. With concepts, your brain simulates so invisibly and automatically that vision, hearing, and your other senses seem like reflexes rather than constructions.
>
> Now consider this: what if your brain uses this same process to make meaning of the sensations from inside your body - the commotion arising from your heartbeat, breathing, and other internal movements? From your brain's perspective, your body is just another source of sensory input. Sensations from your heart and lungs, your metabolism, your changing temperature, and so on, are like the ambiguous blobs of figure 2-1. These purely physical sensations inside your body have no objective psychological meaning.(p29)

Again, we have to caution against accepting literally the Barrett concepts of <concepts>, <predictions> and the idea that "sensations inside your body have no objective psychological meaning."

Barrett's thesis is actually a step back, in some respects.

(1)   That thesis places the brain as the locus of all these processes.

---

[125] although Barrett does not of course use matrixial systems architecture ideas, and denominations

[126] *How Emotions Are Made: The Secret Life of the Brain.* Lisa Feldman Barrett. (2018)

(2)   This corresponds to the Barrett conception of zero
        architecture: that the brain is cut off from the world,
        and even from the rest of our | P | ysiology.

(3)   Yet it's well established as a matter of neuro-anat-
        omy that our gut and heart have massive neural
        networks.

Sadly, we see the important theoretical steps forward
which Barret collates and brilliantly articulates, being
haunted by Banquo's ghost of dualism.

2. | E | *motion Doesn't Care*

Here, we will draw on Chapter 8 of Matrixial Logic:

> We are encultured to regard emotion as the seat
> of Identity. What You$_2$ *Experiences* demonstrate
> evidentially, is what Matrixial Logic derives as a
> proposition. That:
>
> > *Emotions have no self-descriptive state*
>
> What we mean by this admittedly gnomic utterance
> is most easily described by negative comparison.
>
> Our subjective /S/ Scalar axis conducts (+/-
>) examinations of qualities as quantities: more
> pleasurable / less pleasurable. And so on.
>
> These are conceptual constructs, which grow in
> sophistication from the acquisition of language.
> These concepts are, of course, culturally contingent.

This poses problems for views of evolution,[127] and ethics.[128] "Pleasure" is not a fundamental or foundational fact, which can then be used as the substructure for a behavioural or ethical theory.

Pleasure is nothing more than a Scalar $/S/$ interpretation of Ohm Ω states. How that measure is applied, is a social construct.

There is an asymmetry here:
- we are subjects of physically sensed pain and pleasure (a hot stove touch; a cold water refresh)
- we are only describing differences, in retrospect, and in Scalar terms: can can elect to describe such differences differently
- both are real: but reality functions differently in our interactions with externality; and our interactions internally

Emotions do not self-describe. Emotions are mechanical processing of input data: whether provided externally, or internally.

Asking whether one's emotions are "happy" is like asking whether one's blood circulation is "happy". Happy is not the same as functional.

---

[127] Hammeroff; and neo-Darwinian "survivalism"
[128] utilitarianism and its successors

Now, we are able to insert the |capacity| gap "resistor" concept:

> In coming into contact with a |capacity|, which is active through a <resistor>, a <Node> becomes coherent as a <signal>, symbolised as (≥ς*).

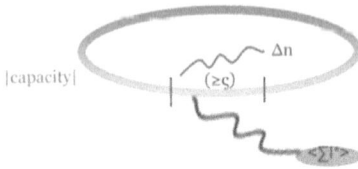

One's emotional mechanics can, of course, suffer disfunction, just as can one's bio-organic processes. The science of such interactions is *Biomorphics*. We will deal with such matters in *Secret Self*.

All this appears, at first sight, deeply counter-intuitive. Surely one's lived reality is comprised exactly of emotional experiences?

We agree. It is. But experience is not the same as a *measure of value*. All sentient life has experiences. How sentience measures experience is the difference between consciousness and awareness.

The Ohm antipoles (ɛ) ≠ (ɔ) are neither opposites nor negations. Therefore, under ML rules, no form can arise.

An obvious example of a (ɛ) ≠ (ɔ) type relationship is the Systolic-Diastolic heart functions:

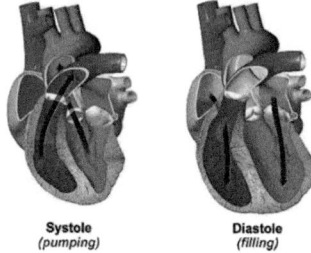

Systole
(pumping)
         Diastole
(filling)

Medicine places these functions under a scalar rule of measurement. Thus we have a regularity of S <120; D <80.

That scalar codification for diagnostic reasons is of no concern to the heart. It jut carries on pumping and filling. Clinical intervention to deal with irregularities in heart function, does of course <Affect> the function: which is why they are carried out.

While the seat of emotion was once thought to be the heart, we have long since known, scientifically, that this is not so. We do know that emotional engagement can have systolic-diastolic consequences. We also recognise that emotional engagement has effects throughout the body.

This provides us with our first clue as to what Ohm Ω actually is.

The Scalar /S/ axis field effects recognition and judgment (quantising and qualifying) in Mentation. These are data (T) equalised in the Theta Θ "shopping basket checkout" function.

The Ohm field performs a *distributed referral* function.

We referred in *(2) Systems,* Segment 20 to the Barrett Model of emotions. We noted the several fundamental issues which we have with the Barrett Model. But also that empirical findings which she ably reports are entirely supportive of the matrixial account of | E | motion:[129]

> Simulations are your brain's guesses of what's happening in the world. In every waking moment, you're faced with ambiguous, noisy information from your eyes, ears, nose, and other sensory organs. Your brain uses your past experiences to construct a hypothesis - the simulation - and compares it to the cacophony arriving from your senses. In this manner, simulation lets your brain impose meaning on the noise, selecting what's relevant and ignoring the rest.
>
> The discovery of simulation in the late 1990s ushered in a new era in psychology and neuroscience. Scientific evidence shows that what we see, hear, touch, taste, and smell are largely simulations of the world, not reactions to it.
>
> Forward-looking thinkers speculate that simulation is a common mechanism not only for perception but also for understanding language, feeling empathy, remembering, imagining, dreaming, and many other psychological phenomena.

---

[129] *How Emotions Are Made: The Secret Life of the Brain.* Lisa Feldman Barrett. (2018)

Our common sense might declare that thinking, perceiving, and dreaming are different mental events (at least to those of us in Western cultures), yet one general process describes them all. Simulation is the default mode for all mental activity. It also holds a key to unlocking the mystery of how the brain creates emotions. (p27-28)

Your concepts are a primary tool for your brain to guess the meaning of incoming sensory inputs.

For example, concepts give meaning to changes in sound pressure so you hear them as words or music instead of random noise.

...Concepts also give meaning to the chemicals that create tastes and smells. If I served you pink ice cream, you might expect (simulate) the taste of strawberry, but if it tasted like fish, you would find it jarring, perhaps even disgusting. If I instead introduced it as "chilled salmon mousse" to give your brain fair warning, you might find the same taste delicious (assuming you enjoy salmon).

You might think of food as existing in the physical world, but in fact the concept "Food" is heavily cultural.

Every moment that you are alive, your brain uses concepts to simulate the outside world. Without concepts, you are experientially blind, as you were with the blobby bee. With concepts, your brain simulates so invisibly and automatically that vision, hearing, and your other senses seem like reflexes rather than constructions.

Now consider this: what if your brain uses this same process to make meaning of the sensations from inside your body - the commotion arising from your heartbeat, breathing, and other internal movements?

From your brain's perspective, your body is just another source of sensory input. Sensations from your heart and lungs, your metabolism, your changing temperature, and so on, are like the ambiguous blobs of figure 2-1.

These purely physical sensations inside your body have no objective psychological meaning. Once your concepts enter the picture, however, those sensations may take on additional meaning. If you feel an ache in your stomach while sitting at the dinner table, you might experience it as hunger. If flu season is just around the corner, you might experience that same ache as nausea. If you are a judge in a courtroom, you might experience the ache as a gut feeling that the defendant cannot be trusted. In a given moment, in a given context, your brain uses concepts to give meaning to internal sensations as well as to external sensations from the world, all simultaneously. (p28-30)

While the matrixial Self has a systems architecture which alters the conceptual content and interactions of the structured concepts Barrett is discussing, the fundamental ideas are sound. As shown in her book, the ideas are collated from a large and growing body of empirical evidence.

The take-home message, is a conclusion which we and Barrett and her colleagues reach, by differing routes:

|E| *motion doesn't care.*

(1)   We have workings of our |W| sensation and |P| autonomic functions. They are real: as real as anything in external reality. But none of them have an <emotional> cadence or valence. They are <emotionally> dumb.

(2)   We formulate subjective concepts in /S/. We attach those concepts to the workings of our |W| sensation and |P| autonomic functions.

(3)   The information we attune in those sensations and functions is utterly real. But the attachment of /S/ concepts to them is discretionary.

(4)   However, we routinely within our /S/ view such attachments as being an embodied reality.

(5)   So far as our /S/ axis field treats something as real, in-

cluding a non-existent paperclip, it becomes real in Theta Θ. But Θ doesn't care either: it is an equalisation function.

(6)   That Θ equalisation has the effect of removing <feelings> from our subjective investment in /S/ axis realities.

When we plug these operants into the Self architecture, we arrive at the dynamics which Barrett is describing:

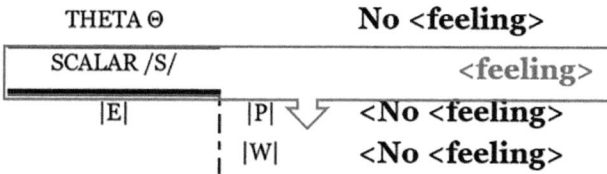

THETA Θ	**No <feeling>**
SCALAR /S/	<feeling>
|E| |P| <No <feeling>	
|W| <No <feeling>	

But what the Barrett model is missing, of course, is the synchronised reality of Θ concurrence with |W| in |T|ime, and thereby space.

We do, of course, culturally see ourself as emotional beings, interacting with the external world. The reality of Self is that our <feelings> are simply <thoughts> attached to |W| sensation and |P| autonomic functions.

And there is a further layer of the architectural 'sandwich'. Our universe of <feelings> is encrusted between the mutual realities of |W|, |P| and Θ. The domain of our emotional freedom is an infinite continuum: bounded by reality.

This is what enables us to be feeling beings, who remain within the boundaries of sanity.

3.   *The Difference Machine*

Continuing the extract from *Matrixial Logic*:

> That process of information selection, however, gives effects to inequality. Our Emotions are a *difference machine*:

$$(\epsilon) \neq (\ni) \, \textstyle\sum \Omega$$

As we said above:

> So now we see that a | gap | is a *Form of Differences*:

- which creates its own reality dimension (the LineScape)
- which "freezes" movement, defining that new stasis by reference to the | gap |.

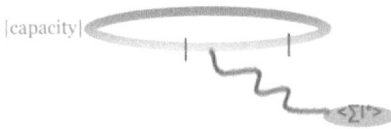

> Here, with the bare wirework, we can see | capacity | in its gapping operation.

Continuing from *Matrixial Anthropics*:

> As we unravel the inner complexities of the Ω field function, we begin to appreciate the raw power of this equation. Unbounded by form, it is the summing of differences which allows the application of Scalar /S/ evaluation.

It is apparent that $(\epsilon)^n$ values are Nodal, or Δ^n Interactions.[130] When we apply the inequality equation dynamics in full, we begin to see something very interesting: Chaos functions, as they become determined by interaction with bounded infinity, assume the properties of probability functions.

Indeed, given the temporal function of Ω, that is hardly surprising. Our Mentative Experiences are $\sum$probability functions, in $|\mathfrak{C}$ present time $[T]^n$ of Ω referral distribution operations. This explains much about a lot.

This open-textured character of the Ω function may call into question its utility. To answer that, beyond the thumbnail presented here, is the labour of an entire book: *Secret Self*.

What may well have seemed obscure in that Matrixial Logic explanation, due to its summary nature, can now be understood in its layers of meaning.

The Exclusion Function is a difference machine. It processes unilinear <signal> types, by factoring their inequalities as a function $\int[x]$. That difference is expressed as a quantitative output.

---

[130] see Chapters 4 and 6

It is then for Ω to collate quantitative outputs in qualitative referrals. Whilst we have reiterated this quantitative=> qualitative system, we have still not entirely explained what distinct role Ω plays.

We will have to wait for Chapter 3 fully to explore those temporal implications of the Ω function.

4.   The Limits of Everything

We need to mention a factor which makes little appearance in classical accounts of "emotion".

In cosseted metropolitan life, or in rural monotony (as experienced by the vast majority of earth's population for at least 12,000 years): nothing much happens.

Looked at in a macro or large scale of comparison, your daily live is filled with the same experiences. Same:

- house
- job and work routine
- family and family routines
- playtime and hobbies
- bed and pillow.

This is the mundanity of everyday life. We're describing, not criticising. It's an achievement of human civilisation in history that billions of people can live like this.

So, the "pool" of potential sense experiences is very small.

That's of course why people travel and do new things: to inject a new pool of experiences.

But then the old saying comes in: it's the same old You that you're taking abroad.

So, when we're talking about I W I => I c I interaction, the universal term I W I needs to be read in the context of the actual limits of the Self in which I c I operates:

- we have limited sense experience in the world
- there are definite limits to what human senses can experience

We restate a core proposition of *Secret Self*:

Mentation

How we can think governs what we can think

Emotion

What we can emote governs how we emote

What we can emote, is limited by:

- environment
- our physiology.

We've mentioned the environmental continuities. They are so obvious as not to need further discussion.

The physiological limits of our senses are also obvious. Our zone of olfactory variation is miniscule, compared to a dog. But we have more sensitive skin than a rhino. It is what it is, and comparative physiology has well established facts of the matter.

Whether you are newborn onto a hospital bed in London, Chicago, Shanghai, or a reed bed in the Amazon, baby You has the same | W | => | c | interaction.

There is, in principle, a whole world out there. Baby You simply exercises the | capacity | mechanics for the | P | hysiological needs of baby life. And adult You does just the same.

The result is that any theory which seeks to draw an arrow of causation or consequence, from the limited and repetitive indents of ordinary daily sense experience, has it fundamentally wrong.
We all have, within geographical and social variations, the same raw material of sense data. We don't sense "the world". We sense infinitesimally small bits of it, in a tiny narrow band (bound by biological limits) and the same bits over and over again.

This, in turn, makes philosophically grand theories of "the a priori"[131] appear ridiculous. You see what you see of that tiny bit of the world in front of you day by day. You don't see anything else. But you can think thoughts about anything.

---

[131] Platonic; Kantian; Hegelian; and other universalist projects

So, any theory of <emotion> has to take into account that, while we can paint whatever shapes we like, in whatever proportions and spacings we like, the colour palette is limited: environmentally; and physically.

The result is that we cannot locate the foundation for variation in emotive thought at the interface of the |W|=>|c| interaction, save in extreme cases (being in battle, other seriously life-changing environments).

Even then, we can only filter |W|=>|c| within the established mechanical processes of our |c|: ands those were set at birth, with augmentation over the next 18 months or so.

The importance of these points will become more apparent in later Parts of this Volume.

(2)   MEETING THE SUBJECTIVE MIND

1.   *Introductory Survey*
In *(2) Systems* we had the task of laying out the processes of each of:

$$|W| \quad => |EF| = \Omega$$
$$|P| \quad => |EF| = \Omega$$
$$/S/ \quad => |EF| = \Omega$$

Under this heading, we focus more on how these Systems

appear from the perspective of our thinking, subjective Selfs.

Whereas *(2) Systems* was a task of construction, these Segments are more a matter of deconstruction: of getting us used to seeking out <thinking> and <feeling> as operating in a continuum of infinity, yet bounded by the systems architecture:

$$\frac{\text{THETA } \Theta}{\text{SCALAR /S/}}$$

$$|E| \qquad |P|$$
$$|W|$$

Time for Lights

We are going to do something very important in the next segments. We have journeyed through this landscape:

We appreciate that it has been, to a certain extent, frustrating. External and internal <nodes>, transforming into <signals>, then qualitative output in Ω^n. Processes in Systems, without meaning: which is exactly what they are.

This is all making Secret Self, less secret. We see the outlines of the Self. We see *Systems* running inside the *Architecture*. But:

> when do we get to see our Mind. The subjective <self>. The Me. My Personality. The buyer and reader of this book.

These are perfectly fair questions. We tend not to mind waiting, if it was worth the wait.

We have been extensively involved in examining Input Systems. We have discovered the Systems under which information about our external world, and about our physiological processes, become available to our /S/ subjective <self>.

It's been a bit like investigating bees doing their thing in various gardens, internal and external habitats. Then disappearing into a "black box" hive. We can see the *Architecture*, and the *Systems*. Now, it's time to turn the lights on:

Dark Architecture   Illuminated Architecture

2.   *Asymmetry In and Out*

We can digest the *(2) Systems* information into two simple graphics:

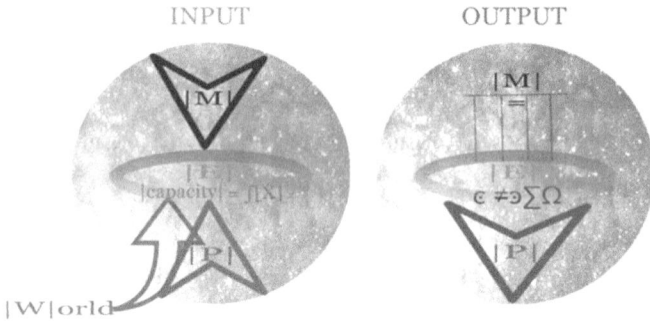

We can notice immediately that the input and output is asymmetric.

- |E| inputs are <Nodes>, whatever the origin:
  1. the |W|orld (via physiological senses);
  2. autonomous |P|hysiology;
  3. |M|entation

but:
- |E| outputs are modulated by the relevant receiving architecture.

That asymmetry is, however, mediated by the same Exclusion Function: whichever of the 3 origin sources.

<Nodes> are transformed by |capacity| into <signal>, which meets <potential>. The quantitative outputs can then function as qualitative <emotes> (ɛ) ≠ (ɔ) in the Ohm $\sum \Omega$ equation.

It is, hopefully, self-evident that | M | entation and | P | hysiology interact differently with $\sum \Omega$.

This input / output asymmetry is what | E | motion actually is. | E | motion is not a type of feeling, or a state.

$| E |$ *is a distributed referral system,*
> taking in <Nodes> and
distributing <emotes> (ɕ) ≠ (ɘ) $\sum$>

There is no point looking for "meaning" in these processes. Although these processes only occur in you as an individual, there is no subjective significance in them.

Like any clinical physiological process, we can by empirical investigation assemble aggregates of these processes, and make scientific predictions based on the results of such investigations.

And, like clinical physiological processes, there is no fact of the matter which is subjective. A well functioning heart can accompany an individual with serious depression. Someone might actually be happy at having a broken leg because they prefer the time off work.

| E | processes are subjective value-neutral. They may function in accordance with aggregate empirical expectations, or not.

That is all clinical, and simple, at least in conceptualisation.

Where it all gets re-complicated is in:

• articulating a domain of <meaning>

and as part of this,

• analysing interaction of the subjective and $|E|$.

3.   *The Subjective and* $|E|$

In *Matrixial Logic*, we had generally set aside the interaction of the subjective Self with $|E|$, in order to focus on the architecture of $|M|$ entation.

That architecture stays the same. What we recognise here, is that $<\sum X^n>$ <Node> outputs from $/S/$ do not simply cohere to $/S/$ inputs. They are mediated by transit through the $|E|$ sphere:

INPUT   OUTPUT

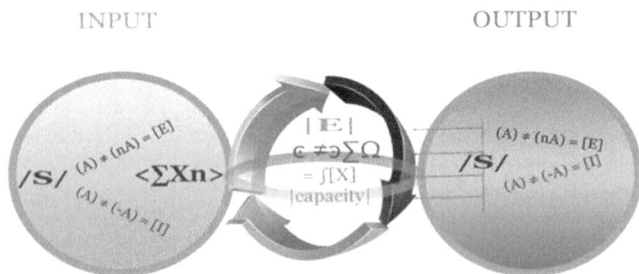

Returning to the table with which we started the voyage of this Chapter:

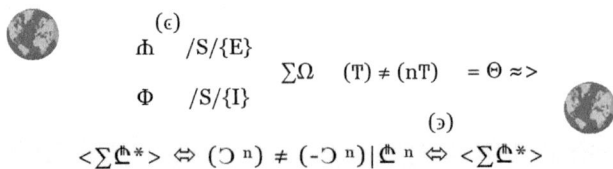

336

the Ohm Ω equation was placed in a distribution around /S/. Now, we can see how deliberate and appropriate that was.

Through the theories of *interoception*,[132] It's becoming a commonplace of psychology and neuroscience, that we do not <think> and <feel> about the world directly. Our thinking reflects the |E| outputs of our 8 Senses.

If the only spheres we had to work with were subjective thought, and emotion: the conflict would be real. These are the only two spheres which neuroscience, philosophy, and psychology try to contend with.

But, what we learned in *Matrixial Logic*, and what we discussed in Section 1 of this Chapter, is that the Theta Θ axis field also exists.

Our |P|hysiology operates within clinically definite boundaries. Our |E| operates functions which are not directly observable, but about which inferences can be drawn with equivalent clinical boundaries. Recall that there are no subjective values in these functions: only a distributed <signals / potentials> $\sum$ referral system.

The Theta Θ axis field is the equalising domain of objectivity. So, we find that the subjective /S/ element of

---

[132] discussed in previous Segments

337

Self is a vital part: but a part, not the whole.

A simple schematic results:

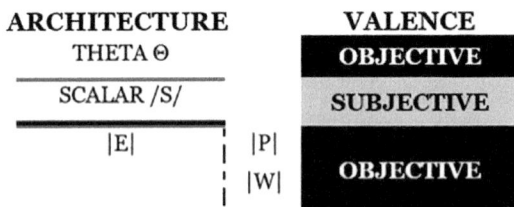

ARCHITECTURE	VALENCE
THETA Θ	**OBJECTIVE**
SCALAR /S/	**SUBJECTIVE**
|E| |P| |W|	**OBJECTIVE**

This table does not attempt to capture the inter-matrixial relationships between elements of the Objective domain, and the Subjective domain. But we have been doing that throughout this Chapter.

If only we could delete that troublesome subjective /S/ scalar domain. But then you would not be You.

This is where we began:

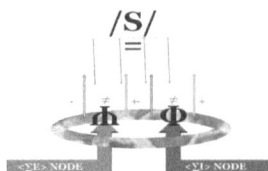

What we have now discovered is that <∑E> and <∑I>, apart from being <Nodes> are the outputs of Exclusion Functions, operating in the domain of |E|.

As we said, halfway through this Chapter: ʃ[x] is not something in itself, or for itself.

∫[x] is a bridge.

The Exclusion Function equation reflects these processes:

- a <Node> is transformed by (variable) resistance in meeting | capacity |
- transformation effects a state change in <signal>
- which interacts with <potential>
- producing a function of that quantitative interaction

∫[x] is a bridge to /S/. Obviously, there is no bridge if = ∫[0]. There is only a bridge if = ∫[x] is a non-zero output.

We are back in very familiar territory: right back to Chapter 4 of *Matrixial Logic*. We have been exploring the derivation of the Phi Φ point:

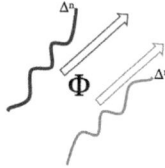

When we plug that much-used *Matrixial Logic* graphic into this Chapter, we see:

∫[x] is not the same thing as Φ

The difference is simple, and fundamental:

some ∫[x] registers in the /S/ axis field under $\sum \Omega$

some ∫[x] does not

but all ∫[x] registers in the Ohm Ω field

In other words, some <signals> functions ∫[x] , enter into Mentation, and some do not. But they all enter into the

Ohm Ω field.

We thus result in this schematic of external influences:

|W| External <Node> In |c| $(\varsigma) \neq (\ni) \int[x]$

Negative =>   No Sensation

Positive =>   Impels Sensation

=>

$(\epsilon) \neq (\ni) = \sum \Omega$

No   No Aferent Feeling

Yes   Potential Aferent Feeling

=>

<Node> in [E] or [I]   => /S/ Equivalance

The same schematic operates for Internal <Node> transmission from |P|hysiology.

4. *Meaning is an Emergent Attachment*

Let's restate the Exclusion Function equations:

$$<(x) \neq (^{NOT}x) = [E_1]> \neq <(y) \neq (^{NOT}y) = [E_2]> \sum E^*>$$
$$\approx \square_1 \neq \square_2 = \sum E^*>$$
$$\text{for a <Node> in [E]}$$

or

$$<(x) \neq (-x) = [I_1]> \neq <(y) \neq (-y) = [I_2]> \sum I^*>$$
$$\approx \Delta_1 \neq \Delta_2 = \sum I^*>$$
$$\text{for a <Node> in [I].}$$

$$>$$

$$(\geq \varsigma_1) \neq (\leq \ni_1) = \int[x_1] \qquad (\geq \varsigma_2) \neq (\leq \ni_2) = \int[x_2]$$
$$> \qquad\qquad\qquad\qquad >$$
$$(\epsilon) \qquad\qquad \neq \qquad\qquad (\ni) \qquad\qquad \sum \Omega$$

Our |E| is a system for:

(1)   receiving <Nodes> in [E] or [I]

(2)   converting them in into \<signal\>: $(\geq \varsigma^{1)}$; which meets extant \<potential\>: $(\leq \ni 1)$

(3)   the result effecting a function $\int[x]n$

(4)   each function then participating as an \<emote\> and its antigone: $(c) \neq (\ni)$

(5)   which aggregate as an Ohm $\sum \Omega$ \<*Affect*\>.

And crucially: our |E| does not discriminate between origins of such \<Nodes\>. Like so much in biology, neurology and molecular biology, it is a "lock and Key" system:

- so long as the referent is of a \<Node\> type
- |capacity| will act as afferent.

It now becomes apparent why we took so much time, both in *Matrixial Logic*, and above, to detail the workings of \<Nodes\>.

All \<Nodes\> are the necessary catalysts of |E| and |M| processes. Human |P|hysiology also works nodally, as the Systolic-Diastolic heart function example demonstrated.

It's not that \<Nodes\> "cause" anything. No more than does the bicycle chain "cause" the rear wheel to move. But, no chain, no movement.

So we say that:

Meaning is an emergent attachment

We attach ideas to Ω referrals, to create \<feelings\>. If there's no Ω referral in a particular matter, there's nothing to attach an idea to.

All referents are emergent. The emergence of Ω referrals is a moment by moment matter of contingency, within the ever-changing[133] circumstances of our becoming.

This is why we feel that we have "no control over our emotions."

That's true in the same sense that we have no control over the weather: and the weather creates conditions in which we experience <Nodes> relevant to wearing a bikini or an anorak.

We do have a degree of environmental control as to how we interact with the weather: which we have been experimenting with ever since life in caves.

It's also true in the sense that we have no subjective control over the systems $|W| => |EF| => \sum\Omega$; and $|P| => |EF| => \sum\Omega$. We can subjectively decide to send <signal> or <potential> to $|EF|$. We can't control the output outcome.

But the horse must come before the cart. So, we also say:
No afferent without referent

---

[133] although in daily life, rather limited

As we explained in Matrixial Anthropics:[134]

> That is not the same as recognition and judgment. Reference involves recognition, but it is not a judgment function. Emotions do not judge: they register. Emotions have no frame of external reference, by which to make judgments. Nor do emotions have a "memory".[135]

Experience: Looky

Look at this graphic:

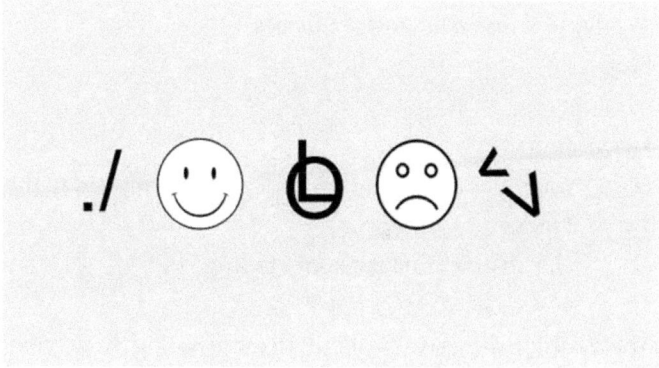

Step 1:

Just think that there will be no questions or instructions about the graphic at all.

Now:

• Just allow your eyes and attention to move between what you can see

---

[134] *Matrixial Logic* Chapter 8
[135] which makes trauma-based cognitive therapy something of a dead duck

- Just relax, and go with whatever comes naturally to your looking

Stop

Discussion:

(1)   Your eyes became more focused on the 2 faces

(2)   It was like you wanted to just see the 2 faces, but you kept getting distracted by the abstract images

Step 2:

Now:

- Try to focus on the abstract shapes

Stop

Discussion:

(1)   Your eyes and attention kept getting dragged to the 2 faces

(2)   The abstract images kept "fading" out

The *Looky Experience* is about demonstrating how your I M I entation functions, without an Emotional Ω input. That is quite hard to achieve: how could you switch off your Ω?[136]

We can achieve part of that effect by giving you comparative stimulus:

- there is no Ω registration for the abstract designs

- there is compelling Ω registration for the happy and sad faces.

---

[136] You can't: instead you can freeze the reaction of your /S/ to Ω input referrals, by fixing these in Shadow Slices: a dysfunctional simulacrum of Theta Θ: see *I Want To Love But* (2019) and Part 2 later

We know this latter datum from early natal development studies. So, for example, the 2008 study by Nagy:[137]

> In most of our social life we communicate and relate to others. Successful interpersonal relating is crucial to physical and mental well-being and growth.
>
> This study, using the still-face paradigm, demonstrates that even human neonates (n = 90, 3-96 hr after birth) adjust their behavior according to the social responsiveness of their interaction partner. If the interaction partner becomes unresponsive, newborns will also change their behavior, decrease eye contact, and display signs of distress. Even after the interaction partner resumes responsiveness, the effects of the communication disturbance persist as a spillover.
>
> These results indicate that even newborn infants sensitively monitor the behavior of others and react as if they had innate expectations regarding rules of interpersonal interaction.
>
> Isn't that fascinating? No matter how old you are when reading this book, you still have exactly the same emotional attachment patterns emergent of your reality (as a human), as you did when just 3 hours old.

Continuing from Matrixial Anthropics:

> Our Emotions discriminate our information acquisition. They choose the focus of our visual and aural attention. Emotions act as channels for sense-Qualia, choosing amongst what we are to notice, and not.
>
> Asking "why" our Emotions function in this way is as helpful as asking why our heart is constructed

---

[137] Nagy, E. (2008). *Innate intersubjectivity: Newborns' sensitivity to communication disturbance. Developmental Psychology, 44*(6), 1779–1784. *https://doi.org/10.1037/a0012665*

as it is. It is the machinery humans are born with: literally, as the above reported experiment shows.

But our emotions are not making Mentative judgments in that selection. Our Emotions don't "think" to themselves:

- I don't want to look at that
- I should look at that
- It's right to look away
- I shouldn't avert my gaze.

Our Mentation can and obviously does train our Emotion to operate programs, by reference to circumstances prescribed by Mentation. That can take a long time: ask any parent.

This brings into notion, an interesting idea. If there is one part of the human process which is most "computer" like: it is Emotion.

- Ω does not reason.
- Ω is a *distributed referral* system: [+ more] information in => [- less] information out.
- Ω runs the default program [+ / -] unless and until instructed to run some other program
- Ω does not consider, appraise, or evaluate the information, in any independent frame of reference
- Ω is no more a reasoning process, than the mechanical action of a flour sieve

> | E | *is a distributed referral system,*
> *> taking in <Nodes> and*
> *distributing <emotes> (ᴄ) ≠ (ᴐ) ∑>*

Ohm $\sum\Omega$ summing of <signal> differences originating in <Nodes>, is distributed *forward in time,*[138]:

- to our physiology
- to our /S/ axis field.

This is what | E | motion does. This is all that it does.

As a matter of daily survival in cosseted metropolitan life, as much as in any "just so" evolutionary biology scenario, our | E | motion has to operate as simple difference machine.

Whereas Mentation occurs in the brain, | E | motion is a *distributed* system. We are seeking to describe with a singe word, that which is a gestalt. Our | E | motion is producing <Affect>, in the inter-dynamic of all of our "8 Senses".

No good comes of trying to make | E | motion a conceptual sub-division of Mentation. That is the path of Freud, ands the delusion of "the subconscious". It is a category mistake.

Whatever has (what Freudian theory would call) a "subconscious" referent, has a "conscious" afferent. Since one illuminates the other by its antigonal opposition, nothing is actually hidden at all.

---

[138] we will come to the importance of this in the next Chapter

Sometimes, an iceberg analogy is used: with <conscious> thought being visible, and <subconscious> "emoting" lying beneath the surface. The analogy is instructive: if you can see the tip, you know the base is there, and you can work out (with deductive reasoning formed from empirical experience) the place, scale and nature of the base.

The appeal to the <subconscious> originated historically in the machine age. It seemed that we knew everything about the external world.[139] That conflicted with our deep lack of knowledge about our internal world.

So, we created the <subconscious> hypothesis. That was an explicit confession of the boundaries of empirical knowledge. It was a false confession.

We cannot unravel every chain of circumstance, of referent and afferent in any manifestation of subjective /S/ thought. But then, we cannot ultimately account for the disposition of the atoms in this keyboard.

We can perform a conditional, and an aggregate accounting, using material data and systems equations. And we are content to declare that to be "material science" and claim that we have thereby explained all that could ever need to be explained about this keyboard.[140]

---

[139] see Chapters 6 and 9 of *Matrixial Logic*
[140] quantum issues aside

Well, the same is true of | M | entation. We can perform a conditional, and an aggregate accounting, using material data and systems equations. We just need the right data exploration tools (the scientific logic of empirical experience) and the right systems equations: the Exclusion Function and Ohm Equation.

With those systems equations, operating as the holistic mechanics of the architectures of | E | and | M |, we can explain all that could ever need to be explained about any product of our | M | entation.

We arrive at this model:

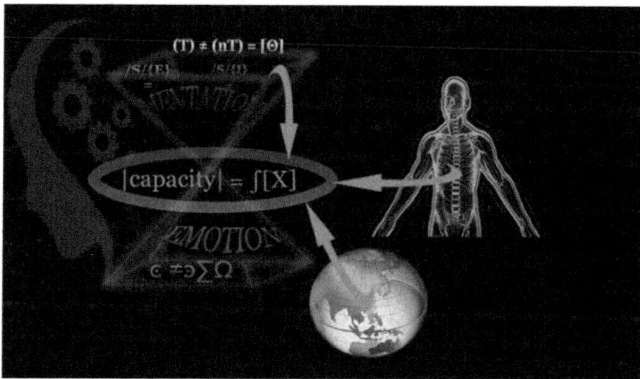

We have explained, and here pictured, the inner workings of | E | motion, and its interactions with | M | entation and | P | hysiology.

5.   *And Feelings Are*

$|E|$ performs no value judgments. Feelings can be produced via the Exclusion Function $>\sum\Omega$ +by:

*   external $|W|$
*   internal $|P|$
*   internal $/S/$ thoughts

All the time, these productions are happening simultaneously.

It may seem strange that, throughout this Chapter, we have not assigned a separate symbol for <feelings>, nor subsumed that notion under an equation.

That's because feelings have reality for us only as manifested, via the Exclusion Function, in $/S/$ or $|P|$. We only experience a reality of <feelings> as:

* $/S/$ thoughts

associating with

* Ω^n referrals.

There is no independent, autonomous, reality of <feelings>.

This is a very challenging idea. We are enmeshed in a model of Self in which a category of "feelings" is granted an autonomous status, such that:

WORLD	FEELINGS	THOUGHTS
➤ things happen	➤ **we Feel**	➤ we think
➤ **we Feel**	➤ we think	➤ **we Feel**
➤ we think	➤ we do things	➤ we do things

This is the *Unilinear Model*. It suffuses neuroscience, philosophy (Western and Eastern), and psychology.

The *Unilinear Model* is a first cause nightmare. It is a circular construct in which cause and effect work as concepts, until they don't. It is the central logic both of materialism and idealism.

The *Unilinear Model* is an absence of architecture. Thoughts and feelings become interchangeable concepts. The very concept of Self becomes so fragile that it can be dissipated by opponents of the ideas of consciousness and free will.

This void, at the centre of thinking about the Self, creates irreconcilable disharmony, which leads to a search for a solution in some "other": spirit; god; organic materialism; physical materialism.

To deny an independent, autonomous role for <feelings> appears, superficially, to be fantastical. The attempt by a logician to eradicate a category of reality which does not fit neatly.

It is the *Unilinear Model* which actuates denial of the reality of <feelings>. Life is real, yet it manifests only in

351

living things. Seeking to grant an independent reality to life is considered to be the scientific quackery of vitalism.

Any post-Victorian scientist or philosopher would turn their nose up at the merest suggestion of a vitalist agenda. Yet the same independent primacy is visited upon the notion of <feelings>. In scientific literature sufficient in volume to fill the Bodleian Library many thousands of times over.

The *Interoceptive Model* has usefully moved away from the *Unilinear Model*. Yet it has simply moved the unilinear concept "up" a stage: instead of the world being the external locus for the Cartesian theatre, human physiology, in interaction with the world, becomes en entangled locus. This is, with respect, a step sideways rather than forward.

We must not, however, elide the denial of autonomous <feelings> into a denial of $|E|$ motion. The function of the Ohm $\sum\Omega$ fields equation is fundamental to the Self.

Yet Ohm does not operate through <feelings> but under the Exclusion Function. It is the interface between $[\int x^n]$ under Ω distribution, and $/S/$ and/or $|P|$, which constitutes what we usually think of as <feelings>.

And so <feelings> are:
> *<thoughts> attached to the emergents*
> *in the interfaces between $|E|$, $/S/$ and $|P|$.*

We don't actually feel autonomous <feelings>. We have <sensations>. These are activations of nerve impulses. We interpret nerve impulses, through physiological, autonomic action, and also through subjective brain functions, /S/, in infinite continuum, bounded by architecture.

6.   *Meeting Our |E|motions*

Generating Feelings With Thoughts

Autonomous, independent <feelings> have no existence. Saying the same thing in techno-speak: there is no epiphenomenon of autonomous <feelings>.

It is not that autonomous <feelings> are somehow "real" but not in a "conscious" way.

All these have a process in |E|: <Nodes>; <signals> ≠ <potentials>; ≠<emotes>. None of them are autonomous <feelings>.

Those processes in |E| are the materials out of which <feelings> can be formed. But <feelings> are only formed when some such material has attached to a <thought> Potential.

Obviously, this attachment happens in every moment, overlapping, layering: and all in the infinity of the /S/ continuum.

We generate <feelings> only with <thoughts>. That is not to deny the vast power which <feelings> can have in us, and over us. Indeed, it is to endow <feelings> with a substrate contingency of *intelligence*. That is the basis of their power.

We can feel this <T | *Attachment* | F> occurring within us moment by moment:

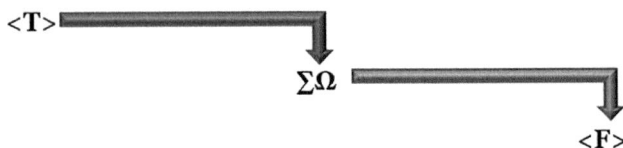

<T> ⟶ ↓
ΣΩ ⟶ ↓
<F>

Intellectually, we can accept that <T | *Attachment* | F> is occurring. But then we want to know *how* <T | *Attachment* | F> works.

Sadly, we can search through the *Interoception Model*, and find no answer.

We find endless assertions, based on good empirical evidence, that <T | *Attachment* | F> happens, that it is indeed how we generate <F> with <T>. That's helpful core data.

We can read about fMRI and EEG experiments which show different parts of neuroanatomy being implicated in different <T | *Attachment* | F> scenes. Again, it's useful empirical data.

Barrett's book has a go at explaining in Chapter 6, which is the fulcrum chapter, concluding:[141]

> Emotions are meaning. They explain your interoceptive changes and corresponding <Affect>ive feelings, in relation to the situation. They are a prescription for action. The brain systems that implement concepts, such as the interoceptive network and the control network, are the biology of meaning-making.
>
> So, now you know how emotions are made in the brain. We predict and categorize. We regulate our body budgets, as any animal does, but wrap this regulation in purely mental concepts like "Happiness" and "Fear," that we construct in the moment. We share these purely mental concepts with other adults, and we teach them to our children. We make a new kind of reality and live in it every day, mostly unaware that we are doing so. (p126-127)

The Author is full of praise of Barrett's work. Her own research and collation of the research work of others provides important empirical data.

But none of it provides a *Systems* explanation: how does a <T> form |Attachment| to an <F>.

The Barrett Model is:
- |P| produces autonomic sensations
- These provide the raw material of <F>
- We then subjectively create <T> and <F> by reference to such raw materials.

This is all fine: as description. But how does that

---

[141] *How Emotions Are Made: The Secret Life of the Brain.* Lisa Feldman Barrett (2018)

attachment work> What is the process?

To this, no answer is given. Instead the Model jinks rather violently sideways into an idealist theory of how "prediction", modelled on the "past", collates the present moments to create "concept" pathways for future thought, feeling and behaviour.

This is neurological Cartesianism: *I make concepts from physiological cadences, therefore I am*. It is the mind as encyclopaedia.

For those who have become familiar with matrixial symbolic usage, there is a big clue in the notation we have just introduced: <T | *Attachment* | F>.

Having become used to the matrixial method, it will be obvious that <T> forms | Attachment | to an <F> by means of <Nodes> entering into an inequality function.

This is where systems architecture becomes completely illuminated by logic.

∑Ohm Process in /S/

We are now going to discover how our /S/ continuum, our subjective <self>, processes Ohm ∑Ω Inputs. To find the light switches and chord connections for our subjective ideations:

We tend to think of <T> as being points, and <F> as waves. <T> as a thing or substance, and <F> as a continuum.

Wee can see how this common sense articulation seeped into Classical logic. In *Matrixial Logic*, Chapter 3, we explained extensively how Aristotle's Categorical Sentences, and Categorical Syllogisms, are in fact failures. They don't work.

Ackrill/Aristotle Categorical Sentence Transitions to ML

	C S	ML Equation	Type
A	Every A is B	$(A) \neq (-A) = B[I]$	Categorical Universal
E	No A is B	$(A) \neq (B) = N[E]$	Reflexive Universal
I	Some A is B	$(A^n) \neq (nA^n) = B[E]$	Reflexive Opposition
O	Not Every A is B	$(A^n) \neq (-A^n) = B[I]$	Reflexive Negation

Table 3.6

Aristotle, and the 2,500 years of logicians who followed him, were unable to see that these illegitimately[142] confuse

---

[142] in a logical frame of reference

[E] logic forms with [I] logic forms.

The idea of <T> as a thing or substance, and <F> as a continuum has been "culturally hard wired" ever since.

But, surely we do experience a "flow of feelings". Surely we think discrete, individual, thoughts. Thoughts that we can break down into atom-like components. As Russell thought, as Dennett-type materialists fondly like to think: as indeed do followers of the *Cartesian Theatre 2.0* Interoception Model.

These are part of the illusions of the /S/ continuum. The reality is:

- <T> is a flow
- the origin of our <F> is Substance: being $\sum\Omega$ <Affects>[143]
- we wrap our <F> in articulations of <T>
- which allow <F> to appear in thought, as if <F> were also continuous: but they aren't.

Experience: Stut
Rest one hand, palm down, on your desk.
Close your eyes
Just feel yourself

Now:
- whatever happens, allow to happen

---

[143] which are Qualitative

Stop

<u>Discussion</u>:

(1)   After a few moments, a finger or fingers started to tap or twitch

You were demonstrating a |P| motor reaction to a rhythm that you began to feel, inside you. Maybe it was your heart beat. Or blood flow pulsing. Or breathing.

A rhythm: think about it. A rhythm is composed of beats, of bits: stut – stut – stut. There are gaps, by definition: gaps between the bits.

This is what <F> are created from. They are bits which happen one after another. Of course, we must imagine overlapping layers of bits, affecting each other in time.

The Exclusion Function $(\geq\varsigma)\neq(\leq\Theta)\int[x]$ creates quantitative output. That is [I] logic, the logic of Moments Δ^n in becoming.

The Ohm Function $(\varepsilon) \neq (\circ) \sum\Omega$, transforms that EF quantitative output in qualitative output: Substance in Form [E].

Each of those outputs is different from every other, all the time. They are each a different substance, produced under the same systems.

Experience: Da

Rest one hand, palm down, on your desk.

Close your eyes

Just feel yourself

Whatever happens, allow to happen

Now, in your head:

- think of a word
- think of words in a short phrase

which, for you, match what you're experiencing

Stop

Discussion:

(1)   After a few moments, a finger or fingers started to tap or twitch.

(2)   Then, as you thought of that word, the rhythm seemed to freeze

(3)   As you articulated in words the phrase, your twitching or tapping, stopped.

Now, this looks like you're halting a flow. It's an example of the common sense intuition.

Yet, it's the words you're using which belong to a flow, a continuum. Those words are associated with all the other words and combinations of words, in your vocabulary.

Suppose that your vocabulary was limited to "da". You could undertake the same *Da Experience*. You'd be experiencing Ohm Function qualitative outputs: blips of substance.

You then take the continuum of "Da", and apply it to different blips. In doing that, you experience:

$$<T> \neq <F> = \{M\}$$
$$<Thought> + <Feeling> = \{Meaning\}.$$

This is not, of course, a proper matrixial logic equation. We are working up to that.

What we are seeing here is *baby talk*. This is exactly how a baby verbalises. Without vocabulary, the baby is attaching word-function sounds to Ω^n.

Vocabulary is a continuum. Any word only means something by reference to every other word. It is an [I] form of cognition:

$$\text{every (A) is (B)}$$
$$(A) \neq (-A) = B \ [I].$$

It is obvious, from this perspective, that Ω^n consist of Substance:

$$\text{some (A) is (B)}$$
$$(A) \neq (nA) = B \ [E].$$

Logic Emerges
We are here in the architecture of Self:

ARCHITECTURE	VALENCE	
THETA Θ	OBJECTIVE	SUBJECTIVE
SCALAR /S/	Theta Θ	/S/ Scalar
|E| |P|	Ohm Ω	
|W|	|P	

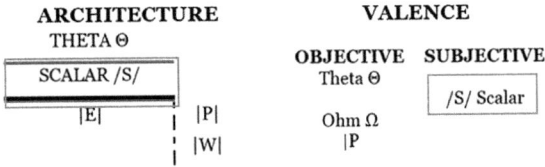

Having surveyed the systems which lead to /S/, we now find the fundamental equations of Matrixial Logic, appearing, as it were, out of the mist of the mind.

We find ourselves recapitulating the very first statements of Matrixial Logic:[144]

> In Matrixial Logic: we are examining types of relationship:
>
> (1)   In E Logic: Things which are **Opposites**, and both exist;
>
> (2)   In B Logic: Things which cause or relate to other things, and which exist, but as a **Process**
>
> (3)   In C Logic: things which do not fall within either category of relationship.
>
> Matrixial Logic seeks to symbolise and explain objects of logical enquiry under the "3H" rubric:

- holistic

---

[144] *Matrixial Logic*, Chapter 2

- heuristic
- hylomorphic

Holistic	The whole is more than the sum of its parts. All parts need to be understood by reference to the whole
Heuristic	Matrices are dynamics of self-learning, by both internal and external reference
Hylomorphic	Forms are the forms of their contents, not merely arbitrary categories

It should be added that the "hylo" is not limited to "things", but includes processes, and paramorphic relations.

We can refer directly to the founding rubrics of ML:

MATRIXIAL LOGIC
AXIOMS COMPARED

IN [E]	IN [I]
Being is the Form of Substances in Extension.	Information is the Form of Moments in Infinity.
Each Substance is a unique event in spacetime.	Each Moment is unique in becoming.
To be a unique event in spacetime, is to be Extended.	To be unique in becoming, is to Become in Infinity.
Extension manifests as Form.	Infinity manifests as Form.
Any Form is the Form of its Contents.	Any Form is the Form of its Contents.
The Content of any Form is Substance in Extension	The Content of any Form is Moments in Infinity

Ω^n Is Substance

To exist, is to be extended in spacetime.
Substance is that which is extended spacetime. The content of any Form in [E] is Substance in Extension.

The Ω^n outputs are Substance. They are extended in spacetime.

Just a moment. Did we just say what we just said? Surely, that's nonsense. These Ω^n outputs are just epiphenomena inside our heads aren't they? Surely they are not "real", like apples and atoms are real?

We are going to call Ω^n outputs, as registered by $/S/: \varepsilon$. The equation for Ω^n outputs as Substance is:

$$(\varepsilon) \neq (n\varepsilon) = \varepsilon \, [E]$$

About that "real" question. The circulation of blood in your arteries. Crossings of the synaptic gap. These are "real", just like apples and atoms. The most ardent materialist wouldn't dispute that.

But of course, that apple isn't an ultimate reality. It's made of atoms. And the atom is certainly not an ultimate reality: comprising sub-atomic particles, then the elements of quantum mechanics, and ultimately: well, the debate still thrives about that one.

But we are all happy: physicists, philosophers, and logicians;

to assign the status of "real" to all these phenomena.

<Affect> which manifest as (ε) has equivalent reality. In the *Stut* and *Nat Experiences,* each (ε) occurred at a definite time, and at a definite co-ordinate point in space.

There may be practical issues with assigning definite spacetime co-ordinates to each (ε): but the same difficulty arises in assigning definite spacetime co-ordinates to the action in movement of each white blood cell in your body.

Yet a proposition that no element of your physical body actually exists in spacetime, would be considered eccentric, whichever chair of science or common sense were occupied by the utterer of it.

In like manner:
$$(\varepsilon) \neq (n\varepsilon) = \text{\euro} \, [E]$$
is a matrixial logic equation of reality.

The equation form:
$$(A) \neq (nA) = B \, [E].$$

can apply to any Substance. All that we do with the = € [E] equation form is specify a particular landscape for the inequality.

<Thought> is Moment
And here we head down an avenue which should by now

be intuitive, in Matrixial Logic.

It is obvious that any <Thought> ($\top$) is a moment in a continuum:

$$\Delta <\top^n> \mid \infty$$

Any $<\top^n>$ is an infinity ∞ of Moments Δ^n in becoming.

Vector Collapse of Infinity Potential

A Form in [E] cannot interact with Moments Δ^n in [I], other than through the creation of <Nodes>. It is <Nodes> which allow crossing of the matrix.

Elementary Matrixial Logic produces the equations:

$$(\epsilon^n) \neq (n\epsilon^n) = \epsilon^n \, [E]$$
$$\neq$$
$$(\epsilon^n) \neq (n\epsilon^n) = \epsilon^n \, [E]$$
$$\Sigma <\epsilon>$$

In classical <Nodal> equation form:

$$[\square \, \epsilon^1] \neq [\square \, \epsilon^n] \, \Sigma <\epsilon>$$

As we said in (C(2)/5:

> Having become used to the matrixial method, it will be obvious that <T> forms ❘Attachment❘ to an <F> by means of <Nodes> entering into a ❘gapping❘ function.

And, here it emerges, right before our mind's eye. as we stated in *Compass*:

A Chi ᵯ <Node> occurs when an
Event
<∑E>, which is a combination of [E]
Forms of Substance contents, interacts
with a course Δ^n of Infinity ∞.

What we called Vector Collapse of Infinity Potential, in
Chapter 5 of *Matrixial Logic*:

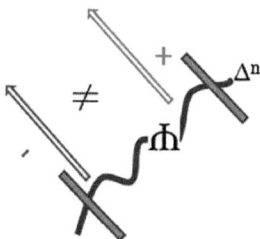

[<T> I Attachment I <F>] is simply the collapse of □[I],
its infinity potential $\Delta<\top^n> I \infty$, by interaction with a
<Node> ∑<€>.

Your $\Delta<\top^n> I \infty$ <thoughts>, consisting of Moments in
infinity, is collapsed by your <Affect> ∑<€>: the rhythm:

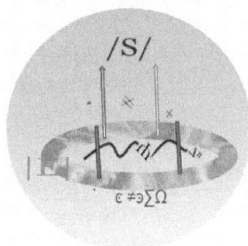

The rivers of your $\Delta<\top^n>|\infty$ <thoughts>, are being disturbed by rocks of $\sum<\epsilon>$ being dropped into them. Yet it is You who are inviting the rock.

Now, there's a massive clue here. For this process to be working, there must be some other aspect of cognitive agency "holding the ring". Of course, there is:

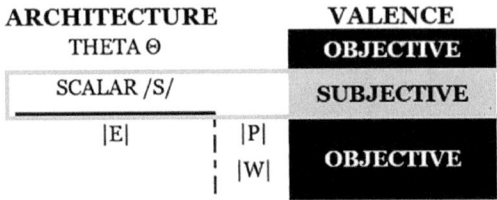

ARCHITECTURE	VALENCE	
THETA Θ	**OBJECTIVE**	
SCALAR /S/	**SUBJECTIVE**	
|E|	|P|	**OBJECTIVE**
	|W|	

but we'll come to that in a few segments.

Plain Thinking

Let's just unwrap the last vital pages, stated in a set of equation propositions, with some plain language narrative.

Think back to the *Stut* and *Nat Experiences*. You allow yourself to be quiet and to experience the <Affect>s occurring:

$$[\square\ \epsilon^1] \neq [\square\ \epsilon^n]\ \sum<\epsilon>$$

Let's just suppose that what became your focus was, if we put a meaningless verbalisation as a sound *Bleep-Blip-Blip*.[145]

It is hopefully obvious that you can't experience an

---

[145] we are just creating this to ease discussion

<Affect> in isolation. The *Bleep-Blip-Blip* can only happen against the "background" of everything else going on in your $|W| => |E| \Leftrightarrow |P|$.

Indeed, if *Bleep-Blip-Blip* is this: $[\square \, \text{€}^1]$, then something else (your heartbeat, breathing, or anything else) is $\neq [\square \, \text{€}^n]$. That's the plurality which allows the <Node>: $\sum<\text{€}>$.

Now, review the history of your head in *Nat*. Slow that review right down. Play your film of that *Experience* in slow motion.

You see what really happened?
- you have awareness of *Bleep-Blip-Blip*
- you spin through different iterations of vocabulary
- a verbal river streaming by
- you interrupt the verbal stream
- bringing *Bleep-Blip-Blip* into the stream at a point.

That's how you verbalise the <Affect> $\sum<\text{€}>$.

The slowmo reality looks very different to what we tend to think we are doing. We have this idea that we are projecting the word= $\neq \text{ʈ}[I]$ into the maelstrom of <Affect>s.

When we speak out loud, projection is what we're doing. But in internal monologue, we apply the <Affect> to the flowing waters of our linguistic moments Δ^n.

We realise an |E|motional <Affect>, as a Subjective /S/ idea. What we will come in later Segments to call an {ident}, under the theory of {identation}.

So, that's why we say:

[<T>|Attachment| <F>] is simply the collapse of $\Delta<\top^n>|\infty$ by interaction with a <Node> $\Sigma<\epsilon>$.

Now, you're entitled to ask why any of this matters. The answers are to be found in the therapeutic intervention analyses later in *Secret Self*.

7. *The Impurity of Thought*

There's a prejudice going back to Plato, that <thought> occupies an ethereal, unemotional dimension. Indeed, the very pursuit of logic is supposed, in culture, to be the antigone of emotional intelligence.

From the perspective of Matrixial Logic, we can now see what Plato was trying to do. He sought to escape the valances of /S/ubjective <thought> by proposing an eternal, objective realm.

That objectivity is real: in Theta Θ:

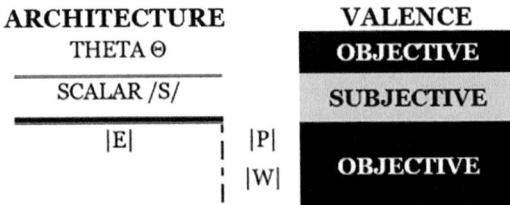

ARCHITECTURE		VALENCE
THETA Θ		**OBJECTIVE**
SCALAR /S/		**SUBJECTIVE**
|E|	|P|	**OBJECTIVE**
	|W|	

It's not a realm outside of Self: it is the means by which Self synchronises with |W|. That interaction is what gave the foundation of reality, to Plato's projections into ideality.

/S/ubjective <thought> is never pure. One of the upsides of the *Interoception Model*, is empirical validation of the thesis that no ₺[I] exists without ∑<€>:[146]

> Every thought, memory, perception, or emotion that you construct includes something about the state of your body: a little piece of interoception.

> A visual prediction, for example, doesn't just answer the question, "What did I see last time I was in this situation?" It answers, "What did I see last time I was in this situation when my body was in this state?" Any change in affect you feel while reading these words - more or less pleasant, or more or less calm - is a result of those interoceptive predictions.

> Affect is your brain's best guess about the state of your body budget. Interoception is also one of the most important ingredients in what you experience as reality.

> If you didn't have interoception, the physical world would be meaningless noise to you. Consider this: Your interceptive predictions, which produce your feelings of affect, determine what you care about in the moment - your affective niche.

> From the perspective of our brain, anything in your affective niche could potentially influence your body budget, and nothing else in the universe matters.

> That means, in effect, that you construct the environment in which you live. You might think about your environment as existing in the outside world, separate from yourself, but that's a myth. You (and

---

[146] *How Emotions Are Made: The Secret Life of the Brain*. Lisa Feldman Barrett (2018)

other creatures) do not simply find yourself in an environment and either adapt or die.

You construct your environment - your reality - by virtue of what sensory input from the physical environment your brain selects; it admits some as information and ignores some as noise. And this selection is intimately linked to interoception. Your brain expands its predictive repertoire to include anything that might impact your body budget, in order to meet your body's metabolic demands. This is why affect is a property of consciousness. (p. 82-83)

As we've previously said, empirical evidence of the continual interoceptive exchange between $|W| => |P| <=> |E| \Leftrightarrow /S/$, and the "body budget" idea, are both useful. We can refer Self *Systems Architecture* to the factual findings of science, without having to jump into the hot air balloon basket of "prediction".

Any $\mathcal{t}[I]$ is an infinity ∞ of Moments Δ^n in becoming. All these Moments are extrusions from the Scalar $/S/$ ubjective plane.[147] As we will see later in the book, they are manifestations of $<I>$.

As such manifestations, they appear to us to have independence and autonomy. That is part of the price we pay for mentative sanity.

Experience: Fluffy
Think of a lovely cure fluffy bunny rabbit
It's in a lovely rabbit run on a well-kept estate
Just lovely and harmless

---

[147] for more detail on this concept, see *Matrixial Logic*, Chapter 4

See the movie in your mind of fluffy bunny, scampering on the grass.

Allow whatever <feelings> that come, to come.

Now:

- think angry thoughts, without words

Stop

<u>Discussion</u>:

(1)   You can't summon <angry>

(2)   Not in <thought> or <feeling>

Review the history of your head, in slow motion:

- we said fluffy bunny
- that was an input from $|W| => |EF| => \sum \Omega^n => \sum <\epsilon>$
- Your $\textit{t}[I]$ became attached to that "emotion".

The Scene precipitated an "emotional" response, which then fixed upon the rolling river of your thoughts: at a definite point.

Once that had happened, you couldn't "unhappen" it. Now let's take a closer look at this happening.

8.   *<Thought> Potentials and <Thought>*

We now need to draw a distinction between <thought> potentials:

$$\Delta<\top^n>\,|\,\infty$$

and actual <thoughts>:

$$(\top) \neq (-\top) = \textit{t}[I]$$

Here, we illustrate the /S/calar continuum.

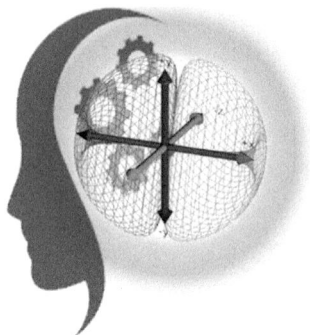

The 3-dimensional torus described by the 3 co-ordinate axes, is the infinite continuum of <thought> potentials: $\Delta<\top^n>\,|\,\infty$.

These ideas are difficult to communicate. How do we think and write about that which is potential thought?

Perhaps an analogy which works, is to consider the potential of a muscle nerve to contact. We understand that easily enough: the nerve is passive until an activation event, which causes firing of the nerve and contracting of the muscle.

In physics, potential energy is well understood too. Obvious applications are: a boulder at the top of a slope, water at the top of a waterfall, electrons ready to propagate across a circuit.

We've already discussed how words are connected to all other words, by associations. That association is possible precisely because all <thought> potentials: $\Delta <\top^n> | \infty$ are extrusions in the /S/calar continuum, from the /S/calar plane.

Now, we don't mean by this that <thought> potentials: $(\top) \neq (-\top)$ are "atomic". They are quite the opposite of tiny autonomous "thought atoms". They are the currents within a perpetual flow of Moments.

<Thought> Potential is Realised by <Affect>
So, we have rubrics that:
- there are <thought> potentials: $\Delta <\top^n> | \infty$
- which have a <thoughts> Form of <thoughts> $\hbar[I]$
- which extrude from the "3 dimensional" /S/calar plane
- in the /S/calar continuum
- which become associated as $\hbar[I]$

We can say that <association> is the aether in which <thought> potentials: $\Delta <\top^n> | \infty$ propagate.

That leads us to ask what instantiates such <association>? We have already met the answer:

      Your $\hbar[I]$<thought>, consisting of Moments in

infinity, is collapsed by your <Affect> $\sum$<ϵ>: the rhythm:

Now we can add a further layer of accuracy.

- Infinite rivers of <thought> potentials: Δ<$\top^n$> | ∞ become <associated> when they conjunct with <Affect> $\sum$<ϵ>
- the vectored collapse of this infinity potential produces $\pounds$[I]<thought> points.

We can represent the above graphic with this schematic:

$$=\pounds[\mathbf{I}]$$

$$(\bar{\top}) \neq (-\bar{\top})$$

$$\sum<\epsilon>$$

This is one of the most important graphic / schematic sets in this whole book.

It is hyperbole, but not entirely underserved, to state that:

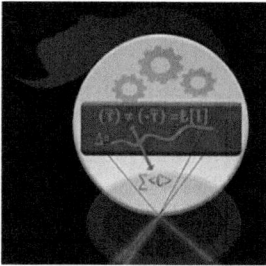

These images represent equation concepts of highest import in Western thought. Ever.

This is the E=MC² of logical philosophy. The holy grail in search of which Descartes wrote *cogito ergo sum*, and in denial of which materialist philosophy has struggled ever since.

Before more blows on that trumpet, let's just unwrap further the implications of these equations.

Extension and Infinity
<u>Extension [E]</u>

After all the Matrixial Logic we have done together, you understand that in (A) ≠ (nA), the inequality [≠] is a <spacetime> function. [148]

---

[148] see *Matrxial Logic*, Chapters 2 and 4

The Form =[E], is the <spacetime>co-ordinate of ≠, yet is no longer simply <spacetime>, but a unique iteration of<spacetime>.

Remember also that a Form is always hylomorphic to its Contents. The Form [E] is created by the opposition of (A) ≠ (nA), and is at the same time, what allows each to exist in<spacetime>.

Thus, in the [E] form of equation, <spacetime> is a potential, which is realised in Extension, and Extension is possible only due to inequality, and manifests as Form of inequality.

Infinity [I]

Infinity ∞ works differently, although the intra-rational equations derivation is the same.

In (A) ≠ (-A), the inequality [≠] is not a <spacetime> function. It is a Δ<A^n>∣∞ <potential> in infinity:

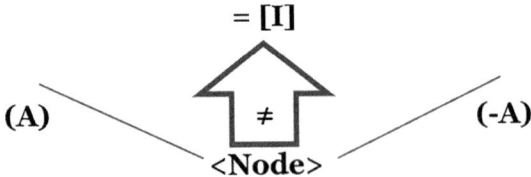

= [I]

(A)   ≠   (-A)

<Node>

That Δ^n <potential> becomes being in existence, that is, within <spacetime>, only upon realisation by a <Node>.

Such <Node> may be :

(i)   another Δ^n <potential>:

A Chi ⷙ <Node> occurs when an Event
$< \Sigma E >$, which is a combination of [E]
Forms of Substance contents, interacts
with a course Δ^n of Infinity ∞.

(ii)   a qualitative <node> formed from <spacetime>
        conjunctions of Forms:

A Phi Φ <Node> occurs when one <set
of Moments Δ^n in Infinity ∞ > meets
another.
This creates an Interference <Node>,
rather than a Point <Node>.

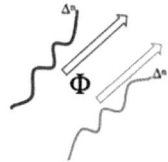

<Affect> and >Thought>

When we consider the <Affect> ⇔ <Thought> schematic,
we can immediately see the equivalent operation of any
[I] Form:

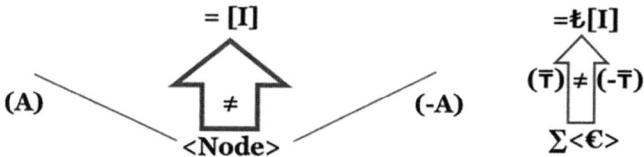

$$= [I] \qquad\qquad = \mathit{t}[I]$$
$$(A) \qquad \neq \qquad (-A) \qquad (\bar{T}) \neq (-\bar{T})$$
$$<Node> \qquad\qquad \Sigma <\mathcal{E}>$$

We have provided countless *Experiences*, in which you
have been invited to operate your thinking in an [I] Frame
of Reference.

We have also provided many *Experiences*, where we have

placed you in Scenes where [I] and [E] have no <node> connection, or we use a <node> which is not hylomorphic to the relevant Contents. This is where you experience being "stuck" in various ways.

In passing, this is also how the Heraclitan, Zenoan and Liar paradoxes work. They are simple tricks in which [I] and [E] contents are disguised under fake forms of "existence" or "movement" or "time"; and so on.

Indeed, the entire edifice of Aristotelian logic, and its successors (Leibnitz, Frege, Russell, Gödel et al),[149] is built out of just such confusions.

These confusions are justifiable. In the Frame of Reference which is the /S/calar subjective axis field, [I] and [E] are indistinguishable.

As we will spend more time discussing in the next Segment, it is a condition of our sanity that it be so.

It is hardly a peculiarity of $\Delta<\top^n>|\infty$ <potential>, that it is "invisible" and unknowable. That is the natural state of the universe of elementary particles, as discovered by quantum physics. Invisible and unknowable that is, until there arises a <node> interaction.

---

[149] see *Matrixial Logic*, Chapter 3

However, that helpful analogy must not be pressed too far. We are not suggesting that $\Delta < \top^n > | \infty$ "exist" as some kind of entangled particle pair in superposition. Whatever quantum physics may ultimately discover to the fact of its elementary particles matters, there are no "elementary particles" of "thought potential" in the human brain.

The idea of $\Delta < \top^n > | \infty$ is an induction from $\hbar[I]$. That may not be worth a lot, in itself. But it is also a deduction from the *Systems Architecture* of Self: which makes it worth everything in human thought. It's the holy grail of humanist thought since 500 B.C.

Process of the Subjective Mind

There is a /S/calar continuum. It is infinite in dimension, in its boundedness by Theta Θ and $|E|$:

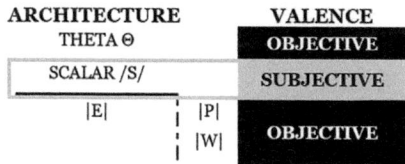

ARCHITECTURE	VALENCE
THETA Θ	OBJECTIVE
SCALAR /S/	SUBJECTIVE
$|E|$ $\quad$ $|P|$ $|W|$	OBJECTIVE

Here, we illustrate the /S/calar continuum:

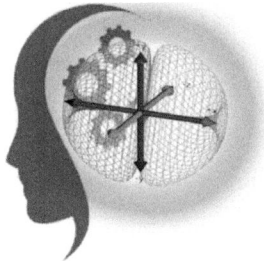

Our *Systems Architecture* in |E|, |P|, \W|, and their interactions, via the |Exclusion Function|, produce in $\sum\Omega$ qualitative <Affects>.

<Affects> operate as <Nodes>. Such <Nodes> interact with an infinity of $[(\top) \neq (-\top)]\,\Delta^n$ <potential>: and in the same way that we can observe such interactions throughout nature, in material science:

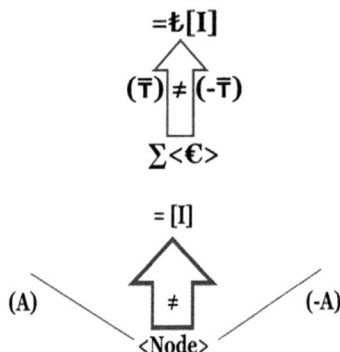

$$=\mathcal{t}[I]$$

$$(\bar{\top}) \neq (-\bar{\top})$$

$$\sum<\boldsymbol{\epsilon}>$$

$$= [I]$$

$$(A) \qquad \neq \qquad (-A)$$

$$<\text{Node}>$$

That vectored collapse of this infinity potential produces $\mathcal{t}[I]$<thought> points.

The <potential> in of $\Delta<\top^n> | \infty$ is <associated> with all other <potential> in $\Delta<\top^n> | \infty$ because all are extrusions from the same dimension of infinity ∞.[150]

It is not that <Affect> $\sum<\boldsymbol{\epsilon}>$ "causes" $\mathcal{t}[I]$, anymore than the bicycle chain "causes" the rear wheel to move.

---

[150] the /S/scalar plane"

Interaction is not the same as causation.[151]

We do not and cannot choose which <Affect> $\sum$<$\in$> interacts with <potential> in of Δ<$\top^n$>|∞. It is random. But we can ascribe any Ƅ[I] we wish to the interaction. That is why Free Will is real, not an illusion.[152]

Such ascription does not need to "make Sense" to anyone except our own Self. And the terms of such sense-making are whatever we choose. After all, nobody else knows, not even our past or future <selfs>.

And all this is occurring in every micro-moment of our lived existence, from birth to death.

9. *Unfaithful Reflections*
We interrupt the continuum of our moments in <thought>, with <Node> $\sum$<$\in$>: <Affects>.

We also send the products of our |Mentation as <Nodes> to our |E|motions. We then use our /S/ equivalence function to interpret |E| outputs.

What we can be certain about, in such |S| => |M| => |S| transitions, is the uncertainty of outcomes. And yet, we know that *Experiences* work as predicted. That seems to be an irreconcilable conflict.

---

[151] which is a circular concept anyway: see *Matrixial Logic*, Chapter 9
[152] very much for another time

Any <Thought> ($\top$) is a moment in a continuum:
$$\Delta < \top^n > |\infty$$
Any $\mathcal{t}$[I] is an infinity ∞ of Moments Δ^n in becoming.
$$(\top) \neq (-\top) = \mathcal{t}[I]$$

When we wish to effect our | E | through thought, we must turn Moments of thought $\Delta(\top)^n$ into a <Node>:
$$[\square \, \mathcal{C}^1] \neq [\square \, \mathcal{C}^n] \sum <\mathcal{C}>$$

At this developed stage of matrixial analysis, we should not need to explain the necessity of a Form=> <Node> transition.

From there, the Systems narrative is fully established. The | EF | Function treats an /S/ <Node>, just as it does a | W | <Node> or a | P | <Node>.

When we send a <Node> from /S/ to | E |, so that it can meet | capacity | and transform into a signal ($\geq\varsigma$), we have no control over what, if anything, emerges as <<Affect>> from Ω.

Narcissus can effect reflection in the surface of the | E | pond. But the | E | output is never a faithful reflection of the /S/ input. Reflections are always approximate: although we can, in our subjectivity, seek to persuade ourselfs that they are realistic.

|E| performs no value judgments. The |EF| is a mechanical system, which transforms differential <Node> inputs into quantised outputs. The Ohm function refers quantised inputs as qualitative outputs.

We are able to shape our subjective thoughts so as to activate $|c| \setminus (ç) \neq (Ə) \int [x]$, just as if a |W| <Node>, or a |P| <Node> had encountered |c|.

We can, indeed, influence our |E| just as can the "real" external |W|orld, and our |P|hysiology. The phenomenon of psychosomatic influence has long been known to medicine, and philosophy.

Yet, within western medicine, there has long been a legacy of objection to mind-body interaction. Part of that objection has rested upon the absence of a medium for such interaction.

The *Matrixial Self* model proffers a solution to the conundrum. It's not that |M|entation effects |P|hysiology directly. Rather, our /S/ subjective thought has the ability to act as a chameleon. To activate our Exclusion Function, as if it were receiving a <Node> from the physical realm.

But, this is not guaranteed to result in a <feeling>. Whether it does, or not depends upon the dynamic process at large, in that moment, in Ohm Ω. Our thoughts do not automatically generate <feelings>.

Ohm Ω is a free transmitter. Once information has been transformed by the Exclusion Function, Ω refers it.

Here's the key point:
$$\sum \Omega \text{ referral involves no judgment}$$

Your Ω acts like a telephone exchange, or an Amazon warehouse robot. Ω does not have a view on what it is delivering.

Ω does not test for meaning: there is no meaning in Ω, only referral function.

In the *Fog Experience*,[153] you noticed that distributed referral occurring. As you read these words, if you just

---

[153] at *(1) Introductory*, Segment 4

allow yourself, you can notice that you are aware of this distributed referral occurring moment by moment.

We might think of it as the "background" noise to your every moment in life. But it's not the background. It's the raw stuff of which your /S/ constructs <F>, and <T> about <F>.

We see in neonates, exactly this process:
- |c| Exclusion Function ∫[x] acts to limit the sense signal effects of |W|=>|c| interaction
- the allowed output in Ω is referred for distribution in |P|
- we can see the baby using Ω <emotes> to learn and grow

In early neonate life, the relatively small /S/ landscape of continuum has only small use of Ω. But, by that [Ω=>/S/=>Ω] reciprocity, the neonate grows its learning.

There are metabolic processes which allow this to occur, then, and throughout life. We come to those in Part 3.

The Neo-Echo Chamber
Let's just park an analogy as a landscape reference. We are well used to the idea that social media, Facebook and the like, has become an "echo chamber". We submit "likes": and the algorithms operate to send us more of what we liked. The infinity of internet output is restricted to our narrow band of expressed preferences:

In like manner, our Ω responds via Emotes, to "likes". The primary response mechanism is of course from our |P| hysiology.

We saw how this process operates in the *Slide* and *Tilt Experiences.*[154]

To anthropomorphise in aid of explanation, say your circulatory system wants |c| mediated information about temperature in your bit of |W|. The information generates "it's getting colder". Your |P| turns your body temperature up. If it gets hypo thermically cold, your |P| will respond to that information by shutting down bodily functions. Your |P| will be shouting at Ω to distribute information about the outside temperature.

In ML terms, |P| is providing potentials ($\leq\ni$) for the Exclusion Function, the outputs of which then provide <emotes> in the Ohm equation: $(\epsilon) \neq (\ni) \sum\Omega$. In our social media analogy, |P| is sending ($\leq\ni$) "likes":

The $\sum\Omega$ function then aggregates $\int[x]$ outputs, and refers as distribution to |P|. And on the cycle goes. Until other information interacts with other elements of |P| producing a counter-cycle.

---

[154] in (*2*) *Systems*, Segment 16.

Now, the above logical analysis is simply an exegesis drawn from clinical medicine. The bedrock of clinical science, established since the days of William Harvey.[155]

Here is where we make the Matrixial Self leap:

- our /S/ functions in exactly the same way.
- /S/ provides potentials ($\leq$Ɜ) for the Exclusion Function.
- This provides <emote> connectivity in $\sum\Omega$, resulting in referral to /S/.
- So $\sum\Omega$ transmissions are received more by /S/, in its "likes".

It's the /S/ "echo chamber".

This is of course a self-reinforcing cycle. Until it's met by a counteracting cycle.

If we want to ask "well, how materially does this happen?", we know the answer: through nerve impulses,[156] transmitted throughout the body.

Let's just restate the landscape, and highlight the paradox. You, a grown adult, have no more sensory machinery $|W| => |c|$, than a neonate. To be fair and accurate, you have developed in some areas, and actually devolved in others.

Remember that we begin with a neural capacity which we could score at 100: then we shed both capacity and

---

[155] Exercitatio Anatomica de Motu Cordis et Sanguinis in Animalibus. (1628). Of course, modified since: but the fundamentals were there.
[156] synaptic and ephaptic

connections from 1 day old through to our mature brain (somewhere around the end of our teenage years). This is an observed neurological fact.

So, it's no good assigning to our subjectivity a phantom ability to draw out of |W| more than a neonate can. Indeed, we get better at shutting out information from |W| as we mature. Selection and discrimination are the metrics of subjective maturity.

The <Node>=> <signals> resource from which we construct <F>, and <T> about <F>, is individual, localised and variant only under the dictates of our constant |P|hysiology. That is the reality.

The paradox, is that out of this narrow and shallow stream, we create all the infinitely varied cathedrals and purgatories of our emotional consciousness.

10.   *The Science of Subjectivity*

Material <Thought>
We should highlight what we have discovered in these C(2) Segments.

Matrixial Logic began its account, in Chapter 2, by saying: there, when we look at the world, that real existing world, the logic that we use in looking at it, and interacting with it, is [E] and[I] and <Nodes> of those Forms.

390

After all these pages of analysis of the Self, its Systems Architecture, we discover that the very formation of the <thoughts> which attach to <Affect>s as <feelings>, operates under the very same logic.

We were perfectly happy to accept that rocks and rivers, out there in the world, exist in spacetime. That rocks are extended as Substance in spacetime. That processes which propagate as waves (sound, light and so on), exist as Moments of spacetime, in infinity. That's all just classical physics.

As we switch on the lights of the Self Systems Architecture, we reflect upon the equivalent reality of that illuminating process.

The *Bleep-Blip-Blip* <Affect>, emergent from our $\sum$Ohm interaction via the Exclusion Function, with $|W|$ and $|P|$:[157] that's as real as our heartbeat. It may well be an awareness of our heartbeat.

That heartbeat is a clinical fact. It is as real as any Substance. It is extended in spacetime. The interaction of $/S/$ with it cannot somehow cease to be extended in spacetime.

That is to suppose that there subsists some phenomena outside spacetime, which can interact with spacetime phenomena. Dennet is right to say that it is simply bizarre

---

[157] and of course /S/ itself

to believe in such a phantasm.[158]

We do not need to believe it. Through patient matrixial logic analysis of Self Systems Architecture, we find that our starting point is our finishing point: in the /S/ubjective /S/ axis field.

We see the |W|orld with exactly the same logic as we see inside our own /S/ continuum. We subjectively (but not objectively) interact with the material worlds, of |W| and |P|, in the very same way that we subjectively understand them.

Our subjective minds are separated from these worlds in exactly the same manner as we are connected to them.

The Science of Self

We said in C(2)/9:

- Infinite rivers of <thought> potentials: $\Delta<\top^n>|\infty$ become <associated> when they conjunct with <Affect> $\Sigma<\epsilon>$
- the vectored collapse of this infinity potential produces $ℓ[I]$<thought> points.

$$=ℓ[I]$$
$$(\bar{\top}) \neq (-\bar{\top})$$
$$\Sigma<\epsilon>$$

---

[158] see *Matrixial Logic*, Chapter 10

This is the E=MC² of logical philosophy. The holy grail in search of which Descartes wrote *cogito ergo sum*, and in denial of which materialist philosophy has struggled ever since.

…

The idea of [(⊤) ≠ (-⊤)] is an induction from ₺[I]. That may not be worth a lot, in itself. But it is also a deduction from the *Systems Architecture* of Self: which makes it worth everything in human thought. It's the holy grail of humanist thought since 500 B.C.

Those *Experiences* which use Theta Θ to alter your interaction, not merely with your /S/ubjective <self> but with your |P| and |W|, are sufficient to terminate both materialist and dualist philosophies.[159]

But now we have discovered the *Systems Architecture* in and through which the continuum of the /S/ subjective mind subsists, neither of materialist or dualist philosophies even get off the ground.[160]

Materialism wishes to deny reality to a subjective "conscious" mind, and its iterations, such as Free Will. There are many varieties of materialism, of course: from the romantic materialism of Dennett, to the Cromwellian materialism of Churchland.

---

[159] as we explained in *Matrixial Logic*, Chapter 10
[160] an inevitable element of Straw Man reduction arises from such summaries

Dualism affirms a reality of some subjective "conscious" mind, with or without its iterations, such as Free Will.

Both operate with the culturally established *Unilinear Model* of World⇔Mind⇔Body. Since the Model is completely circular, it is possible to stand at any point on the circle and define that as real reality, the rest merely being a shadow. This is what both camps actually do.

Metaphorically, they are just arguing past each other around the circumference of a pen head upon which illusory angels cycle.

Now, we know the matrixial logic equations of reality. To selectively state those immediately relevant:

Fundamental Equations

Form in [E]	$(A) \neq (nA) = [E]$	(1)
Form in [I]	$(A) \neq (-A) = [I]$	(2)
\<Node\> in [E]	$\square[E]^n \neq \square[E]^n \sum<E>$	(3)
\<Node\> in [I]	$\Delta[I]^n \neq \Delta[I]^n \sum<I>$	(4)

Modes of Interaction

|W|orld \<Node\>	$\|W\|\sum<I> => \|EF\|$	(5)
|P| \<Node\>	$\|P\|\sum<I> => \|EF\|$	(6)
/S/ \<Node\>	$/S/\sum<I> => \|EF\|$	(7)

Exclusion Function: Quantised

Capacity Gapping	$(\geq\varsigma) \neq (\leq\ni) \int[x]$	(8)
Plurality	$\Delta\int[x]^n => (\varepsilon) \mid \Delta\int[x]^n => (\ni)$	(9)

Ohm Function: Qualitised

Aggregation	$(\varepsilon) \neq (\ni) \sum\Omega^n$	(10)
\<Affect\>	$(\varepsilon) \neq (n\varepsilon) = [€]$	(11)
Referral to /S/	$[\square €^1] \neq [\square €^n] \sum<€>$	(12)

\<Thought\>

Potential	$\Delta<\bar{T}^n> \mid \infty$	(13)
VCIP	$\sum<€> (\bar{T}) \neq (-\bar{T}) = t[I]$	(14)

We could of course add the equations for $/S/=>|EF|$, and so on. However, with the essential equation forms and functions understood, we find that all Self *Systems* operate under iterations of them.

The material sciences are constituted by theories, founded in empirical observations, which are codified in equations.

We do not suppose that any of the theories or equations are "real". They describe, in different ways, realties which are observed.

We are content to conclude that the objects of such theories, observations and equations are real. We justify that conclusion on the basis that:

- the empirical observations are verifiable or falsifiable, within (arbitrary) experimental limits
- the body of knowledge allows predictions which, which can be implemented so as to affect the material world.

We observe, and through conclusions drawn from observation, are able to act so as predictably to effect verifiable change. This is scientific materialism, or just "science".

Matrixial Logic is science in exactly the same way. The object of ML science is the interaction, and means of interaction, between each human being and everything else in the universe.

The equations of ML are derived from observation and empirical experiment. They are the codifications of by theories, founded in empirical observations. As the ML *Experiences* prove:

- the empirical observations are verifiable or falsifiable, within (arbitrary) experimental limits
- the body of knowledge allows predictions which, which can be implemented so as to affect the material world.

Reductionist materialism, which seeks to comport the entire universe into a misunderstood apparition of {substance}. In doing so, it is no less dualist than overt dualism. It simply lends qualities, attributes and processes to misdescribed and misunderstood {substance} apparition: which real Substance, extended in spacetime under an [E] Form, cannot posses.

Dualism seeks to comport the entire universe into a misunderstood apparition of {moment}. It similarly lends qualities, attributes and processes to misdescribed and misunderstood {moment} apparition: which real Moment, a potential in infinity under an [I] Form, cannot posses

ML observes that ours is a universe of Substance and Moment. Each has a different logic, but each logic operates under the same processes as Forms of Inequality.

Fundamental Equations

Form in [E]	$(A) \neq (nA) = [E]$	(1)
Form in [I]	$(A) \neq (-A) = [I]$	(2)
\<Node\> in [E]	$\square[E]^n \neq \square[E]^n \sum\text{<}E\text{>}$	(3)
\<Node\> in [I]	$\Delta[I]^n \neq \Delta[I]^n \sum\text{<}I\text{>}$	(4)

Modes of Interaction

|W|orld \<Node\>	$\|W\|\sum\text{<}I\text{>} => \|EF\|$	(5)
|P| \<Node\>	$\|P\|\sum\text{<}I\text{>} => \|EF\|$	(6)
/S/ \<Node\>	$/S/\sum\text{<}I\text{>} => \|EF\|$	(7)

Exclusion Function: Quantised

Capacity Gapping	$(\geq\varsigma) \neq (\leq\Theta) \int[x]$	(8)
Plurality	$\Delta\int[x]^n => (\epsilon) \mid \Delta\int[x]^n => (\ni)$	(9)

Ohm Function: Qualitised

Aggregation	$(\epsilon) \neq (\ni) \sum\Omega^n$	(10)
\<Affect\>	$(\epsilon) \neq (n\epsilon) = [\text{€}]$	(11)
Referral to /S/	$[\square\,\text{€}^1] \neq [\square\,\text{€}^n] \sum\text{<}\text{€}\text{>}$	(12)

\<Thought\>

Potential	$\Delta\text{<}\bar{T}^n\text{>}\|\infty$	(13)
VCIP	$\sum\text{<}\text{€}\text{>} (\bar{T}) \neq (-\bar{T}) = t[I]$	(14)

As we move from Equation (1) to Equation (14) in the Table, we do not at any point alter the perspective in reality: in the material world.

A \<thought\> is as real as a rock, or a daisy, or a sub-atomic particle. The same equations describe the being and becoming of each of these: and everything else.

Now that we understand, through matrixial analysis, codified in equations, how \<thoughts\> become Form, the /S/ubjective mind is transparent.

We do not suppose that any of the equations are "real". They describe, in different ways, realties which are observed. They are codifications of observations of empirically verifiable reality.

The philosophical, psychological and neurological disciplines remain enmeshed within a 2,500 years old cultural legacy of <self>. Which treats "the mind" as a black box.[161]

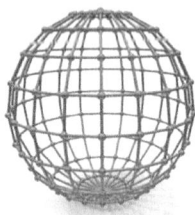

Matrixial Logic proves that there is no black box at all. Simply a Systems Architecture, which operates with processes which we can codify in a simple set of equations.

The equations work in exactly the same way, whether we are considering a rock, a daisy, or operations of the human mind.

There is no "hard problem" of consciousness. All of that thought, by brilliant minds, is as relevant to actuality as the ponderings of the Church Fathers.

We will reserve to later discussion, the puncturing of those

---

[161] Affective neuroscience simply seeks to draw inferences from supposed cause and effect afferents, which are assumed to run "through" the black box

thought bubbles: all the stuff about *what it is like to be a.*

Now that the lights have been turned on for the Subjective <self>, the old problematics have disappeared. They arose only from obscurity.

To be unfair, these theorists have deliberately engineered an intellectual investment in a black hole, which never actually existed.

To be more fair, their theorising has reflected the prejudices which the /S/ubjective <self> creates about its own identity.

Thinking about <thought> suffers much the same disadvantages as the observation of quantum materials. To observe thinking, is to change it.

If we were truly stuck in a unidimensional /S/ubjective universe of <self>, this would be an unsolvable problem, and the "hard problem" of consciousness devotees might have something of a point.

Dark Architecture   Illuminated Architecture

But that is not the Architecture of the human mind. This is:

The Systems process from | E | to /S/ is, once understood, elementary. The relationship of <thought> to "external" reality is a matter of transparent scientific analysis. It is no more scientifically mysterious and unknowable than the relationship of electrons to a circuit, or sunlight to a daisy.

Every element is "material", in the sense that it is accessible to material science. It is only a cultural dissonance which treats 'mind' as something different, because of how the /S/ubjective looks from inside itself.

But | M | entation is bigger than that. It is Theta Θ, in its external synchrony, which allows /S/ to appear as separate from Self.

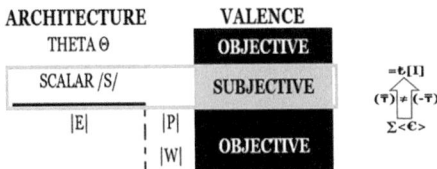

ARCHITECTURE	VALENCE	
THETA Θ	OBJECTIVE	
SCALAR /S/	SUBJECTIVE	=t.[1]
		$(\mathbf{T})|*|(-\mathbf{T})$
|E| |P|	OBJECTIVE	$\Sigma<\mathbf{C}>$
|W|		

SECTION D: REALISATION

1. *Subjectivity Under Objectivity*

> *Subjective <Thoughts> and <Feelings>*
> *are types of cognitive fictions, which are our reality*
> but:
> *the Self is a reality, which we perceive through illusions*

We repeat this aphorism, as the way-station to our next destination.

In Section A, we took off where Matrixial Logic left off, surveying the overall framework of |M|entation.

In Sections B and C, we provided a detailed scientific account, a text book of the Systems Architecture for:

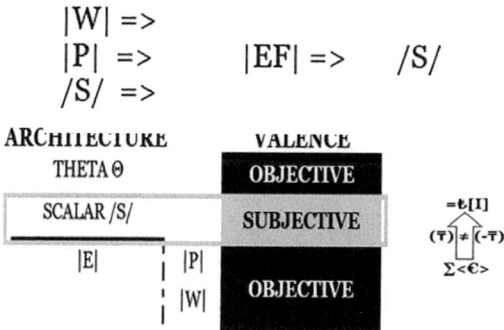

$$|W| =>$$
$$|P| => \qquad |EF| => \qquad /S/$$
$$/S/ =>$$

ARCHITECTURE	VALENCE	
THETA Θ	OBJECTIVE	
SCALAR /S/	SUBJECTIVE	=t[I] (T)≠(-T) Σ<€>
|E| |P| |W|	OBJECTIVE	

In a plain English narrative metaphor:
(1)   The Top Floor (Theta Θ) is the communications equipment. This links directly to the outside world.

It's communications have *synchronous coherence*[162] to the outside world.

(2)   Your subjective /S/ <self> is here, on the ground floor.

(3)   There is a special ceiling mirror between the Top Floor and Ground Floor: like a police interview room. Top Floor can see /S/: but /S/ can't see into the Top Floor. When /S/ looks up, or around, all /S/ sees is reflections.

(4)   The basement is |E|. There's a hard floor between /S/ and |E|. Nothing can be seen of |E| by /S/.

(5) |E| communicates with /S/ through the <Affect> vector <node> $\sum<\text{€}>$.

(6)   This collapses infinity <potential> $\Delta<\top^n>|\infty$, which gives $=\text{₺}[I]$.

(7)   /S/ communicates with |E| in <Nodes> of <thought>, which are not the same as <thought>.

(8)   There is |P| physiology, which is part of the external |W|orld. Of course, |P| is a semi-autonomous operation within the landscape of the |W|orld: but then so is a rock or a single celled organism.

The building metaphor describes a "sandwich". It is /S/ which is sandwiched between Theta and |E|.

Another paradox: our /S/ubjective <self> is locked in a permanent prison of its own being in becoming, yet the

---

[162] see the next Chapter

honeycombs of that prison, are a multiversal landscape of infinity.

Connected Separateness

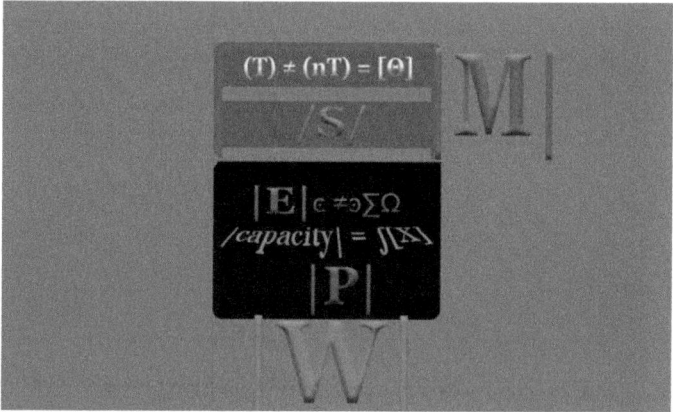

This graphic strips to the bare architectural layers the *Matrixial Self*.

In previous Segments, we have shown:

- how the different architectural layers communicate with each other
- how /S/ is in a "ground floor" continuum, receiving inputs from |E|

Here is the connected separateness of Θ and /S/:

$$\frac{\text{THETA } \Theta}{\text{SCALAR /S/}}$$

Self uses Θ as a resource:

- to transmit to the world | W |
- to provide languaging for otherwise mute / S / notions

What we now need to look at is

- the use of Θ Constructs to generate the language for / S / {idents}
- how we work with a system of information transmissions, and / S / equivalences.

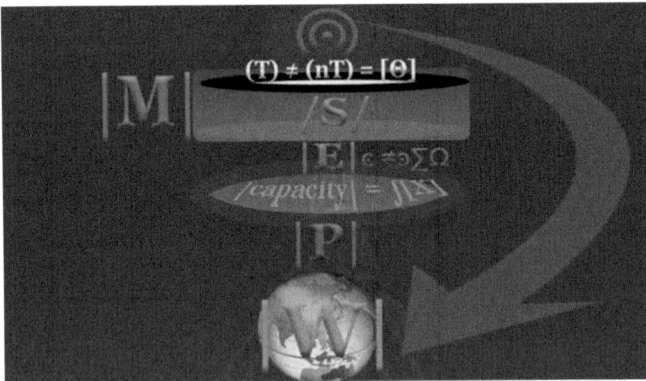

Θ is the Equaliser. Θ effects equalisation by the use of <Constructs>. These <Constructs> are then used to effect communication, and synchronisation.

If you want to communicate a particular suite of ideas to another Self, you might paint a picture, or write a set of logic equations.

These are just different <Memetic> methods which Θ

uses to effect its communication function.[163]

We don't /S/ubjectively experience Θ <Constructs>. The only reality which we consciously[164] experience: in relationship to which we have self-awareness, are {idents}.

- /S/ operates an equivalence function: part logic, part intuition. /S/ makes mistakes all the time, makes inspirational linkages of equivalence and occasionally sparks genius. That is all rational.
- The exercise in rationality is assisted by drawing on the Θ resource. But in so drawing, Θ loses its equalisation quality and becomes just another ident in /S/.
- /S/ also handles ʃ[x] outputs. These are "rational", insofar as they concern interaction with the needs of |P| and imperatives of the real |W|orld.
- /S/ can try and does try to cohere ʃ[x] outputs to the /S/ equivalence landscape. In so doing. those ʃ[x] outputs lose their <Node> source connection to |P and |W|: they become more /S/ {idents}.

By analogy: rain is a reality, but we don't get rain without all the other conditions which constitute "weather", and the nature of that "weather" conditions what sort of rain we get.

---

[163] *Matrixial Logic*, Chapter 5
[164] which includes the non-existent category "sub-conscious"

Self Without Theta

Classical Accounts in philosophy, psychology and neuroscience might perhaps find wiggle room to manage with this landscape:

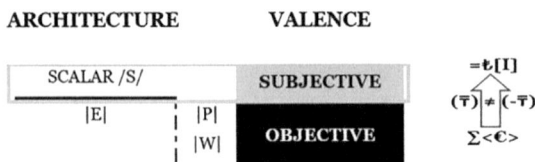

ARCHITECTURE   **VALENCE**

SCALAR /S/	**SUBJECTIVE**
|E| |P| |W|	**OBJECTIVE**

$$=\text{t}[I]$$
$$(\top) \neq (-\top)$$
$$\sum<\text{€}>$$

Indeed, this looks sufficiently dualistic to allow at least the *Interoception Model* to maintain an appearance of integrity.

Were a matrixial sceptic to look closely at this unfinished Architecture, a problem should arise. If the /S/ubjective is the only dimension of |M|entation, then how is this *System* process possible at all?

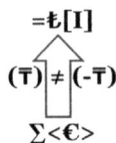

$$=\text{t}[I]$$
$$(\top) \neq (-\top)$$
$$\sum<\text{€}>$$

If one is prepared to accept the logical integrity of Forms of Inequality, then one must accept the impossibility of:

$$\sum<\text{€}> (\top) \neq (-\top) = \text{t}[I]$$

being the resolving equation, in:

Fundamental Equations

Form in [E]	$(A) \neq (nA) = [E]$	(1)
Form in [I]	$(A) \neq (-A) = [I]$	(2)
<Node> in [E]	$\Box[E]^n \neq \Box[E]^n \sum<E>$	(3)
<Node> in [I]	$\Delta[I]^n \neq \Delta[I]^n \sum<I>$	(4)

Modes of Interaction

|W|orld <Node>	$\|W\|\sum<I> => \|EF\|$	(5)
|P| <Node>	$\|P\|\sum<I> => \|EF\|$	(6)
/S/ <Node>	$/S/\sum<I> => \|EF\|$	(7)

Exclusion Function: Quantised

Capacity Gapping	$(\geq\varsigma) \neq (\leq \partial) \int[x]$	(8)
Plurality	$\Delta\int[x]^n => (\epsilon) \mid \Delta\int[x]^n => (\ni)$	(9)

Ohm Function: Qualitised

Aggregation	$(\epsilon) \neq (\ni) \sum\Omega^n$	(10)
<Affect>	$(\epsilon) \neq (n\epsilon) = [€]$	(11)
Referral to /S/	$[\Box \: €^1] \neq [\Box \: €^n] \sum<€>$	(12)

<Thought>

Potential	$\Delta<\overline{\top}^n> \mid \infty$	(13)
VCIP	$\sum<€> (\overline{\top}) \neq (-\overline{\top}) = \text{\textit{t}}[I]$	(14)

Whilst it is logically acceptable that the <Affect> vector of <node> $\sum<€>$ collapses infinity <potential> $\Delta<\overline{\top}^n> \mid \infty$, that actually leaves unanswered: what is the dimension in which $=\text{\textit{t}}[I]$ subsists?

While any:

Form in [I] $(A) \neq (-A) = [I]$

is of course hylomorphic as the Form of its Contents, it is axiomatic that an [I]nfinity can only subsist under a domain of :

Form in [E] $(A) \neq (nA) = [E]$

Now, we cannot simply resolve $=\text{\textit{t}}[I]$ in $\sum<€>$, for that is circular.

In this Section, therefore, we are going to answer the question: but how is this *Systems Architecture* possible?

So we will consider:
- how /S/ communicates within the /S/ continuum
- the relationship between Θ and /S/.

2. /S/ubjective Muteness

Our cultural view is that it's our subjective <self> which transmits to the |W|orld. It doesn't. Our subjective <self> is completely mute. Let's see.

Experience: Nice
Look around your room.
Choose an object.
Focus on the object.

Now, while looking at the object,
- say in your head *That is nice*

Stop

Discussion:
(1)   In order to say even that simple phrase, you had to de-focus from the object.
(2)   We are so used to looking and thinking, that you probably didn't notice the effect: so please re-run the *Experience* and notice what happens.

It's anecdotally interesting that we think it's good for a person to have "eye contact". Yet if a person is maintaining a visual focus, it means that they are not thinking anything.

It's one of the rubrics of NLP,[165] that eye movement correlates with "self-talk" and other brain "access processes".

There's a bit more to it than that:

Experience: Nicer
Look around your room.
Choose an object.
Focus on the object.

Now, while looking at the object,
• 	say Out Loud *That is nice*

Stop

Discussion:
(1) 	You can speak, and maintain focus on the object.
(2) 	Speaking can actually feel directed at the object, making the connection more vibrant.

The *Nice* and *Nicer Experiences* provide data. What does it mean? To show that, we need to take a step further:

---

[165] Neuro Linguistic Programming

Experience: Paste

Look around your room.

Choose an object.

Focus on the object.

Step 1:

Now, while looking at the object:

- hear or hum some tune in your head

Stop

Discussion:

(1)   You can speak, and maintain focus on the object.

(2)   The audio sensation doesn't generate more "connectedness".

(3)   You do have to concentrate a little to maintain visual focus.

Step 2:

Now, while looking at the object,

- tap your fingers (to a rhythm or randomly)
- do some deep breaths

Stop

Discussion:

(1)   You can tap and breathe, and maintain focus on the object.

(2)   The actions don't generate more "connectedness".

(3)   The actions help a little to maintain visual focus.

Step 2 in Paste uses the NLP technique of "anchoring".[166] We mention this because NLP works: until it doesn't. But it's a useful paradigm for explaining what's going on in these Experiences.

Your /S/ is mute. It is an equivalence function, a pattern recognition system. And much more besides. But you don't actually have <thoughts> in grammatical language.[167]

You can test this by asking how much language appears in your dreams. The answer from most people is "sometimes, a bit, but not much." We dream in thoughts of images: that is, in <thoughts>.

We see the reality of our <thoughts> most clearly when we dream. That's a disturbing and counter-intuitive idea. We are here treading on later landscape in *Secret Self*, but let's just put it out there:

The only difference between sleeping and waking thoughts, is disconnection from the continuum of reality

The physiological – neurological condition of sleep is that our brain "locks off" our subjective mental process from external, and so far as clinically possible, internal

---

[166] a modification of it. We will discuss NLP elsewhere
[167] contrasted with simple naming words

sensation. That is a basic datum of the sleep science.

The |W| orld is still going on around you, but there is a halt to communication of output from your Exclusion Function.

During sleep, what correlates to that quieting of your Exclusion Function, is the limitation of your Theta Θ axis field function. The Equalizer takes a break from equalizing.

What's left is:

THETA Θ		
SCALAR /S/		
	|E|	|P|
		|W|

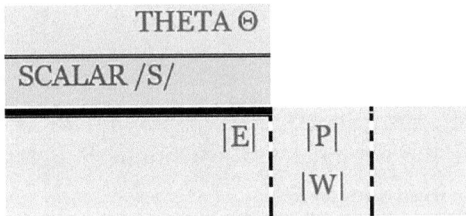

This is what you experience when there is just your subjective scalar /S/ <self>.

We mimicked that condition in the *Nice and Nicer Experiences*:

Nice

(1) Theta Θ is what grants language to your <self> notions.

(2) When you want to engage Theta Θ to provide language for self-talk, you are directing Θ inwards.

(3) /S/ is simultaneously putting s stop notice on visual signals from |E|. The object <Node> is still of course

interacting with the Exclusion Function, and ∫{x} output is being referred. But the "letterbox" is closed.

(4)   That's why your visual focus averts, just to say *That is Nice*.

Nicer

(5)   Now, you are projecting into the world. You are in "transmission" mode.

(6)   So you keep your "letterbox" open for ∫{x} output referral.

(7)   Indeed, you are making that a priority, as you want to address your remark to the correct point in spacetime.

(8)   That spacetime co-ordination effects *synchronous congruence* of your Θ axis field function.[168]

Paste

(9)   Here, we are interrupting your default system for use of the Θ axis field function for languaging "inner dialogue" /S/ <thought> / <feeling>: the one we sent you to in *Nice*.

(10)   We are keeping your ∫{x} output => /S/ "letterbox" open, by getting you to maintain active "down signal" from /S/, via |E|, to your |P|.

Let's do more in this suite of Experiences, to demonstrate further:

---

[168] see Chapter 3

Experience: Dit

Look around your room.

Choose an object.

Focus on the object, in its landscape.

Now close your eyes, and see the object, and its landscape in your head

Step 1:

Focus on the object, and its landscape in your head

Now:

• hear or hum some tune in your head

Stop

Discussion:

(1)   The audio is really distracting.

Step 2:

Focus on the object, and its landscape in your head

Now:

• tap your fingers (to a rhythm or randomly)
• do some deep breaths

Stop

Discussion:

(1)   Both of these are really distracting.

Experience: Scrip
Keep the object and landscape from *Dit*.

Again, close your eyes, and see the object, and its landscape in your head

Step 1:
Focus on the object, and its landscape in your head

Now:
- say in your head *This is nice*.
- repeat the phrase a few times.

Stop

Discussion:
(1)   This is very easy to do.

It is incredibly natural. But there's something going on here that you don't usually notice. Re-run the history of your head. Ask yourself to notice "where" the words are, in relation to the image:
a)   "in" the image
b)   "next" to the image, kind of like a side-title
c)   in some other "room", with a window through to the image.

Let's find out:

Step 2:
Just as for Step 1.

Now:
- see the words and the image
- move the words around the image in a circle

Stop

Discussion:
(1)   You saw that the words appear next to the image.
(2)   It was easy to "move" the words

Step 3:
Just as for Step 1.

Now: see the words and the image

Now:
- move the words in some other "room", with a window through to the image

Stop

Discussion:
(1)   That is really hard.
(2)   You can have the words adjacent to the image, or have the words in their own "room"; but not both.

Reading the last few pages, and doing these *Experiences*, you may well have intuited a growing sense of discomfort. That's because your cultural <self> understanding was undergoing a challenge which your linguistic machinery was not keeping up with, so as to articulate it.

We said, before launching you into the *Experiences*:

> Your /S/ is mute. It is an equivalence function, a pattern recognition system. And much more besides. But you don't actually have <thoughts> in language.

Now, if we had stated that:

> your *feelings* are mute. They are an equivalence function, a pattern recognition system. And much more besides. But you don't actually have <feelings> in language:

you would have thought and said: sure, so what? Of course feelings are dumb, that's why we need thoughts to interpret them.

The problem is, we have opened some windows for you onto the realisation that your <thoughts> are dumb. They are unlanguaged.

So:

- your <feelings> are dumb: not new information
- your <thoughts> are dumb: new information

what then is the difference between your <thoughts> and your <feelings> ?

The answer is: nothing except how we choose, /S/ ubjectively, to categorise them.

- If by "feelings" we mean the sensations in |E|, which we discussed in Sections B and C, then we are fooling ourselves, with an imaginary projection: there's nothing going on in |E| which /S/ can seperately perceive, as a "witness".

- If we mean the unlanguaged receipt of <Affect> <node> $\Delta<\top^n>|\infty$, then yes we can "feel" that. But is not any specific "feeling".

- Certainly, it has a valance in /S/, which we might call pleasant or unpleasant. But in trying to call that valence anything, we are seeking to use a sea anchor from a boat on the shore.

- That valance is only crystallised as "a feeling" when the <thought> potential $\Delta<\top^n>|\infty$ (our infinite series of possible anchors) is specified in $\sum<\epsilon> (\top) \neq (-\top) = \text{\textsterling}[I]$: which is where our "boat" enters the waters.

But are we not rational, feeling beings? Yes, we are. Yet that is only how we appear to ourselves, as the emergent facets of Self *Architecture*. That appearance is a reality. But it is an architecturally conditional and conditioned reality.

In these *Experiences*:

- You witnessed the difference between notions and language

- You witnessed how you have notions without language; and, that
- once you imprint a notion with language, that connection becomes "sticky".

We have already run through this, but just to reiterate:
- your senses are not "feelings"
- they produce <signals> under | capacity |
- they interact with <potentials> to create quantised $\int[x]$ outputs
- and those are not "feelings", either.
- $\int[x]$ outputs become qualitised as <emotes> under the $\Sigma\Omega$ function: they are not "feelings" either
- only in Σ<€> $(\top) \neq (-\top) = \text{ƚ}[I]$, do <feelings> arise.

So then we ask: what and where are these "feelings", which you entirely accept are dumb?

The Matrixial Self answers:
> Your <thoughts> and <feelings> are just different methods that /S/ uses to effect its equivalence function.

It's not that <thoughts> and <feelings> are the "same" thing. Obviously they are not. They are tools which the same subjective /S/ equivalence function uses to generate {idents}.

3. *{identation} Theory*

We have already met {idents} in Chapters 4-5 of *Matrixial Logic*, and right at the start of this Chapter. The {idents} are what emerge in the /S/ axis field:

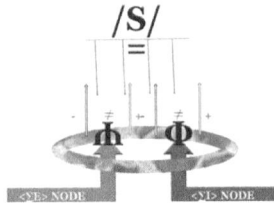

We say that <thoughts> and <feelings> are {idents}. This is not an equation, it is a classification.

It is manifest, from personal experience, and from psychology and neuroscience that:

- <thoughts> associate with <feelings>
- <feelings>associate with <thoughts>

There are habits of association, which we can observe in ourselves, and from the reports of others. But there are no rules.

The /S/ axis field can be described as a self-organising anarchy of equivalences.

Experience: It
Setup:
We used a random word generator (for nouns)
We then found an image on the internet to match the word:

Look at the image

You can put a copy of the image in your head, if you wish

Just keep looking, and

Now:

- think whatever you think and feel whatever you feel.

Stop

Discussion:

(1)   This is very easy, and natural, to do.

(2)   We do it all the time

The point of the *It Experience*, was to illustrate the diffuseness and randomness of {ident} associations, from a single starting point.

<thoughts> and <feelings> are just different types of {ident}. A bit like a knife and fork, they are tools we use. A better analogy might be: easting by using a different type of chopstick in each hand. And by constantly changing the characteristics of chopsticks, even while we are using them:

Your <thoughts> and <feelings> are just different methods
that /S/ uses to effect its equivalence function.

Helpfully, we are not the first to say this about <T> and <F>. The Allostasis and Interoceptive Models[169] now take it as a datum that <thoughts> and <feelings> are outputs of the same system, and just represent modes of cognition which we Subjectively see differently

Although that seeing is inconsistent: both within the same person from moment to moment, and as between individuals.

We can expand the taxonomy of {idents} beyond <thoughts> and <feelings>. We can categorise and sub-denominate all academic year long.

We can assign the category <thought> to one sort of {ident} and <feeling> to another. And swap them around. And create a set of rules for doing all this.

So far as {ident} associations demonstrate habits, or patterns, then we can use the regularity to effect manipulations: to an extent. Because one person's meat is another person's poison.

And even within one person: you love minty chocolate,

---

[169] *How Emotions Are Made: The Secret Life of the Brain.* Lisa Feldman Barrett. (2018); and see Section B(1)/5

so I get you an Easter egg full, but on this occasion you wanted orangy chocolate instead. I predicted your choccy {ident} association perfectly, but still got it wrong, because it changed.

This is the /S/ubjective world of arbitrary {ident} associations which we all individually live in. This is our lived experience, moment to moment. It is our undeniable reality.

That we associate {idents] is not new information in psychology or folk-wisdom. Carl Jung was lecturing on "The Association Method" in 1910.[170]

Association of {idents} is how advertising works. As Edward Bernays, the father of public relations, wrote:[171]

> The conscious and intelligent manipulation of the organized habits and opinions of the masses is an important element in democratic society. Those who manipulate this unseen mechanism of society constitute an invisible government which is the true ruling power of our country. We are governed, our minds are molded, our tastes formed, and our ideas suggested, largely by men we have never heard of.... It is they who pull the wires that control the public mind.

Other manipulations strategies work also through association of {idents}: much of magic; fake spiritualism; NLP therapies; combinative strategies used by Derren Brown.

---

[170] http://psychclassics.yorku.ca/Jung/Association/lecture1.htm
[171] *Propoganda* (1928)

That's also why such strategies work very effectively: until they don't. One is dropping a pebble in a multiverse of rivers. By trial and error, and induction, we can generate a Bell curve of probabilities: of summing over differences to elucidate patterns of /S/ coherence to the pebble impact: the <Node> point.

But the best we can achieve is temporary influence. We can't assume control, because it's impossible to know all of the factors in the multiversal continuum which is /S/.

Unmeasured Matching

We've done a couple of *Experiences*, to generate the insight. Can the reader please try some free-form *Experiences*.

Experience: Roll

Try this:

(i) with eyes closed (ii) with eyes open

Step 1:

Just allow yourself some moments of "feeling". Whatever it is.

Now:

• choose a word or words which match the "feeling"

Stop

Discussion:

(1)   This is easy. We do it constantly.

Step 2:
Now, slow this down in your head.

Really slowly:
allow yourself some moments of "feeling".

Now, Slowly:

• choose a word or words which match the "feeling"

Stop

<u>Discussion</u>:

(1)   Again, this is easy. We do it constantly.

What you notice, in slow motion is this: various words roll round in your head, like revolving scenery.

Like ducks in a duck shoot at a fairground:

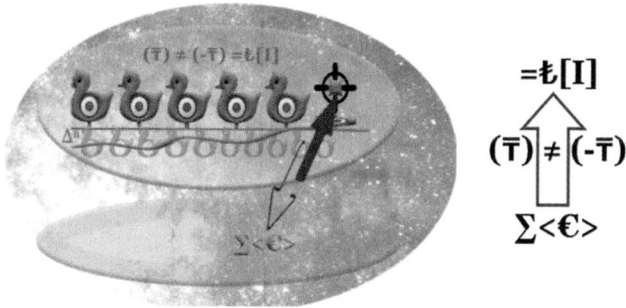

You then target one of those words with the feeling. You choose the closest word you can get to the feeling.

That realm of <Affects> has endless, overlapping landscapes. They are repopulated moment by moment. You target the rolling scenery of "duck target" words with the the best situated mountain top: the best match.

This still leaves more behind than we can bring into words.

We know this. Our artistic forms are modelled around our inability to match our rolling scenery of words, with our endlessly changing landscape of <Affects>.

And, once we have target a word "duck", it's too late to change. We can repeat the exercise, and we do: constantly. But that same interaction will never ever occur again.

Our <thought> =₺[I] creation is a procession of unique events.

Just About
The targeting of <thought potential> by <Affects> is an affair of approximation.

There are no right or wrong target solutions. Yet, it's very rare that we can match, to our own standards, <thought potential> to <Affect>.

Even when we do the best we can, there's also something of the mountain landscape left behind.

This is a self-taught skill, which we improve as we mature from the neonate stage. We can continue to improve it throughout life.

We can take in lessons from others, about how better to exercise that skill. But even the very best practiced in the skill, must always leave something of the mountain behind.

This is another paradox of the /S/ubjective <self>:
*we can never entirely think what we can feel
nor, therefore, can we say it*

Truth and Reality
The classical understanding of concepts like "truth" and "lies" function in a *Unilinear Model* of /S/ubjectivity.

The unscientific prejudice which underlies the Unilinear Model, is that there is a unimorphic relationship between /S/ubjectivity and the |W|orld, such that:
- the is objective truth in the |W|orld
- our /S/ubjectivity can, as a matter of choice, reflect that truth, or not.

This unilinear logic has termination points like Russell declaring in 1954 that the only real word is "The".[172]

This is not the place for a full discussion of truth concepts

---

[172] see *Matrixial Logic*, Chapter 3

in relation to the Self. There are useful applications of the truth and lies concepts, but these must embody the *Systems Architecture* of Self. Otherwise, they become illogical metaphysics of confusion.

/S/ Logic and {idents}

In the world | W | there is Substance under extension in [E] and Moments in becoming in [I]. These are the logical forms of that which exists independently of any of us.

No such logical form applies to /S/ {idents}, but they are the only reality we each have. We can certainly think /S/ subjectively in [E] or [I] forms. Clearly, we do arrange our {idents} under such Forms.

/S/ Logic is arbitrary: *withing the limits of a continuum of infinity*.

We can use any logic we choose in the arrangement of /S/{idents}: and we do. We can do entirely without logic, or just invent our own logic: and we do.

/S/ is an equivalence function. It is not a logical equaliser. We arrange our {idents] however we wish. It is the ultimate domain of freedom, and hence Free Will.[173]

There is a confusion which we need to avoid. You are reading

---

[173] more on this elsewhere

a book. With words. But these are words operating under rules of grammar. More than that, they are Memetic.[174]

Grammar and Memetics are objective tools, or methods, of inter-Self communication. They are not how the internal, /S/ubjective Self works.

We do, of course, use Θ <Constructs> (which we will discuss in detail in a moment) in our /S/ubjective self-talk. But those <Constructs> lose coherence within the /S/subjective domain. They become randomised, arbitrary: subjective.

Our {idents} have no inherent logic. They are not Substance in <spacetime>. They are not even Moments in infinity. They are assemblages under equivalence of unique <thought> $=Ł[I]$ creation, which do occur in <spacetime>.

They are the un-material reality of our becoming, but our being resides elsewhere.

Instinctively, we want to say that <feelings> {idents}: <F>{i}, are like Moments in becoming, and <thoughts> {idents}: <T>{i}, are like Substance.

We can see the resemblance. But the distinction is arbitrary.

---

[174] see *Matrixial Logic*, Chapter 5

An $<F>\{i\}$ without a $<T>\{i\}$ is shapeless. Whereas an $<T>\{i\}$ seems like it can subsist without an $<F>\{i\}$: but must have an association with another $<T>\{i^n\}$

In nature: a rock was deposited by a glacier movement, a wave of ice: a Moment in becoming. The rock has stood there, in that spot, for a hundred millenia. The rock is Substance: it does not need the Moment. And vice versa.

In other words, | W | is a composite universe of contingencies: all being is becoming, and becoming produces being.

But there is contingency in the /S/ continuum only under the conditions of the reality checks.

In plain words:
   we don't subjectively think like the logic of the world is.

Yet, it is a condition of our sanity that we engage in pretence of doing exactly that.

We will return to this at the latter Segments of this Section.

The Limits of /S/ Logic
As we stated in *Compass*:

A Chi m̄ <Node> occurs when an Event
<∑E>, which is a combination of [E]
Forms of Substance contents, interacts
with a course Δ^n of Infinity ∞.

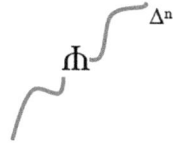

A Phi Φ <Node> occurs when one <set
of Moments Δ^n in Infinity ∞> meets
another.

This creates an Interference <Node>,
rather than a Point <Node>.

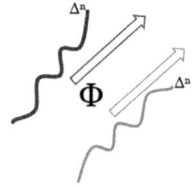

It would be neat to be able to assert that Chi m̄ points give
rise to <thoughts>, and Phi Φ points give rise to <feelings>.
But that would be to instigate a causal explanation of
what is actually a phenomenon of coherence.

What we saw in *Compass*, and in Section A *Mentation*, in
this Chapter, were the operative limitations on our /S/
ubjective <thought>:

How we can think governs what we can think.

Identity

Our {idents} are mute: they are unlanguaged.[175] They are
also unmeasured. We construct {idents} as equivalences
and patterns of qualities. That's why word association
works. It's really nothing to do with the words at all. They

---

[175] that is to say, lacking rules of grammar

are just labels for {ident} associations.

We might say that the words tell us which "door" an {ident} assemblage lies behind, but not what is actually in the room.

It's interesting that, as soon as we begin to analyse our thinking about {ident} associations, we generate ideas which resonate with the Copenhagen interpretation of quantum physics.

This is not accidental. By stripping back the appearances of the natural world to the analogous {ident} continuum of fundamental forces, particles and fields, we find ourselves staring into a mirror. The Bohr "mysticism" has enduring appeal precisely because it involves seeing the essence of the material world just as we seem to see ourselves.

We think that $<I>$ is the continuum of {idents}: $|C|\{i^n\}$. Put another way, that $|C|\{i^n\}$ is our personality: what makes each of us a $<self>$.

This immediately raises the Heraclitan problem of homologous substance,[176] also wrestled with by Aristotle, and plaguing thought ever since: if $<I>$ is the continuum of {idents} $|C|\{i^n\}$, then how can there be a $<self>$ at all?

---

[176] see Chapter 3 of *Matrixial Logic*

We answer that by stating:
- $<I>$ is not the continuum of {idents} $|C|\{i^n\}$ at all.
- $<I>$ is something completely different.
- The continuum of {idents} $|C|\{i^n\}$ is Me $<self>$.

There is a continuity, a permanence, of $<I>$ through time and space. That's because $<I>$ is the personification of Θ.

There is no continuity or permanence of Me $<self>$. The continuum of {idents} $|C|\{i^n\}$, has habits, crystallised from repeated patterns. In each moment, that continuum is different. That's what makes the subjective human mind alive, and capable of novelty.

We will examine $<Me>$ and $<I>$ in more detail in Part 2.

{identation} Analytics
We refer to the association of {idents} as *{identation}*.

The core rubric in {identation} theory is:
Your $<thoughts>$ and $<feelings>$ are just different methods that /S/ uses to effect its equivalence function

This rubric has profound consequences: for neuroscience, philosophy, and psychology. It allows us to unravel {ident} associations in novel and useful ways.

{identation} doesn't have work through logic. But it does operate under *Systems Architecture*. Our understanding of *Systems Architecture* allowed the invention of *Matrixial Healing* strategies, using *Psychotectics* and *Biomorphics*.[177]

Matrixial Healing strategies work through the Self *Systems Architecture*.

(1)   We accept the reality for any Self of {identation}.

(2)   We say that you can't use {identation} to alter itself.

(3)   That you in fact try to do this all the time, and this ends up with Shadow <constructs>.[178]

Positively, we accept an understanding that the *Systems Architecture* with which we are born, is perfect, by nature. That's a good thing: because there's nothing we can do to change it.

Psychotectics and *Biomorphics* are |**Congruence**| strategies:

•   we minimise the /S/ function by effecting <coherence>

•   we allow interaction between |W|=>|P|=>|E| by using Θ, rather than using /S/

•   in Biomorphics, we effectively silence /S/ temporarily, so as to allow an organic rebalance.

Essentially, we understand and accept that there is an automatic dissonance between the reality of *Systems Architecture* and the reality of {identation}. The more one tries, though {identation} the more dimensioned the dissonance becomes.

---

[177] there will be much more about these in later Parts

[178] more on this later

Now, we have just summarised an entire volume of explanation in three bullet points. These are markers for later. But they are also written to indicate that "it doesn't have to be like this".

Towards Reality

We cannot escape the *Architecture* of the Self:

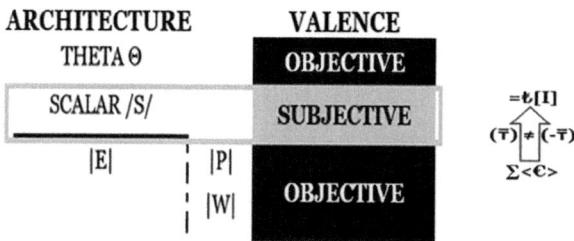

Our /S/ubjective <self> has existence only within the confines of that ground floor" continuum. We can construct {idents} which allow us to project unto imagined infinity. There is nothing real about these {idents}. But they are the only reality for each of us. That is the paradox of reality for the /S/ubjective <self>.

Philosophy and science has, hitherto, stopped at that point. Lacking Psychotectural Constructs, everything has been ladled into the realm of /S/. Then entirely arbitrary divisions are sought to be imposed on that continuum: categorical constructs to allow the running of one theory or another.

By their nature, all such theories are circular. Circularity is then sought to be countermanded by doctrines of cause and effect. Rather than curing the circularity problem, these make it worse.

It will reasonably be objected that this analysis leaves the continuum of {idents} as an inexplicable, incoherent, and ultimately irrational chaos.

Yet we know there exists both randomness and order in the human psyche. Whilst it may be acceptable to assign randomness to the /S/ continuum, from where, it may be asked, can the order come?

What gives potential to order, is that all {idents} are extrusions from the same /S/calar axis field. They have the "mind print"[179] of the lived experience of that Self.

What crystallises that order, is staring us in the face, from the repeated *Architecture* graphic, and the *Experiences* we have undertaken.

That order is provided by:
(1) $|W| => |P| => |E|$: which is a contingent order
(2)   by synchronisation of Θ <Constructs> with $|W|$.

These are the reality checks on /S/ubjectivity.

_____

[179] by analogy with a fingerprint

4. Reality Checks

So, we're blobby blobs of arbitrary |W| & |P| =>
contingency, in an endlessly cycling continuum of the
/S/ubjective. Tell us something we don't know.

One of the fascinating things about Psychotectics, is that
the pursuit of equations derived from *Architecture* always
brings us back to the "self" which we already knew.
We just see it differently, and with new capacities for
coherence and control.

Our /S/ {idents} can travel freely in projection. But that
continuum:

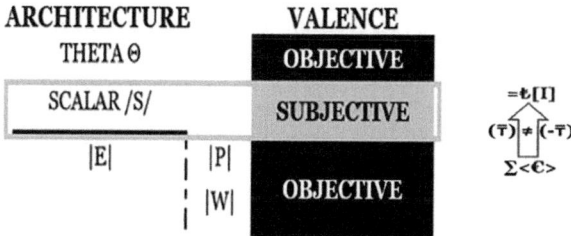

ARCHITECTURE	VALENCE
THETA Θ	**OBJECTIVE**
SCALAR /S/	**SUBJECTIVE**
|E| |P| |W|	**OBJECTIVE**

$$=t[I]$$
$$(\bar{T}) * (-\bar{T})$$
$$\Sigma <\mathfrak{C}>$$

is sandwiched between a quasi-computational Θ and
material reality |P| and |W|.

We actually have multiple reality checks upon /S/ and its
associative {idents}:

- |E| interactions through <Nodes> with |P|} External
- |E| interactions through <Nodes> with |P|} Internal

Those |P|} External interactions happen, of course

through interactions between |P| and |W|: between our physiological senses and the world.

These interactions are occurring in a timescape in which a millisecond is an infinity. It may or may not be that the Planck unit of time is the smallest quantisable unit. That's interesting, but not directly relevant to the fact that out {ident} formations are glacial in motion, compared to the organic processes of our body.

Picture a mountain stream source. A tiny rivulet dripping, dripping from a fissure in the stone. The droplets forming into a tiny slivered mountain stream. Flowing with gravity into a river course, then widening until it reaches the sea, channelling out into a world ocean.

Now, run that movie backwards. That's how {idents} are created. Or rather, the associations of {idents}.

Both of these are rivers that we can never tread in twice. But we don't need to. We can recycle {idents} perpetually. They are different each time, but unless we choose to notice the difference, they aren't.

Different how? Different in time and space, certainly. But also different to the material realities of our |P and |W|, and their interactions.

These interactions are our |E|=> /S/ reality checks.

That's how sensory deprivation is so uncomfortable. It can drive us clinically insane. It's why we've categorised the use of that technique as "torture" in international law.

Sensory deprivation removes these reality checks. Sure, our |P| is still functioning. Having <Node> interactions with |E|, and so on in that process. But with an utterly limited, unchanging |W|, our /S/ continuum becomes un-naturally unbounded. We are bouncing a ball off prison walls which aren't there any more.

In other words, we can't actually *reference* our {ident} associations to anything external in |W|. We absolutely rely upon the reality checks, to mediate the /S/ continuum.

We don't like to be told what to think. But we need to know that there are conditions to our thinking, which exist independently of us: to which we can refer our {ident} associations. When such conditions are not available in reality, our /S/ invents them.

We can reverse engineer these observations. Reality tells us not to {ident} about sticking our hands in a fire, or trying to walk through walls. Or if you like, neurobiological "just so" stories about staying away from sabre-toothed tigers.[180]

---

[180] what's objectionable about this Neo-Darwinian nonsense is not the "... and so..." reasoning; it's the Psychotectural blindess which results in re-locating perfectly ordinary psychological phenomena of the every day into some ante-diluvian fairyland

Reality compels us to create cohering "survival" {idents}. Adding the neurobiological idea of "survival" only adds a useless layer of complication.

Let your coffee cool down first, don't step into the road without looking, and always brush after eating. The trivia of every day metropolitan life provide quite sufficient menus of reality checks for each of us to create cohering {idents}.

Unless you happen to be on active duty in Afghanistan (or any urban setting in the USA, these days), or other like circumstances, "survival" is the least of our worries. The neurobiological agenda of trying to ascribe human self function to "survival" drives, is both fantastical and useless.

Our reality checks derive from the humdrum circumstances into which we are born. They are our parents' reality check circumstances, and as we mature, those of our wider, but still small society.

That's why people from the same street or school or job or club are like the other people. They have common reality checks and so they create {ident} associations which are similar.

But just similar: full stop. It stops there. There is no commonality below that superficiality. That superficiality is itself an emergent from the /S/ continuum, which is not only individual: it has no consistency or coherence within that individual <Me>.

You can go further in exploring the reality check | W | background. You can go all the way down to genetics, and then more helpfully to epigenetics. You can find all manner of commonalities between individuals. And all of that is real in | W |.

But there is no direct "string" pulling between any of | W | and anything in /S/. There can't be. Any Substance or Moment in | W | must pass through the Architecture and Systems to reach /S/:

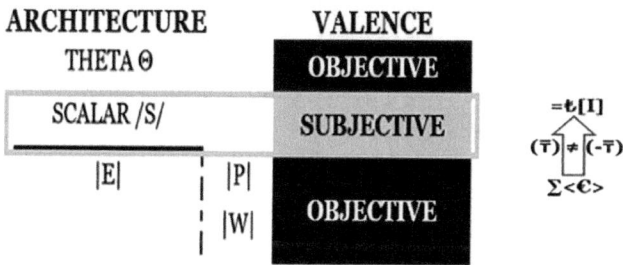

ARCHITECTURE	VALENCE	
THETA Θ	**OBJECTIVE**	
SCALAR /S/	**SUBJECTIVE**	
|E| |P|		
|W|	**OBJECTIVE**	

$$=t[I]$$
$$(\mathsf{T}) \neq (\text{-}\mathsf{T})$$
$$\Sigma <\mathbf{\epsilon}>$$

That passage necessitates a <Node>, meeting | capacity |, becoming translated in to <signal>, interacting with <potential>, being summed in the Exclusion Function. Only then does the ∫[x] quantised output become available via $\Sigma\Omega$ equaliisation, to /S/. At which point, /S/ performs its equivalence function.

Now be honest, every time we say this, part of you goes "it can't really be all that complicated can it? How on earth do we get by from moment to moment?"

To which we reply: make a 50 millisecond movie of all that's going in in your physiology. That's a whole medical library.

By comparison, our $|W|=>|P|<=>|E|<=>/S/$ is a simple process. Neuroscience has proven that stimulus-effect time (in what we would call $/S/$) is of the order of <500 milliseconds to >50 milliseconds, depending on the complexity of the stimulus.[181]

Our inherently arbitrary $/S/$ continuum is being reality-checked in a continuum of overlapping dimensions of external reality. Except when we are asleep. There, we use the same {ident} chopsticks. It's just that we are eating in the dream café.

---

[181] Dainton, Barry, "Temporal Consciousness", *The Stanford Encyclopedia of Philosophy* (Winter 2018 Edition), Edward N. Zalta (ed.), URL = <https://plato.stanford.edu/archives/win2018/entries/consciousness-temporal/>..

5.   *Equalizing Reality*

Back in Chapter 5 of Matrixial Logic, we introduced:

{Θ} **Theta Axis Field**

$$(\top) \neq (n\top) = \Theta$$

This is the realm of the Objective. Or, as we more functionally and glamorously say, the Theta Axis is:

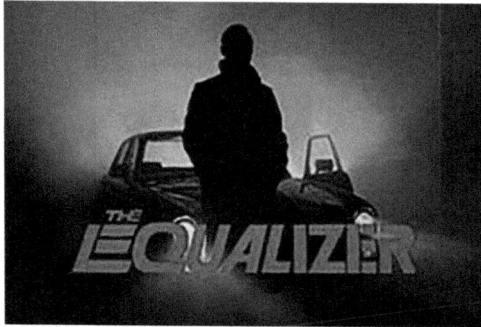

Universal Television (1985-1989)

The Θ Theta Axis takes Subjective states, which are Scalar /S/ modified from the original disparate subjective sea inputs, and *equalises* them.

Nowthatwehaveexplainedthe | W | => | P | <=> | E | <=> | M | coherence process, we can finally focus on Theta Θ.

Certainly, we have been referring to Θ throughout. Now, we focus on this relationship:

THETA Θ
SCALAR /S/

/S/ is the subjective realm of equivalence. Of {ident} associations. Where the continuum of {idents} | C | {i^n} is Me <self>.

How we can think governs what we can think.

We start by noting that Θ is like a computer, in that it processes information, such as to equalise it. But is unlike a computer, in that it can process non-existent data: that is, data about things which do not exist.

Θ functions primarily as a transmitter. The equalised components of its axis field are communicated: internally to /S/; and externally to | W |.

Use of Θ also has the remarkable ability to cohere | P | without going "back down" through /S/ and | E |. *Experiences* such as *I-Pen, Noming, TimeCart, Mirror,* and others, illustrate and indeed prove this ability.

Here, we have a further paradox of Self:
- Θ synchronises via <Constructs>, with | W |
- that coherence allows Θ indirectly to control | P |

and
- Θ also provides integration to /S/{idents}
but:
- in doing to loses its equalisation coherence.

Now, we need to explain how Θ interaction actually operates.

Synchronisation and Simulation Illusion

From some of the latest Interoception Models, all the way back to Plato, we have entertained the notion that the human mind processes, not reality, but a simulation of reality.

These ideas arise from the attempt to model Self│W│ interaction without the benefit of a Systems Architecture of Self. They also arise naturally from how the /S/ ubjective <self> mirrors itself in everything.[182]

/S/ relies upon sensory input and then performs its equivalence function: a function which is subjective, approximate and riven with inaccuracies as {idents} associate freely with each other.

By contrast, Θ has no idents. It only has Theta particles: ⊤, which are equalised.

Θ is synchronised to the external world │W│. This is in a way, the most mysterious capacity of Θ. Yet it is that │W│ synchronisation which explains the transmission function.

---

[182] see Chapter 6

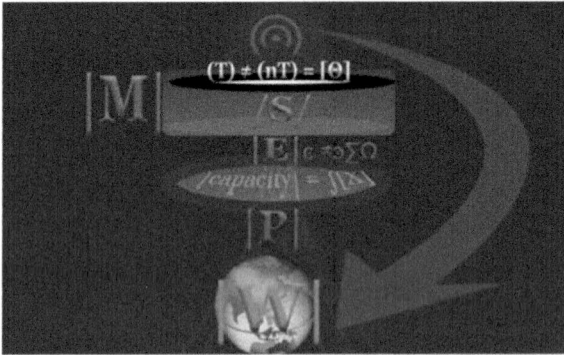

Θ is the Equaliser. Θ effects equalisation by the use of <Constructs>. These <Constructs> are then used to effect communication, and synchronisation.

That Θ=>|W| synchronisation is invisible. We can detect it only through the use of time and motion synchronisation strategies: such as |T|ime based *Experiences*.

That synchronisation appears to our /S/ubjectivity as if it were a simulation. Animals, not having /S/, aren't impelled to imagine a simulation. Trapped as we are in our /S/ubjectivity, it's the only way that we can perceive synchronisation.

To further explain this phenomenon, we can look to the natural world. Take the example of bat echo-location. The bat is transmitting an audio signal to the environment: the reverberating signals are mapped in the bat brain by reference to the slightly different times of receipt by the two ears. It's like an auditory Cartesian co-ordinate system.

Human Θ uses a very similar, natural, function:

- The Θ transmission system is already synchronised in spacetime to |W|. That is so from the moment of birth.
- Θ does not need to "bounce" signals off |W|.
- Instead, Θ produces the effect of a <spacetime> map of |W| and locates human interaction within that map.

We can, as an approximation to the reality, think of this as a "virtual world", like a 4D computer simulation: ΘЮ|W|

- The senses then react to that |Ю|, just as they react to a computer simulation. You really are in the "matrix".
- So, in a sense, Θ "hijacks" the |P| => |E| process of <self> by creating a synchronised "illusion" of reality |W|. But it's not an illusion. It's just not how /S/{i} interprets the world.
- Those /S/{i^n} associations are the illusion: yet we are forced by the architecture of Self to deal with those /S/{i^n} illusions as our reality.

You may notice our use of the term "4D". That gives a clue to what's really going on. It is the |gapped| synchronisation of |☪| which actually creates the "spatial" map. The ultimate reality is that it is a multiple |T|imes "map", which co-ordinates Extension in <space>, which together create <spacetime>. That's a lot to unwrap.

I-Pen Experience Synchronisation
Let's start here, taking the *I-Pen Experience* as our paradigm

of Θ synchronisation.[183]

This *Experience* is so valuable as a demonstration because you don't just witness alterations in your own |M|entation: you actually see tangible, verifiable physical evidence of that alteration in the real world, through altered manipulation of your |P|.

We use the anthropomorphising of You$_2$, to effect the alteration. There are good reasons for this:
- if we simply said "allow access to your Theta", you couldn't, unless you had already experienced Θ induced |Ю|.
- we need to engage your /S/{i^n} so that it invests |Ю| with subjective reality. You have to "accept the matrix program".

Once an individual has become subjectively convinced of the reality of |Ю| (and it is absolutely real), and its access pathway through Θ: then an individual can allow access to Θ at will.

So, with I-Pen:
- you write to 100% capacity with your normal hand A B C
- then you try writing that with your non-normal hand: with the expected scrawl

---

[183] see Section A, Segment 3

We then get you, through You$_2$, to allow Θ to "take over"

- your non-normal hand instantly performs at >80% of calligraphic function of your normal hand.

You sit back, amazed, and ask "how on earth did that happen".

Respondents acknowledge, when asked to recapitulate the experience in the history of their head is:

- it felt like someone else, not me, was using my hand
- it felt like my self was disconnected from the process
- I felt in a zero emotion state, while doing it: though once I saw what I'd achieved, I had a rush of good feelings.
- I also felt a contest going on, where it was like "me" was struggling not to re-assert control

When we analyse these responses, we can see clearly that the $\Theta | \text{Ю} |$ construct has completely bypassed $| E |$. The writer's entire physiology is reacting to the virtual world $| \text{Ю} |$, not to $| W |$.

The <Nodes> being received at $| E |$ | capacity | are being controlled by the interposition of $| \text{Ю} |$. These translate into signals ($\geq_\varsigma$) which are perfectly[184] balanced in Ohm potentials ($\leq \ni$). So there is a "wave reinforcement" function $= \int [x]^2$.

---

[184] or near perfectly

The Ohm Ω equation automatically qualitises that predictable quantum, and effects $\Rightarrow |P|$.

It's really hard to see how our $|E|$ works in normal life. It's like a goldfish trying to analyse its own bowl.

But, when we subjectively experience a complete loss of emotional stimulus, while performing a complex motor task, in which our subjective $/S/\{i^n\}$ is experienced to be a bystander: then we attain clarity.

The matter of $\Theta|W|$ synchronisation was taken up in Chapter 7 of *Matrixial Logic*. We will be returning to it in Chapter 3 here.

For now, what we need to appreciate is that we are only in contact with every moment of reality $|W|$ in a specifically quantised temporal conjunction.

Equivalence and Equalisation
Our $/S/$ <self> appears invested in a belief that $|W|$ is a continuum, like $/S/\{i^n\}$. It is correct that $/S/\{i^n\}$ is a bounded continuum, unaware of its own boundaries in architecture.

$|W|$ is not like that. $|W|$ is quantised, and our $|P|$ has temporal point interactions with it.

We should not think of $|W| \Rightarrow |P|$ as being like rivers flowing constantly into a sea. Instead, $|W| => |P|$ is an overlapping series of incidences: like a light flickering, or an atomic decay. Again, on proper inspection, our very life has more in common with the universe of quantum phenomena, than we are used to believing.[185]

$|P|$ sensations create a series of "dots". Transformed as <signals> in $|E|$, $/S/\{i^n\}$ "joins the dots". Using equivalence, patterns and habits.

This is not to disregard that $|P|$ also includes vital autonomic functions: taking in 0_2, and expelling $C0_2$, for example. $/S/$ doesn't need to direct autonomic functions.

Similarly, the operation of gross motor functions (walking and balancing) can all occur without $/S/$ involvement.

Θ has a completely different way of assembling the "dots", a way inaccessible to $/S/$:
• $/S/$ estimates.
• Θ equalises

In *I-Pen*, Θ is "transmitting" the simulacrum $|\text{Ю}|$ of a sensory dot matrix to $|W|$. It is creating a virtual world in which an 'A' looks like an 'A', not the squiggle that $/S/$ estimates as being an 'A'.

---

[185] even under the Copenhagen interpretation

It's really tempting to think that Θ is taking "control" of your motor function. We do present You$_2$ in that manner, so as to better allow you to access Θ. But that's not what's going on.

Your pen and the pad are in the world, and operating in the world |W|. What graphically appears at your open tip is <Node> information effecting your |capacity| via your sense inputs (feel, sight).

Θ <Constructs>

Your Θ Ю is transmitting a <Construct> of the sensory "dots" which your |capacity| is responding to, and sending appropriate ∫[x] data via ΣΩ to your |P| fine motor system.

To say it again, your |P| is responding to the Θ|Ю| <Construct> transmission, mapped onto the actual |W| of your sensory experience.

Some readers will have experienced this Θ|Ю| projection in other areas:

- clay pigeon shooting, golf putting, karate moves: those moments when you already know you have "hit it" before you physically act
- the Ouija board phenomenon
- knowing what time it is, without checking a clock

There are many more examples. We tend to put these

down to "instinct".[186] The Psychotectural reality is that they as far removed from "instinct", which we understand as spontaneous unthought reaction, as you can get.

There is, however, another way of looking at "instinct". Matrixial Self analysis proposes as a theory that:

- all cellular life forms operate some version of Θ.
- they are controlling their behaviour by the use of an epigenetic Θ | Ю | projection.

This theorem is capable of accounting both for acquired characteristics and for the acquisition of behaviour modifications which cannot be ascribed to inheritance.

Without teetering at this stage into a minefield of debate, let us simply suggest that this provides a materialist (or naturalist) basis for explaining the undeniable (since experimentally verified) phenomena which Rupert Sheldrake ascribes to morphic fields and resonance.[187]

It can be taken as a datum that the Author can alter your Θ | Ю | simply by transmitting to you a small set of instructions.

Most of these instructions are actually designed to get your /S/{i^n} out of the way (by limiting it to a narrow channel of <coherence>), so that Θ | Ю | can go about its

---

[186] perhaps not Ouija boards
[187] https://www.sheldrake.org/research/morphic-resonance

virtual projection work. In the non-human realm, there is no /S/{i^n} to get out of the way, in the first place.

To summarise:
|W| *Input*

(1)   We have no actual continuum of interaction with the real external world |W|.

(2)   We engage in a series of overlapping point interactions: <Nodes>.

(3)   Wee create qualitised coherence in our $\sum\Omega$ function, which is then referred to |P| and /S/

Ю *Input*

(4)   Θ is an equaliser. It transmits equalised <Constructs> as a virtual framework |Ю|.

(5)   Θ is synchronised with external |W| spacetime.

(6)   To our |P| motor control system, input referenced to |Ю| is indistinguishable from input referenced to |W|.

(7)   Input referenced to |Ю| is (by reason of the Θ equalisation function) coherent in $\sum\Omega$ function, compared to the arbitrary quality of input referenced to |W|.

The result is that our |P|, in interaction with |W|, can be controlled by referencing the |Ю| virtual framework.

This is not the same as some kind of neo-Buddhist mind-body interaction, producing physiological changes.[188] It's

---

[188] which are relatively small, and take years to achieve even that

not that Θ is taking over nerve functions, and thereby altering physiological processes. Those $|P|$ continue as they always would. It's that they are referencing a different virtual world, to the one they usually reference.

And let's just build out that last point. As a condition of our sanity, our subjective continuum has us enmeshed in a perspective wherein we interact with the world seamlessly, in a matched continuum of $|W| \Rightarrow /S/\{i^n\}$. It is a rational delusion.

It's rational because if we had to stop and analyse every actual point interaction with $|W|$ we would be unable to function at all.

Our interaction with $|W|$ is not, in reality, a seamless continuum. It is an overlapping and arbitrary series of point interactions through <Nodes>. Then "dots" are created by the Exclusion Function, as <Nodes> meet $|$capacity$|$. This is quantisation.

The first "dot assembly" is then in $\sum\Omega$. It is a virtual $|W|$, not $|W|$ itself. A virtual $|W|$, created by <Node> interactions in $|E|$. Now the reader can see quite why we spent so long on this explanation of the mechanics.

The Ohm distributed referral system sends its outputs: to $|P|$ or $/S/$, as appropriate.

So far as ($\in$) outputs are referred to /S/, we then assemble in >50 <500 millisecond times our /S/{i^n} maps, as equivalences of pattern comparisons, operating in habits.

Theta Θ transmissions present a different virtual |W| to |E|. Theta Θ <Constructs> matches the actual |W| in spacetime synchronisation.

We might say that the matrixial logic of the world |W| is processed in Θ, without the intermediation of /S/.

The result is Θ|Ю|: a virtual world which is spacetime synchronised with |W|. It is from these <Nodes> that "dots" are created by the Exclusion Function.

There is no <potential> ($\leq\ni$) in Ohm $\sum\Omega$ which correlates to anything in /S/{i^n}. That's why you feel "emotionless" while You$_2$ is operating.

That's also why you have the feeling that <Me> You, is struggling to stay quiet and not interfere. The space between the "ceiling" and "floor" of the /S/ continuum is being "squeezed". That part of Self which is <Me> is being negated, overlooked. We don't like that:

> *Our /S/ likes an unbalanced dynamic*
> *in the direction of <coherence>*
> *but finds actual <coherence> uncomfortable*

The Θ|Ю| assembly is "seamless" in the way that

ordinary I W I <Node>=> I capacity I is not.

Thus, in ΘIЮI <Construct> transmission, we are replacing our usual I W I origin virtual reality experience, with another. The results we attain in doing that, can be astonishing.

We experience the world in a virtual reality.
We can alter our virtual reality
Which changes our experience

But ΘIЮI transmission has a limited repertoire. We don't get originality, novelty, invention out of ΘIЮI. We only get reality-consistent iteration. For animals, that's all they need to survive. For our human sanity, and creativeness, we need more. We need the subjective continuum.

6.   *Computing the Incomputable*

So now we can ask:

(1)   what are the constituents of Theta particles (T) ≠ (nT)?

(2)   how does a /S/{i} become <T>?

You may have noticed that there are no equations in /S/: although the ability of /S/ to access I W I is limited.

That's because:

*   {idents} associate in equivalence, not identity
*   /S/ doesn't need equations: who can you think your unlanguaged <thoughts> and <feelings> to, except you?

Ю I **W** I **Synchronisation**

Theta, by contrast is nothing but equation:

$$(T) \neq (nT) = \Theta$$

You'll notice that the Theta equation is almost exactly the same as the elementary [E] equation:

$$(A) \neq (nA) = [E].$$

There is no equivalent of the [I] equation in Theta, because there is no need for it.

- Theta is an equalisation axis.
- It is a <Construct> without parts.

Θ is synchronised with spacetime. It is I W I expressed in the logic of spacetime itself.

These are unfamiliar and challenging concepts. It's difficult to provide metaphor and analogy. But let's try this:

Experience: Linker

Look into the room

See two Balls floating in the air, a few armlengths away:

Next: visualise these tangential lines connecting the Balls:

Now:

- make the Balls disappear
- float the Lines around
- make the Lines longer and longer, the apex disappearing, until you can no longer see it

Stop

Discussion:

(1)   All of this is easy to do

(2)   The Lines appear without effort to link the Balls

(3)   Then, you don't need the Balls

(4)   You can work with the Lines directly

But, here's the thing:

Experience: Alley

Look into the room

Now: visualise those tangential lines , floating free in space

Stop

Discussion:

(1) Unless you were anchoring the lines to something (the wall, for example), this visualisation just would not happen

So we see **Lesson (1)**:

- You need $/S/$ {idents} to create $(T) \neq (nT) = \Theta$

But:

- once a Θ <Construct> subsists, it coheres Ю to ｜W｜, without needing the {idents}.

Experience: Inner

Read the directions then close your eyes

Step 1:

Inside your head, eyes closed:

See two Balls floating in your head:

Next: with your eyes closed:

inside your head: visualise these tangential lines connecting the Balls:

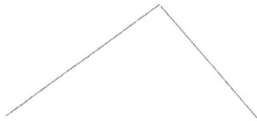

Now:
- make the Balls disappear

Step 2:
Forget the balls
Just visualise the Lines

Now:
- make the Lines longer and longer, the apex disappearing, until you can no longer see it

Stop

Discussion:

(1) Inside your head, you can't detach the Balls from the Lines.

(2) With the Lines on their own, you can vary them a little, but it takes real concentration, and they keep threatening to just disappear.

What you did here was to make an /S/ {ident}. No Θ was involved. You were trying to make a "Shadow <Construct>". We will be discussing this a lot in Part 3.

So we see **Lesson (2)**:
- we can only create <Constructs> in Θ
- if we try to move a Θ <Construct> to /S/, that <Construct> cannot maintain coherence

Which gives **Lesson (3)**:

- Θ <Constructs> are formed from /S/{idents}
- Θ <Constructs> subsist in coherence independently of /S/ {idents}

But:

- Θ <Constructs> subsist at all only in Ю coherence with <spacetime>

With the *Linker Experience*, you may now be able to see more clearly what a Θ<Construct> is:

- the Balls are {idents}
- the Lines are Θ <Constructs>
- which become coherent when the Balls disappear
- the Lines are now a Ю framework

That's fine, but that [Θ <Construct> Ю] must be connected to something, somewhere. Something is giving the Lines their coherence. We know it can't be the {ident} Balls, since they have gone; and the Lines and apex can just move freely.

Ю ∣ **W** ∣ **Synchrony**

We have already stated the answer, many times over and in different ways, And from different perspectives.

Now that we are focusing just on the Θ field axis, we can finally provide a literal statement.

That which synchronises [Θ <Construct> Ю]

is ∣ ♔ ∣ <spacetime> itself.

462

For readers who have done the *Experiences* of *Noming*, *Soundspace*, *Ropetime*, and *Timecart*, from *Matrixial Logic*, this rubric will have a quality of meaning, which may not be apparent to readers only of this book. We will be taking you through these *Experiences* in Chapter 3, as they are so important.

As we said in C(2)/8:

> Extension [E]
>
> After all the Matrixial Logic we have done together, you understand that in (A) $\neq$ (nA), the inequality [$\neq$] is a <spacetime> function. [189]

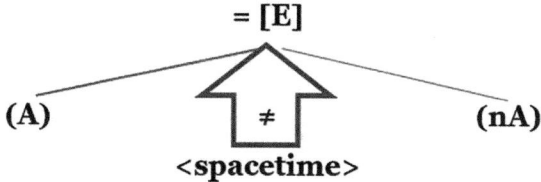

$$= [E]$$

(A) $\neq$ (nA)

<spacetime>

> The Form =[E], is the <spacetime>co-ordinate of $\neq$, yet is no longer simply <spacetime>, but a unique iteration of<spacetime>.
>
> Remember also that a Form is always hylomorphic to its Contents. The Form [E] is created by the opposition of (A) $\neq$ (nA), and is at the same time, what allows each to exist in<spacetime>.

---

[189] see *Matrxial Logic*, Chapters 2 and 4

Thus, in the [E] form of equation, <spacetime> is a potential, which is realised in Extension, and Extension is possible only due to inequality, and manifests as Form of inequality.

The solution to [Θ <Construct> Ю] coherence is that:
in (T) ≠ (nT), the inequality [≠]
is also a <spacetime> function.

Graphically, we can try to represent these concepts like this:

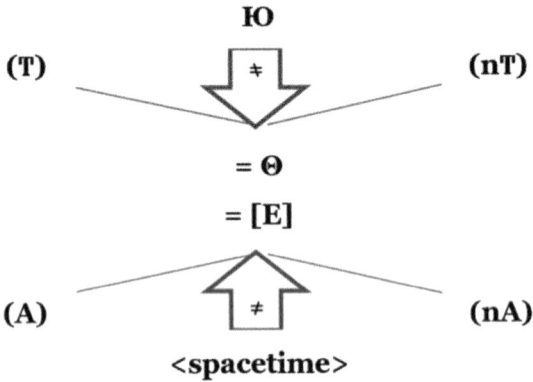

There is an asymmetry here between Ю and <spacetime>. This is because Ю is synchronised with =[E] through | T | ime. It is that | gapped | synchronisation[190] | ℭ | which creates the coherence.

---

[190] see Matrixial Logic, Chapter 7, and Chapter 3 later

This is not a hylomorphic relationship of Substance with Form, under Extension. It is the super-position of Extension in synchronisation.

We cannot avoid setting out, in advance of Chapter 3, the following:

(1) | T | ime is not a dimension with extension.

(2) | T | is quantised.

(3) | T | manifests in Extension in | W |, which is an infinite, overlaying, procession of | gapped | <times>

(4) | T |, under Extension in | W | creates <space>; or to put it this way, Extension is the spatial manifestation of | gapped | <times>.

Which allows us to state:

(5)   Ю is the Extension of | T |, in relation to Self.

(6)   Θ is the inter-spatial manifestation, in Extension of | gapped | <times>.

Thus:

(7)   The creation of <thought>: $\sum$<€> $(\top) \neq (-\top) =$ ₺[I] occurs as <spacetime>.

(8)   It is obvious that {idents} do not have a <spacetime> co-ordinate reference: they have reality only in our /S/ubjective sense of {time}, which

•   ultimately depends upon our Selfs being and becoming in <spacetime>;

but

•   is not co-ordinate referenced to it; nor

- synchronised to it.

(9) Θ is synchronised, by |T|ime to <space> in |W|.

Although you can't see it, the *Linker Experience*, where the Lines float and transform in what we perceive as <space>, are actually Ю |W| interactions in |T|ime.

We can quickly prove that, by noting that the landscape you are looking at, when you float and transform the Lines, is actually (and always) in the past. About 12 milliseconds away from your retina, and a further >50 milliseconds in neurological activity.

What you are actually doing in the *Linker Experience*, is manipulating the Θ<Construct> in |T|ime.

If you're not familiar with Chapter 7 of *Matrixial Logic*, we fully expect that what we have written under this heading may not make a great deal of sense, for now. Insofar as the meaning of the words comes, though, it may well seem like utter nonsense.

Please reserve judgment on that, and return to these pages after Chapter 3. Hopefully, the following pages should also assist in clarification.

/S/ {idents} for Θ
As we have said, /S/{idents} have no intrinsic or necessary logic.

So, what draws {ident} information from /S/ to Θ? The answer is: whatever is required to function in the morphological interaction of Θ and |W|.

You can feel that morphological interaction occurring in the *Nicer Experience*. To remind us:

> *Experience: Nicer*
> Look around your room.
> Choose an object.
> Focus on the object.
>
> Now, while looking at the object,
> • say Out Loud *That is nice*
>
> Stop
>
> Discussion:

(1) You can speak, and maintain focus on the object.
(2) Speaking can actually feel directed at the object, making the connection more vibrant.

By contrast, in the *Nice Experience* of silent speaking, you can't keep visual focus on the object.

In speaking "to" the object, your morphological interaction is drawing into the Θ linguistic grammar function, elements from /S/{I^n}.

Let's do some more examples. Notice what is happening in your head as you do this *Experience*.

Experience: Val

Look around your room.

Choose an object.

Focus on the object.

Summon /S/{I^n} <thoughts> and <feelings> about *cheapness, worthlessness*

Step 1:

Now, while looking at the object,

• say In Your Head *That is cheap*

Discussion:

(1)   Nothing much really happens.

(2)   You might even feel a slight sense of frustration that the object can't experience your /S/{I^n}.

Step 2:

Now, while looking at the object,

• say Out Loud *That is cheap*

Stop

Discussion:

(1)   You can sense the /S/{I^n} being transmitted "at" the object.

(2)   Yet, you can notice that the Θ transmission plays in

your head very differently to Step 1.

That difference you notice is due to the transformation of $/S/\{I^n\}$ into:

$$(T) \neq (nT) = \Theta$$

Your $/S/\{I^n\}$ is not "yours" anymore. It "belongs to" the world. What was before only in your head, has acquired morphological interaction with $|W|$.

Now, run the *Val Experience* again. This time vary it, so that you perform Step 1 and Step 2 with each of the following phrases:

• That is expensive
• That is funny
• That is serious

What's happening here is that:

(1)   We are modelling the morphological interaction of Θ and $|W|$, by this book acting as $|W|$.
(2)   That is (albeit artificially) drawing a response from you.
(3)   You are formulating an {ident} association in $/S/$.
(4)   Those particular idents then come into the Θ cashier "shopping basket".
(5)   There is not the least reality (in $|W|$) of those {idents}.
(6)   But that is irrelevant to the Θ equalisation function.
(7) Θ then transmits.

(8)   The transmission occurs within a Θ।Ю। frame-work.

(9)   So your ।P। responds.

(10) You articulate the phrase.

And you'll notice that, in your head, it's almost like the object is describing itself to you. That's the consequence of the transmission Θ।Ю। framework shaping the <Node> information being registered by your ।capacity। in ।E।. The "other virtual reality".

We've used the phrase *morphological interaction with* ।W।. We should clarify.

If you've read Chapter 7 of Matrixial Logic, then what we mean by morphological (literally "shape reason") will already be fairly clear. Chapter 3 in this book will lend further clarification. For now, let's just assert:

(1)   Our Θ has the capacity to synchronise in time with ।W।.

(2)   To synchronise in time is to co-ordinate in space, since they are dimensions of the same phenomena.

(3)   Synchronisation is structural: not hylomorphic.

(4)   Noting here that $/S/\{i^n\}$ are hylomorphic, and (T) are not.

To make these ideas a little more clear, let's follow this.

Experience: String

Look around your room.

Choose two objects which have more than a foot of space between them

See both the objects (Object 1; Object 2)
then
Focus on Object 1

Step 1:
Now, while looking at Object 1:
- visualise Object 2 moving to where Object 1 is

Discussion:
(1)   This is easy.
(2)   It's like Object 2 creates "ghosts" of itself and moves to where Object 1 is.
(3)   It takes some concentration, and as soon as you relax, Object 2 "snaps back".

This happens because your your /S/{I^n} is creating {idents} to support your intended visualisation.

Step 2:
See both the objects (Object 1; Object 2)
then
Keep your focus on both objects at the same time

Now, keeping your focus on both objects at the same time:

- visualise Object 2 moving to where Object 1 is

<u>Discussion</u>:

(1) It won't move.

(2) You can't create "ghosts" of either Object.

This is because the two objects together are being seen by you in a spatio-temporal relationship. The architecture of your | M | entation is governing what you can think.

Your Θ is in *morphological interaction with* | W |. It's the same room, the same objects. The same pair of your eyes. We instructed:

> See both the objects (Object 1; Object 2)
> then
> Keep your focus on both objects at the same time

So, you *equalised* the two objects. You made them be, for you, co-ordinate points an a spatio-temporal map, in your head.

> co-ordinate points an a spatio-temporal map in Θ
> $$= | Ю | =$$
> *morphological interaction with* | W |.

Whatever the 2 objects actually are, which you chose, (say a bottle and a lamp): those ideas just became labels Θ = | Ю | = | W |.

You'll notice that we have a new equation form:

$$Θ = | Ю | = | W |$$

It's not really an equation, of course. It's a description of an equalisation.

There are equations behind Θ and |W|. But [=|Ю| =|] is a meeting point of all those equations. It is not an inequality (≠) because it is not hylomorphic to any Substance or Moment. It is an equality in the virtual reality framework which is |Ю| .

By changing the inequality equations (that is, what the equations represent) behind Θ and |W|, we automatically alter |Ю|. Let's see.

Experience: Bar
Setup As in *String*:
Look around your room.
Choose two objects which have more than a foot of space between them

See both the objects (Object 1; Object 2)
then
Keep your focus on both objects at the same time

Now, keeping your focus on both objects at the same time:
- visualise both Objects moving around the room together
- keeping the distance between them the same

<u>Discussion</u>:

(1)   This is fairly easy.

(2)   Notice that, as you succeed in the visualisation, you don't create "ghosts" of the two Objects. It's like the Objects and the distance between them make up a portable "box"

You are (in your imagination) changing the co-ordinate points an your spatio-temporal map. This "moves" | Ю | .

You don't get any "ghosts" because your your /S/{Iⁿ} isn't having to create {idents} to support your intended visualisation. Your Θ | Ю | is shifting instead.

It's a bit like when you are using an area function on a rental properties map. As you move the area of interest from one part of the map to another, different properties pop up. Or, another analogy: using a magnifying glass and moving it from one part of an image to another.

Experience: Back
Setup As in *Bar*:
Look around your room.
Choose two objects which have more than a foot of space between them

See both the objects (Object 1; Object 2)
then
Keep your focus on both objects at the same time

And:

keeping your focus on both objects at the same time:

- visualise both Objects moving around the room together
- keeping the distance between them the same

and

- move them halfway across the room

Now, keeping your focus on both objects in their new place:

- try to visualise where they used to be

Discussion:

(1)   You can't.

(2)   You can either have the Objects in the middle of the room in $\Theta | \text{Ю} |$; or "see" them where they used to be: but not both

The Objects are now "locked" in their new co-ordinate points an a spatio-temporal map, in your head: in $\Theta = | \text{Ю} | = | W |$.

Step 2:

Put the two Objects back where they were, halfway across the room

See them in their new $\Theta = | \text{Ю} | = | W |$ position

Now, relax

let them be where they used to be

and

- try to see the "space bar" between them
-

Discussion:

(1)   It's really hard.

(2)   Back in Step 2 of *String*, it was easy to visualise the Θ I Ю I . You just let Θ equalise the co-ordinate space. It was automatic.

(3)   But now, when you try to repeat it, something is "nagging" you that the Objects are in the wrong place.

(4)   When you try to visualise the "space bar" between them, it's like that "space bar" now is real only in the middle of the room.

We coined the term "Θ is in *morphological interaction with* I W I". We said this literally means "shape reason".

Experience: Shaple

Look around your room.

Choose two objects which have more than a foot of space between them (the ones you used previously will probably be "neutral" again now, so you can use them for this)

See both the objects (Object 1; Object 2)

then

Visualise a Circle, with its circumference edge touching each object

Now:

•   move the Circle around the room

•   have fun moving the circle anywhere you like

- including back to between the actual Objects

Stop

Discussion:
(1)   This is so easy.
(2)   You have created Θ | Ю | and given it Form in a Circle.

Morphological Interaction

Now you can see why we say *morphological interaction*. In dealing with this spatial relationship between physical objects in | W |, your Θ is homologising (equalising). Θ is analysing their Extension in spacetime, placing that under a Form, and equalising that with | W |.

And what is Substance? It is of course: $(A) \neq (nA) = [E]$. Your Θ is taking the $\neq$ from your | S | [C]{i^n} and making that a (T).

The part of (nT) is played by the rest of the spacetime continuum.

Let's work through the detail. Say that your two Objects were a <bottle> and a <lamp>. Those are objects in the world, but they could as well be objects that you are just imagining.

We know very well by now how any actual objects get into your /S/. Imaginary objects are simply {idents}, which bear whatever ultimate relationship they do to things in the actual | W | orld.

Now, you don't need to turn {idents} into <Nodes>, in order that Θ can use them. Because Θ isn't using the "substance" of the {idents} at all: Θ is using the morphology (the shape reason) of the {idents}.

In other words,

Θ is using the $\neq$ between {idents}:
not the {idents} themselves.

You have witnessed this going on in your own head in the recent *Experiences*.

$$(X) \neq (nX) = [E_1] \mid (Y) \neq (nY) = [E_2]$$
$$>$$
$$(T)$$

The term (nT) is derived from | W |. This is the synchronous element of Θ. In spacetime co-ordinates, (nT) is all the points which are not (T).

This is not surprising. It's how any co-ordinate system works:

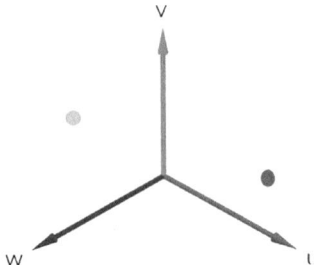

$(X) \neq (nX) = [E_1] \mid (Y) \neq (nY) = [E_2]$

$>$

$\sum(T)$

$$(V) \neq (W) \neq (U)$$
$$<$$
$$\sum(nT)$$

$$=$$

Θ (Yellow Thing Co-Ordinate)

Now, the $\Theta \mid$ Ю $\mid$ is obviously made up of "stacked" co-ordinates. So Θ runs the same "program" for the Grey Thing.

Remember that $\mid$ Ю is a manifestation of gapped $\mid$ T $\mid$ ime: $\sum \mid$ ₵ $\mid$. Perturbations of $\mid$ gapped $\mid$ time create spatial relationships.

We thus end up with:

$$\frac{\Theta^n = \mid Ю \mid = \mid W \mid}{\sum \mid ₵ \mid}$$

And that's how you hit the tennis ball, catch the baseball, walk through a door. And all the other mundane complex spatial co-ordinate activities which fill daily life.

That's why you get the notion of having "hit it" before you've even moved.

Analytically, we could wish to say that $\mid$ Ю $\mid$ is the ultimate expression of ≠ inequality. But that wouldn't be correct. | Ю | does not transform into anything else. as we said above, | Ю |:

> is not an inequality (≠) because it is not hylomorphic to any Substance or Moment. It is an equality in the virtual reality framework which is | Ю | .

This is to consider | Ю | only in its spatial domain. Looked at in this limited perspective, it really looks like a "cheat". A super luminary intrusion of some sort of equality in a universe of inequalities.

Once we add in the $\sum$| ₵ | temporal quality of | Ю |, that "cheat" disappears. That apparent "equality" in | Ю | is itself only the manifestation of "gapped" or quantised Time.[191] Equalisation is the form by which extension in space appears under quantised time.

We appreciate that these last sentences, especially if the reader is not familiar with *Matrixial Logic*, Chapter 7, are difficult to make sense of. We can't go further at this stage without writing Chapter 3 of this book right here. So please do come back to this section after Chapter 3.

---

[191] we explored this in *Matrixial Logic*, Chapter 7

7. *Down is Up*

The last layer is, looking at how Theta Θ interacts with the Scalar /S/ continuum /S/ of {idents}.

We're going to try to explain with a slightly odd *Experience*.

Experience: Roo
Look at your room
Focus on anything in it

Just allow yourself to look at the thing
Allow yourself to feel whatever you feel
Allow yourself to have whatever wordless thoughts you have

Step 1:
Now:

• Name the thing in your head: just the name

Step 2:
Now:

• Think of a simple sentence about the thing and your experience
• Say the sentence to yourself, in your head.

Discussion:
(1) Review the history of your head.
(2) When you named, the name was already "there" in your head.

(3)   When you formed the words sentence, it was like you were "pulling" the non-name words from a shelf somewhere.

We had to do this experience without giving you a specific set of sentence words. Otherwise they would have come in being in | W |. That would have sent them in the circuit | W | => | P | => | E | => /S/. They would have become, via Mimesis, part of your {idents} landscape.

Instead, we made you apply grammar, which is the Theta Θ equalisation which makes language possible.[192]

This brings us to the rubric: we don't need Θ to function in /S/{I^n}: until we do.

We can name <T>{i} or <F>{i}. Indeed, we can't really work with them in /S/{I^n}, until we do name them: however contingently or temporarily. We don't need Θ grammar for names of <T>{i} or <F>{i}.

But, as soon as we want to make *existential statements* about <T>{i} or <F>{i}, that is, statements which place them in a landscape of "is", of "being", then we have to use Θ "map making" facilities.

The key difference is that | W | out there, is real. When Θ

morphogenic ally interacts with | W | in | Ю |, that creates an equality, a fixedness.

There's no material reality within the /S/ continuum. It's subjective, contingent, equivalence based approximation and association. It's whatever you want it to be, or not to be.

So, when you bring (T) from Θ "upstairs" down into /S/ /S/, it stops being (T). It loses Theta coherence. It becomes just another {ident}.

If you want to put the {idents} association out into the world, then you need to pass their inequalities into the Theta Θ equalisation program: and out comes grammatical language.

And let's finally just consider that for a moment. You know what it's like to say just about anything out loud. What you hear yourself saying, or see yourself writing, is never really quite the same as your <T>{i} and <F>{i} associations.

You can never express, out loud, what You, as You, "really" think in your feelings. That necessary linguistic equalisation always leaves something behind.

we can say what we want to be understood as meaning; but we can never authentically mean what we are saying.

That's why we have poetry. It's the art form of the spaces

between /S/ and Θ.

Bricks Made of Straw

Associative {idents} are the constituent elements of our notion of the cultural <self>. That's why we are so resistant to denying them the status of "ultimate" reality.

Yet, it's precisely because we have invested culturally in that "ultimate" reality, that we have ended up in the mutual dead ends of: materialism, dualism, idealism, deism, and panpsychism.

After 400 years of enquiry in philosophy, logic, linguistics,[193] and latterly neuroscience and neurobiology, and trillions of data points: we are quite as stuck today as Rene Descartes and Spinoza were. And indeed Plato, Aristotle and Galen.

The reason for all this, has two fundamental layers:

(1) the cultural dependence on trying to visualise a functioning organic machinery, by starting from <thoughts> and / or <feelings> as the ultimate human realities[194]

(2) by trying to formalise an equivalence function in /S/ as the logical law of identity (A=A): which effected a 2,500 year confusion between Θ and /S/ functions.

---

[193] and much more
[194] in opposition to the deism and animism of Medieval and Classical paradigms

Our cultural investment in these two fundamental notions has led us to amazing insights, analyses and understandings: but by accident.

Indeed, it's exactly because (1) completely contradicts (2) that the fissure between them has enabled constructions of genius in science, art and humanities.

To borrow and modify the Frankfurt School phrase: the brilliances of Western thought have germinated in the soil between the dialectical walls of unreason.

It's the forms of inequality which rescue us from this impasse. In the /S/ domain nothing "equals" anything else.

This is an objectively correct perspective, since no thing is the same as any other thing: every Substance under extension is in opposition to any other Substance; and every Moment in becoming is in negation to any other Moment:

$$(A) \neq (nA) = [E]$$
$$(A) \neq (-A) = [I]$$

Remember that the aequalis does not mean "equals", as in mathematics, but instead means "interacts, or transforms as".

The forms of inequality unlock the /S/ domain. They liberate it from its necessary continuum of confinement.

However, we have already said, and because of its mental health imperative, we'll keep on saying it:

> We can use the equations which illuminate and activate the architecture of Self. We can use the diagnostic and therapeutic methods which the architectural equations show to us. But we must not try to live in our minds outside the /S/ continuum of confinement. To do so, is to put sanity seriously at risk.

In *I Want To Love But*, we met categories of person who do almost live outside the /S/ continuum of confinement. We will see in Chapter 7 the techniques which all of us use, all the time, to try and live outside the /S/ continuum of confinement. None of it ends well.

The agenda of *Secret Self* is to reveal that which is hidden from us, so that we can better embrace, not reject, our Selfs.

8.   *Logic of the /S/ Continuum*

We do interact with the world *under a relation to* our feelings and thoughts, but not under the *Unilinear Model*.

{idententation} has the necessary and unavoidable effect that we can only looks at out <F>{idents} with <T>{idents}.

We invent all manner of folk and scientific paradigms of how such interactions are supposed to work. All of that is supported by the undeniable fact that, when we apply our awareness to the external, or internal world, we seem to be using that awareness, and it seems to be accompanied by feelings.

The categories <thought> and <feeling>: both of these are illusory. They are the reflections of architecturally defined systems interactions with other reality. We accept the reflections as actually being reality because there is no other way we can function in sanity.

| E | motions Do Not Know Themselves

We desperately want to believe in the reality of <feelings> because, well, surely we can just *feel* them.

Even if, intellectually, we can accept the structures of matrixial Self architecture, and the reality of the *Experiences*, we still want to feel that we feel.

What's going on here is:

we want to think that we know we have feelings

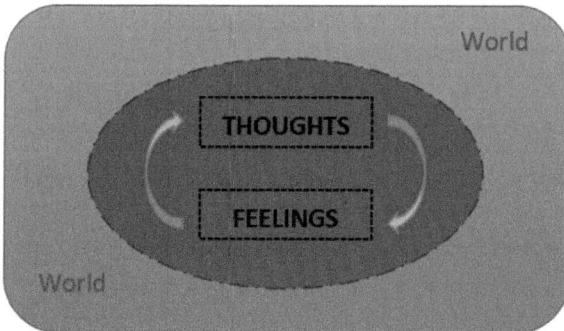

That's a snapshot of the circular mentative process. It's circular, because we want to think that we interact with the world through our feelings and thoughts.

We want to think that, because we want to think we have control, or at least influence over that interaction: and we think that only be thinking these thoughts can we be possessed of such control, or influence.

This {identation} is what grants such power to the *Unilinear Model*, which has founded Western thought for 2,500 years.

We have traversed and made transparent the *Systems Architecture* of the Self:

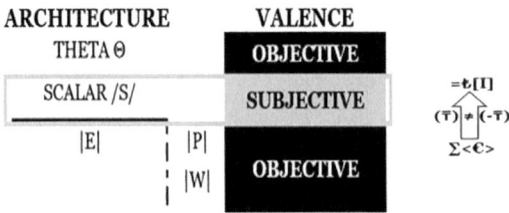

ARCHITECTURE	VALENCE	
THETA Θ	**OBJECTIVE**	
SCALAR /S/	**SUBJECTIVE**	$=\textbf{t}[\text{I}]$ $(\text{T})|\neq|(\text{-T})$
|E| |P| |W|	**OBJECTIVE**	$\Sigma <\text{€}>$

We now understand that there is no "meaning" in the sphere of |E|. It is all *Systems* process.

There is "meaning" only at the point where <thought> creation occurs in <spacetime>: $\Sigma<\text{€}>(\text{T}) \neq (\text{-T}) = \textbf{t}[\text{I}]$.
But that meaning is /S/ubjective. It is meaningless: where "meaning" is supposed to confer privileged status upon {ident} by reference to some superior connection to "reality".

When we confer "meaning" on $=\text{ʤ}[I]$, we are merely constructing associations of {idents}, and by other {idents}, conferring /S/ubjectively privileged status upon them.

The /S/ Law of Identity

/S/ operates under an equivalence function.

Self does not need to use any kind of logic in performing equivalence. It just amounts to an internal judgment that <A> is like something else <Z>.

Yet, the /S/ logic of identity is intrinsic to the operation of the /S/ equivalence function.

We derive our sense of order, which is necessary as a condition of sanity, from the submission of our subjective landscape under [A=A] logic:

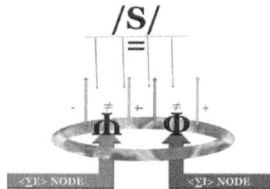

This is where we began the analysis. We chose *Experiences*, which demonstrated to you, that in order for identity logic to work, you need to be presented with information under Forms of Inequality.

We were showing you that there is a disjunction between

the way that we naturally, in our /S/ubjectivity, think that we think, and how {identation} actually works.

We build our lives around /S/ identity logic. It is elementary how /S/ identity logic works.

Experience: What
Think of an apple and an orange.

Now:
• think of a Form of Identity [A=A] for them

Discussion:
(1)   You might have thought of "2" or "fruit", or indeed both.

You're doing what human kind has done forever: placing {idents} under a /S/calar equivalence.

To quote from Chapter 4 of Matrixial Logic:
> Unlike the First/Higher Order logic divide, ML is holistic: *hylomorphically reciprocal*. In plan English, ML works as the interaction of its parts.

> It may be worth addressing, at this point, the phenomenon of *atomism*. Russell's system, like Leibnitz's was explicitly *atomic*: blocks constructed of single elements, and arranged into a model.

> In both models, the essential building block is

[A=A]: the law of identity. With its congruent laws: non-contradiction and excluded middle.

Essentially, these *atomic models* take:

$$\forall = [A=A]$$

as the atom, and then build from there, through the linear portal of:

$$Every \; \forall \; is \; B.$$

$$\approx$$

$$\forall \, x: P\,(x)$$

This gives you Set Theory,[195] and on to to *modern logic*, syncopating around Wittgenstein, Gödel and Tarski.[196]

In an *atomic model*, the atoms are undifferentiated, save as to linguistic "colour". Each atom has existence independent of the curriculum in which each atom appears. Each atom is unperturbed by its inclusion in a curriculum. There is erected a structure, a lattice, of such atoms.

The atomic lattice is uniplanar. As if each lattice were written on a sheet of paper, and the sheets of paper marshalled upon a table top. So conceived, the derived frames of reference are both arbitrary, and fixed.

---

[195] Boole, Cantor, Frege, Peano, Russell, Hilbert

[196] Just the space between some landscape peaks, not the landscape

- They are arbitrary: since you may shuffle the latices around as you please. That is, after all, why you engaged in the construction of the atoms in the first place.
- But they are fixed by the assumed existential property of each atom.

What the atomic model achieves is a bounded infinity. It is a *shadow* of infinity ∞.

It ought then, perhaps, to be unsurprising that the enterprises in logic derived from the assumed existential atom have proved:[197]

- incapable of solving the paradoxes of movement, of dynamic
- to create their own paradoxes[198]
- incapable of representing the world of the real, whether in psychology, biology, physics or quantum mechanics

ML works differently. A fundamental principle of Matrixial Logic is that:

nothing Is

Less obscurely, that any Thing which Is, enjoys that property of Existence only in plural juxtaposition to that which is not (nA), or negates (-A).

---

[197] repeatedly and since inception in 350 BC
[198] the empty set, the set of sets, and so on

Existence is no more a property of abstraction into an *atomic* entity, then the necessary plurality of Things (^{NOT}) / (-), which populate existence.

Existence in neither a void, nor a plane, from which extrude (or are intruded) these (Things^{NOT} $^{/ \cdot}$). Existence and (Things$^{NOT / \cdot}$) are reciprocally inherent features of each other.

To posit $\forall = [A=A]$, is to posit a nullity. To operate with that nullity in logic, is to generate a fiction: a shadow of an (A*)*.

This is exactly what you did, intuitively, in the *What Experience*: placing {idents} under a /S/ calar equivalence.

/S/ identity logic [A=A], is logic works only by violating its own rules. It's the logic of the Aristotelian Categorical Sentences and Syllogisms.[199]

It's no good trying to defend identity logic as being the fulcrum of the materials sciences. They simply ignore identity logic in performing their technological and empirical feats: then dress the knowledge back up in identity logic paradigms. Which then gives rise to whole heaps of trouble.

----

[199] see *Matrixial Logic*, Chapter 3

The /S/<coherence> Illusion

Our /S/ubjective sanity, sandwiched by the actual conditions of our objective *Systems Architecture*, seems to require us to live our subjectivity in a landscape where:

- <feelings> are real and autonomous of <thought>
- <thought> is genuinely ordered by identity logic
- we can use one to engage the other in philosophically and psychologically useful ways.

This is the /S/ubjective <coherence> illusion. It achieves what it does, mainly by disregarding the rules under which <coherence> is supposed to function.

Yet, it is an illusion, only by reference to the objective elements of the Self *Systems Architecture*. Within the /S/ continuum, that illusion is our inescapable lived reality, from the moment of our birth.

The Theta Θ axis is a procession of <constructs>. We can't locate our /S/ubjective mental life in those <constructs>: even though they are the synchronicity of Self and reality.
Our /S/ubjective illusions are what allow us to live under Objective reality.

Leter, we will explain the distinction between <coherence> and |congruence|.

9.   Secret Architecture and Sanity

As we have previously stated:

> *Subjective <Thoughts> and <Feelings>*
> *are types of cognitive fictions, which are our reality*
> **but:**
> *the Self is a reality, which we perceive through illusions*

> *we don't subjectively think like the logic of the world is.*
> *but:*
> *Yet, it is a condition of our sanity that we engage in pretence*
> *of doing exactly that.*

As we previously said:

> As a condition of our sanity, our subjective continuum has us enmeshed in a perspective wherein we interact with the world seamlessly, in a matched continuum of $|W| => /S/\{i^n\}$. It is a rational delusion.

We are heavily invested in cultural concepts of Self. Science and practical personal psychology all press us towards a combination of concepts: from which we derive distinct, but fundamentally equivalent, models of Self.

The cultural <self> seems to be supported by our direct personal experience. It is. The cultural <self> is our reality.

The cultural <self> model, with variations is this:

Landscape:

- there is a world out there
- there are humans in the world
- humans have consciousness, or what looks like it[200]

Operational:

- humans receive sense inputs from the world, and from their physiology
- we have thoughts and feelings
- physiology triggers thoughts and feelings
- thoughts and feelings can trigger each other
- thoughts can trigger physiology, maybe[201]

Internal:

- we are only aware of little bits of our thoughts and feelings: that is conscious awareness
- the rest is subconscious
- our dream state shows the difference between conscious and subconscious

Interactive:

- Each brain is a solitary world, cut off from all else
- We connect to the external physically, or through language
- Maybe we have other connections: quantum; energy; psychical[202]

_____

[200] the materialist / idealist / panpsychist split
[201] depending how far down the "Eastern" or Hameroff paths one is prepared to go
[202] and all the variants

From the scientific perspective of matrixial logic, the cultural <self> is, frankly, superstitious nonsense. It's a collection of self-contradictory folk intuitions. A set of invisible balloons tied together with ragged rationalist string.

If we had told you at the outset of this Chapter, that we were going to take you through *Experiences* and analyses which would challenge the above bulleted cultural <self>: you probably would have resisted.

Not for want of curiosity, or academic rigidity. But because we are conditioned by our own experience not to be able to see the conditions of our experience.

- In doing the *Experiences* which make you meet the limits of your Subjective architecture, you become very uncomfortable.
- In doing the *Experiences* which compel you into subsuming your /S/ to "You$_2$" (which is really just your Theta Θ axis field), you feel that conflict. That struggle to "just let go" and allow Θ to take over.

You are right to feel uncomfortable and to struggle. The delusion that your subjective /S/ type of |M| entation is actually you Self, is the price of your continued sanity: of your functioning as a consciously aware human.

We have had to build out the architecture of Self slowly. We proceeded like this:

(1)   We accustomed you to shutting down your /S/ func-

tion. Not entirely, but by showing you some limits of it. The various *Experiences* posted mirrors on the walls of the actual enclosure in which /S/ operates.

(2) This energised your **Coherence Function**. In Part 3, we'll explore this in depth. Simply put, at this stage, your *Coherence Function*, is what maintains the "circus show" of your subjective <self>. You will do whatever you can to support your *Coherence Function*, including ending your own life.

(3) Your *Coherence Function* acted to repress the expression of your subjective <self>. To deny the use of your usual subjective <self> coping strategies. That's why you felt "paralysed". And it was uncomfortable.

(4) Then, we took you on an electrical engineering tour of your sensations, and how they operate inside you. You may have found it interesting, tedious, or thought it wrong. But none of these activated any defence systems inside your /S/.

(5) Then, we hit the punchline that <feelings> don't autonomously exist. They are simply <T | *Attachment* | F> for the emergent manifestations in Ω^n <Affects> of interactions which do happen in reality.

(6) As soon as we made that statement, your cultural <self> probably became defensive. This was a direct challenge to our operational and internal cultural <self> model.

(7) But by then, we had re-iterated the idea of thinking about <self> processes in terms of <Nodes>.

We can, with matrixial logic, see the hidden *Systems Architecture* which allows this cultural <self> to subsist. Given the absence of *Systems Architecture* and the matrixial logic which powers it, thinkers about thought had no choice but to pursue the avenues which they did.

This is the central paradox of the *Secret Self*:

Mentation

How we can think governs what we can think

Emotion

What we emote governs how we can emote

Yet, we can't go live our minds in that *Systems Architecture*. We can't live our mind's life in Theta Θ: to do so would quickly drive us insane. Yet our sanity comes at the price of a vested delusion of the cultural <self>.

10.   *<coherence> and | congruence |*

We now need to focus on two key concepts:

* <coherence>
* | congruence |

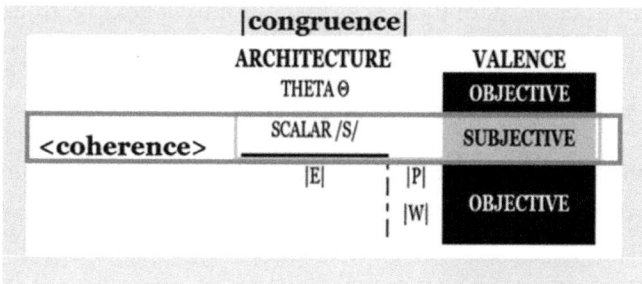

Our {identation} functions best in congruence
We are born with systems to ensure that it is

We have mentioned these concepts in previous pages of this Chapter. But, until we had fully developed the *Systems Architecture*, and its operating equations, in Self, we couldn't provide the picture on the puzzle box.

Now, the terms <coherence> and |congruence| are arbitrary. We could just as well use other words. These words do, perhaps, capture the essential elements and differences of process involved.

The whole of this Chapter has been the struggle to replace culturally deep-seated concepts of <coherence>, with novel concepts of |congruence|.

The cultural legacy is not something merely historical, social or religious. It arises from the natural workings of the Self.

Another sector of the Self, is that our life experience, from birth, inures in us the essential concepts of <coherence>.

Our /S/ubjective |M|entation engages in a perpetual movement through <coherence>. It is the fulcrum of our sanity. It is what makes our Selfs appear to each of us as <self>.

<coherence>

What we mean by /S/ubjective <coherence>, are the core processes which occur within the /S/ continuum:

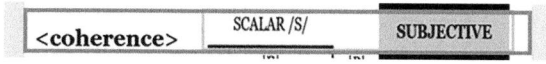

<coherence>	SCALAR /S/	SUBJECTIVE

We engage /S/<coherence>:

- by {identation}
- treating <F>{idents} as "subjective"
- treating <F>{idents} as objects of <T>{idents}
- abstracting from <T>{idents} to create iterations of [A=A] logic: the law of identity

then, creating an illusory dialectic, in which, [A=A] logic engages (usually argumentatively) with some non-logical rationality of <F>{idents}.

We justify belief in rationality of <F>{idents}, by claiming that these more truly represent the "real" world out there, and our lives in it.

This dialectic commonly performs under the rationale: "our emotions are real, and our thoughts are abstracted attempts to divine and order that reality."

This is description, not criticism. We cannot avoid thinking in {idents}. We can't avoid a belief in the dialectic of <F>{idents} rationality, and <T>{idents} identity logic.

Humans have engaged our /S/ubjective I M I entation under this dialectic, for as long as we have have had the capacity for /S/ubjective thought. Every child develops from neonate to infant, by more sophisticated engagement of this dialectic.

We seek to replicate that order which is innate in the world, in its arbitrary interactions with us, through a simulacrum of order: identity logic.

The /S/ dialectic of <coherence> is the wonder of the universe. It is the original anthropic miracle: reflected in the *Genesis* story of Adam and Eve.[203] That miracle is born again in every neonate. It is the biography of every <Me>.

It's just that the /S/<coherence> dialectic is incapable of solving the problems which it finds in the Self. The society of human kind, our history and future, all pay a terrible price for that intrinsic, and unavoidable failure.

I **congruence** I

What we mean by I congruence I, is the objective *Systems* under the *Architecture* of which, /S/ functions.

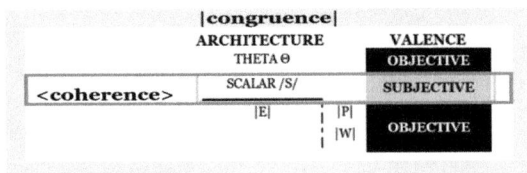

|congruence|		
	ARCHITECTURE	**VALENCE**
	THETA Θ	OBJECTIVE
<coherence>	SCALAR /S/	SUBJECTIVE
	|E| |P|	OBJECTIVE
	|W|	

---

[203] and knowledge acquisition myths throughout early civilisation: Sumeria, Egypt and so on

We can perceive the operation of |congruence| in every moment of our lives. It is |congruence| which creates and maintains <I>: the awareness of self-identity.

The primary difficult with using |congruence|, is that the moment Θ<Constructs> are "down-layered" into /S/<coherence>, they lose their Θ quality.

They become {idents}, and thus implacably subject to the railroads of the /S/<coherence> dialectic.

This is exemplified by the ever-unresolved debate in philosophy, neuroscience, and psychology over self-identity.

- The objective *Systems Architecture* of Self in |congruence| forms and maintains self-identity as <I>. That is absolute in every moment, and perpetually re-established in quantised |T|ime.
- Yet, we can only <T>{ident} or seek to <F>{ident} the |congruence| of <I> under the /S/<coherence> dialectic: which innately depletes <I> identity of its |congruence|.

We can only {ident} <I> as <Me>

However, we can use |congruence| to alter the conditions under which the /S/<coherence> dialectic operates. We have been doing this repeatedly, in the *Experiences*: both in this book and in *Matrixial Logic*.

We are bound to understand and express the *Systems Architecture* of |congruence| through {idents}. The very nature of |congruence| allows us to commune with objective reality, without the use of {idents}.

In Parts 2 and 3, we will explain the *Organic Systems* which govern |congruence|.

In Volume 2, we will explain the practical, therapeutic *Methods* of allowing |congruence| to be effective. These are the connected sciences of

- *Psychotectics*

and

- *Biomorphics.*

We'll explain what works, how and why it works, and allow you to *Experience* for yourself, the results.

All of this is made possible by this new science of Self. The application of *Matrixial Logic* to, what has still largely remained to this day, a *Secret Self.*

11.   *The Matrixial Self*

After over 50 Segments of analysis, set under 4 Sections. it's time to pause and summarise.

What We Have Discovered

We have discovered an entirely new way of constructing

Logical Rules governing the *Systems* under which our Selfs have an *Architecture*.

The *Architecture*:

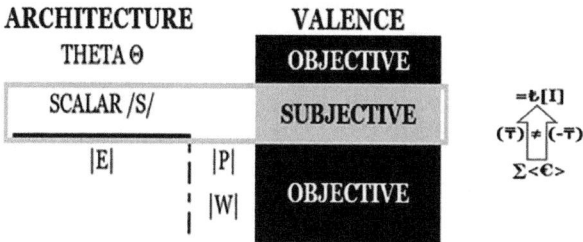

The Equations under which the *Systems* operate:

Fundamental Equations

Form in [E]	$(A) \neq (nA) = [E]$	(1)
Form in [I]	$(A) \neq (-A) = [I]$	(2)
<Node> in [E]	$\Box[E]^n \neq \Box[E]^n \sum <E>$	(3)
<Node> in [I]	$\Delta[I]^n \neq \Delta[I]^n \sum <I>$	(4)

Modes of Interaction

|W|orld <Node>	$\|W\|\sum<I> => \|EF\|$	(5)
|P| <Node>	$\|P\|\sum<I> => \|EF\|$	(6)
/S/ <Node>	$/S/\sum<I> => \|EF\|$	(7)

Exclusion Function: Quantised

Capacity Gapping	$(\geq\varsigma) \neq (\leq\partial) \int[x]$	(8)
Plurality	$\Delta\int[x]^n => (\varepsilon) \mid \Delta\int[x]^n => (\ni)$	(9)

Ohm Function: Qualitised

Aggregation	$(\varepsilon) \neq (\ni) \sum\Omega^n$	(10)
<Affect>	$(\varepsilon) \neq (n\varepsilon) = [\text{€}]$	(11)
Referral to /S/	$[\Box \text{€}^1] \neq [\Box \text{€}^n] \sum<\text{€}>$	(12)

<Thought>

Potential	$\Delta<\bar{T}^n> \mid \infty$	(13)
VCIP	$\sum<\text{€}> (\bar{T}) \neq (-\bar{T}) = \mathfrak{t}[I]$	(14)

Theta Axis

<Constructs>	$(T) \neq (nT) = \Theta$	(15)
[T]	$\Theta^n = \|IO\| = \|W\|$	(16)
Synchronisation	$\sum\|\mathfrak{C}\|$	

Systems Architecture **Narrative**
<u>The Classical Account</u>

There is /S/ubjectivity in our heads, or all of us as organic beings. This contrasts with the "out there" objectivity of the IWIorld. And, somehow, one relates to the other:

Philosophy

- The Materialist says its all one substance, all the way down from thoughts to quarks. Anything else is not part of material reality, and only material reality exists.
- The Idealist says there are two different Substances: one material and one Conscious. They are both real and both exist.

Neuroscience

All agree that neurology maps real structures and measurable events in the brain.

- Behaviourists, or reductionists say that all manifestations of Subjectivity can be ascribed to neurological functions which we have discovered, or can in principle discover.
- Interoception Models say that neurological functions cannot be separated from organic physiology. That Subjectivity organises itself through predictive concept networks, which are not reducible to neurological function.

Psychology and CBT

- Our Subjectivity is absolute in each of us, but conditioned by our real word circumstances.
- Our Subjectivity consists of layers.

- The primary distinction is between rational thoughts and irrational feelings.
- Another distinction is between Conscious states and Sub-Conscious states.
- We have behaviours and memories which can burden us, by residing in the Subconscious.
- We can effect change in our Conscious behaviour and perspectives by rational dialogue, and this can have positive effects on our Subconscious, thus improving our life.

The Straw Man reduction of these complex and often overlapping theory perspectives, is unavoidable in a such summary.

That really doesn't matter, because Philosophy and Neuroscience are labouring under the false premise of a *Unilinear Model* of existence:

$$\underline{|W|=>} \qquad /S/=> \qquad \underline{|W|}$$
$$\text{Objective} \qquad\qquad\quad \text{Objective}$$
$$\text{Spacetime} \qquad\qquad\quad \text{Spacetime}$$

Philosophy and Neuroscience remain in the 400 year old grip of Descartian paradigms, operating in a quasi-Newtonian universe of spacetime: which provides the objective landscape for everything we wish to theorise about.[204] The inevitable results are dualism and circularity.

---

[204] The Hameroff-Penrose Orch-OR theory comes closest to breaking out of the straightjacket.

It's difficult to be even that gracious about CBT. It has nothing to do with cognition, or behaviour. It's primary precepts are illogical and self-contradictory. Nevertheless, it is still stuck in a *Unilinear Model*. Since Freud, it has become an amalgam of fantasies and folk-wisdom.

The apparent utility of the *Unilinear Model* derives from the reality that you can get out of it whatever you put into it.

But that's all you get: a mirror of wishes, ideas, hopes and delusions. And a distorted mirror at that. As engineering, it is inefficient circularity. As logic, it is putting <A> in one end and getting <A> {+/-} (depending upon your delights) out of the other.

Then pretending that [=] is the same as [equivalence]. Functionally: they are. Logically: they aren't. And logic is the science of our | M | entation in reality.

The Bridge

Matrixial analysis allows us to understand how and why this merry-go-round ever got spinning, and why after at least 2,500 years, people with brilliant minds are still jumping on board.

The /Subjective/ <self> can see only its own continuum. It is a goldfish in an infinity of ocean. Every ocean is bordered by that which is not wet:[205] but no goldfish can ever realise that, such is the aquatic nature of the organism.

Even Matrixial Logic must be written in {idents}. And {idents} are how all Selves with /S/ubjectivity identify themselves. That is a matter of compulsion, not choice: a Self cannot be other than its own becoming.

All this infinity of {idents} constitute extrusions from the /S/ continuum, which is, with the Architecture of the Self, an axis field. An endless river, with banks (to alter the aquatic analogy).

It is the *Experiences* which best demonstrate to the /S/ ubjective <self> that there are limits on the /S/ continuum. Once that is realised, then the unreality of [A =A], even in the /S/ axis field of {idents} drives analysis beyond the boundaries of the /S/ domain.

The Experiences reveal the existence and operation of the Θ axis field, and of the ∑Ω function. Revealed also, is the synchronisation of | gapped | time: the understanding that | T | ime is quantised, and the corresponding revelation of Θ synchronicity in | ♎ | with | T | ime.

These concepts leak everywhere into Classical Accounts.

---

[205] even a planetary ocean

But they are taken to be iterations of the /S/ubjective, whereupon they lose their coherence. They become just more {idents} swilling round in a whirlpool[206] of /S/ubjective circularity.

The Matrixial Self Narrative

You have a Self awareness that you feel things, and that you look out at the world. Maybe you think of your own body, or brain as part of the world, or part of you: which is separate from the world, but connected to it.

This is the common starting point of all Classical Accounts. In this framework, there's: You, made up of your body and your thinking, feeling, mind; and the world out there.

This is a chicken and egg framework. No amount of neurology, philosophy or psychology, will get us anywhere, in that framework.

We need to come to an understanding of the core messages of *Secret Self*:

Mentation
How we can think governs what we can think
Emotion
What we can emote governs how we emote

This is because our |M| and |E| share a parallel

──────────────
[206] aquatic metaphors are working overtime in this Segment

Architecture: but are governed by different *Systems*.

It is the architecture of each part of the Self globe, which constrains:
- what we can think
- how we emote.

These ideas do run counter to what we are encultured to believe. That's why it takes so much detail, and levels of meta-analysis, to establish firmly the concepts of this complex matrix.

We start here: your Subjective mind is not the only system in your Mentation. We can prove that to you by showing how your Subjective mind only works under certain conditions.

Your Subjective Mind needs <Nodes> to operate. Without those <Nodes> your Subjective Mind becomes paralysed, or incapable of effective thinking.

We can prove that those <Nodes> are not just "in" your mind, because we can can change deliberately the circumstances in which you think: and that changes what you can think, and how you can think it.

The same is true of your feelings. That, we didn't have to prove, because everyone implicitly accepts that circumstances alter feelings.

So, we can conclude that there are matters about the world which have scientifically predictable effects on our thinking. This means that our thinking must take place under *Systems*, and in an *Architecture*.

Now, we have taken our first crucial step. We have realised that our Subjective Mind is limited. But that we usually don't notice those limits. When confronted with them, we become very uncomfortable. Our Subjective Mind acts as its own mirror.

We can see beyond the mirror, but we need to escape from the conventions of our Subjective <self> thinking, to achieve that.

So, let's perform the narrative of a Subjective mental interaction with the world:

- There's something out there in the world: a thing, a process, and event.
- To be able to perceive Subjectively that reality (in our thoughts or feelings), the information about that reality needs to reach us in a certain way: through <Nodes>.
- We obtain that information through our Senses: everyone is on common ground there.
- Our Senses then pass that information to a sorting centre. What we call the Exclusion Function.
- The Exclusion Function transforms information which comes to us via our Senses (and internally produced information too).

- That transformation turns all incoming information, from whatever source, into <signals>. That is, into quantities of + / -. It quantises them.
- The output can range from zero to infinity. It depends on how the signals combine.
- The quantised signal interference information then appears on a readout: like a shadow on the wall from a light bulb. That readout is the Ohm distribution function.
- Ohm then refers the "shadow" within the self. Where is refers to, depends on where there is a "lock" for that "key".
- All of this is automatic. It happens within us from the moment we are born.

Then:
- Using our Subjective mind, we can by trial and error, create pathways of habit through the Exclusion Function and Ohm.
- Our Subjective Mind is a procession of potential thoughts.
- Ohm refers information (which we call an Affect) to our Subjective Mind. We then choose where in that potential, the Affect targets.
- Once an Affect is matched to a thought potential target, that's it. Game over: we have had a thought or a feeling.
- Feelings are simply thoughts.
- We have awareness of the Exclusion Function and Ohm processes. We are aware of them all the time. They seem to have valences within us: pleasant, unpleasant, mixed. And all going on all the time.

- But these are not what feelings are, any more than sunshine or rain is what weather is.
- It's only when Ohm Affect is matched to a thought potential target, that we have a feeling. And we can't have a feeling without a matching thought.
- This doesn't mean that we match thought and Affect "correctly". There's no rules about this. It's entirely free Subjective choice.

So, there's a narrative of an interaction between the world and the Self.

But that's only half the story. The other half is the reality checks: the way that our Subjective Mind is both infinite in itself, and utterly bounded by the *Architecture* in which it resides.

Like all sentient life, we have a Theta Θ function. This is a set of constructs which synchronise with the objective, external world. That synchronisation works through time.

If time was just a big universal blanket, or a force, then some 3rd thing would need to interface between <spacetime> and the Self. We have spent millenia looking for that 3rd entity in gods, spirits and anything else other-worldly.

Fortunately, the development of the material sciences has allowed us to see that there is no such thing as "time".

There are times. And we can see that time is a quantised phenomenon, just like matter.

Putting it simply, we are born with a clock. Kind of like your iPhone international clock, it can match time with lots of different time zones.

The world is filled with different times, and what the Theta Θ function does, is match time with the relevant time in the external world. This is what co-ordinates space.

Much of these last words, are for the next Chapter to explain. But what's important, at the end of this Chapter, is to appreciate simply this:

our ability to think and feel Subjectively depends upon an Objective Architecture, and Material Systems.

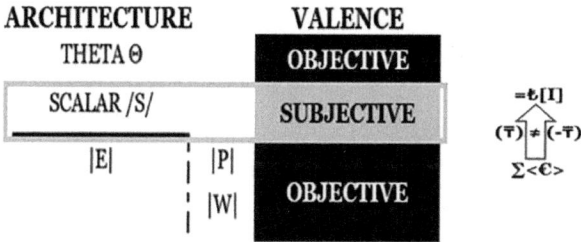

ARCHITECTURE	VALENCE	
THETA Θ	**OBJECTIVE**	$=t[I]$
SCALAR /S/	**SUBJECTIVE**	$(\top) \mid * \mid (-\top)$
$\mid E\mid$ $\quad$ $\mid P\mid$ $\mid W\mid$	**OBJECTIVE**	$\Sigma<\varepsilon>$

The Objective "layer" of Theta Θ is made up of Constructs: these cohere with the external world; they are also what allows our Subjectivity to tend towards <coherence>.

They give those random thoughts the structure of

515

language. Theta Θ is what allows us to communicate language-based information to each other.

Your internal, Subjective, self-reflections are a secret: but only up to a point. There are trillions of circumstances, which we can replicate by scientific experiment, in which you can't think certain things and can't feel certain things. And under which you're compelled to think and feel certain things.

Your Self is a prisoner of the *Systems Architecture*, which is what allows you to be a Self at all. And within the bounds of that *Systems Architecture*, you have the utter freedom of a continuum of infinity.

Mentation
How we can think governs what we can think
Emotion
What we can emote governs how we emote

The Self is a paradox: but only partly a secret.

CHAPTER 3

TIME

We have discussed aspects of | T | ime in previous Chapters.

Now, we'll focus on | T | ime. In the big picture of the matrixial Self, we see | T | ime like this:

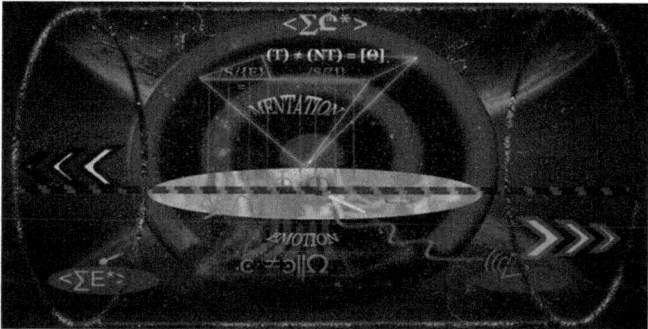

In *Matrixial Logic*, Chapter 7, we gave a full account of this vital element of the matrixial universe. It is the fulcrum of our Self in its objective relation to the | W | orld.

In this Chapter, we restate the essential concepts of Chronal Field Theory. We then focus on how CFT allows us to understand how the Self is an identity, in synchrony with the external | W | orld.

SECTION A: |T|IME CONCEPTS

1.   Chronon Field Theory

In this Segment, we reiterate key principles of Chronon Field Theory.

The basic unit is:

[*Chrone* (ɔ^n)] [and ≠] [*Anti-Chrone* (nɔ^n)]

Plural: *Chronons*

Each Chrone (ɔ) is a perturbation in a *Local Chrone Field* ("LCF"). Each LCF is created by its Contents (eg currents within the sea of visual perception). These LCF's are Chronal Tensor[207] Fields.

Chronal Equations

The basic equation is:

$$(ɔ^n) ≠ (nɔ^n) \mid ♨^n$$

(ɔ^n)	≠	(nɔ^n)	|	♨^{n}
Chrone	meets	Anti-Chrone	mutually 'annihilating'	Creating a temporal "gap"

This equation is a *Chronogap*. But this is an inferred theoretical state-change only.

---

[207] a multi-dimensional array

Time presents in space only as Events, with the potential to become Nodes:[208]

$$(Ɔ^n) \neq (nƆ^n) \mid \text{♘}^n \, [\text{LCF}^1])$$
$$\neq$$
$$(Ɔ^n) \neq (nƆ^n) \mid \text{♘}^n \, [\text{LCF}^2])$$
$$=$$
$$<\sum \text{♘}^*>$$

Nodes of course interact with currents in infinity Δ^n. Thus manifesting more perturbations $(Ɔ^n)$ and $(nƆ^n)$.

To explain the mutual annihilation $\mid$ concept:

- Chronons are not energy or mass and not carriers of energy or mass.
- They are spatial modifiers. They are the manifestation of what is not matter or energy.
- We are using the word "meet" figuratively. What we mean is that a chrone becomes co-ordinate with another chrone, thereby creating a space-time event: $<\sum \text{♘}^*>$
- At this point, the time "wall" in each chrone is "destroyed" by the other wall.
- This creates a temporal gap (a fissure), which allows the reconfiguration of spacetime.

This can be visualised just like the "quantum foam" of the universe. Where perturbations represented by quarks (with plus and minus charge) are being created

---

[208] upon interaction with an Infinity ∞ of Moments Δ^n

and annihilated. Or by the QED model of particles and anti-particles being mutually annihilated. These are approximations by analogy.

Time is neither mass nor energy, but is the product of both. Upon a chrone ≠ anti-chrone event ♛, the chronons "exhaust" each other.

Returning to the quantum field example, we would not characterise the "appearance" of a Q^+ as $(ↄ^n) \neq (nↄ^n) \mid ♛^n$. Rather, that Q^+ is a Node $<\sum♛^*>$: a composite of Chronogaps.

Don't worry about what these equations mean, for now. How we use them will become clear in following segments.

2. |T|ime Is Quantised

As the Chronal equation states:

$$(ↄ^n) \neq (nↄ^n) \mid ♛^n$$

This is, at first glance, a surprising formulation.

Now that readers are becoming familiar with ML equation formulation and manipulation, it appears strange that the equation for time is not couched in $(A) \neq (-A)$. After all, what could be more intuitively a flow of Moments Δ^n in Infinity ∞ : than Time?

The reason is simple: and deeply counter-intuitive to

everyone who has grown up in western traditions of culture and science.

Time is not a flow. It is not a river. Time is a series of beats. And not even the same beat. There are different beats, contingent upon the state of matter in which time manifests.

Matrixial Logic, Chapter 7, sets out in detail the scientific support for the proposition that | T | ime is quantised.

3.   *Chronon Field Synapses*

In the Annex, we will meet the new neuroscience of mind. A physical explanation, based on empirical data, of *where in the brain Chronon Field Synapses subsist and of what material they are made*.

Our world is *Fields*. They are the foundation of everything. This is a common enough viewpoint in the the material sciences: electromagnetism, QED and so on.

The "sea" in which <spacetime> events[209] occur, can be viewed as a Vector Field:

> A vector field in the plane (for instance), can be visualised as a collection of arrows with a given magnitude and direction, each attached to a point in the plane.

---

[209] local spacetime: see later

There are *chronological localisations within Vector Fields*

Events in a Vector Field are cognised under Scalar Field Axes: /S/{E}; /S/{I}. In physics, a Scalar Field is defined as:

> a field whose value at a particular point in space and time is characterized only by a single number.

Now, we can't use the "number" concept, except as a placeholder.

Theta Θ operates as a tensor field:

> As a tensor is a generalization of a scalar (a pure number representing a value, like length) and a vector (a geometrical arrow in space), a tensor field is a generalization of a scalar field or vector field that assigns, respectively, a scalar or vector to each point of space.

In Chronon Field Theory, we refer to *Chronon Field Synapses*.

Thus:
- Each Chrone ($\supset$) is a perturbation in a *Local Chrone Field* ("LCF").
- Each LCF is manifested in its Contents (eg the currents within the sea of visual perception).
- These LCF's are Chronal Tensor Fields.
- Chronal Tensor Fields interact at Chronon Field Synapses

4.   *Matrixial Time Machines*

Each of us operates a collection of "clocks".

While this succession of | congruence | events will occur under the same process for each of us, we will each undertake that process at different speeds: in different durata of times.

There's a dog in the kitchen. Nancy registers seeing the dog at a different "time" to Nick. They can both agree to feed the dog at 12.30 pm. That does not in itself create some objective time, nor is it a reference to an objective time. It is a mutual synchronisation of activity by reference to a form of time measurement.

What we need to disassociate, are the concepts of: (i) "reality"; and (ii) "time as an objective frame of reference". It is precisely this assumed association which has caused so much philosophical trouble, for 2,500 years.

Nancy processes the (now past) visual image of the dog in (say) 50 milliseconds.[210] Nick takes (say) 65 milliseconds. These are psychometric facts: matters of reality.

We don't notice them, in ordinary daily life. But when the car heads towards the dog in the road at 60 mph, such that the vehicle is covering 88 feet per second (0.88 feet

------

[210] in her Subjective /S/{E} axis field

per millisecond): then the /S/ timing difference of 15 milliseconds between Nancy and Nick does matter. Did doggy manage to just evade the edge of the car bumper, or not?

In this scenario, we have no difficulty in agreeing that the different /S/ time perceptions of Nancy and Nick map onto reality.

But: on what basis do we arrive at this agreement?
How can our subjective, individual, sense of time, map onto the temporal order of reality?

Because we each have a matrixial time machine.

Recall that the basic Chronal equation is:

$$(\text{Ɔ}^{\,n}) \neq (n\text{Ɔ}^{\,n}) \mid \text{℔}^{\,n}$$

$(\text{Ɔ}^{\,n})$	$\neq$	$(n\text{Ɔ}^{\,n})$	$\mid$	$\text{℔}^{\,n}$
Chrone	meets	Anti-Chrone	mutually 'annihilating'	Creating a temporal "gap"

This equation operates in the Theta Θ Chronal Tensor Field, but not in the /S/subjective continuum. The operation of the Chronal equation is the time machine by which Self synchronises with external reality.

In the following Segments. we'll experience it in action.

5.   *Temporal Synthesis*

We are accultured to seeing time as a flow of Moments Δ^n in Infinity ∞.

We can accept relativity theory, which privileges the speed of light and makes frames of reference relative to light speed. So that time dilation and spatial contraction, and so on, can accommodate the necessity for light speed to remain constant in the universe.

Quantum experiments have revealed increasing problems with the relativity model, not least in the tangled matter of entanglement.

/S/ Times

For now, let's draw closer to home:

Experience: Flicks
Just look around the room you're in
or Look out of the window.

You can move your gaze (field of view)

You can sense yourself making "snapshots" of whatever you're seeing

Just carry on

Now:

- Count the number of times your mind makes a snapshot

Stop

<u>Discussion</u>:
(1)   You can't.

The visual saccades model has been known for over a century.[211] We see, not as a visual continuum, but in little flicks: like still frames of a movie.

Although the basic saccades phenomenon is not in doubt, questions have been raised about the reliability of reference models, using the concept.[212]

What's important for the current analysis, is the fact that you can't keep count of the number of times your mind makes a snapshot.

This is because you are trying to count in your /S/ ubjective mind. But /S/ operates under an equivalence function, not as a calculator.

Time, for your /S/ubjective <self> is just another thing. You can compare time intervals, and estimate equivalences.

---

[211] For a useful review, see https://www.ncbi.nlm.nih.gov/books/NBK10991/
[212] Is the eye-movement field confused about fixations and saccades? A survey among 124 researchers Roy S. Hessels Diederick C. Niehorster Marcus Nyström Richard Andersson Ignace T. C. Hooge Published:29 August 2018 https://doi.org/10.1098/rsos.180502

The common sense element of this is not new information. We all get that we have our own times. That they vary all the time. Sometimes a minute drags slowly, sometimes at lightning speed.

Time, for the Self, just seems to be whatever we experience it as feeling like, from time to time.

The common sense view of time, as Selfs perceive it is right: and fundamentally wrong.

The /S/ continuum includes an endless procession of senses of times. These are realities for the /S/<self>, as is everything else in the /S/ continuum. But they have no synchronous relationship to temporal quantisation in |W|.

This is, of course, the standing problematic of time. There are clocks in the world, which measure "objective" time. Then infinite numbers of "subjective" clocks inside us, that aren't really clocks at all: just effervescences of temporal-like senses.

Yet, we are in time, and we are born with the capacity to synchronise Self |T|ime with |W|orld |T|ime.

Theta Θ |T|ime
This *Experience* is vital to understanding Θ Synchronised |T|ime.

Once you awake to this understanding, the rest is just filling in the analysis of implications.

Experience: Noming
Preparation:

- Google "30 bpm"
- choose a metronome (YouTube or any will do)
- Make sure the Metronome has a seconds time clock counter
- Be ready to press Play (don't Play yet)

You will then have an audible 30 beats per minute: one beat every 2 seconds.

Test that you can hear the beat.

A 10 Beat takes 20 seconds: check the time from 0.00 on your YouTube clock (your YouTube clock will show 18 seconds of count: that's because the next Beat occurs on the 20th second).

Activity:
Step 1:

- get one finger ready: to tap on the table, or your leg
- play the metronome
- try and tap your finger in time with the Beats

Discussion:

(1)   Unless you trained as a music student, or gymnast,

you find this very hard.

(2)   You seem to get "lost" between the beats.

(3)   You feel like you are waiting for the sound, then tapping: but anticipating the next beat seems like an accident.

Step 2:

Close your eyes and focus

Engage You$_2$: your Theta Θ brain function

- get one finger ready: to tap on the table, or your leg
- play the metronome
- try and tap your finger in time with the Beats

Discussion:

(1)   Now, it seems easy.

(2)   You feel like there is an automatic synchrony between your finger and the audible Beats.

(3)   It's almost like "You" are not there at all: like some other person is tapping out the Beats and you're just observing.

Recall the *I-Pen Experience* ("IPE"). It's the same You$_2$ feeling.

Step 3:

Now: ***turn the metronome sound off***

Close your eyes and focus

Engage You$_2$: your Theta Θ brain function

- get one finger ready: to tap on the table, or your leg

press Play [spacebar or mouse]

and
- play the metronome, *silently*
- tap your finger in time with the Beats
- for 10 Beats (18 seconds of time)

Press Stop [spacebar or mouse]

Now: check the YouTube clock counter.

Discussion:
(1) Now, it seems easy.
(2) You feel like there is an automatic synchrony be-
     tween your finger and the audible Beats.
(3) It's almost like "You" are not there at all: like some
     other person is tapping out the Beats and you're
     just observing.

This is evidence, not proof. It's evidence that we have two
completely different internal "clocks":
- effervescing our Scalar /S/ subjective times
- creating our Theta Θ Chronon Field "objective" time
- interacting with |W| at Chronon Field Synapses

You can practice on your phone by downloading an App

like *MIDI Rec.*[213] Repeat Steps 2 and 3. Use the piano keypad (with or without sound). Reset to 0 each time. You can film the playback with a phone screen recorder App. So, you can check if you are hitting the key at the correct 2 second intervals. Then, try it with different metronome beats.

It is the Theta Θ clock which is able to synchronise with the YouTube second counter. That counter is of course a digital representation of the "second" determined by the "atomic clock".

New studies conducted over the last decade, in the wake of the Libet Experiment,[214] provide scientific support for just such Theta Θ clock function:

Results from Emmons et al. (2017) suggest that such ramping activity encodes self-monitored time intervals. This hypothesis is particularly pertinent given that self-monitoring of the passing of time by the experimental subjects is intrinsic to the Libet et al. (1983) experiment.

If time is a flow, a "river", then two rivers can never mix, without losing their flow integrity. They can be bridged, but that is to create a form in alienation from the rivers.

But where time is not a flow, but a quantised apparition of $(\mathfrak{O}^n) \neq (\mathfrak{n}\mathfrak{O}^n)$ |, then each Event $\mathfrak{C}^n$ can *synchronise* with its negation in Nodal *annihilation*:

---

[213] a free App

[214] *Readiness Potential and Neuronal Determinism: New Insights on Libet Experiment.* Karim Fifel. Journal of Neuroscience 24 January 2018, 38 (4) 784-786; DOI: 10.1523/JNEUROSCI.3136-17.2017

As the Chronal equation states:
$$(\mathcal{C}^n) \neq (n\mathcal{C}^n) \mid \mathcal{C}^n$$

In the *Noming Experience*, you felt that │annihilation happening. Review the history of your head and go back into the *Experience*. Or just repeat the *Experience*.

You will sense that each synchronised Beat (which is an │annihilation) seems to "reset" your internal counter to zero (0). You feel liberated to feel the next │annihilation. You can sense "when" it is coming.

It is not your /S/<self> which is doing the sensing. It is your Ohm Ω function: more on that later.

The quantised property of time, in the world and in your head, explains a perennial mystery: how animals can act in unison. For example: birds in flight.

Since birds do not have a Scalar /S/ field,[215] there is nothing to "get in the way" of the operation of the avian version of a Theta Θ type axis. Thus, the birds synchronise their Theta Θ time. Time, speed and distance are intrinsically relational. The individual bird in a flock of birds does not need to know "where" is "now", at every moment: merely to have the same "now" by reference to the same metronome, as the other birds in a flock.

---

[215] will, if they do: it is very small and <coherent> compared to humans

6.   *Matrixial Synchronics*

The *Noming Experience* has been validated, as a repeatable and verifiable experiment. Such that Theta Θ axis "clock" and "clocks" in the external world may synchronise: and such that this is a scientific datum.

Let us call this the Theta Clock Observation ("TCO").

The TCO tells us that, for any time event $<\sum \mathfrak{C}_1>$, there can exist a time event $<\sum \mathfrak{C}_n>$, such that the two events can assume a Nodal value (+ / -) in any configuration of $|\Leftrightarrow|$

Thus:

- Your $<\sum \mathfrak{C}_1>$ can configure with the BPM $<\sum \mathfrak{C}_2>$, in a [= 0] configuration of $|\Leftrightarrow|$
- Your $<\sum \mathfrak{C}_1>$ can configure with the YouTube $<\sum \mathfrak{C}_3>$, in a [= 0] configuration of $|\Leftrightarrow|$

Since every human alive has a Theta Θ clock: Your $<\sum \mathfrak{C}_1>$ can configure with $<\sum \mathfrak{C}_x{}^n>$, of any other human, in a [= 0] configuration of $|\Leftrightarrow|$.

What this entails is that (by analogy) an orchestra can play without a conductor: no baton being required to be waved by the hand of god, nor by any universal Lorentzian[216] time.

---

[216] or Einsteinian

That relativistic time is subject to dilation, does not render it any the less a universal constant. Indeed, that was the position which Einstein fought for before and after the infamous Solvay Conference of 1927.

We arrive at a description of the universe which is much less counter-intuitive, and much more useful than QED, or relativity.

Let's spend some moments describing the Matrixially Synchronic universe.

(1)   There exists within the elements of any system, the potential for synchronic configuration: at Chronon Field Synapses.

(2)   Until the potential is actualised, the system is open and chaotic.

(3)   Actualisation can occur between Local Chrone Fields: (i) by conscious will, for those entities possessed of such;[217] (ii) by genetically determined behavioural gestalts;[218] (iii) by circumstantial imposition;[219] (iv) by interactions of categories (i) to (iii).[220]

(4)   Upon actualisation, [=0] configuration of $\left| \Leftrightarrow \right|$ occurs: or to put it more accurately, the arising of [=0] configuration of $\left| \Leftrightarrow \right|$ is exactly actualisation.

(5)   Actualisation occurs without any universal flow or

---

[217] human beings
[218] animals
[219] the inanimate universe
[220] for example, in a 2-split quantum apparatus

account of time т.

(6)   Indeed, the idea of т is antithetical to TCO actualisation.

(7)   There is no single temporal mode of TCO actualisation. Each is a form of the forms of its interaction (reference the Nodal formula).

(8)   Any form of forms has an apparitional property, which partly accounts for the illusion of "time". (That which completes the account is discussed below).

Let "H" stand for any human being^n.

(9)   Any H has potential to actualise $[(\supset^n) \neq (n\supset^n) \ | \ ]$ with any other H^n.

(10) Such actualisation creates a $\sum H$ temporal frame of reference $|T|$, which is fixed in some externality.

(11) Externality is any function of Substance extended in spacetime.

(12) In other words, $|T|$ is not an abstract or non-contingent emergence or property.

(13) Nor is $|T|$ an Infinity ∞.

(14) $|T|$ is a succession of annihilations. That which lies between $|T|^n$ is no kind of order, but Chaos [=C].

(15) That Chaos [=C] may be granted apparitional form: as anything. That apparitional form is freely culturally contingent.

One can take the view that quantised matter creates quantised time, or vice versa, or that both are emanations of something else.

Rather than getting bogged down here in that debate, the important take home for understanding Self, is that we are not merely prisoners of arbitrary /S/ubjective senses of times.

We are temporally "plugged in" to the matrix of external |T|ime, as it manifests in material processes and events in the |W|orld.

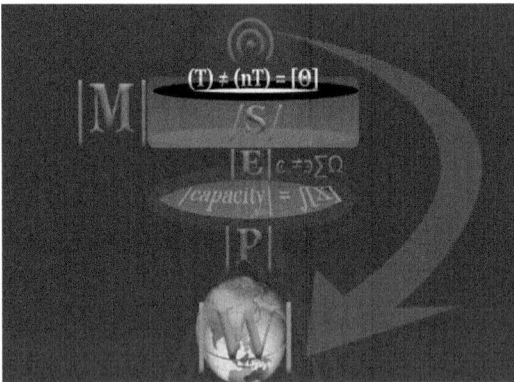

We saw this graphic in the previous Chapter. Now, we can appreciate its significance as a matter of |T|ime

7.   *Two Timing*

This brings us to the realisation that there are two sorts of "time" which we experience:

• Subjective time in our Scalar /S/ axis field
• Objective (in the sense of externally synchronic) time, in our Theta Θ Chrone field.

Our "subjective" time, is the time which actualises in our personality matrix.

- what makes a film pass quickly for one H and interminably for another
- what makes the summers appear shorter as we age
- our very perceptions of ageing

By contrast:

- Objective (externally synchronic) time $|T|$ is quantised.
- It is the quantisation of time which accounts for the precepts of relativity, and for entanglement in quantum theory.

It is also that quantisation which allows us to cohere with external time.

In other words, quantisation, which for 100 years has seemed to furnish only counter-intuitive advances into unreality, is the simple foundation of the ultimate proof of our own subjective reality.

Our "objective" time, is not just something that we engage though Matrixial Logic *Experiences*. These *Experiences* are merely deployed in order that we can externalise our perception of what occurs automatically. In every moment of our lives.

From our moment of birth, our Theta Θ Chrone field carries the potential to be actualised in interactions with the world.

Imagine two children running around. They move chaotically, in relation to each other, and the world. Then, without necessity of communication, they engage in synchrony of the Theta Θ Chrone field in each of them.

Now, they co-ordinate in time, and thus in movement (velocity and distance). They have created space-time: a frame of reference. Without observing or corresponding to any outside "clock" measuring any universal "time".

That which was chaotic has become determinate, in the mutual frame of reference of $<\sum \mathfrak{C}_1> [=0] <\sum \mathfrak{C}_2>$. That $[=0]$ Nodal point is itself an externality, by reference to which all of space and time can, in its infinity of moments Δ^n, become bounded: but only in reference to that $[=0]^x$.

Each other $[=0]^n$ creates its own spacetime. Thus a continuum of spacetime appears, but only as apparition of its elements, not as a thing or force in itself.

Entanglement Ideas

Why can't we travel faster than the speed of light C? Because any velocity creates its own frame of reference $[=0]$ which binds the time in which C can subsist. So, in fact, we can in a sense travel at super-luminal speed, but the time which is available for us to do that reduces ultimately to Planck time.[221] We can chase our own tail but the faster speed we

---

[221] or something of that order: see the papers referenced above

achieve, the more foreshortens the tail we are chasing.

If this be so, then the calculations of relativity remain in effect.

We simultaneously glimpse an answer to to the fundamental problem of quantum mechanics. There are waves and particles, as entities with $[=0]^x$ time function, which, when actualised to a different frame of reference $[=0]^y$, subsist in that actuality differently to the initial observation.

The entangled photon are not communicating at super-luminal speed ($= D/T$). It is that their quantised time $|T|_0$ is necessarily different to the $|T|_{+\backslash-}$ which is the frame of reference of the equipment.

That equipment, being local to the observer, appears to fall within the same frame of reference: although at the Planck scale level, is actually not.

To put it another way, т is not a singular phenomenon. т subsists both as quantised Substance relations in [E], and as unquantised Process infinity ∞ in [I].

When we bring these т subsistences together, we create new time {t}, which is a simulacrum of [E] $|T|_0$ (in this experiment).

But this is a process in nature and in the macro-world. We can experience it. We have had that experience it in

Noming and will again in *Ropetime* and *TimeCart*.

Thus, rather than an Everett "many worlds" interpretation, in which the wave function invests the entire universe, producing infinite numbers of new universes at each interaction, we have something much simpler. And more coherent with observation.

There are simply "many times" $< | \mathbb{C}^n >$, each extinguishing upon the advent of the next:

$$(\mathsf{כ}^n) \neq (\mathsf{n}\mathsf{כ}^n) \ | \ \mathbb{C}^n$$

Successive extinctions:

- preserve multiplicity, which avoids the requirement for Schrödinger wave collapse

yet

- do not result in that cumulation of hypothetical states, which makes the many worlds interpretation so distasteful to many.

All we are doing in small-particle experiments, is dealing with phenomena so close to the Planck scale interaction of the speed of light, and the size of the particle, that the gaps $< | >$ become so small that the phenomena appear to violate FTL law, and thus instantiate non-locality.

But they don't do either. On this basis, it can be said that Einstein was right all along, for the wrong reason.

It lies at the level of preliminary suggestion, at this stage, to submit such a radical re-interpretation in operation of the Schrodinger wave equation. But it works. Fundamentally, we are able to explain why the insertion of any "observation" appears to collapse the wave function.[222]

It is not because the superposition of particles in a probability wave (the spread of which cannot be determined), is collapsed.

It is because the interposition of the observation[223] actualises temporal state $\{<\sum \mathfrak{C}_1> [=0] <\sum \mathfrak{C}_2>\}_z$ which is different to the initial temporal state $\{<\sum \mathfrak{C}_1> [=0] <\sum \mathfrak{C}_2>\}_a$ and is different not on any scalar axis, but a new and entirely distinct $|T|$ time.

One could analogise this and say that the Bohmian pilot wave interpretation works, and without non-locality, if one substitutes a conceptualisation of $<|\mathfrak{C}^n>$, for the pilot wave. There can then, of course, be non-locality in the trivial geographical sense of simultaneity at a distance: but that is only simultaneity from the FoR of the "observer", not within the temporal FoR of the entangled particles.

Indeed, we end up with the best of Everett and Bohm. Interactions of quantised temporal FoRs provide:

- the same operator function as Pilot Waves plurality,
- thereby preserving the wave function, but via extinction rather than multiplication.

---

[222] or rather, doesn't: instead a different Chronal Field is instantiated
[223] the 2-slit device

What's more, the divide between the quantum and the classical, and indeed the cosmological, disappears. It is no longer needed. The same mathematics of $|\mathbb{C}n$ inequality function can[224] describe each plenum.

Let's consider the journey of two tennis balls:[225]

(1) they are each poured from a single tin, from the same factory, down an incline plane.

(2) at $|T|_1$ each ball has a temporal state $\{<\sum \mathbb{C}_1> [=0] <\sum \mathbb{C}_2>\}_{a\,b\,c\,n}$

(3) at the split-screen, that creates a Node for potential event $|T|_1$.

(4) there is now actualised a new $|T|_2$.

(5) ball hits screen, creating a new $|T|_3$.

(6) 2nd ball undergoes the same process.

(7) the split-screen acts like the YouTube beat-meter and You in the *Noming Experience*: there is actuated the same temporal actuation $|T|_2$.

(8) 2nd ball now shares in that temporal actuation, when it hits the screen.

We could express this in other words:

• the split-screen actuates a specific Chronon Field Synapse, in interaction with subject Events.

• Local Chrone Fields are "carried" as Chronal Tensor Fields by each of the balls, and

• actuate at Chronon Field Synapses.

---

[224] it is thought: but not yet proven
[225] this is a surface-skimming explanatory; not an analysis

To continue the analogy, the split-screen interaction "coats" all balls (that have the same elementary properties) with the "impressum" of that new null $|T|$ field [=0]. That is why the balls manifest an apparition of the "coating" at the final screen.

The Bell inequality is still preserved by non-randomness in non-temporal qualities of the entangled particles.

This further explains why the added imposition of moment measuring devices "cancels the interference": because we are trying to image a ghost.

- The $|T|_z$ state of even a single particle simply does not exist in the $|T|_x$ state in which our "camera" is operating.
- Not least, because our visioning is by definition occurring at a different lightspeed C than the reference object. And so on, for the imposition of the screen.

These are not probability functions, as probability assumes a single $|T|$ frame of reference. This explains why, without "normalisation", probability functions tend to infinities: that which is a $|T|$ frame of reference does not, without an intervention, submit to any other $|T|$ frame of reference. Each is contingently independent of the other.

The difference with Self, is that it can function in a domain of choice and will. You do not have to join the dance. Non-conscious nature admits of no choice, only contingency.

This datum explains also why the "observational" actualisation of different $|T|$ states came to be (mis-) associated in popular culture with some consciousness interaction. That which is non-conscious cares not the least whether we do, or do not, observe.

By our conscious actions, we can so effect external states of affairs such as to actualise different $|T|$ states. But effect requires material intervention and imposition.

A further matter which arises from the *Noming Experience* is the multi-chronologic nature of time $|T|$. We notice the 2 BPM pattern and have to engage Theta Θ with deliberation, because it is not a pattern we are used to.

There is no reason to think that, in the universe, there exists some supra-regulatory "beat". We have good reason, from empirical physics investigations, to consider Planck time as a minimum unit of $|T|$ quantisation.

Beyond that, we have no obvious basis for assuming that the contingent event time $|T|^n$ of any events correlation, is the same. There are obvious inferential reasons for assuming that it isn't.

This is helpful. It is what makes the detection of Theta Θ $|T|$ so accessible with a simple *Noming Experience*.

SECTION B: SELF | T | IMES

1.   Emotional Future, Subjective Past
Look at anything in your room, or outdoors.

It's not there now. It's never there now. Because, for the /S/ subjective <self>, there is no now.

Say the object you're looking at is 12 feet away. Light is taking around 12 milliseconds to reflect from it and enter you eye. Process of information through your visual cortex then takes around >50 milliseconds.

If that object were on the moon, it would take around 1.25 seconds for the light to reach your eyes. It takes 499 seconds (1 AU) for light to travel from the sun to earth.

Whatever you see, or sense, is a past event.

Experience: Bell
Visualise a front door bell button.
A front garden path leads to it.

The door bell is connected by wires which distribute signal to various parts of the house.

The signals fire, when the doorbell is pushed.

Step 1:

A finger moves to press the doorbell
- what is the "now" in this Scene?

Discussion:
(1)   You probably said: at the moment the finger pushes the bell button

Indeed, this seems to be the only sensible version of "now" in this Scene. But this is an external, imagined view.

Step 2:
You are in the attic room.
A bulb will light, if the doorbell button is pressed

A finger moves to press the doorbell
- what is the "now" in this Scene?

Discussion:
(1)   You probably said: at the moment the attic room bulb lights up.

This seems to be the only sensible version of "now" in this Scene. Yet you know that the attic "now" has a past. There was some other "now" at which the bell button was pushed.

There's an idea within *Interoception Models*, that we create predictive maps, in our /S/ubjectivity. That these link the doorbell push "now" and the attic "now". Let's see

Experience: Pasting
Step 1:

- Look around you at the room you are in.
- Take a few relaxed normal breaths.
- Relax.

Now:

- Imagine, there in the room, a paperclip
- Just let the paperclip be in the room
- Move it around. Make it bigger and smaller
- Feel your control over it

Stop

Discussion:
(4)   The paperclip appeared.
(5)   It was easy.

Step 2:
Now:

- Look around that room

and:

- See the paperclip there in the room

Now: Focus

> *Make the paperclip appear 5 Seconds in the Past*
> in the room

Stop

Discussion:

(1)   You can't do it

(2)   The harder you try, nothing happens.

(3)   You actually feel like you're frozen.

Step 3:

Now:

- Look around that room

and:

- See the paperclip there in the room

Now: Focus

Make the paperclip appear 5 Seconds in the Future

in the room

Stop

Discussion:

(1)   This time, you can kind of do it

(2)   It's like a ghostly image of your the paperclip that you definitely can make appear in the present.

(3)   But it feels emotionally unsettling.

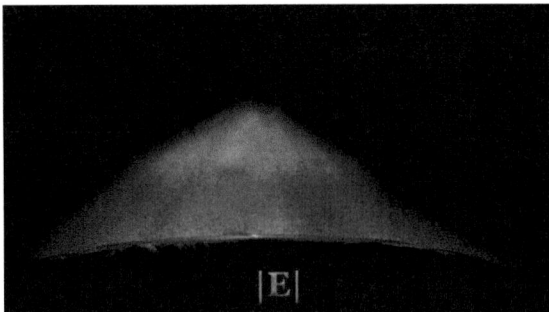

Our | E | motional processes are like the headlights on a car: they are directed towards the future.

Our | E | *Systems Architecture* is oriented to the future:

- <senses> sense the doorbell push: Then
- Exclusion Function convers kinetic energy, into <signals> output; Then
- $\sum\Omega$ function qualitises | EF | output, and refers in distribution <Nodes> to | P | and / S /; Then
- / S / receives.

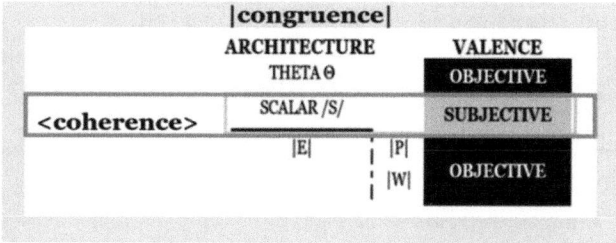

	congruence		
	ARCHITECTURE	**VALENCE**	
	THETA Θ	OBJECTIVE	
<coherence>	SCALAR /S/	SUBJECTIVE	
	|E|	|P|	
		|W|	OBJECTIVE

Recall the *Systems Architecture* of Self:
We can now add the final layer, which illustrates the *Chronal Congruence* of Θ⇔ | W | :

	congruence			
	ARCHITECTURE	**VALENCE**		
	THETA Θ	OBJECTIVE	♻ n	
<coherence>	SCALAR /S/	SUBJECTIVE		
	|E|	|P|		
		|W|	OBJECTIVE	♻ n

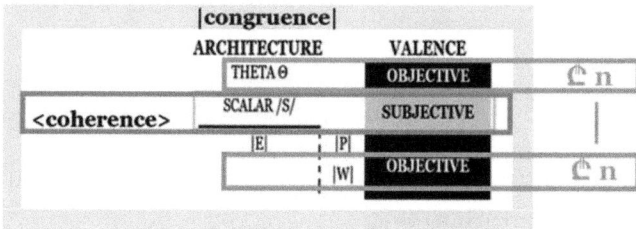

Now, compare the / S /ubjective perception of | T | ime. This is a rear-view mirror:

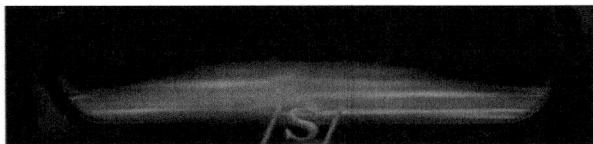

The perspective of /S/ is illuminated by the past lights from |E|.

Experience: Thirst

Imagine yourself being really thirsty.

Maybe imagine that feeling in a context of being in a desert, or in the middle of the ocean on a raft.

Just allow your imagination to sink into the feeling, until the feeling becomes powerful in you.

Step 1:

- think of 5 seconds in the Past
- think of a cup of water
- locate that cup of water at that 5 seconds in the Past

Now:

- try to see yourself reaching for the cup and drinking

Stop.

Discussion:

(1)   You can't reach the cup

(2)   It's like there's an invisible barrier stopping you from reaching it

Step 2:

- think of 5 seconds in the Future

- think of a cup of water
- locate that cup of water at that 5 seconds in the Future

Now:

- try to see yourself reaching for the cup and drinking

Stop.

Discussion:

(1)   Now it's easier

(2)   There's no barrier. It does feel "blurry", as if you can't quite complete the reaching / drinking experience.

This *Experience* illustrates the *temporal* role for emotion:

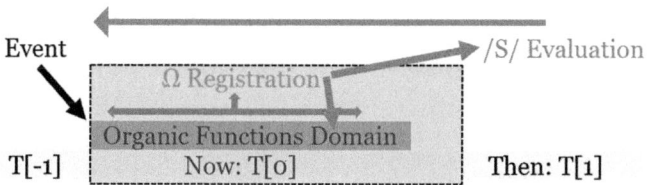

(1) You self-simulated your Exclusion Function: $/S/ => |EF| => \sum \Omega$

In Step 1:

(2) your $/S/$ evaluates backwards in time: so envisioning the 5 seconds Past cup is easy

(3) but: your Ω cannot "see" the Past

In Step 2:

(4) your $/S/$ envisions a present state projected as a "future" state

(5) your Ω functions as a referral-to-the-future (your /S/ evaluation) function. In other words, your Ω is always *forward looking* in its referral function.

(6) so, your Ω can engage with that fictive "forward" experience

Once we understand and acknowledge that /S/ can only function as an evaluation of past experiences,[226] we appreciate the necessity of the |Exclusion Function| sieve.

Without it, we would see everything and nothing. An indiscriminate, undifferentiated landscape of the past. With referential axes or points: a landscape from which we could not learn.

2.   *There Is No Now*

We began Chapter 2, *Globe*:

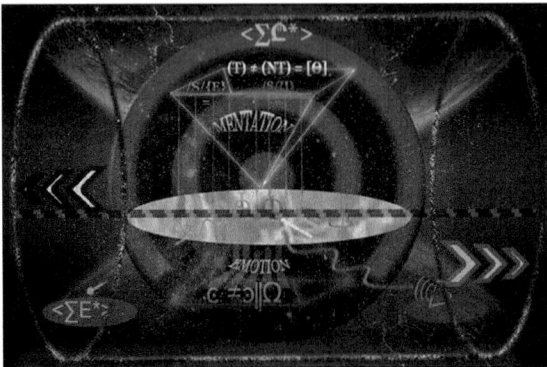

---

[226] *past* including the domain of the millisecond

$$\text{ꟸ} \quad \text{/S/\{E\}}^{(\epsilon)}$$
$$\Phi \quad \text{/S/\{I\}} \qquad \sum\Omega \quad (T) \neq (nT) \quad = \Theta \approx>$$
$$\langle\sum\text{₵}^*\rangle \Leftrightarrow (\supset {}^n) \neq (-\supset {}^n)|\text{₵}^n \Leftrightarrow \langle\sum\text{₵}^*\rangle$$

This is the map. With the primary equations for the map dynamics: the equations which provide the compass.

We can now see the purpose of the equator line, dividing the Globe of Self, with the tri-band arrow heads:
- our |E| "spins" forwards, always oriented to the future
- our /S/ "spins" backwards, always oriented to the past.

The Myth of Now

It's quite disconcerting to realise that our entire /S/ ubjectivity is limited, in the *Systems Architecture* of Self, exclusively to the past.

Certainly, we can know facts about the past, about:
- historical events
- autobiographic events.

These facts are important to us. But we do not shape our /S/ subjective daily lives around them. Such facts may be important to our cultural identity.

But it's not what we mean when we report:
- "I'm feeling "xyz"; or
- "I felt "xyz"; or
- "I remember feeling "xyz".

These are the feelings, noted in our temporal /S/ subjectivity, which seem to drive us as personalities. It is to these feeling states, that psychology and CBT looks, in order to analyse and remedy.

This has all the analytical rigour, and the same prospects of success, as line fishing in an ocean, while blindfolded. Even if the weight on the line tells the analyst there's a catch on the hook, there's no way of knowing what it is. And no way of replicating the procedure.

Those spiritual awakening gurus, and other CBT theorists, who counsel "living in the now", have plainly never encountered a doorbell system.

We cannot live in the "now", if that is supposed to mean that moment when |W| interacted with |E|. That is always in the past, whenever our /S/ gets around to considering it.

We can't even live in a "now" in within the /S/ continuum. Every [t]hought is itself a temporal emanation. Infinity is a landscape of /S/ cognition, not |T|ime.

What these misguided analysts are actually counselling, is that you try to turn those headlights around. Instead of illuminating y0ur future, you should seek to make them beam into your imagined now.

That is doubly misguided:

- it cannot actually work: it's like trying to turn your feet backwards, or invert breathing in and breathing out
- the attempt to do it, give rise to many serious psychological problems.

Indeed we try reverse | E | motional reference all the time, in our /S/ imagination. We use a fictitious "emotional now reality" around which to arrange an order of {idents}.

Where we realise the process of {identation} which we are undertaking, it becomes harmless, and thus pointless. But, if we persist in telling our | Exclusion Function | that we will experience <thirst>, we can get | E | responses.

These are *Unfaithful Reflections*, as we noted in Chapter 2, Section C(2)/9. However, since /S/ operates under an equivalence function, we can assign a false reflection to a category of the true, if that's what we want to do.

There is no "now". Not for our /S/ubjectivity.

The Reality of Now
Chronon Field Synapse is constantly being created in:

- | W | => | E |
- | P | => | E |
- Θ => | W |

We see the latter in Chronal Congruence of $\Theta\square$ | W | :

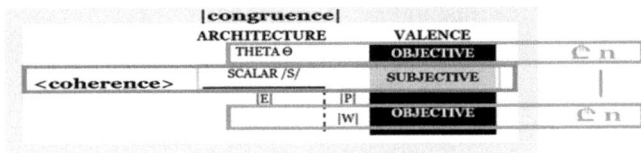

We have already explained the Architecture of this Chronal System.

You experienced it in *Noming*. Now, you can witness the difference between /S/ | T | imes, and Chronal Congruence.

Experience: TimeCart

Setup:

Get your by now familiar blank sheet of paper

Get ready to imagine a load of paperclips

Step 1:

- Pour a load of paperclips over the sheet
- Cover the sheet
- Until you have a mound of paperclips

Now

- Count the paperclips

Stop

Discussion:

(1)   You can't.

(2)   You try, but after the first few items, the whole
       thing started phasing in and out of your focus: it
       was like manipulating ghosts.

Step 2:

Setup:

You will need:

-    a metronome, as in *Noming*
-    set it to 1 BPM
-    to imagine a little conveyor belt taking the clips
     away from the pile, one at a time.
-    a pad and pen: you are going to be making / / /
     marks on the pad, in rows
-    to be ready to switch your You_2 on, as in *Noming*

Now:

•   Pour a load of paperclips over the sheet (don't try to keep
     a count as you do it)
•   Cover the sheet
•   Until you have a mound of paperclips

Next:

•   set your metronome beating
•   switch on You_2 and match your [T] Node, with the BPM count

Now:
- count each paperclip away
- keep the pile in your head
- make a / mark on your pad each time

Do this for as many beats as you like

Stop

Discussion:

(1)   This is actually very easy now

(2)   The only effort is to keep the pile in your head

(3)   But you can see it reducing

An extraordinary thing is that, you can even project forward. It's like you can run the beat as a fast-forward movie, and see the clips disappearing one by one: while still keeping a count.

You're using synchrony: $<\sum ₵^{n}>$, to arrange your interaction with the material world.[227]

The succession of Chronogaps between each extinguished $<\sum ₵^{n}>$ Chronal Node, is part of the fabric of that organisation. These are the experienced manifestations of Matrixial Synchronics.

---

[227] The *Experience* would obviously work just as well with real paperclips

3.   *Temporal Psychotectics*

Psychotectics is a new word in the therapy lexicon.[228] It signifies the science which involves:

> *using the Architecture of the Self, in conjunction with the logic of reality, to allow therapeutic intervention.*

In this Segment, we want to demonstrate, through Experiences:

- more of the reality of your Theta Θ Local Chrone Field; \<synaptic\> with
- $|W|$ Local Chrone Fields.

This lays the groundwork for understanding being and becoming, as matters of: philosophy, neuroscience and psychology.

With this understanding, we can then see how *Psychotectics* can be used to effect therapeutic interventions.

Recall the *Noming Experience* from Section A, Segment 5. We showed that your Theta Θ Local Chrone Field is able to synchronise with an external time beat $|T|^n$ at a procession of Chronon Field Synapses

The very reason you can do this is because this is not a scalar universe, ruled by scalar time: a metric. Ours is a living universe, operating dynamically through forms of inequality.

---

[228] Googling it beings up some strange stuff from *Star Trek*

You don't need to be able to plot every point of the compass on a scientifically Olympian map. You simply need to be able able to match your "now" to any other "now: and you can. We've proved it.

Certainly, we can map points and paths of expectation. That's what quantum field theory, and life experience are for. But the map is not the thing, nor even representational of the thing. It expresses the structure of the gaps between things. The map is what scales inequality.

/S/ Dimensions

In the next *Experience*, we're going to explore more limitations within the /S/ continuum.

Remember the rubric:

>   *How we can think governs what we can think.*

Experience: Maptime

Keep your eyes open.

Just look around the room you're in.

Look to your left

Preparation:

- Imagine yourself, about 2 arm's lengths away. With Silhouette You ("S-You"), having its back to you. Standing upright, on the floor.
- You can be perfectly aware of the surroundings of S-You
- Walls, and other such obstacles don't exist for S-You. It can walk through any of them, just like a ghost

Step1:
- Looking at the back of S-You
- Make S-You move in straight line forward

Stop

Discussion:
(1)   S-You won't move
(2)   It's like trying to push S-You through drying wet concrete.

Step 2:
- Looking at the back of S-You

Now:
- Feel the distance between You and S-You
- See that in your mind's eye like a thick, stiff, length of rope

Now
- Place that rope length in front of S-You
- Make S-You move in straight line forward
- Repeat

Stop

Discussion:
(1)   S-You moves immediately to the end of the rope length
(2)   At instantaneous speed

Step 3:
- Looking at the back of S-You
- See again the rope length between You and S-You

As before in Step 2
- Place that rope length in front of S-You
- Make S-You move in straight line forward

Now
- With S-You at the end of a rope length, from any previous position of S-You
- Make S-You come back Half (½) a rope length

Stop

<u>Discussion</u>:
(1)   S-You won't budge
(2)   The best you can do is get a shadow of S-You to hover at the half-way mark, but then disappear, under the force of S-You

Step 4:
- Looking at the back of S-You
- See again the rope length between You and S-You

As before in Step 2
- Place that rope length in front of S-You
- Make S-You move in straight line forward

Now
- Snap your fingers and make the rope length disappear

Stop

Discussion:

(1)   S-You instantly snaps back to its starting point.

Congratulations: you have just experienced being an electron.[229] Your self-movement was quantised. S-You was not able to travel at all, until you provided the natural unit of movement: an S-You Length ("SYL").

Once provided with SYL, S-You could travel, in SYL steps, all the way to infinity. But S-You could only move, forwards or backwards, in SYL steps. And, once you removed the SYL frame of reference, S-You transmuted instantly back to base state.

Theta Θ Local Chrone Fields

Now, let's see what happens when Θ LCF interact <∑🕐> with I W I LCF.

Experience: Soundspace

Keep your eyes open.

Just look around the room you're in.

Look to your right

---

229   that's a quantum joke

Preparation:
- Prepare S-You, just as in *Maptime Experience*
- Google "30 bpm"
- choose a metronome (YouTube or any will do)
- Be ready to press Play (don't Play yet)

Step1:
- Looking at the back of S-You
- If you start thinking of the rope-length, wash that out of your mind
- Make S-You move in straight line forward

Stop

<u>Discussion</u>:
(1)   S-You still won't move
(2)   It's still like trying to push S-You through drying wet concrete.

Step2:
- Looking at the back of S-You

Press Play
- Allow yourself to fall into the rhythm of the beat
- "switch on" You$_2$ see the *Noming Experience* in Chapter 7
- Nod your head, or tap your finger in time

Now:
- see S-You
- just focus on S-You
- whatever you experience
- just keep focusing on S-You

Discussion:

(1)   Without you even thinking of it, S-You moved

(2)   S-You just started "walking", in time with the Beat

(3)   On every Beat, S-You moved another step

(4)   It was always exactly the same distance

(5)   Yet you weren't thinking out the distance, as in a
       rope length: it just happened on its own

So, now distance and speed are being quantised by packets
of time | T | beats. Welcome to quantised momentum.

You can re-run the *Soundspace Experience* in your head. You
can see your in awareness that there is no possibility you
could make S-You take half a step. Or walk backwards.

Do now re-run the *Soundspace Experience* in your head.
You can see in your awareness, that if the Beat speeded
up, then so would S-You. But, if the Beat got to infinity ∞,
S-You would freeze.

Space or Time: Not Both

We mentioned in *Globe* that <spacetime> is an awkward
concept, which has to be used with care.

In this *Experience*, we see that Local Chrone Fields in
interaction <∑🜨> create (or manifest, if you prefer)
<spacetime>: but that the annihilation of Chronal | gaps |
does not allow for supervention of <spatial> dimensions.

Experience: Ropetime

Keep your eyes open.

Just look around the room you're in.

Look left or right

Preparation:

Get your Beat metronome ready

Get S-You in place

Get your rope length from S-You ready

Step 1:

- Press Play
- Move S-You
- Try and use the rope-length in time to the Beat

Stop

Discussion:

(1) It doesn't work

(2) You can use the rope length

(3) Or: use the Beat

But:

(4) You can't do both

(5) As hard as you try, it all just become "mush". Everything collapses

(6) S-You won't move.

As Dirac effortlessly put it:[230]

---

[230] Dirac, P. A. M.. *The Principles of Quantum Mechanics*. (1930) (4th Ed 1957). At 4: *Superposition & Indeterminacy*. The Author's appreciation of Dirac's style does not commit the Author to endorsement of all the substance

> The non-classical nature of the superposition process is brought out clearly if we consider the superposition of two states, A and B, such that there exists an observation which, when made on the system in state A, is certain to lead to one particular result, a say, and when made on the system in state B is certain to lead to some different result, b say. What will be the result of the observation when made on the system in the superposed state? The answer is that the result will be sometimes a and sometimes b, according to a probability law depending on the relative weights of A and B in the superposition process. It will never be different from both a and b.

> The intermediate character of the state formed by superposition thus expresses itself through the probability of a particular result for an observation being intermediate between the corresponding probabilities for the original states, not through the result itself being intermediate between the corresponding results for the original states.

This is all elementary: yet philosophy, neuroscience, and psychology (in particular) seem not to have caught up with the necessary implications.

In *Psychotectics*, we take these scientifically robust elements of Self understanding, and apply them in therapeutic frameworks.

4. | T | *Ime, Becoming and Being*

Classical Accounts in philosophy, psychology and to a lesser extent neuroscience, don't have an integrated approach to the | T | ime.

Yet | T | ime is the grand unifying factor which integrates the Self into universal reality.

Let's use this graphic:

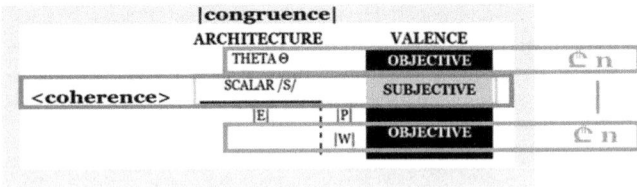

|congruence|	
ARCHITECTURE	VALENCE
THETA Θ	OBJECTIVE
SCALAR /S/	SUBJECTIVE
|E| |P|	
|W|	OBJECTIVE

<coherence>

Contingent Objective |T|imes

Any of these interactions takes place at a definite <spacetime>:

|W| => |P|

|P| => |E|

|E| => /S/

When, according to any clock, any of these events happens, is a matter of contingency.

As a simple example, your alarm clock goes off at 8am. The sound waves interact with your auditory system: |W| => |P|. Your auditory senses pass the input to your |Exclusion Function|: |P| => |E|. Your $\sum\Omega$ refers qualitative output to your mind: |E| => /S/.

Each of these events takes place at a definite point in <spacetime>. What point that is depends, of course, upon the temporal frame of reference, in accordance with relativity.

Atemporal /S/ Continuum

Neither the creation of {idents} nor their combinations, is a <spacetime> event *capable of being perceived as such within /S/*. There is no objective reference frame within the /S/ continuum.

All we can do within the /S/ continuum, is use {idents} as an approximate frame of reference for other {idents}.

We can, of course, look to an external I T I ime measure: a clock. But that external clock cannot tell us when any {identation} is taking place.[231]

Our /S/ubjective sense of time is the temporal continuum of our *Becoming*.

This Becoming {identation} of <time> does not work, in our minds, as real objective time does. Objective I T I ime is a procession of temporal annihilations: of gaps <♚n> I <♚n>.
/S/ {identation} of time is a matter of approximated repetition: of equivalences sought to be {idented} between <then> and <now>.

We need to believe in these equivalences. It's a condition of sanity: of being able to function as a thinking being. But the {ident} mirrors which we use in our heads, to orient ourselves, between or on either side of them, are

---

[231] which is what the Libet experiments, and the updated versions, actually tell us

not a reality of |T|ime. They are the reality of our /S/ continuum within the Self *Systems Architecture*.

Classical Accounts were unable to establish "bridges" between /S/ and the domains of the objective. Except by materialist reductionism, which seeks to state /S/ only in terms of the objective; and unavoidably implicates itself in dualism, in the attempt.

With the benefit of the matrixial *Systems Architecture* of Self, we know better.

Objective Chronal ∑₵ Synapses

The *Experiences* in this Chapter have demonstrated to you, how your |M|entation does actually synchronise with the external |W|orld.

That <₵ⁿ>|<₵ⁿ>, the occurring of Synapses between Local Chrone Fields, is a reality.

We have spoken before in the the metaphor of /S/ being in a "sandwich" between layers of objective reality. In the same way, /S/ is sandwiched between layers of objective temporal reality.

All the events which happen to the Self, as an entity, happen contingently, in externally referable |T|imes: from the time of our birth. From that time, our Θ functions, allowing each of us to synchronise with external |T|imes.

This *Self Synchrony* is the fulcrum of our *Being*.

As *Beings*, we are ever in objective synchrony with | T | ime and the <space> which relates to it. This is how a Self has the quality of <I>.

We *Become*, as Self only in <Me> <time>. We are Self in *Being*, only as <I> in temporal synchrony.

There cannot be one without the other. The differences are visible in the *Systems Architecture* of Self. It is chronological synchrony which allows that Self to exist, and which coheres the material subsistence of that reality.

PART (2)
ENGINEERED TO PERFECTION

CHAPTER 4

ELECTRICITY

(1) Geography

In Part 1, we established the *Systems Architecture* of Self. We explained how |T|ime is fundamental, providing not merely correspondence, but |congruence| between Self and the world.

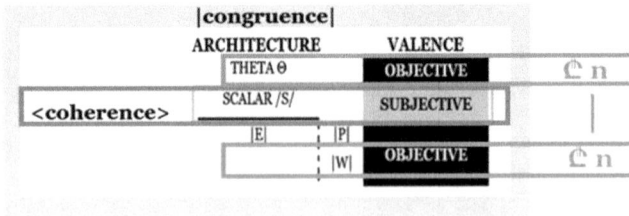

|congruence|			
ARCHITECTURE		**VALENCE**	
THETA Θ		**OBJECTIVE**	ℭ n
<coherence>	SCALAR /S/	**SUBJECTIVE**	
|E|	|P|		
	|W|	**OBJECTIVE**	ℭ n

In this Part, we look at the *Processes* which underlie the operation of the /S/ continuum.

The first of these is the Anxiety Soothing Rhythm (ASR"). Functioning of the ASR is fundamental to the science of *Biomorphics*.

This is what allows therapeutic interventions, which have remedial effects:

- instantly
- without hypnosis
- without having to think directed thoughts
- without having to emote in accordance with directed thoughts.

The second is Coherence Quotient Dynamics ("CQD"), which we more commonly call "Slices Dynamics".

We covered these concepts in detail in *I Want To Love But… Realising The Power Of You*. In this Part, we want to locate those concepts within the *Systems Architecture* of Self.

So, this Part is not a diagnostic manual. It's a geographical guide.

(2)   The Anxiety-Soothing Rhythm ("ASR")
I Want To Love But… Realising The Power Of You, uncovered and explored the working out in our | E | motions and / S / ubjectivity of a natural cycle, with us from birth.

The core concept:

> *The Anxiety-Soothing Rhythm is a*
> *Learning Experience in Self-Balancing*

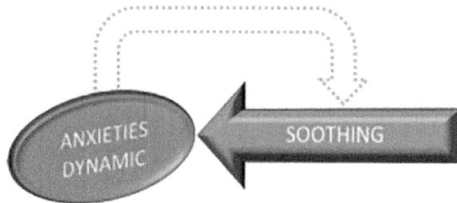

There's no good purpose in repeating here all the detailed analysis of this Process concept.

Instead, we want to focus on locating the ASR Process in the *Systems Architecture* of Self, so that it has a firm scientific basis.

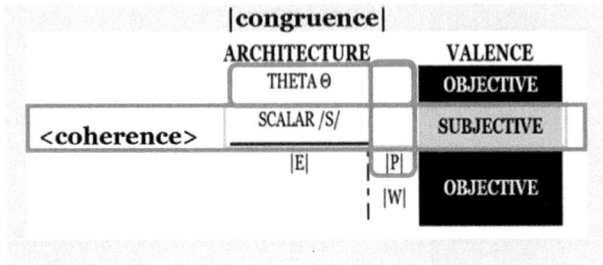

The ASR is a Process which links our organic | P | hysiology, with our Theta Θ domain.

The ASR is the dynamic which regulates the interaction between <Affect> and {identation}, under | congruence | .

The ASR acts through our /S/ ubjectivity, and at the same time effects order in it. This is not the sort of "order" we get by marshalling our {idents}. That's just piling bricks made of transparent jelly, one atop another.

Instead, with the ASR, we re-empower the essential internal Process of Self.

The ASR begins at birth. It's the way that neonates engage

their dynamic relationship with the world. A new born doesn't have a rich and varied emotional or intellectual lexicon. It's vital that a neonate be able to communicate its needs to the I W I orld: so how is that achieved?

Anxiety

Say baby is hungry. The stomach doesn't have a voice. So that hunger needs to activate an acting out by baby, to get attention.

In the *Systems Architecture* of Self:
<hunger> I P I => I Exclusion Function I =>$\sum\Omega$<€>=>/S/

Now, baby can't at this stage form any but the most basic {idents}. These formations come from experience, and the translation of experiences into equivalences.

So, <€>=>/S/ channels through very basic {idents} into a Θ<Construct>: <anxiety>. It is this channelling through from which a "chain reaction" of {idents} becomes created in /S/.[232]
<hunger> I P I => I Exclusion Function I =>$\sum\Omega$<€>=>/S/
$$>$$
$$(T) \neq (nT) = \Theta <anxiety>$$
$$>$$
$$\Theta|Ю|=|P|$$

In Matrixial Healing analysis, <anxiety> hasn't the same

---

[232] more in this later

meaning as its popular version. In popular culture, and in psychology / CBT, anxiety is seen as a problem.

As we'll see later, this is because psychological symptoms of disfunction between the ASR and the /S/{idents}, are being misdescribed as "anxiety" problems.

The reality is not that a person is suffering from excess "anxiety", but that disfunction between the ASR and the /S/{idents}, is manifesting in other problems: ranging from manias (panic attacks) to depression: and everything in between.

In the ASR, <anxiety> is a completely natural function. It's how the new born activates its necessary interactions with |W| (including the parent).

Recall how we explained that Θ<constructs> create an Ю interaction with |W|. Sort of like a virtual reality construct, which activates |P| responses to stimulus:[233]

> Theta Θ transmissions present a different virtual |W| to |E|. Theta Θ <Constructs> matches the actual |W| in spacetime synchronisation.

> We might say that the matrixial logic of the world |W| is processed in Θ, without the intermediation of /S/.

---

[233] Section D/(5) *Equalizing Reality*

The result is $\Theta \mid HO \mid$: a virtual world which is spacetime synchronised with $\mid W \mid$. It is from these <Nodes> that "dots" are created by the Exclusion Function.

There is no <potential> ($\leq \ni$) in Ohm $\sum \Omega$ which correlates to anything in $/S/\{i^n\}$. That's why you feel "emotionless" while You_2 is operating.

That's also why you have the feeling that <me> You_1 is struggling to stay quiet and not interfere. The space between the "ceiling" and "floor" of the $/S/$ continuum is being "squeezed". That part of Self which is <me> is being negated, overlooked. We don't like that.

The $\Theta \mid HO \mid$ assembly is "seamless" in the way that ordinary $\mid W \mid$ <Node>=> $\mid$ capacity $\mid$ is not.

Thus, in $\Theta \mid HO \mid$ <Construct> transmission, we are replacing our usual $\mid W \mid$ origin virtual reality experience, with another. The results we attain in doing that, can be astonishing.

> *We experience the world in a virtual reality.*
> *We can alter our virtual reality*
> *Which changes our experience*

But $\Theta \mid HO \mid$ transmission has a limited repertoire. We don't get originality, novelty, invention out of $\Theta \mid HO \mid$. We only get reality-consistent iteration. For animals, that's all they need to survive. For our human sanity, and creativeness, we need more. We need the subjective continuum

As you undertake *Biomorphic Experiences*, you'll understand in your Self, how all this fits together.

So <anxiety> is acting as a connection (via /S/) between |P| and Θ. The Θ<construct> is creating a |P| response:

- crying
- wriggling
- other baby acting out behaviours.

Soothing

Acting out results, sooner or later, in satisfaction of the baby's needs.

Now, if there were no mechanism to abate <anxiety>, a baby would become a self-destructive pressure cooker. The <anxiety> mechanism needs a reciprocal calming mechanism.

This is the <soothing> function.

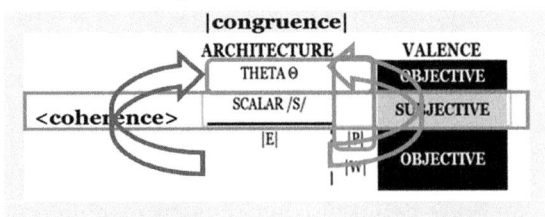

<anxiety> [orange] : <soothing> [green]

Obviously, <soothing> follows the same process pathway as <anxiety>:

<-hunger> | P | => | Exclusion Function | =>$\sum\Omega$<€>=> / S /

$$>$$

$$(T) \neq (nT) = \Theta \text{ <soothing>}$$

$$>$$

$$\Theta|Ю|=|P|$$

In matrixial logic, we have a reciprocal wave effect, operating at the core level of the | Exclusion Function |.

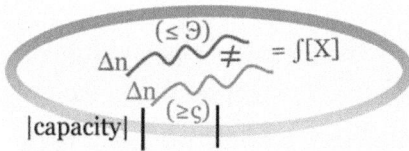

We said in Section B, Segment (10):

The *Temp Experience* also illustrates an example of:

Internals}			
=> from |P| or |S| Internal}		=> from |P| or |S| Internal}	
$(\geq\varsigma_1) \neq (\leq\Theta_1) = \int[x_1]$		$(\geq\varsigma_2) \neq (\leq\Theta_2) = \int[x_2]$	
>		>	
(€)	≠	(э)	= $\sum\Omega$

You used Internal}<Nodes> to generate $\int[x]$ outputs in $\sum\Omega$. This is a deeply important and interesting dynamic under the /S/ ⇔ | E | architecture.

When we explained the | Exclusion Function | in Segments (10, (18) and (19) of Chapter 2, Section B we focused on its quantised nature. The symbols (≥) and (≤) deliberately indicate an integer scale 0 to ∞.

Thus, the larger the <anxiety>, the bigger that <signal> (from 0 to ∞), so must respond the <soothing>.

The |P|hysiological origination of any <anxiety> reflex will obviously be different from time to time, even within the same system: say gustatory (hunger). And different again as between different reflex origins (hunger, absorption, excretion).

Even a newborn is not of course simply limited to these elementary functions. A newborn wants sights, touches, smells, sounds.

All of these involve different |P| systems. A magic of our Self *Systems Architecture*, is the operation of the |Exclusion Function| to transform all of these qualitative mixes, into <signal> interactions: reciprocal wave effects.

This of course entails that we have a (≤Ɔ)<anxiety>potential born into us. And similarly, a <soothing> potential.

Neonate science has actually been able to see these <potentials> in foetal development.[234] We are born with these <potentials> ready to activate.

[234] *Mothers and Infants and Communicative Musicality*. Stephen N. Malloch. DOI: 10.1177/10298649000030S104 Musicae Scientiae 2000 3: 29; Chapter 12 *From the Intrinsic Motive Pulse of Infant Actions to the Life Time of Cultural Meanings*. Trevarthen C. In: *Philosophy and Psychology of Time* (pp.225-265).

(3) | Congruent | Equalisation

A central rubric in *I Want To Love But,* was that <soothing> always equalises <anxiety>.

There's no point repeating here all those pages of analysis.

We know from our detailed analysis of Self *Systems Architecture* that equalisation if the mechanism of Theta Θ <Constructs>; while equivalence is the mode of operation of the /S/ubjective.

So, it's axiomatic that the ASR is effected by | congruence | of Θ | Ю | = | P | . This is what grants the ASR its power in Self.

This understanding is what allows us to intervene therapeutically. We simply devise behaviour copying models which trigger that ASR | congruence | .

This is how babies manage their interactions with their care environment. It's how a mature Self does it too: except that other things get in the way.

(4)   Learning

Neonate learning arises in the delay between <anxiety> and <soothing>, and in differences between expectation and satisfaction.

Just imagine a baby whose every need is satisfied instantly

and exactly in match with the baby's needs experience. Such a baby would never learn, because baby would not need to. In effect, baby would be stuck in a foetal life experience.

Using this graphic model:

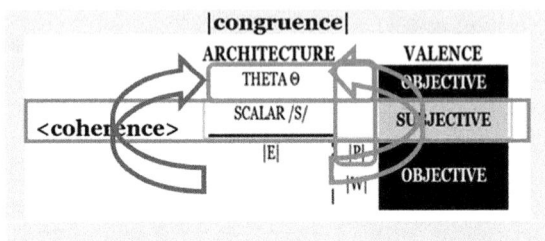

<anxiety> [orange] : <soothing> [green]

baby learning arises in the gap between <anxiety> and <soothing>. The <anxiety> process generates behaviours. /S/ develops {idents} from that generation.

You can feel that process happening, in real time, right now.

Experience: Ants
You're going to close your eyes, and breathe
You can stimulate your own Anxiety just by thinking about it.

If you put two fingers of either hand to the side of your tummy and press gently, this will help.

Now:
- Allow that anxiety to build inside you for a few seconds

Stop

Discussion:

(1)   You felt that familiar effect. It's like ants scurrying around inside the top of your head

This is a neurologically normal response to that <anxiety> stimulus. You're recapitulating what baby You does automatically.

Your /S/ is shuffling through {idents}. Trying to find an equivalence for the [=>∑Ω<€>=>/S/] which is coming up from |P|.

That scurrying "ants": that's your synaptic relays buzzing at hyper-speed, trying to find an {ident} solution. You are *learning*.

In this case, there's nothing to learn, because it's a false alarm. We triggered a <signal> increase in [<anxiety>|P|=>|Exclusion   Function|]   artificially, through *Biomorphics*.

By the way, your <soothing> response happened automatically, while you were reading that. The simple distraction of reading allowed Θ <soothing> |Ю|=|P|, to go into effect.

Both <anxiety> and <soothing> effect a "tunnelling" through /S/ from |P| to Θ. In baby You, that's easy. There's not much /S/ {identation} to interfere.

You may remember us saying: [235]

> Thus, in Θ|Ю| <Construct> transmission, we are replacing our usual |W| origin virtual reality experience, with another. The results we attain in doing that, can be astonishing.
>
> *We experience the world in a virtual reality.*
> *We can alter our virtual reality*
> *Which changes our experience*
>
> But Θ|Ю| transmission has a limited repertoire. We don't get originality, novelty, invention out of Θ|Ю|. We only get reality-consistent iteration. For animals, that's all they need to survive. For our human sanity, and creativeness, we need more. We need the subjective continuum

So, that ASR tunnels through /S/. In doing so, it stimulates the production of /S/{idents}. The ASR is not a heuristic in itself. It never learns anything. It just repeats, with naturally born regulation and equalisation.

But it's the ASR which provides the crucial dynamic for heuristic {identation} in /S/. The ASR stimulates self-learning.

Yet, in another central paradox of Self, it is that very creation of /S/ {identation} which creates the fundamental psychological need for <coherence>.

The perpetual search for that <coherence> is what leads to love, to genius, and the psychological disfunction.

(5)   Neonate Science
The central role of the ASR in early /S/ development has become well supported by neonate developmental science.

Let's take just two examples from a vast new field of research.

In *The Early Development of the Autonomic Nervous System Provides a Neural Platform for Social Behaviour: A Polyvagal Perspective*,[236] Stephen W. Porges and Senta A. Furman postulate:

> We present a biobehavioural model that explains the neurobio- logical mechanisms through which measures of vagal regulation of the heart (e.g. respiratory sinus arrhythmia) are related to infant self-regulatory and social engagement skills. The model describes the sequential development of the neural structures that provide a newborn infant with the ability to regulate physiological state in response to a dynamically changing postpartum environment. Initially, the newborn uses primitive brainstem-visceral circuits via ingestive behaviours as the primary mechanism to regulate physiological state. However, as cortical regulation of the brainstem improves during the first year of life, reciprocal social behaviour displaces feeding as the primary regulator of physiological state.

---

[236] Inf. Child. Dev. 20: 106–118 (2011) DOI: 10.1002/icd

The model emphasizes two sequential phases in neurophysiological development as the fetus transitions to postpartum biological and social challenges: (1) the development of the myelinated vagal system during the last trimester and (2) the development of cortical regulation of the brainstem areas regulating the vagus during the first year postpartum.

Colwyn Trevarthen and Kenneth J. Aitken, in *Infant Intersubjectivity: Research, Theory, and Clinical Applications*, [237] report:

We review research evidence on the emergence and development of active "self-and-other" awareness in infancy, and examine the importance of its motives and emotions to mental health practice with children. This relates to how communication begins and develops in infancy, how it influences the individual subject's movement, perception, and learning, and how the infant's biologically grounded self-regulation of internal state and self-conscious purposefulness is sustained through active engagement with sympathetic others. Mutual self- other-consciousness is found to play the lead role in developing a child's cooperative intelligence for cultural learning and language. A variety of preconceptions have animated rival research traditions investigating infant communication and cognition. We distinguish the concept of "intersubjectivity", and outline the history of its use in developmental research.

The transforming body and brain of a human individual grows in active engagement with an environment of human factors—organic at first, then psychological or inter-mental. Adaptive, human-responsive processes are generated first by interneuronal activity within the developing brain as formation of the human embryo is regulated in a support-system of maternal tissues. Neural structures are further elaborated with the benefit of intra-uterine stimuli in the foetus, then supported in the rapidly growing forebrain and cerebellum of the young child by experience of the intuitive responses of parents and other human companions. We focus particularly on intrinsic patterns and processes in pre-natal and post-natal brain maturation that anticipate psychosocial support in infancy.

---

[237] *J. Child Psychol. Psychiat.* Vol. 42, No. 1, pp. 3–48, 2001 Cambridge University Press

The operation of an intrinsic motive formation (IMF) that developed in the core of the brain before birth is evident in the tightly integrated intermodal sensory-motor coordination of a newborn infant's orienting to stimuli and preferential learning of human signals, by the temporal coherence and intrinsic rhythms of infant behaviour, especially in communication, and neonates' extraordinary capacities for reactive and evocative imitation. The correct functioning of this integrated neural motivating system is found to be essential to the development of both the infant's purposeful consciousness and his or her ability to cooperate with other persons' actions and interests, and to learn from them.

The relevance of infants' inherent intersubjectivity to major child mental health issues is highlighted by examining selected areas of clinical concern. We review recent findings on postnatal depression, prematurity, autism, ADHD, specific language impairments, and central auditory processing deficits, and comment on the efficacy of interventions that aim to support intrinsic motives for intersubjective communication when these are not developing normally.

We don't have to look far to find the neurophysiological pathway for the ASR. The vagus nerve features repeatedly in neonate development studies:[238]

The vagus nerve is a mixed sensory and motor nerve with many functions that include immune response, heart rate, digestion, and mood control. As the longest of the cranial nerves, cranial nerve number ten (CN X) travels from the brain to the abdomen, also innervating parts of the face, throat, and thorax, and acting as a sensory, special sensory and motor nerve.

Vagus nerve function is split into four groups according to the type of nerve fiber: sensory, special sensory, motor, and parasympathetic. Although primarily an afferent nerve that brings sensory information from the body to the brain, the vagus nerve is also an efferent (motor) nerve that brings messages from the brain to muscle. Smooth muscle control is regulated within the parasympathetic nervous system. The vagus nerve originates in the medulla oblongata of the brainstem:

---

[238] https://biologydictionary.net/vagus-nerve/

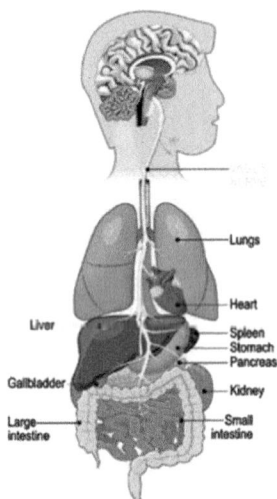

Recall the *Ants Experience*. Now you can see why, when we want to stimulate your <anxiety>, we have you place a little pressure at the base of your vagus nerve.

(6)   Biomorphics, <coherence> and |congruence|
Using the ASR to modulate your /S/ {identation} is one of the major elements of Biomorphics science.

Much of our individual psychological problems come from interference in the ASR.

To function with psychological health, we need to able to allow the ASR to do its work. That's a perpetual dynamic, with us every moment of our lives from birth to death.

The ASR dynamic allows /S/<coherence>, at the

perpetual price of decoherence:

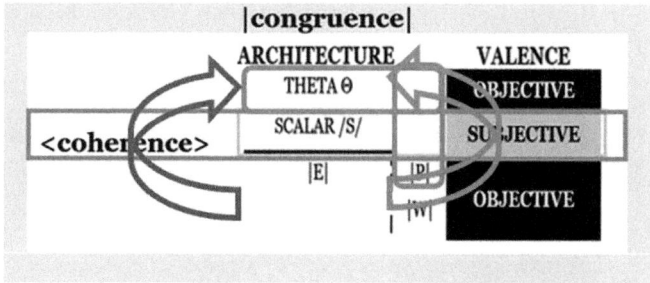

This dynamic is the core of what psychological science and spiritual learning seeks to describe as "Peace":

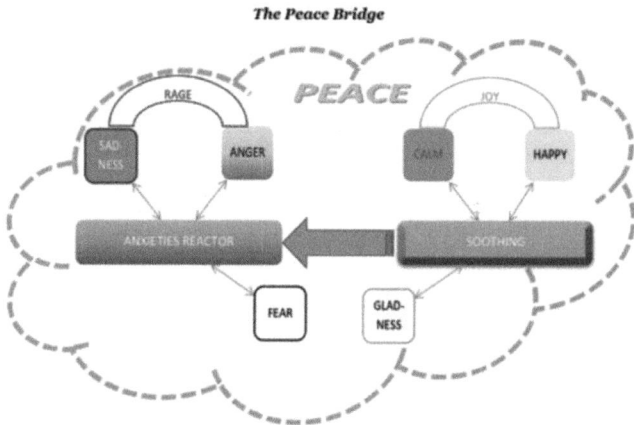

The Peace Bridge

Peace is not a place. It is an emergent idealisation in {idents} of the movement which occurs from one moment of <coherence> to another: a series of bridges.

The ASR lives in disturbance. By |P| tunnelling through /S/ to stimulate Θ<Constructs> which effect equalising Ю|P| interaction.

Within the *Architecture* of Self, /S/ is an infinite but dimensioned continuum: a layer in the "sandwich". /S/ is limited by the architectural conditions of its own infinity.

By contrast, |P| is in infinite dynamic with the universe. The body replaces all of its atoms over the course of every 7 years.

We can and do create disturbances in our sea of {idents}. That's what <T>{i^n} and <F>{i^n} consist of. Yet we seek to contain novel {idents} in frameworks of <coherence>. For a fascinating example, see the phenomenon of visual prism adaptation.[239]

When we experience difficulty in achieving <coherence>, then we resort to other devices. This is the route to psychological Pain.

Here, we need to differentiate between pain which us the result of physiological injury: a break, a burn. And what is often referred to as Emotional Pain.

---

[239] Li A. Experiencing visuo-motor plasticity by prism adaptation in a classroom setting. *J Undergrad Neurosci Educ*. 2008;7(1):A13-A18.

The Pain Gap

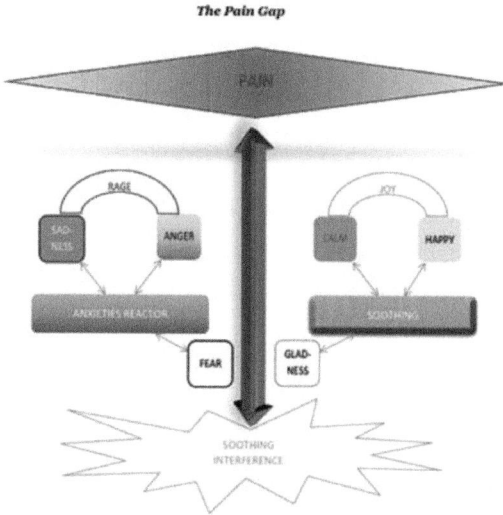

Pain is a place. Pain is failure of movement.

However, since both acts through signals in the I Exclusion Function I, the phenomenon of psychosomatic pain is as real to You, as externally attributable injury pain.

Indeed, it can be more enduring: many I P I hysiological injuries will heal, by themselves or with clinical treatment. But <coherence> induced pain is self-fulfilling.

It is an alignment of <coherence> to deal with life experience. In visual prism adaptation, special glasses invert left and right sight. Over some days, the wearer becomes used to the inversion. But then when the glasses are removed, a new <coherence> has to be established.

The wearer knows that it is "all in the mind". But that cannot stop the <coherence> function from orienting itself to sensory experience.

The fundamental dynamic of addiction issues lies in misaligned <coherence>. The problem is not the substance: it is the pain experienced by rigified alignment of <coherence>, which repeats a dynamic of discomfort: "emotional pain".

The substance is of use only to blot out the pain: to effect temporary <decoherence> by having neurophysical effects. These are, of course, only temporary, and with various substances produce diminishing effects.

In all of this, what is being lost is the natural born dynamic of the ASR. <anxiety> is not being allowed to regulate <Affect>. This prevents the <soothing> dynamic from engaging reactively. The result is a "frozen" place of Pain.

We see here another of the paradoxes of Self:

- Our /S/ubjective <self> layer needs to create and multiply {idents} in order to allow our Personality lattice to become whole: to become a <Me>.
- We perpetually seek <coherence> so as to shape that explosion of {idents}, so as to create the core {idents} of <Me>. In other words, to establish homeostasis of <self> recognition.
- Yet, it is that very dynamic which tends towards

dislocation and suppression of the ASR. We can see that most clearly in the journey from infant to maturity.

We judge maturity by capacity for self-control. Yet that type of control is secured through ASR suppression, using powerful cultural Mimetics.

This is not to suggest that the healthy state of <coherence> is at war with the ASR: that being an emotionally incontinent individual is a truer "self".

On the contrary, the attribution of /S/{ident} <coherence> to ASR activity, is exactly what best provides control: because that control arises dynamically from the process itself: without necessity for <coherence> of $<T>\{i^n\}$ or $<F>\{i^n\}$.

It's how baby You learns. It's actually how the mature Self learns also. It's the most powerful heuristic available to the Self.

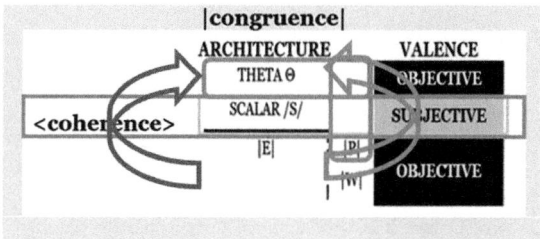

The science of Biomorphics concerns the location of pathways which energetically activate the ASR, without "challenging" <coherence>.

This recalibrates |congruence|. That re-assertion of the *Architecture* within which the /S/ continuum enjoys {identation} infinity, automatically alters the self-reflection of <cohered> {idents}.

It's not so much that Biomorphics alters {idents}, it alters the angles of their /S/ continuum Mirrors. That inevitably then alters the dynamic cycles of {ident} ideation: but from the inside, rather than attempts to do so from the outside.[240]

---

[240] in Talk Therpaies and the like

CHAPTER 5

STEERING

(1) The Slices of Personality ("CQD")

Another key concept in *I Want To Love But*, is how our personality is formed in a dynamic of 5 "Slices":

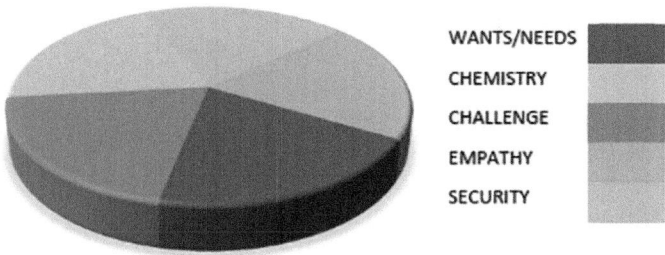

WANTS/NEEDS	
CHEMISTRY	
CHALLENGE	
EMPATHY	
SECURITY	

We give this the technical name of *Coherence Quotient Dynamic* ("CQD").

The 5 Slices are a way of understanding how the Anxiety-Soothing dynamic, and our individual interference patterns and habits, manifest themselves in our personality: and in our life choices.

The key concept here is dynamic harmony: not equality. A metaphor may be the gravitational harmony of differently size orbiting objects. The balance arises from their difference, not from a hypothetical equality.

Indeed, such is the basic law of matrixial logic: *inequality is Form.* The Personality Matrices which we can easily identify from different ordinations of the 5 Slices, are simply those Forms of CQD inequality.

(2)   Slices Cycle

We saw in the last Chapter how:

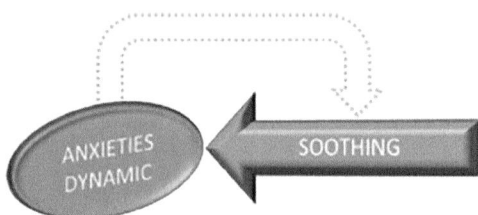

The ASR is the dynamic which regulates the interaction between <Affect> and {identation}, under | congruence |.

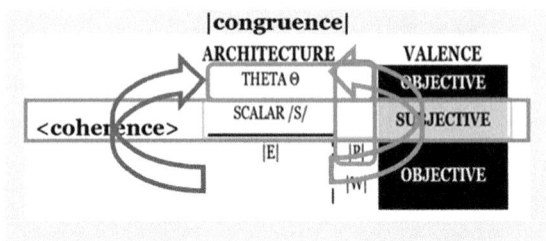

By empirical observation of reported <Affect>, {identation} and observed behaviour, we can by induction create a dynamic template: of how the Self steers.

We need to say at the outset that this dynamic template is a theoretical construct. It averages empirically observable tendencies. So it's not a scientific description of reality, as the ASR is. It's a dynamic model of ideas which relate to innate tendencies in the personality nexus.

That said, it is very powerful in therapy. It is the core of *Psychotectics*: techniques which involve recalibrating elements of the dynamic model of Personality. Not so as to control them: but to liberate them.

Psychotectics works through {idents}, as contrasted with Biomorphics, which works directly through the ASR and its innate function in *Systems Architecture* | congruence | .

Psychotectics assigns [<Affect>{identation}]] dynamics under model categories: the 5 Slices.

We can see, underlying the different Slices, the momentum of the ASR:

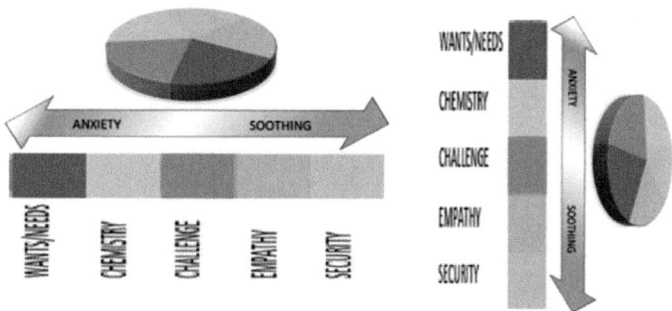

It is our elementary [needs], from birth, which engage the <anxiety> reflex. Satisfaction engages our <soothing>

response: equalised under *Architectural* | congruence |.

With the development of Personality: the <me> | <I> lattice, /S/ {idents} produce {wants}: complexes of self-stimulated <Affect> and cohering {idents}.

One can see some superficial similarity to Maslow's famous *Hierarchy Of Needs*. The problem with the Maslow hierarchy is that it consists entirely of ex post facto ideations of types in stasis. Or rather, moving from one homeostasis to another. It's the archaeology of personality, not a dynamic model for intervention so as to allow re<coherence> of personality under | congruence |.

We can see how Satisfaction signals are part of the Security slice. We have to learn when to start (or accept) a conflict, and when to stop: when matters are Satisfied.

When we are not Satisfied (which is always, after a Satisfaction event has passed), we Need or Want: and the Slices Cycle begins again.

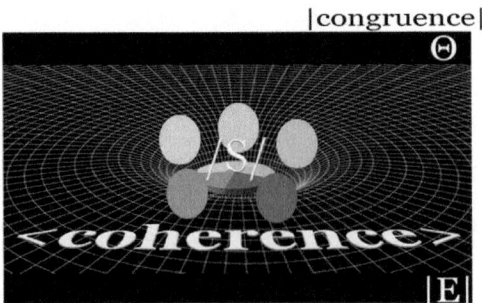

The Slices Cycle is how You live your life. Every moment of every day. Your Slices Cycle has been created since your first breath on earth.

It is unique to You, in your personality lattices. Yet that cycle demonstrates both continuity over time (which can be marked by discontinuity) and an averaging into the model Slices: under the "gravitational" force of the /S/ continuum innate need for <coherence>.

(3)   Autonomic Balancing
Our Slices dynamic is effected under the ASR:

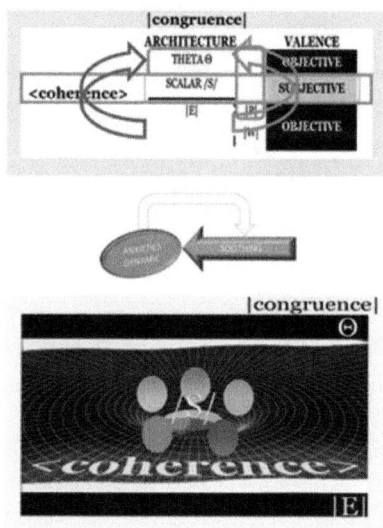

This is an *Autonomic Balancing*. It operates from the moment of our birth. It's how we neonates manage to survive at all.

This *Autonomic Balancing* is our primal and primary Self-survival mechanism. It ultimately involves the dynamic balance of our |Need| and |Security|:

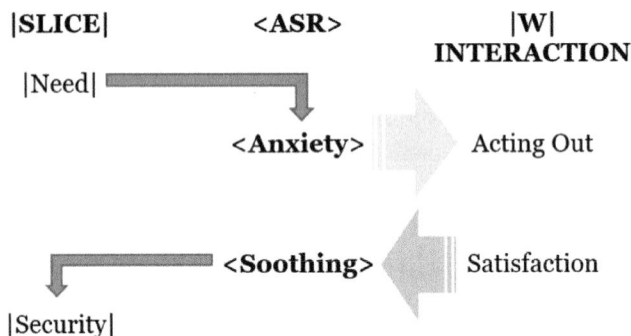

|SLICE|	<ASR>	|W| INTERACTION
|Need| ⟶		
	<Anxiety> ⟹	Acting Out
	<Soothing> ⟸	Satisfaction
|Security| ⟵		

You may notice an important asymmetry here:

- <Anxiety> is engaged by Primal Need (and very soon after birth, /S/ubjective Want).
- Both of these come from inside Self: although both of course can relate to contingent interactions with |W| and |P|.
- <Soothing> is engaged by external |W| interaction.

We are born with a functioning /S/ continuum. It is now established empirical neonate science that our /S/ is diffuse: unorganised.

As neonates, we have massive {ident} capacity, which is later subject to synaptic pruning. But we have limited {idents}. Our Mirrors exist. We inevitably project {ident} light at them.

- the projections are limited

- our {identive} proficiency in analysing the reflections, is also limited.

It is development in this capacity for light projection, and increasing proficiency in reflections analysis, which charts the path of our growth as <Me>.

We achieve, over time, trial and error, a reflective <coherence> in /S/.
We become in reflection.
We will consider this rubric in much more detail in the *Mirrors* Chapter, in this Part.

(4)   Para-Autonomic Balancing

This graphic:

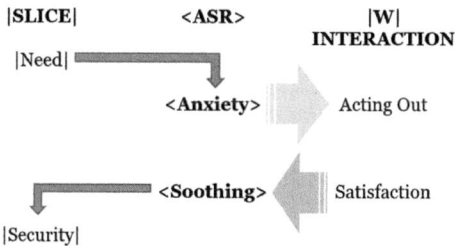

is able to represent any sentient life, which has ASR capacity.   This is why we are so readily able to see ourselves in other sentient creatures: we share the same primal pathways.

But there is much more going on in the human Self:

601

|P| <ASR>   INTER |W|
                        FACE   Acting
                                     Out

Hunger

        <Anxiety>   ΘIO   Objective
                                     Behaviour

        |SLICES|
        |Need|
|Chemistry|
|Challenge| /S/   Subjective
|Empathy| Response
        |Security| to
                             Stimulus

|W| |P| <ASR>
Supply

Objective   Satisfaction

                        <Soothing>

                        |SLICES|
                        |Need|
                |Chemistry|
                |Challenge|
                |Empathy|
                        |Security|

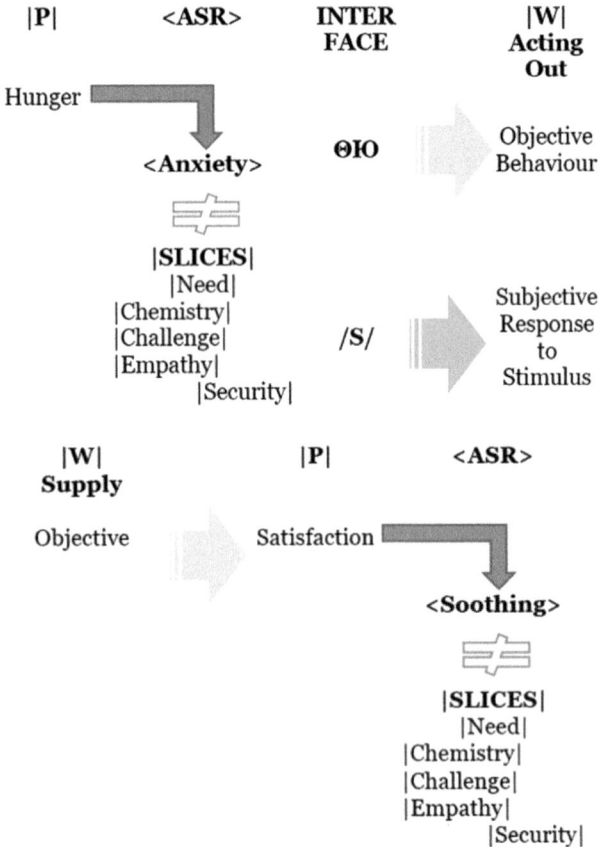

We are each born with obvious personality dispositions. This was obvious to the ancient Greek philosophers, as it is obvious today.

We describe the Slices dynamic as *para-autonomic*, because our /S/subjective {identation} can and does affect that dynamic.

Analytically, we reflect these differing dispositions in the 5 Slices dynamics.

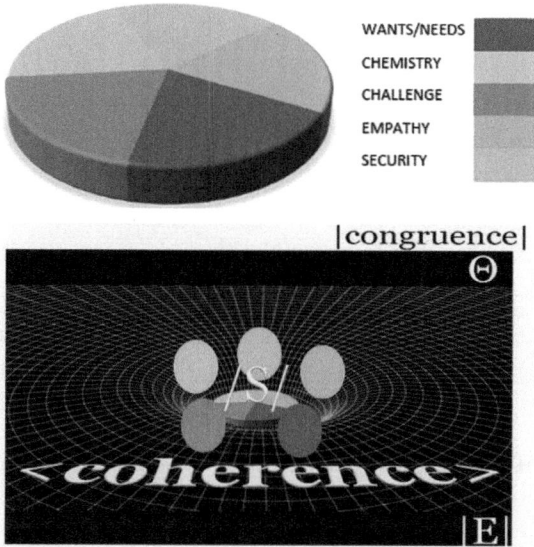

In our standard Slices graphic, we represent the Slices as having equal proportions.

This is for graphical convenience only. It would be a very odd state if each of the Slices were in equal proportion. Indeed, this would make dynamic change impossible.
Our Personality dynamic depends upon imbalance between its component Slices.

It is the different "weights" or "sizes" of the Slices relative to each other, which:

- anchor our Personality
- how we act out out Needs
- how we respond to Supply.

There's no objectively right dynamic balance. Whatever works for each individual, from time to time, works. And what works today, may not work tomorrow.

This is yet another reason why the objective prescriptions of classical psychotherapy are useless or harmful. These prescriptions stem from a failure to understand that the Self is born with a perfect self-balancing ASR.

The ASR acts with the para-autonomic Slices. The relationship between the Slices can be supportive of the ASR function, or get in the way.

Which of these is going on, is all that we need to concern ourselves with, as a therapeutic matter.

With understanding of the para-autonomic Slices dynamics, we can use therapeutic techniques to assist You to balance your Slices, as you need them to be balanced.

This is not about telling you to think or feel certain things. It's about devising experiences which allow you to use the self-reflective processes of your /S/ continuum Mirrors[241]

––––––––––––––––

[241] see later Chapter

to illuminate the gravitational forces between the Slices. If all in /S/ were unbounded infinity, then this task would be forlorn. But of course that is not the position.

/S/ is bounded by a Systems Architecture:

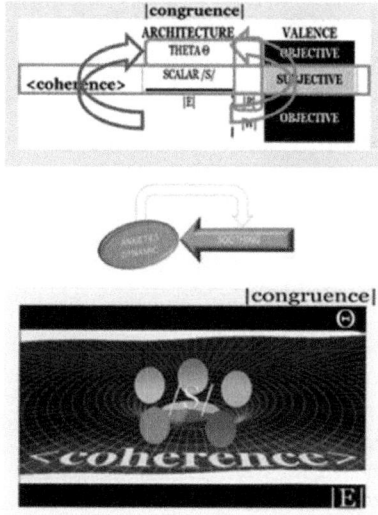

Primal Needs and primary Wants act through <Anxiety>:

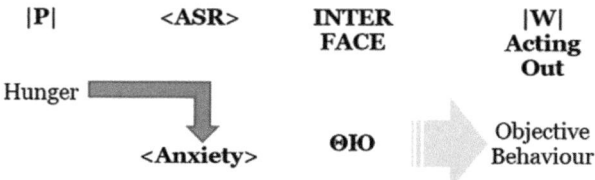

they impose <Coherence> in /S/, which allows their rapid propagation through "waves" of /S/{idents} into Θ.

Θ<Constructs> create Ю | congruence | with | W | and | P | .[242]

We can therefore call the acting out which accompanies this ASR process "Objective Behaviour".

In a neonate, there is not much more going on than this Objective Behaviour. In a 40 year old, under a life threatening situation, there suddenly comes to be little more going on, either.

The "more going on", in infant development, and then throughout life, is illustrated in this part of the graphic:

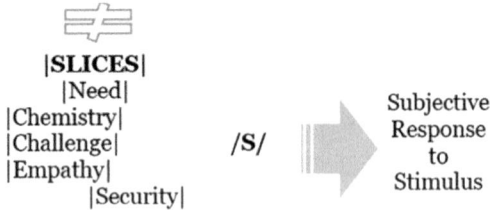

|SLICES|
|Need|
|Chemistry|
|Challenge| /S/   Subjective
|Empathy| Response
     |Security| to
                         Stimulus

Whether Objective Behaviour and Subjective Response work together constructively, destructively, or indifferently: well that's all human life right there. It's 7.8 billion universes of possibilities, changing moment by moment.[243]

---

[242] as explained in Part 2
[243]https://www.prb.org/2020-world-population-data-sheet/#:~:text=The%20 2020%20Data%20Sheet%20identifies,2020%20population%20of%20 7.8%20billion.

The same is true of the reciprocal ‚Soothing> side of the ASR:

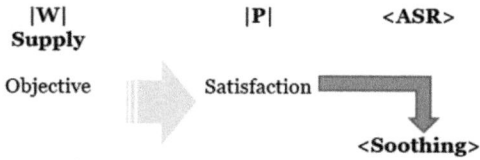

|W| **Supply**	|P|	<ASR>
Objective	Satisfaction	
		<Soothing>

In primal Needs, |P| is satisfied (or isn't). That's an objective reality:

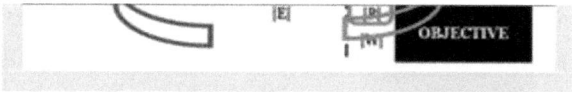

How /S/ responds to (€)=> is subjective reality. With 7.8 billion universes of possibilities, changing moment by moment:

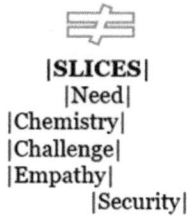

|SLICES|
|Need|
|Chemistry|
|Challenge|
|Empathy|
|Security|

The more that we are concerned with Wants, rather than, or wrapped around, Needs, the greater the scope for /S/ ubjective intervention, at both ends of the ASR.

The Slices dynamic shapes how we act out our Wants, and how we respond to the supply of their Satisfaction.

When we express "emotional" Wants, it's obvious that we are engaged in attachment of |E|<Affect> to <Thought> potential.

607

In doing that, we are "letting in the ASR". Not that the ASR ever goes away, but in the sense that we are deliberately manufacturing an <Anxiety> trigger.

Equally obviously, the strength of the <Anxiety> stimulus in /S/ is limited if we have "large" <Security> Slice: and contrarily so in the inverse.

We may indulge in intellectual wants, which are simply {ident} associations with no particular <Affect> attachment. Characteristic of that acting out behaviour is control, and absence of expectation.

These are merely examples of the general principles. What matters is only the relationship between the Slices: their "gravity".

Simply put, the Self experiences the life of the Self better, when the Slices have *dynamic harmony*. Which means that there is *constructive association* between Objective |congruence| and /S/ubjective <coherence>.

You know how to achieve that. If you didn't know, you'd never have made it out of the cradle.

The task of therapy is simply to design techniques, founded in this understanding of Self, which can assist You to experience that *constructive association*: however that works for you. And only You know.

(5)   Born Perfect

All human kind is born with the ASR. It functions perfectly. It is dependent for that function upon the sensory mechanisms, and their interdependence with neurological function.

Where there are deficits in either or both of those, our sensory and neurological systems will seek to compensate. But the ASR nevertheless functions in the same way. I congruence I models in exactly the same way: it's like a 3 wheeled car instead of 4 wheeled.

Both Biomorphics (bottom up therapy) and Psychotectics (top down therapy)[244] work with that born perfection. We are concerned, with these therapeutic interventions, to stimulate the access of your personality to the perfection which is already inside you.

That access is effected in the ASR tunnelling through the /S/ continuum, which results in <coherence> being recalibrated under Θ I congruence I .

---

[244] both of these are crude intuition pumps, of course

Each Slice is a dynamic. It is in the process of constant adjustment. Growth in each Slice grows and shapes the others. Shrinking in each Slice shrinks and shapes the others.

Of course, we use the {idents} of "growth" and "shrinking" merely to communicate the idea of force within the dynamic.

We might consider another metaphor: of the Personality Slices as instruments in a quintet. Each instrument is different, with differing internal dynamics. Together, they can be concordant or discordant. Each needs to play at the right time and at the right volume to produce *harmony*: the music of the Self.

Let's suppose You want to achieve something in the world, like a new opportunity in work:

- You Want something
- Chemistry matters: with colleagues, boss, others your work relates to
- enhancing Empathy with relevant decision makers is important
- Challenging your abilities to make the Opportunity work
- Conflicting with your current safety, but feeling the Security to go for it.

Maybe you can already see the ASR in action here. The powerhouse driving the 5 Slices dynamic, and allowing You to realise when your {want} is satisfied.

It becomes even clearer, when we take away those parts of the Slices Cycle which rely on the adult brain and its associated brainwaves. There's no longer any doubt, following the last two decades of neonate research, that a baby has wants, as well as needs. Wants such as: attention, communication, reaction.

However, we can see a baby's needs (for food, changing and so on) activating the ASR, and being soothed under the ASR.

What we also see, in concordance with those developing {wants}, is growth in self-stimulation of the | Exclusion Function |, thereby triggering the ASR and the phenomenon of self-soothing.

In the Second Volume of Secret Self, we will show how:
• Biomorphics induces physical and emotional state changes, without the need for a Subject to try and adjust thoughts or feelings;
• Psychotectic adjustment of Slices produces profound and helpful changes in Personality dynamics.

Some important examples of Biomorphic and Psychotectic techniques are also include din this Volume.

Biomorphics operates therapeutically to engage the ASR, while inducing <coherence> in /S/ .

Psychotectics uses the Slices as <coherence> ranges. Capacity of {identation} is infinite within the boundaries of the /S/ continuum: we can think whatever we wish to think, except always of course that:

Mentation

How we can think governs what we can think

Emotion

What we can emote governs how we emote

Thus, Psychotectics uses the plasticity of {identation} within the /S/ continuum, to effect self-stimulation of the |Exclusion Function|.

This is directed at matching the pathways tunnelled by the ASR. So, we find /S/<coherence> becoming recalibrated by the *Systems Architecture* of Self |congruence|.

To put it simply: you become more You.

CHAPTER 6

MIRRORS

We have previously in the book referred to the Mirror aspect of /S/ubjectivity.

This is an incredibly important process within /S/

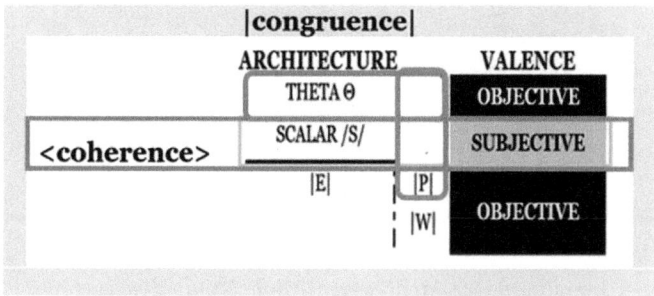

(1)   <coherence>
The pursuit of <coherence> is the essence of <Me> self.

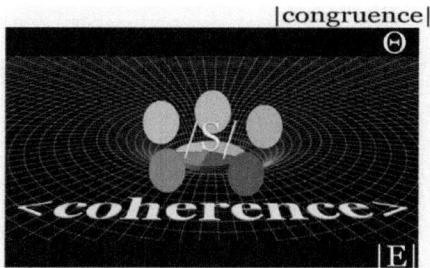

This Slices gravity graphic demonstrates dynamic balance, not <coherence>.

What is necessary for <coherence> is the capacity to reflect. That is exactly what is provided by the very Systems Architecture of Self:

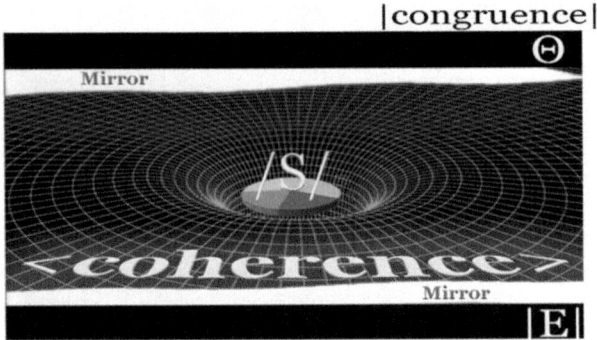

Mirrors are intrinsic to the operation of /S/ubjectivity:

- /S/ is a continuum of infinity, which is bounded by the congruence Architecture of Self. That is the central paradox of Self.
- It is that "sandwiching" that innately imposes Mirrors in /S/ubjectivity. You might thing of the "floor" and "ceiling" of the /S/ lawyer, as being made of Mirrors.
- Indeed, it is that opposition to objectivity, which is the foundation of <Me>: the sense of personhood.

We are bound to use those Mirrors in pursuit of <coherence>. So we send {ident} "lights" to bounce off those Mirrors, as reflections. All the time. Every moment of our lives.

It is this "Self-Reflection" which is the fundamental

process that underlies both:

- our common individual experience of Self
- the Classical Accounts and debates over Self.

In philosophy, the Descartian answer to scepticism about the existence of the Self *cogito ergo sum*, expresses this fundamental process.

It amounts to saying "I see reflections of a my-self, therefore something must be doing that seeing."

In the centuries since, philosophy has hardly doubted the reality of the reflections, since these are {idents} which allow discussion of the very subject. So philosophy has sought to understand what constitutes the seer.

For dualists, it's the separate subjective self, in a cartesian theatre. For materialists, the self is reducible layers of animate but non-subjective entities. Trapped in a Unilinear Model of Self, these diametrics are circular. This Secret of the Self remains unsolved.

In the matrixial *Systems Architecture* of Self, there is paradox, but no secret.

(2) Reflective Introspection

Superficially, and under identity logic, self-reflection is inherently antagonistic to <coherence>, for obvious reason: {idents} projected "at" Mirrors cannot be intrinsically equivalent to {idents] which are reflected back.

The different {ident} sources, by definition, preclude identity:

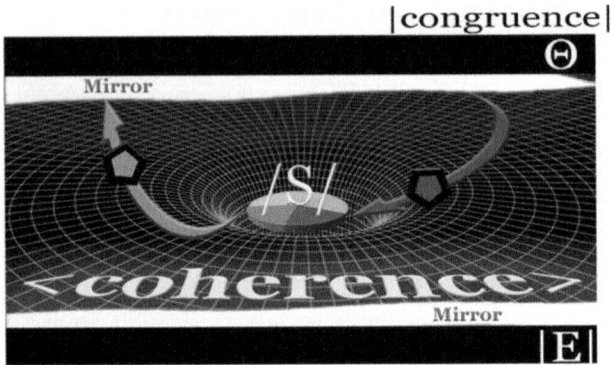

Yet, this inequality is the actual foundation of reflective introspection:

[Sent Light] ≠ [Returned Light] = Form.

That is so, whether the Output {ident} and Return {ident} be Content in [E] or [I].

What is also obvious, is that both of the Output {ident} and Return {ident} must be capable of being Contents under the same Form, and thus either acting as Substance or Moment.

If they do not, then no <coherence> is possible. And <coherence> is what we seek.

So, we find that:

/S/ *<coherence> manifests in forms of inequality:*
in forms of differences between
Output {ident} and Return {ident}.

Not because some homunculus "wants" to seek it. But because <coherence> is necessary as the neurological function of /S/ in its continuum of infinity, bounded by Objective Architecture layers.

Most cellular based life forms emit signals to the environment and react to feedback. We don't suppose that there's an independently intelligent homunculus in a paramecium. We recognise that it is the objective necessity of how the Output=>Return<= system works.

The difference with human Selfs is that our unique synaptic capacity grants us the ability to choose Output {ident} to be sent. We don't choose all of them. Our autonomic functions under the ASR acts, paramecium like, outside of our choosing.

(3)   Formless Consciousness

Where Output {ident} and Return {ident} do not have the capacity to act in inequality as Contents under a Form, there is no <coherence>.

This does not render such {idents} of no account. It is simply that they do not have *visibility in Form* in the /S/ continuum.

And, with that elementary understanding, formulated with such simplicity, we grasp the mystery of the unconscious.

The matrixial Self denies the unconscious, or sub-conscious, as special domains contrasted with "conscious". Theories of the unconscious are empirically untestable notions anyway. They have no claim to the mantle of science.

The /S/ continuum, in its Architecturally bounded infinity, is what there is, and all there is. There are no other dimensions or layers. What we can distinguish is:

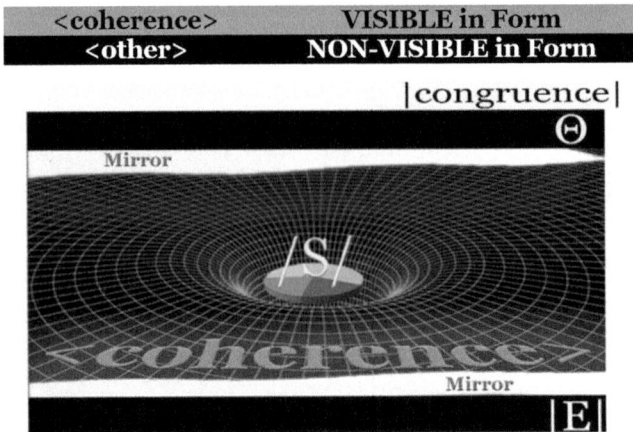

We need to explain what "Visible in Form" means.

/S/ <coherence> manifests in forms of inequality:

in forms of differences between

Output {ident} and Return {ident}.

That manifestation is what we mean by "visibility".

We need to appreciate that visible and non-visible are aspects of the same continuum: we cannot have one without the other.

So, in the above graphic, the gridlines are possible only because of the ungridded areas.

Experience: Torch
Close your eyes.
Imagine a torchlight.

Now:
• try to make disappear that which is not the light

Stop

Discussion:
(1)   You can't.

The Light and not-Light are together a Form in a continuum:

$$(L) \neq (nL) = [E]$$
$$>$$
$$(L) \neq (nL) = \text{Visibility } [E]$$

Visibility is not what the light is. Visibility is the Form of inequality of the Light in darkness (not Light)

By contrast, imagine a Red light beam, crossing a Blue light beam:

https://maggiessscienceconnection.weebly.com/visible-light--color.html

There, we encounter interference:

$$(R) \neq (B) = \text{Magenta } [I]^{245}$$

So:

$$\langle \text{visible}^1 \rangle \neq \langle \text{visible}^n \rangle \sum \langle \text{coherence} \rangle \, [\text{Form}]$$

$$\langle \text{visible}^1 \rangle \neq |\, \text{non-visible} \,| \Rightarrow /\,\text{continuum}\,/$$

But:

$$|\, \text{non-visible}^1 \,| \neq |\, \text{non-visible}^n \,| \sum \langle \text{coherence} \rangle$$

Consider this analogy.

- To water ski requires the coherence of two skis, in parallel, at the correct spacetime co-ordinates to allow balance, under momentum. The skis must have coherent visibility.
- To function as skis, the slats need water, which is a coherent medium. The water needs to be visible to the skis.

---

[245] strictly, these are $[\Delta R^n]$ etc Nodes interfering.

There is no "unconscious" which we cannot see. Or of which we have no "aware" perception. There is simply the /S/ continuum, which is a composite of <coherent> and non<coherent> events.

Some <coherent> events are visible in their Form. Becoming Form requires the obliteration of its Contents as separate entities. The Red and Blue lights are not coherent in Magenta: their Form. They are obliterated in Magenta: yet without the Red/Blue Contents there is no Magenta Form.

This is not unique to {idents} in the /S/ continuum. It is the matrixial logic of all knowable reality.

|non-visible| events are not visible in Form. But they conjoin in <coherence>. That <coherence> is not what we are aware *of*: that <coherence> is what *enables* awareness.

We might say, by analogy, that our eyes[246] are the <coherent> |non-visible| event awareness in which <coherent> light propagates.

To say that the light is conscious but the means of awareness is not (or vice versa), seems silly. Manifestly, the light is useless to us without the means of sight.

---

[246] visual response systems

It is just an odd notion, valued only by a century of mistaken usage, that seeks to assign categories of "conscious" and "unconscious" to either.

<visible> and <non-visible> coherents are the interdependent elements of Reflective Introspection.

We also do not mean to imply that the elements of a <non-visible> coherent, cannot become elements of a <visible> coherent. Of course they can. If, how and when this occurs is the /S/ubjective contingency of You.

(4)   Slices Reflections

We use the "light" bouncing off the Mirrors to reflect our Slices dynamics.

Slices "gravity", to borrow an Einsteinian metaphor, "bends" the light. By adjusting the relative "orbits" of the Slices, we alter the gravitational effect on <coherence>.

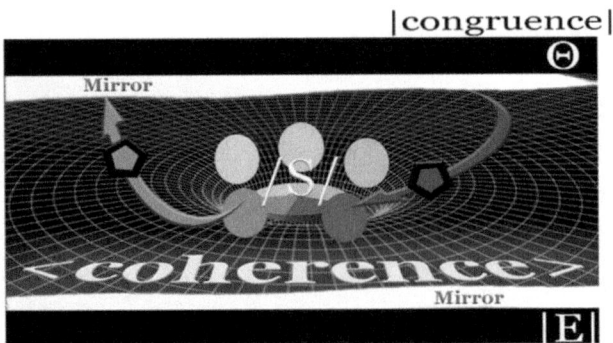

We can't 'see' the Slices'. We can only see the light reflections, and make inferences based on what we see.

To reach Θ, <Anxiety> must engage (€)=> <Thought> Potential in /S/. <Thought> Potential {idents} bounce to and from /S/ Mirrors.

The relative forces of the Slices gravity shape the {identation} light which we transmit to our Mirrors, and similarly shape the {identation} light which we receive from our Mirrors.

Experience: Lightroom
Imagine an empty room, with uniformly blank surfaces, around the size of a squash court:

Consider what you "see" in that empty room:
You see the walls, floor, ceiling.

Step 1:
Now, imagine a line, like a laser light in museum security system. It must cross the room, in a straight line
- Now imagine 2 lines
- Now multiply the lines
- Keep multiplying them

Stop

Discussion:

(1)   You can do the first few lines, easily

(2)   But, as you multiply the lines, eventually they start to bend: they become spaghetti

(3)   If you kept going long enough with the multiplication, you find the light lines turning into a homogenous liquid, just filling up the room space.

(4)   That works for a while, but as the lines radiate in a *field of potential Frames of Reference*, they become jumbled and entangled, and eventually lose their coherence completely.

Step 2:

Now, imagine a ball in the room.[247] A basketball size ball.

*   Now, project a laser light out from the ball
*   Keep projecting more laser lights from the ball

Stop

Discussion:

(1)   Now it is easy.

(2)   You picture lines, connecting the ball to the walls, ceiling and so on.

(3)   The lines stay straight. They remain coherent.

(4)   After a while it is like the ball just will not let you insert any more lines.

Step 3:

Now, imagine a single atom in the room. A tiny point,

---

[247] floating free, or located anywhere

which is visible only to your mind's eye.

- Now, project a laser light out from the atom
- Keep projecting more laser lights from the atom

Stop

Discussion:

(1)   This works just like Step 3.

(2)   It seems to make no difference what size the object is: just so long as there is an A (the object) and a B (the room).

Conclusions:

1.   The empty room is blank canvas.[248] The only FoR is the bounded room space.

2.   There is a *potential intersection* of FoR's, but the potential is unfulfilled.

3.   Coherent 'light' cannot maintain its coherence, when it is merely a product of that single FoR. In other words, coherence cannot sustain in unbounded infinity ∞.

4.   The introduction of the Ball (that which is not empty space), *collapses that potential into a specific intersection of FoRs.*

5.   Now ∞ becomes bounded by the intersection of FoR's.

6.   When you use the atom as the "anchor" for this 2nd

---

[248] please mark this idea: we will return to it

FoR, that works too. In fact, you find that populating the room with coherent, straight laser lights to be the easiest exercise.

7.   The atomic laser light shows that the FoR intersection which bounds ∞ is not a box, or container: it is a *point*. It could be the tiniest imaginable point in the quantum universe. So long as it is there.[249]

Those who have read *Matrixial Logic*, may recognise this as a version of the *Roomed Experience*, from Chapter 3 Categorical Transformations.

That Chapter concerned defects with the fundamentals of classical logic, derived from Aristotle. Yet here we see the same issues turning up at the core of the /S/ubjective Self.

Expectation: What If?

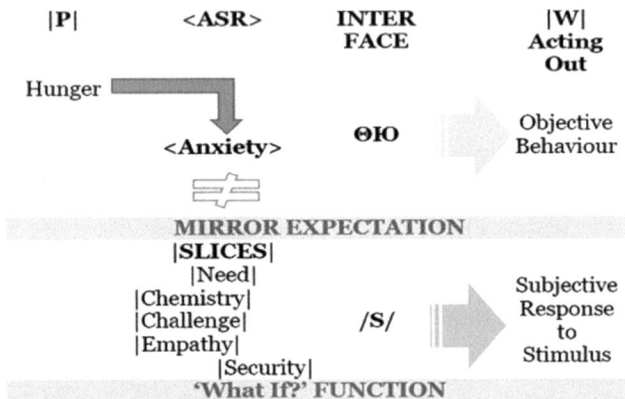

|P|	<ASR>	INTER FACE	|W| Acting Out
Hunger			
	<Anxiety>	ΘΙΟ	Objective Behaviour

MIRROR EXPECTATION
|SLICES|
|Need|
|Chemistry|
|Challenge| /S/
|Empathy|
|Security|
'What If?' FUNCTION

Subjective Response to Stimulus

---

[249] yes, we have just meta-explained the "big bang"

In order for "what if?" reasoning to have any sense, there must be a comparator: an objective substrate.

The Systems Architecture of Self provides exactly this. The ASR interface in <Anxiety> promotes Objective Behaviours.

We grow and learn in the Expectation gap. As a neonate:
- Hunger triggers <Anxiety>
- |Need| is activated in /S/
- "narrow band" <coherence> in /S/ creates Θ<Constructs>
- with Ю|W| interface
- baby acts out.

Now, there is an opportunity for {identation} to Mirror project: shaped by the Slices gravity, and altering the Slices dynamic harmony:
- what did I do?
- will it work?
- what if I did something else?

We're not saying that these sophisticated ideas are rattling around the head of a newborn. But the {ident} associations which will, over the next 18 months come to form these ideas, are being formed in the neonate brain.

In the Expectation gap, we are learning how to project: how to imagine alternatives. This is the heuristic of creation. We are learning to create our Self-image: our sense of <Me>.

The Expectation function has its analogue in the Interospection Model of mind. As you may recall from previous Chapters,[250] that Model claims that all thought is expective:[251]

> Simulations are your brain's guesses of what's happening in the world. In every waking moment, you're faced with ambiguous, noisy information from your eyes, ears, nose, and other sensory organs. Your brain uses your past experiences to construct a hypothesis - the simulation - and compares it to the cacophony arriving from your senses. In this manner, simulation lets your brain impose meaning on the noise, selecting what's relevant and ignoring the rest.
>
> The discovery of simulation in the late 1990s ushered in a new era in psychology and neuroscience. Scientific evidence shows that what we see, hear, touch, taste, and smell are largely simulations of the world, not reactions to it.
>
> Forward-looking thinkers speculate that simulation is a common mechanism not only for perception but also for understanding language, feeling empathy, remembering, imagining, dreaming, and many other psychological phenomena.
>
> Our common sense might declare that thinking, perceiving, and dreaming are different mental events (at least to those of us in Western cultures), yet one general process describes them all. Simulation is the default mode for all mental activity. It also holds a key to unlocking the mystery of how the brain creates emotions. (p27-28)

The idea of mental Simulation is useful. But it can't explain itself, without circularity.

This passage, brilliant though it is in its narrative power,

---

[250] see especially Chapter 2, Section C.1(2)
[251] *How Emotions Are Made: The Secret Life of the Brain*. Lisa Feldman Barrett. (2018)

demonstrates very clearly that the Simulation mechanism of the Interospection Model is stuck in the hall of Mirrors of /S/.

By contrast, in the Self Systems Architecture, we can see:

- dynamics of the ASR
- the interaction of {ident} <coherence> (visible and non-visible)
- under the gravity of the Slices
- bounded by interaction with the Mirrors.

So, we can see how and why that Simulation takes place.

Which enables us to develop appropriate therapeutic interventions.

Examination: How, Why?

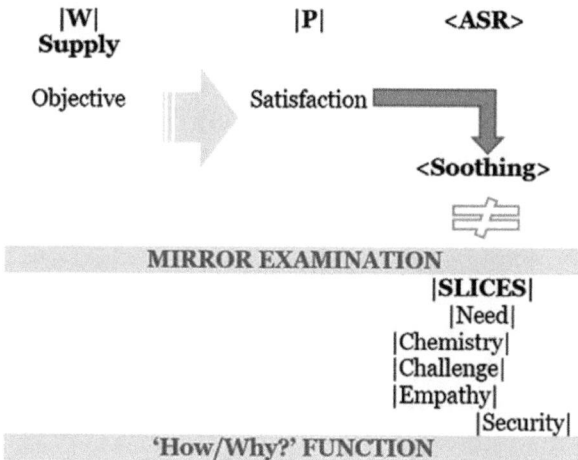

|W| Supply |P| <ASR>

Objective   Satisfaction

<Soothing>

MIRROR EXAMINATION

|SLICES|
|Need|
|Chemistry|
|Challenge|
|Empathy|
|Security|

'How/Why?' FUNCTION

In the same way, the supply of Satisfaction to us, enables comparison with our Objective <Soothing> function.

We are prompted to ask:

- why did (or didn't) our acting out work?
- how did (or didn't) it work?
- what as the difference between our Expectation and our Receipt?

We are learning to think empirically: to test expectations against results.

The Expectation and Examination comparators promote our early learning. As we learn, the Slices gravity becomes more powerful, because it is a gravity formed from the movement and association of {idents}.

So, we now see that the Systems Architecture of Self, and the Mirror function for {idents} shaped in their association by the gravity of the Slices in dynamic harmony: together these automatically opportune creativity and science; the core features of human civilisation.

Practice at Becoming

As we become more practiced at using our /S/ continuum Mirror function, we develop our individually unique dynamic harmony of the Slices.

Yet we're expert amateurs. Expert, because nobody else

knows our /S/ubjectity: only each of us does. Amateur, because the methods we use in bouncing {ident} lights off the Mirrors, are uninformed by science: they are just guesswork.

Often we prejudge what we want the reflection to look like, so we are not really caring to observe the reflection at all. This, by the way, is describing: not criticising.

Biomorphics and Psychotectics are empirically validated therapeutic interventions. Their foundational purpose is to give You the techniques to be more You.

Because You were born with the same Systems Architecture as everyone, and the same perfect ASR, we can derive objective generalised techniques, which you can use.

But those techniques do not impose on You and external prescription. They work only through the modes of becoming which You choose.

(5)   Classical Failure

/S/ *<coherence> manifests in forms of inequality.* This understanding is antithetical to Classical Accounts of introspection. In that model, what we understand as <coherence> is muddled with an idea of "accuracy".

The Classical Accounts don't use that term, but it's the essence of what they're talking about. The big idea is that introspection should be "true" or "faithful". This idea is taken for granted in philosophy of mind, but a core value in psychotherapy.

The suffering Subject is supposed to seek alignment of Output {ident} and Return {ident}. The psychotherapist helpfully imposes utterly arbitrary constructions of "aligned thinking". The sort of thing you see in social media memes, and self-help books everywhere:

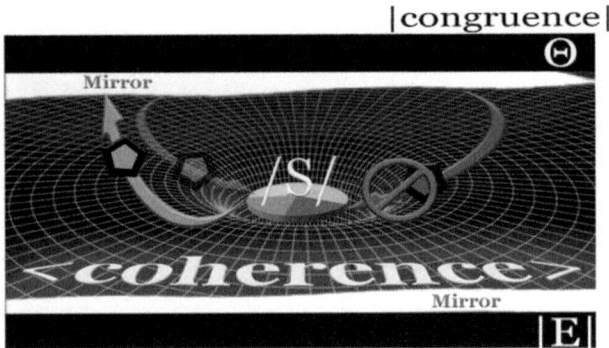

You are supposed to practice aligning Output {ident} and Return {ident}, to match these prescriptions. Then you will be happy (or however the therapist arbitrarily defines success).

Clarity compels us to a little lack of kindness here. This is /S/ubjective savagery. No doubt well-meant. But it's difficult to conceive a prescription which could simultaneously be so useless and so damaging.

In order to comply with the prescription, the Subject is bound to manufacture Shadow Slices: *an association of {idents} which is unaffected by the dynamics of the Slices.*

We will examine Shadow Slices in detail in the next Chapter.

What we will state here, is that we all have the constant urge to create Shadow Slices, in our pursuit of <coherence>.

Disciplines, techniques and persuasions are offered by a psychotherapy which induces us to create more, and more layers, of Shadow Slices.

Such psychotherapy is equivalent to medical practices based on the four humours, and the wisdom of blood letting by leeches.

Where it works, it is by accident. It cannot work without damage. And, at least medieval medicine did not generally blame the patient.

Yet that is the patronising, elitist perspective of psychotherapy. The overarching idea that there is a better You. Over there, way away on that high mountain top. If you just swallow the prescriptions of principle and practice the techniques for long enough, you too can walk the narrow path to self-salvation. It's a rocky road, but have faith you will arrive there: one day.

To which must Subjects, sooner or later, say "Sod it".[252] And they are perfectly right to say it.

All this irrationality is founded in:

- failure to understand the Systems Architecture of Self
- obeisance to a useless Unilinear Model
- trying to fashion therapeutic interventions out of identity logic.

To be fair, the philosophers have long been at the same game. Just with longer sentences.

Zombie Philosophy

Suppose that one were a Zombie, or otherwise bereft of /S/ubjective function. The *Autonomic Balancing* would continue, independently of any /S/ubjective adjustment.

This fact explains the whole corpus of Zombie philosophy ("ZP"). ZP is seductive, because we can see from our own self-experience, and from experiencing others, that ZP ideas bear some relation to those experiences.

We can see a commonality about how all individuals go about being individuals. By simple reductionism, we can then derive a conclusion that this "X-ness" which they have in common, is what is their irreducible core: what they "really" are. As an exercise in identity logic, given

---

[252] matrixial technical term

the premises, the conclusions entirely follow.

But ZP makes a simple category mistake. ZP is confusing the behavioural patterns attributable through /S/ responses to to *Autonomic Balancing*, with the entirely different processes of the /S/ continuum.

That mistake is just another consequence of the Unilinear Model of self: where there is just World, Body, Mind and their interactions.

CHAPTER 7

SHADOWS

Our daily lives as psychological beings consists of encounters with /S/<coherence>. It's our primary psychological relationship. What we often popularly call "making sense": of ourselves, of others, of the world.

Now, the mountain range of matrixial Self appears through the clouds into sunlight. The established theories and practices of individual psychology and inter-personal relations all operate in this dimension.

This is the dimension where:
* you read the memes about "brighter tomorrows" from CBT practitioners in social media
* relationship guides on how to love, and everything else crowd the bookshelves
* psychology from Freud and Jung through to the moderns conduct their dialogue

This is also the dimension in which the last 400 years of philosophy of mind operates. The dimension in which operates the *Philosophical Foundations Of Neuroscience* critiqued by Bennett and Hacker.[253]

---

[253] 2003. Malden, MA: Blackwell Publishing

It is tautological to say that we undertake in the /S/ continuum all {identation}: the association of {idents} and the construction of ideas, concepts, theories. Where else can the mentive products of /S/ubjectivity appear than in that subjectivity?

/S/{idents} appear in /S/, of course. That seems to be the subjective experience which makes the idea of the cartesian theatre so intractable.

But the origin of /S/{idents} is outside /S/. As we have shown over the previous Chapters. And what allows the Cartesian theatre to appear to exist is the <Constructs> function of Theta Θ.

It's Θ <Constructs> which supply the rules of grammar that actually allow Shakespeare's characters to conduct their dialogue in the theatre. It's the |W| |=>|P| processes which allow the elemental {idents} to arise, and which grant them meaning in lived reality.

And its ΘЮ=>|W| in Mimetics and |T|ime, which allow the solipsis of /S/ubjectivity to be conveyed to any audience.

As we said in Chapter 4:
    We see here another of the paradoxes of Self:
- Our /S/ubjective <self> layer needs to create and multiply {idents} in order to allow our Personality lattice to become

whole: to become a <Me>.

- We perpetually seek <coherence> so as to shape that explosion of {idents}, so as to create the core {idents} of <Me>. In other words, to establish homeostasis of <self> recognition.
- Yet, it is that very dynamic which tends towards dislocation and suppression of the ASR. We can see that most clearly in the journey from infant to maturity.

We perpetually interfere with our Slices dynamics. Remember that the Slices represent /S/ aggregates of the ASR function.

The perpetual struggle for /S/<coherence> is not a "bad thing". It's not something we ought to try and stop. If we ever did succeed in stopping it, the outcome would be serious psychological impairment.

Shadow Creation
/S/ is illuminated by mirrors. Reflection is the essential process for establishing equivalence.

We reflect one association of {idents} off another, and thereby scale their difference or similarity: good / evil; right / wrong; truth / lies.

We create templates of these {ident} associations, and then use those as reference points. We attach <Affect> to {ident} associations, to make them more powerful. These become our "emotional layers": what we think of as the fundamental elements of our emotional personality.

It's neither easy or automatic for the 5 Slices to relate in dynamic harmony. All the circumstances and vicissitudes of life conspire to de-harmonise, to interfere with the natural "gravity" of our personality.

We find that the mirroring function doesn't work, or just doesn't seem to work. That perception is probably justified. There's no immutable law of science or nature which dictates that we, as /S/ubjective <selfs> must be able to understand our life experiences.

We create understandings: and those are more or less efficient to the circumstances of our life.

To maintain <coherence> what we all do is create *Shadow Slices (Ш)*.

> *A Shadow Slice Ш is an association of {idents} which is unaffected by the dynamics of the Slices.*

Ш subsist within the /S/continuum. So, what sort of {identation} creates Ш, as contrasted with other {idents}?

To answer that, we need to have regard to Chapter 2, Section D, Segment (7) *Down Is Up:*

> This brings us to the rubric: we don't need Θ to function in /S/{I^n}: until we do.
>
> …

There's no material reality within the /S/ continuum. It's subjective, contingent, equivalence based approximation and association. It's whatever you want it to be, or not to be.

So, when you bring (T) from Θ "upstairs" down into /S//S/, it stops being (T). It loses Theta coherence. It becomes just another {ident}.

If you want to put the {idents} association out into the world, then you need to pass their inequalities into the Theta Θ equalisation program: and out comes grammatical language.

And let's finally just consider that for a moment. You know what it's like to say just about anything out loud. What you hear yourself saying, or see yourself writing, is never really quite the same as your <T>{i} and <F>{i} associations.

You can never express, out loud, what You, as You, "really" think in your feelings. That necessary linguistic equalisation always leaves something behind.
we can say what we want to be understood as meaning; but we can never authentically mean what we are saying.

That's why we have poetry. It's the art form of the spaces between /S/ and Θ.

To use Θ<Constructs> in ordering {ident] associations (under rules of grammar, say), is one thing.

Ш arise when we create synthetic [constructs].

Once again, exploration of the Self leads us back to the fundamentals of matrixial logic.

We make synthetic [constructs] by seeking equalisation. To create forms of forms of forms (and so on) abstracting ever further, until we empty, as far as we can, ultimate meta-Forms of any Content relationship.

We can't really get to true equalisation. Only in the Θ field function is equalisation real. Instead, we create a "balloon", and manufacture longer and longer string.

Experience: Balloon

Look into your room, or an outside landscape

Visualise a balloon on the floor

Visualise a little ball, floating inside the balloon

Visualise the balloon rising into the air

Now:

• pop the balloon

Stop

Discussion:
(1)   Either: you couldn't pop the balloon at all; or
(2)   once you popped it, the little ball disappeared as well

Experience: String
Look into your room, or an outside landscape

Visualise a balloon on the floor

Now: you're holding the string which is attached to the balloon

Visualise the balloon rising into the air
There's loads of string. The balloon can rise as high as it needs to

Hold out your hand, as it holds the balloon string

Now:
•   pop the balloon

Stop

Discussion:
(1)   Now you can't pop the balloon at all

These *Experiences* are metaphors for what happens with Ш. The balloon is a classic example of Form almost without Content.

In Step 1, the Form (balloon) is referenced to a Content (ball), but in a strange way. You have an instinct to preserve the ball, so it's difficult to pop the balloon. You can put some force behind popping the balloon, but then you lose the ball as well.

We are seeing here the lesson that Ш are very resistant to interaction with other {idents} and associations. In *I Want To Love But*, we used a metaphor of Ш being "up in the attic" of your /S/. We resist that otherwise useful metaphor, as it's difficult to visualise in the context of the Self *Systems Architecture*.

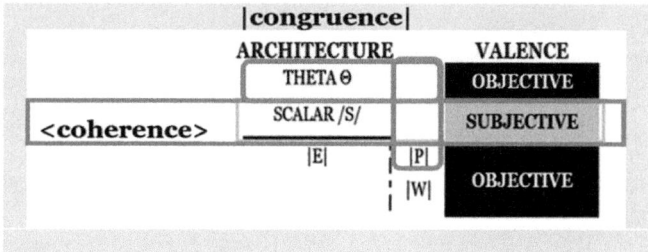

|congruence|			
	ARCHITECTURE			**VALENCE**
	THETA Θ			OBJECTIVE
\<coherence\>	SCALAR /S/			SUBJECTIVE
	|E|	|P|		OBJECTIVE
		|W|		

A more architectural visualisation, is to take the /S/ continuum:

Let's recall and repeat this Experience from Chapter 2, Section A, Segment (1):

Experience: Already

Setup:

Look at this simple picture. Lots of ordinary things in here, from a perfectly ordinary part of the real world

And a non-ordinary thing.

Just look at the picture, with your eyes open:

Step 1:

Take the whole picture of the Landscape into your head

Close your eyes

If you need to refresh your memory by looking a few times, that's fine

And: when you're sure you have the Landscape in your head

With your eyes closed:

Now:
*   Look around the Landscape in your head

Stop

Discussion:
(4)   Static imaging the Landscape, behind closed eyes, in your head, is easy
(5)   But the strange Symbol:

just won't reast easy in your head.
(6)   It's like your head keeps being pulled back to look at the picture, and Symbol, to try and resolve the conflict.

We have the explanation as to why this is happening:
*   If /S/ cannot recognise the data *by reference to what is already in /S/*, then /S/ rejects it as an input.

The Symbol was deliberately designed as an abstract with no obvious reference to anything in our experience.

As we said:

Your subjective /S/ scalar domain can do almost anything. But there are limits.

If you review the history of your head, you'll see that your Mentation held the Symbol apart from the Landscape. Your /S/ axis field "parked" the Symbol in a "to be determined" box, separate from the familiar room landscape.

The *Already Experience* sees your /S/ trying to grapple with an externally generated equivalent of Ш. Indeed, in this Experience, you easily move the strange symbol to your /S/ "attic".

What we are dealing with in Ш is *self-creation* of {idents} which operate in our /S/ continuum like this strange symbol.

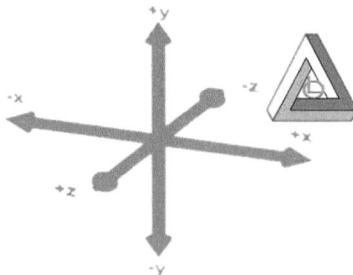

These are *Obsession Anchors*. They are the marker points in our mental map of discomfort. Through processes of logic, we externalise Ш. That Ш comes to be held in our /S/ like an actual |W| object which we don't recognise.

A metaphor for the real underlying process is that we are creating a balloon, and holding onto its string. We might figment some other thing inside the balloon. We float the balloon. It can expand in size: it can rise in its height level in our /S/.

But we just can't pop the balloon:

> Ш *is unaffected by dynamics of the Slices.*

There's a vast range of Ш, and within each individual, Ш can come, and go, and morph. What all Ш have in common is that:

- they are extremely abstracted {idents}
- so they can participate in <Affect> attachment very easily.

We looked at <Affect> attachment in Chapter 2, Section C, Segment (8) *<Thought> Potential and <Thought>*.

$$=\mathbf{t}[\mathbf{I}]$$
$$(\overline{T}) \neq (-\overline{T})$$
$$\Sigma <\mathbf{\epsilon}>$$

\<Thought\>

$$\Delta<\top^{n}> \mid \infty$$

$$\sum<\text{€}> (\top) \neq (-\top) = \text{₺}[I]$$

Recall the duck shoot: where a rolling canvass of \<Thought\> Potential is "hit" by an \<Affect\> [$\sum<\text{€}>$].

In the usual /S/ continuum, that \<Thought\> Potential canvass is infinity ∞. Where Ш is in operation, we have an utterly abstract idea: a Form with barely any connection to Content.

Technically, [$=\text{₺}[I]$] has been multiplied in \<Nodes\> and meta-Forms of \<Nodes\>.

You know from working in matrixial logic, that \<Nodes\> are very unstable. They collapse under interaction with \<Affect\> vectors very easily.

However, these Ш subsist in dimensions of /S/ removed from

the ordinary rules of /S/{identation} attachment to <Affect>.

We can see why the detailed technical analysis in Chapter 2 was so necessary. It allows us to dissect and understand the actual processes occurring within the Self *Systems Architecture*:

(1) To try and solve thinking and feeling problems, in pursuit of /S/<coherence>, we formulate Ш.

(2) Ш are abstracted meta-Forms of <Thought> Potentials.

(3) Ш subsist within the /S/<continuum>.

(4) But the innate logic of their creation makes them inaccessible to other {identation} within /S/.

(5) So, it's like Ш are in an "attic" or sub-dimension.

(6) Because Ш are meta-Forms, created by layers of <Nodes>, they barely have any relation to actual {ident} Content.

(7) So, Ш are stable.

Our Slices work to cohere our {identation}. They are the 5 gravitational forces which act to provide <coherence>: that <coherence> for which we perpetually strive in our /S/ubjectivity. What we experience as sanity.

But, our Ш seems to grow outside our control. Our Slices gravity has no effect on them. We can't get them to submit to <coherence>.

They are Ш *Shadow Slices*. Our /S/ubjective {identation} creates them: yet like a Frankenstein monster, they seem

649

to acquire controlling power over us.

Shadow Power

The result is that our <Feelings> and <Thoughts> churn. We fee upset and unbalanced. The Ш sits in our "attic" headspace, as if surrounded by emotional fires and sirens.

Whatever we think and feel, we can't shift the Ш obsession. We are *obsessed*. And possessed by the powerlesness we feel.

The process of <Affect> attachment to <Thought> potential is going on perpetually, every moment of the day:

$$\textbf{<Thought>}$$
$$\Delta <\bar{T}^n> | \infty$$
$$\Sigma <\text{€}> (\bar{T}) \neq (-\bar{T}) = \text{Ƅ}[I]$$

But this is not so with Ш.

Ш appear out of our ordinary efforts to acquire {identation} <coherence> in relation to the unfamiliar. We manufacture Ш without positively intending to do so.

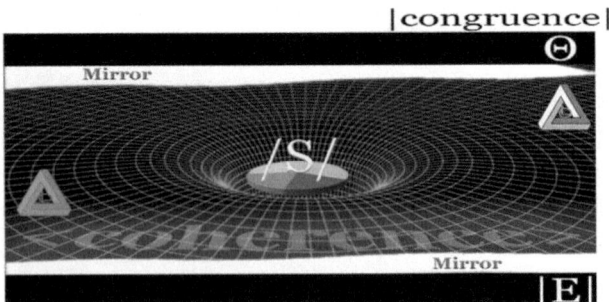

What we then discover is that we can power Ш by undertaking active suppression of the ASR:

- Our <Anxiety> is going about its usual autonomic business.
- But, within /S/, we are deliberately suppressing normal <Affect> attachment to <Thought> potential.
- We are thereby reducing the gravitational force, or size, of the Slices.
- The Mirrors become "starved" of reflective {ident} input, and thus output less reflection.
- We thus alter <coherence>.
- <Anxiety> is not reaching Θ<Constructs>.
- Our Ш gains more relative size.

So, our Objective Behavior is being altered:

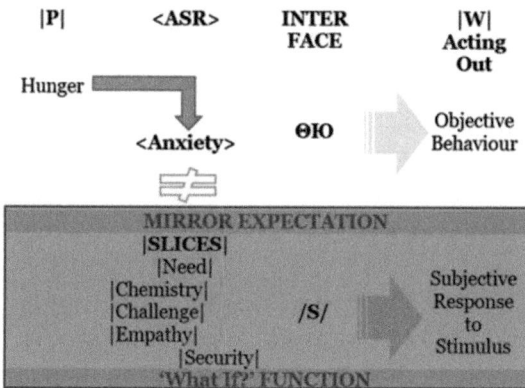

This affects our /S/ ability to {ident} in Mirror Expectation: to undertake the "what if" function.

In like manner, it affects our "how, why?" function:

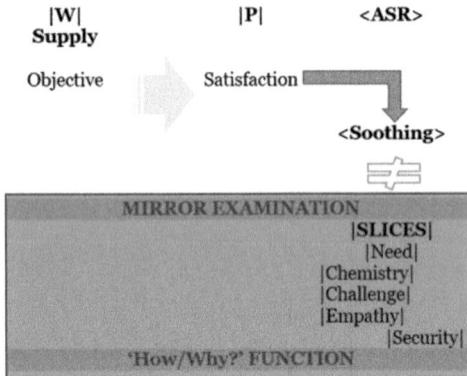

It is commonplace to notice these aspects of Ш, of obsession:

- We become "unidimensional".
- Our ordinary Personality appears to others[254] to become more narrowly focused.
- Emotion and Thought appear disconnected.
- We can appear highly emotional, or emotionally repressed, but the obsession endures.

We obtain an important clue from this commonplace presentation: we can see that Ш act as analogues of Θ<Constructs>.

Removed from the ordinary Slices gravity and Mirror function in /S/, these Ш are trying not to act under

_____
[254] Personality is a social phenomenon, not an individual one

equivalence. They are trying to mimic Θ equalisation <Constructs>.

As we said above:

(6)   Because Ш are meta-Forms, created by layers of <Nodes>, they barely have any relation to actual {ident} Content.

(7)   So, Ш are stable.

We see this in the proto-logical madness of obsession.

This is <Me> trying to copy <I>. The Θ<Constructs> in <I> have permanence through | T | ime. Just as Ш pretend to permanence, despite what is going on in and around us. So we see another enduring characteristic of obsession.

We see also another characteristic: the sense that Ш is part of the fabric of "my" being. "I" cannot let that Ш go, without losing myself: or such part of myself as I sense to be the "real" me.

Ш As Obsession

So, we see the dominance characteristics of Ш:

•   separated from <Affect> attachment
•   outside the gravitational force of Slices on {idents}
•   stable in meta-Forms
•   mimicking Θ<Constructs>
•   acting as a proto <I>
•   disconnected from the ASR

It's strange that Ш can acquire such seeming dominance in our |M|entation, when they ought to be so fragile. They are disconnected from the ASR: the process which is born into us as our primary survival mechanism, and as our heuristic fulcrum.

These Ш are fragile. That's why we protect them by undermining the normal process in /S/: by suppressing the ASR.

Suppression takes effort. To aid the suppression, we turn to pharmaceuticals and behaviours: processes which can disrupt the ordinary functioning of the ASR.

But that effort takes effort. And we are fighting an ultimately losing battle. We are trying to use artificial imposts, to suppress an ASR that is born into us, and which is the electricity for our operating System.

No wonder then that enervation of the ASR symptomises in: lack of energy; listlessness; torpor; depression.

Insomnia is another obvious feature of obsessive Ш. We cannot allow our guard down. We can't let the ASR go about its usual energetic business in /S/. It takes deliberate effort to suppress the ASR. So we sleep fitfully, with one eye open.

There's the picture of Ш obsession: depressed,

unidimensional, pouring energy into distraction, yet insomniac and exhausted.

Healing Ш Obsession

Understanding these dynamics provides the key to unlocking Ш obsessions: to release suppression of the ASR.

We can't:

- think our way out of Ш. If we could, they would simply be normal {idents}, subject to Slices gravity.
- "feel" our way out of Ш, because that's just another flavour of {identation}.

We can't challenge Ш by using our /S/ubjectivity. All that talk therapy and its CBT variants which try to spin effective Ш challenge out of /S/, are not only wasting everyone's time, they tend to make the problem worse:

- The more you look at Ш, the bigger it gets.
- Trying to ignore Ш, makes it bigger too.

Experience: Ness

Imagine something small that doesn't usually sit on your desk, or coffee table.

Let's agree to imagine a snail shell.

Visualise the Shell somewhere on the surface top.

Move it around.

Hover it in the air, and play with its movement.

Set it back down anywhere on the surface top.

You know it's there.

Now:
•   tell yourself to ignore it

Distract yourself for a few moments.

Again:
•   tell yourself to ignore it

Stop.

<u>Discussion</u>:
(1)   The Shell did not go away.
(2)   The more you tried to ignore it, the stickier it be-
       came.

You've created a Ш:

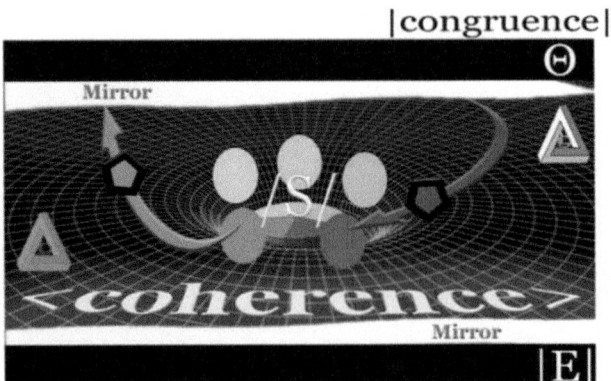

- The Shell has no business being where it became in your mind, until we put it there.
- Your <coherence> pushed the Shell into its own little Penrose Triangle: as in the graphic.
- But, once there, it became dimensionally immune to your Slices gravity {idents}.

However, this Ш is hardly obsessional. You're not striving to suppress your ASR to maintain the Ш. So, it will just fade away. It probably already has, by the time you read this. Now there's just a ghost of a shadow.

This is how we heal Ш obsession. We simply restore ASR function. That's really not difficult. The ASR is the motive energy of your entire Self becoming, and has been since the moment of your birth.

We use *Biomorphic* techniques, to interrupt ASR suppression. It only takes a few moments. Because the ASR is the life of Self. We simple restore your *Biomorphic Autonomic Balance*

We were engineered to perfection. All the vainglory of Ш meta-Forms, mimicking Θ<Constructs>, are helpless when exposed to the momentary force of unsuppressed ASR.

A Spectrum of Shadows

We have focused[255] on Ш as obsession, in order to clarify explanation.

Of course, we have a whole spectrum of Ш. There was the harmless snail Shell earlier. We live our lives creating Ш. We can't bring all of our life experiences into <coherence> and there's no reason we should.

Ш only become problematic when we start trying to suppress our ASR, in order to maintain them.

From the matrixial logic of Self, we transition suddenly from dry equations and technical explanations, to revelation of the secret processes which create obsessions that drive human kind. Love, hate, and everything beyond and in between.

These processes of Self are no longer secret, but they remain a paradox:

Mentation
How we can think governs what we can think
Emotion
What we can emote governs how we emote

By understanding how these paradoxes are formed, we uncover the therapeutic intervention techniques which actually heal the Self.

---

[255] not obessively: joke

CHAPTER 8

PERSON

8.   Self In Perception

We spend our lives in Self perception. We have devoted much ink and treasure (in philosophy, neuroscience and psychology) to the investigation of what makes each Self a person: to each self, and to others.

Just seeking to understand what a person is, forms part of that quest. Trying to form social theories of persons, is another. We also seek pathways to being a better person, in oneself, and for others.

We have now established:
- the *Systems Architecture* of Self that that functions organically, in | T | ime and <space>
- the {ident} processes within / S /
- the <Constructs> process within Θ
- their respective relationships, both internally and externally
- what powers the Self: the ASR
- what fundamentally steers the Self: the Slices dynamics

These established analyses make it easy to consider core issues about personhood. We don't need to go round endless circles of contingent and arbitrary reasoning: all within the / S / hall of mirrors.

All that is useful is to delineate between <I> and <Me>. This is not a distinction which particularly matters. We can live, think and feel well enough without it.

9.   Self As <I>

We begin here, because it is the most simple of the aspects of the Person:

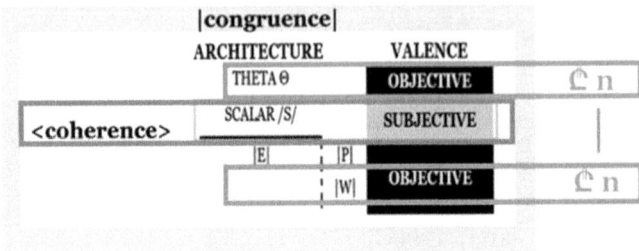

The Self as <I> is the objective Self. That Self which has interactions with objectivity, an objective frame of reference.

This is most easily seen in the synchrony between Theta Θ and |W| under the operation of |T|ime Synapses.

As a Self, you are interacting with the |W|orld in an objective temporal nexus, every moment of your life. We usually do not, in our /S/ continuum grant visibility to that nexus. Of course, when we do, that objectivity is transformed into just another {ident}.

However, as so many *Experiences* have shown, we can by design demonstrate to your /S/ubjectivity, the reality of that objective temporal nexus.

The <I> of Self inures in this relationship:

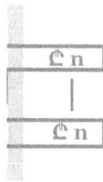

```
┌─────────┐
│   Ĉ n   │
└─────────┘
     │
┌─────────┐
│   Ĉ n   │
└─────────┘
```

This is what grants | congruence | to the Self as a being *of* | T | ime. Note that we say "of" not "in". Each of us is a temporal being. That is what "existence" is.

The *Systems Architecture* of Self presents itself as the solution to that perennial problem: *how is the identity of the Self maintained through time?*

Classical Accounts get stuck in trying to link the Self and external temporal reality, as if they were two parallel rail tracks, each travelling in infinity.

- That problem framework produces the subsidiary problem of how such rail tracks can indeed parallel at all: and how can we actually tell if they are parallel or not?
- This then originates the spiritualist type solutions, which posit that subjectivity can be overcome, by surrender to some domain in which you can become one with the other rail track.

There are not two rail tracks. There isn't even one.

(1) | T | ime is not a river into infinity ∞.

(2) | T | ime is a procession of quantised <spacetime> events.

(3)   Our Θ synchronises with those events, on a moment by moment basis.

(4)   That is the permanent identity which is <I>.

There is no other external frame of reference for <I> ⇔ | W |. The relationship is one of perpetual superpositions becoming realised, thereby vanishing, and the process occurring again. And again. That indeed is a process of infinity ∞. A true infinity, and not merely an order of integers on a scalar plane. It is infinity without existence. We might put it like this, in a simplistic analogy.

- The Self as <I> is a movie.
- It plays only as successive individual frames, and is being projected upon a screen which appears, so as to reciprocate the projector beam, then vanishes. Only to reappear again for the next frame. And so on.
- What is real in the | W |orld is each frame. But each frame can only be seen as a moving image.

<I> is the Self as Being. Being is realised temporal potential, which can only be experienced as existence, as <is>.

Then here comes the paradox:

- <I> is the Self in being, maintained permanently in momentary Ю interaction in time and space

Yet:

- we cannot see our <I>, except as reflected in others, and as we mirror it in /S/.

We live in a goldfish bowl: the surface of which is <I>: but we can only see in associate {identation} that bowl and the space outside, from inside the bowl.

10.   Self As <Me>

It's easy to define the Self as <Me> by exclusion. It's what isn't <I>.

The Self as <Me> is the Mirror continuum of {idents} generated by us, in every moment of our lived experience. These are what make the Self, a Person.

We can create {idents} about the Self as <I>. Of course, we do that all the time: both in ordinary life and academic theory. By necessity of our *Systems Architecture*, whenever we articulate the objective in {idents} we strip it of its very objectivity.

By analogy, we could say that:

- the Self as <I> is how the basic vehicle comes off the production line. With all the relevant engineering parts.

- the Self as <Me> is how we style the vehicle, and where and how we choose to drive it.

Understanding the difference between the Self as <I> and <Me>, as resolved by our *Systems Architecture*, is useful in devising Psychotectic and Biomorphic interventions. To the benefit of the whole Self.

Still a paradox, but no longer a secret.

11. Personality

Our Personality is a social phenomenon, not an individual one. It is also a relative spectrum.

The "engine room" of our Personality is summarised in these already seen graphics:

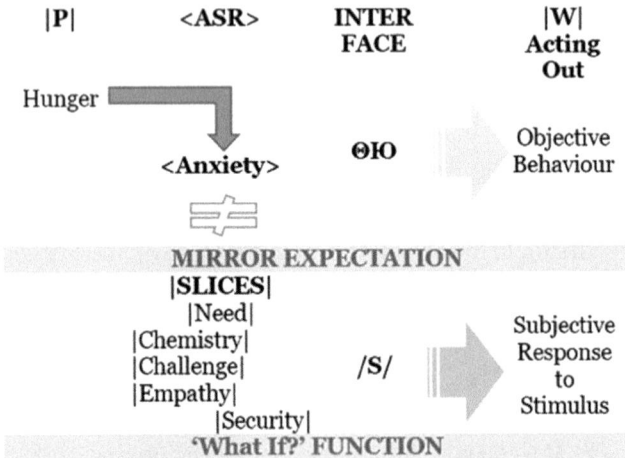

|W| Supply	|P|	<ASR>
Objective	Satisfaction	
		<Soothing>

MIRROR EXAMINATION

|SLICES|
|Need|
|Chemistry|
|Challenge|
|Empathy|
|Security|

'How/Why?' FUNCTION

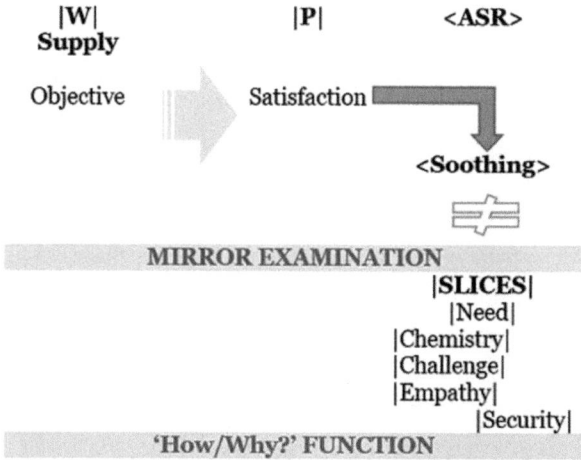

We can introspect judgments about our Personality, but those are inevitably comparisons between how we see our Self, in relation to other Selfs.

We will discuss this further in the *Relating* Chapter.
The relevance of this to Matrixial Healing, through Biomorphics and Psychotectics, is that *we assist Persons, not Personalities*.

The task of Matrixial Healing is to facilitate /S/<coherence> in Θ |congruence|. The mission is not to change your personality: only to help You to be more You.

CHAPTER 9

BIOMORPHICS

Biomorphics is the science which sets out empirically observed principles of how the ASR autonomically regulates <Affect>, in |congruence| with Θ: Biomorphic Autonomic Balance ("BAB").

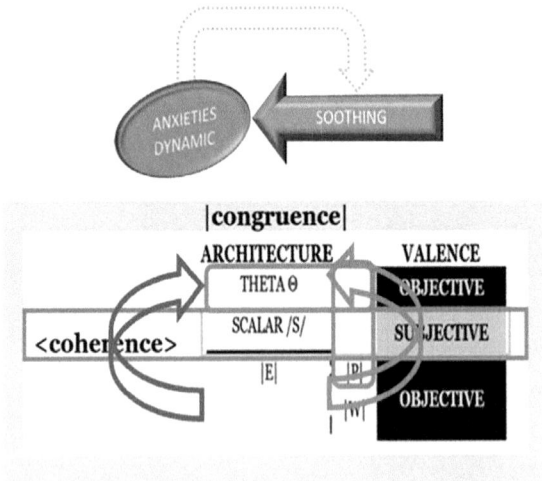

We can then observe how the operation of BAB impacts the /S/ubjective continuum.

Biomorphics then provides therapeutic interventions to restore BAB:

- by stimulating the ASR.
- by displacing /S/ interference in the ASR.

- by reducing the interference energy input available to /S/ so as to produce and maintain Shadow Slices.
-

The core of Biomorphics is understanding that:

(1) We are born with a perfectly functioning ASR, which creates and maintains BAB.

(2) The ASR is common to complex sentient life.

(3) In humans, the Vagal Nerve is central to ASR operation.

(4) What differentiates humans, is the existence of the /S/ continuum, and the complexity of its neurological system.

(5) This complexity grants power to /S/ to interfere in the ASR in a way not available to other complex sentient life.

(6) It's through interface between /S/ and the ASR that we learn in /S/ubjectivity, and that we develop a <Me> personality.

(7) That which is <Me>, moment to moment, is constrained by the limits of BAB.

(8) When we try to subvert, alter, or push beyond BAB, we induce trauma in the Self.

(9) We absolutely cannot think ourselves better. We cannot improve on the ASR perfection endowed in us by nature.

(10) Encouraging us to use /S/{identation} to interfere more in the ASR is irrational.

(11) Therapy which seeks to use {idents} within the /S/ continuum to heal, challenge, or change other

{idents}, by reference to external objectivised Mimetics, has either zero, placebo, or harmful effects.

(12) Biomorphic techniques are explicitly directed at
restoration of BAB.

Empirical observation (experiment) has demonstrated that
simple hand and breath movements have immediate effect:

- to restore BAB
- to minimise /S/ interference.

We have also discovered that 3-5 repetitions of a Biomorphic
Exercise, are sufficient to engage │congruence│, such that
Θ<Constructs> can be accessed by volitional /S/{idents}.

The result is that you can achieve some of the effect in ASR
on BAB simply by recapitulating in your │M│entation,
the Biomorphic Exercise.

Practices

Fortunately, we have a resources to which we can direct
the reader.

On YouTube and at www.paulchaplin.life is a library of
Biomorphic Exercises:

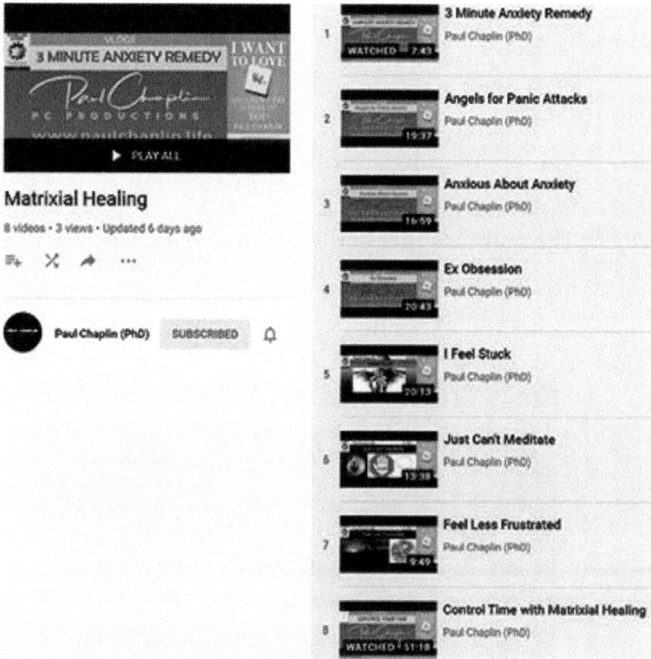

		3 Minute Anxiety Remedy
	1	Paul Chaplin (PhD)
		WATCHED — 7:43
		Angels for Panic Attacks
	2	Paul Chaplin (PhD)
		19:37
		Anxious About Anxiety
	3	Paul Chaplin (PhD)
		16:59
		Ex Obsession
	4	Paul Chaplin (PhD)
		20:43
		I Feel Stuck
	5	Paul Chaplin (PhD)
		20:13
		Just Can't Meditate
	6	Paul Chaplin (PhD)
		13:38
		Feel Less Frustrated
	7	Paul Chaplin (PhD)
		9:49
		Control Time with Matrixial Healing
	8	Paul Chaplin (PhD)
		WATCHED — 51:18

https://www.youtube.com/
playlist?list=PL51Rj0JrpYF14Rfv2CeU09KjPJXakp8mC

In this section, we will talk you through one of them, and explain the Biomorphic science which informs it.

3 Minute Anxiety Remedy
The reader will need to watch this 7.4 minutes video, so that the following explanation will make sense.

https://www.paulchaplin.life/vlog-1/
qk5dgdwb09utzoh1vqofd7o2q9ybqa

Now, let's explain the science.

The Problem

1. You're suffering from what is commonly thought of as <anxiety>.

2. The reality is that you're using /S/ to suppress operation of the ASR.

3. You've created Ш:

|congruence|

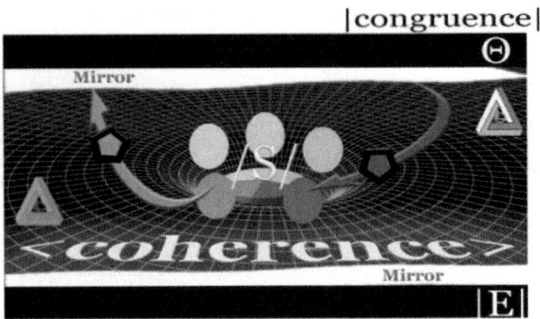

4. There could be an infinite number of "reasons": {idents} which you could call forth in /S/ to explain, or justify such suppression. None of them matter. So "talking" to them, is pointless.

5. It's that suppression which is preventing your natural Soothing dynamic to be effective.

6. That suppression keeps Anxiety going, but you're frustrating, impeding, its natural operation.

7. Your Θ is being denied Anxiety stimulus (via /S/), and so is unable to create <Constructs> which match your underlying Biomorphic Autonomic Balance.

Biomorphic Solution

<u>Step 1</u>

8.   We ask you to close your eyes. This limits $|W| => |E|$ interaction.

9.   We attach 2 fingers of each hand to those points in your body which are approximately close to the "top" and "bottom" of your Vagus Nerve.

10.   The reason we don't attach all your fingers, is that this would create a fixation. Test that: just place all your fingers of one hand on your leg, right now; then place only your 2 longest fingers; feel the difference between fixation and connection.

11.   We say "feel that connection between your fingers." This is a deliberate distraction focus, with sensitisation:

(a)   we focus /S/{identation} on a process which has no {ident} reference;

(b)   that distracts attention from the remaining /S/ {ident} continuum;

(c)   we sensitise /S/ to that $|P| => |E| => (\epsilon)$ input;

(d)   we enhance tunnelling of <Affect> through /S/, into Θ;
      thus

(e)   by intensifying <coherence> as a limited part of the /S/continuum, we begin to restore $|$congruence$|$.

12.   We allow this process to augment: to increase in intensity.

13.   That tunnelling is increasing the gravitational force of the Slices dynamic. Imagine strange and dys-

671

functional orbits, becoming more <coherent>:

|congruence|

14. That increasing <coherence> promotes even more effective tunnelling.

15. During this augmenting process, your /S/ubjectivity "inside your head" begins at first, feeling foggy and incoherent. Then, your head comes to feel sharp, and to cohere with the "heat" and "static electricity" which you seem to feel is passing between your fingers. These are simply suggestive metaphors which we deploy to allow your /S/ {idents} to self-justify what you're experiencing.

Step 2

16. Around 90 seconds into this ASR augmentation, we induce a sudden stop.

17. We ask you to breathe in deeply and hold the breath for 3 seconds.

18. It's a simple survival mechanism, an autonomic reflex: when your brain declares a state of non-oxygenation, that triggers in brain function outside the

neo-cortex,[256] a panic button response.

19. Your entire |P|, |E|, |M| Self goes into intense focus on solving the problem of an anticipated oxygen starvation.

20. Your Vagal stimulus stops. Instead the Vagal nerve is placed into an anticipation state, ready to respond to autonomic direction from the brainstem.

21. Your /S/{idents} understand what "3 seconds" means, and that you're not going to die. But the sudden interruption of your autonomic breathing function send a signal to that system, which has no conceptual apparatus.

22. The result, in essence, is a momentary shut down of the whole /S/ function.

23. Remember:

(a) the problem is that you're using /S/ to suppress operation of the ASR;

(b) we have now achieved suppression of that /S/ function, under the 90 second period; and

(c) we achieve shout down of /S/ to all but vestigial function, for 3 seconds.

24. That 3 seconds may not sound like a lot. In the millisecond landscape of human brain experience, and in the |T|imescape of quantised chronal interfaces, this is an equivalent to eternity. That's certainly how /S/{identation} experiences it.

25. For these 3,000 milliseconds, /S/ is receiving fo-

---

[256] your high function thinking brain control centre

cused ASR =>(€) input. The most basic human need is: oxygen.

26. All of our amazingly sophisticated /S/{ident} creations are suddenly helpless, and useless.

27. What it feels like inside your head is a sudden emptying. Your /S/{identation} production stops: save for its vestigial function as a channel to Θ.

Step 3

28. After the 3rd second, you breathe out.

29. We've removed the 2 fingers set up, and replaced it by a single hand over your chest.

30. We press this against the chest. We do this in ordinary life, instinctively, when we have a shock. It's a Biomorphic attachment to the autonomic lung function. Almost a "prayer" to the restored function.

31. We accompany this with allowing the body to fall backwards: into a chair, or onto a bed (from a seated position).

32. The usual response is to "pass out". The /S/ continuum pauses all but its vestigial functions. But now, that is happening without "external" stress on /S/ (whether from the ASR, or from the brainstem).

33. It is similar to a meditative state: but we did not use /S/ to get there.[257]

---

[257] trying to use /S/ to control /S/ simply does not work. That's why people find meditation techniques so difficult

Recovery Phase

34.   The recovery phase can take anything from 30 seconds to 3-5 minutes.

35.   You feel amazingly relaxed, yet alert. It's a nice place to stay.

(a)   You are experiencing unsuppressed flow of the ASR.

(b)   Gravitation distortions of the Slices have been reduced.

(c)   ASR is no longer "tunnelling through" /S/. Instead /S/ is using {ident} waves, shaped by the Slices gravity, to propagate ASR =>(€) input to Θ.

(d)   Θ<Constructs> are being used by /S/ in relatively undistorted <coherence>.

You feel great! When you attribute {idents} to what you are sensing, you report feeling:

- calm

- peace

- balance

- control

- energy

- power

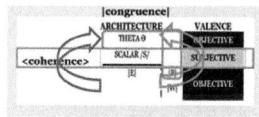

As we said:

> Biomorphics is the science which sets out empirically observed principles of how the ASR autonomically regulates <Affect>, in |congruence| with Θ: Biomorphic Autonomic Balance ("BAB").

We have succeeded, with the Biomorphic technique, in restoring your Biomorphic Autonomic Balance.

We've empirically observed the use of this Biomorphic technique in hundreds of subjects. Once shown how to use the technique, everyone is well capable of using it for themselves.

With repetition, the technique becomes more effective, and more quickly. Simply, /S/ becomes less effective at ASR suppression. The Slices dynamic gravity is less impeded. The Self is having its life experience at a threshold closer to its BAB.

The ASR is a process common to every human being. The BAB is unique to every human being. If that sounds odd, just remember that the ontogenesis of every person follows the same system: but the genetic markers of every human being, are unique.

Repetition also improves the ability of /S/ to cohere {idents} which correspond to Θ<Constructs>. Or to put it another way, to allow <coherence> to propagate ASR

=>($\in$) input as coherent waves to Θ.

The result is that you can simply "think" the Biomorphic technique, and your Self responds, just as if you ran the experience in real time.

This isn't "thinking yourself better". It's not a matter of constructing /S/{identation} for use in |congruence| interference: it's the opposite. It's like switching on your You$_2$ avatar.

It's important to note that we achieve all this, without trying to manipulate your /S/ubjective process, with words and ideas. The only words we actually spoke were:

(1)   Simple mechanical instructions for elementary manual movements;

(2)   basic guidance words which allow your /S/ {idents} to attend to the autonomic vagal response;

(3)   a 3 second breath holding, and exhalation instruction.

The guidance words are only spoken to speed up the process, and to normalise your /S/{ident} response. Even without them, the process happens. It's just more uncomfortable for the first few seconds.

We can, by persuasion, explanation and argument, challenge subjective ideas, with other ideas. But the problems that psychotherapy is supposed to treat, are not problems with ideas at all. They are problems with

ASR suppression and Slices dynamics: the two being intrinsically linked.

Classical Psychotherapy
It's important to recognise that none of the processes effected in Biomorphic Exercise, are imposed from the outside. You are not asked to think or feel anything, by reference to an external metric of meaning.

You've seen those endless "tomorrow is a better day" and so on memes on social media. Together with potted explanatories, by reference to which you can alter your /S/ ideas about things. So that you can change your "negativity".

We reject entirely that corpus of therapy, which seeks to persuade You to think and feel something different. You are Perfect already.

You were born with a perfect ASR. The ASR promotes BAB. The external world can impede neonate maintenance of BAB: by starving you, for example. Or by infectious disease, which either your |P|hysiology cannot cope with, or which is not successfully medicated.

Apart from these boundary conditions of |P|ysiological well-being, it is only your own /S/ {identation} which has the faculty of interference with the ASR.

In Chapter 2, Section B, we explained how self-stimulation of the |Exclusion Function| operates. In Section C, we explained the process by which <Affect> attaches to <Thought> potential.

It is by both of these means that we interfere with the ASR. Further interference, by Mimetic promotion of {idents} cannot in principle work, and demonstrably does not work.

We are engineered at birth, to perfection. The augmentation capacities of our higher brain functions, with which we are also endowed, are the soil of our human civilisation. Together with all its human-made suffering.

We regain our birth gift of Biomorphic Autonomic Balance perfection, not by thinking more: but by allowing ourself unimpeded becoming in the ASR dynamic of that perfection.

PART (3)
DREAMS AND MEMORY

In Part 1, we set out in detail the *Systems Architecture* of the Self. We explained that the /S/ubjective <self> is an infinite continuum, yet is "sandwiched" between layers of objectivity: |W|, |P| and Θ.

We explained the Systems under which these aspects of Self Architecture interact.

The existing paradigms of philosophy, neuroscience, and psychology (apart from spiritual, noetic or morphic fields theories) are founded upon the axiom that the brain and its |M|entation are *locked in a black box of the skull and body*."

We showed through matrixial analysis, and empirical *Experiences* which use "You$_2$", (the interaction of Θ and |W| through Ю interfaces) that the brain and its |M|entation are not so confined.

On the contrary, it is the objective interface ΘЮ|W| in quantised |T|ime which actually secures the very integrity of the Self. It is what allows the /S/ubjective Self to exist at all.

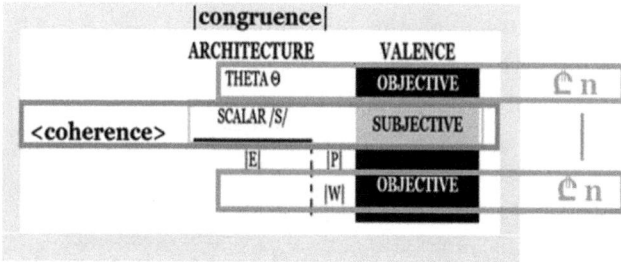

We also importantly demonstrated the Systems derivation of what we commonly think of as our /S/ubjective <self>: our "thoughts" and "feelings".

In common with 21st century work in Interoception, we showed that "thoughts" and "feelings" are all {idents}, formed under exactly the same System, and relating to each other under an equivalence function in an /S/ continuum of layer-bounded infinity.

In Part 2, we look at the *Processes* which underlie the operation of the /S/ system. We differentiated between <I> and <Me>:

- <I> is the objective mode of identity: what persists through time and space. The very atoms of our body change over a 7 year cycle. Yet the interaction of ΘЮ I W I in quantised I T I ime is perpetual.[258]
- <Me> is the /S/ubjective {identation} of being an architecturally layered <self>, in bounded infinity.

Personality is framed by the interaction of <I> and <Me>.

---

[258] given the subsistence of an organic entity to manifest it

We then explained the core process of the Anxiety Soothing Rhythm (ASR"). How functioning of the ASR is fundamental to the science of *Biomorphics*.

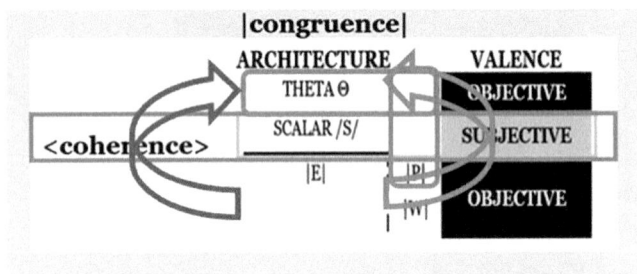

We then introduced the concept of the 5 Slices: the Coherence Quotient Dynamic (CQD).

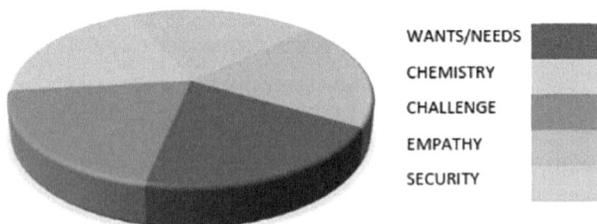

We explained that:

> We perpetually interfere with our Slices dynamics. Remember that the Slices represent /S/ aggregates of the ASR function.

> The perpetual struggle for /S/<coherence> is not a "bad thing". It's not something we ought to try and stop. If we ever did succeed in stopping

it, the outcome would be serious psychological impairment.

The task of Psychotectics is to "think our way into Soothing", by encouraging /S/<coherence> around harmonic Slices dynamics.

Then, we explained the phenomenon of Ш Shadow Slices: what we commonly think of as "obsessions". We explained the dominating role that these Ш come to have in our subjective lives. Their Frankenstein nature, as they evade all efforts to bring them within the <coherence> gravity of CQD.

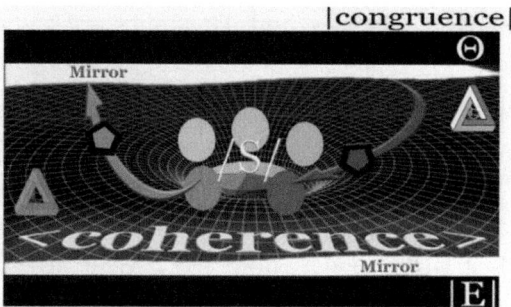

Yet, how they are a product of that very quest for <coherence>, the need we intrinsically feel to "make sense", from inside the /S/ continuum, of that which cannot be understood from within it.

In this final Part, we examine two further dimensions of /S/ubjectivity: Dreams and Memory. We then explore some aspects of Self relations to other Selfs. Finally, we draw some life lessons about *Finding the Power of You.*

CHAPTER 10

DREAMS

A search of Science Direct under the term "dreams"[259] returns over 94,000 results. Theorising about dreams goes back at least to Aristotle's *On Dreams*, written around 350 BC.[260]

For an excellent review of issues outstanding since Athenian thought of the 5th century BC, see Windt, Jennifer M., "Dreams and Dreaming", *The Stanford Encyclopedia of Philosophy* (Summer 2020 Edition), Edward N. Zalta (ed.).[261]

Aristotle thought that dreams were (in matrixial logic notation) an emanation of $|P|=>/S/$. Some 2,500 years layer, that is the model which has been returned to by Interoception. A 2020 paper, *Interoception relates to sleep and sleep disorders* by Yishul Wei. Eus. JW Van Someren[262] suggests:

> The central nervous system senses and responds to afferent signals arising from the body. These interoceptive afferents are essential to physiological homeostatic control and are known to influence an individual's momentary affect, cognition, motivation, and conscious experiences. Both sleep and interoception are tightly connected to physical and mental well-being.

---

[259] https://www.sciencedirect.com/search?qs=dreams
[260] http://classics.mit.edu/Aristotle/dreams.html. JI Beare Translation
[261] URL = <https://plato.stanford.edu/archives/sum2020/entries/dreams-dreaming/>.
[262] Current Opinion in Behavioral Sciences Volume 33, June 2020, Pages 1-7. https://doi.org/10.1016/j.cobeha.2019.11.008

This review outlines the current knowledge about the interactions between interoception and sleep. It is demonstrated that there are complex, dynamic relations between sleep and sensory processes within each modality of interoception, including thermoception, nociception, visceral sensations, and subjective feelings about these sensations.

A better understanding and appreciation of the intricate interrelations may facilitate management of functional somatic symptoms, chronic pain, insomnia, and other sleep and mental disorders.

Or as Aristotle put it, without the benefit of fMRI devices:[263]
From this it is manifest that the stimulatory movements based upon sensory impressions, whether the latter are derived from external objects or from causes within the body, present themselves not only when persons are awake, but also then, when this affection which is called sleep has come upon them, with even greater impressiveness.

For by day, while the senses and the intellect are working together, they (i.e. such movements) are extruded from consciousness or obscured, just as a smaller is beside a larger fire, or as small beside great pains or pleasures, though, as soon as the latter have ceased, even those which are trifling emerge into notice.

But by night *i.e. in sleep* owing to the inaction of the particular senses, and their powerlessness to realize themselves, which arises from the reflux of the hot from the exterior parts to the interior, they *i.e. the above 'movements* are borne in to the head quarters of sense-perception, and there display themselves as the disturbance (of waking life) subsides.

The matrixial model of Self only moves a small dimensional step in understanding.

It is common ground across all disciplines which consider dream states and functions, that <sleep> is a biologically

---

[263] op. cit Part 3

defined state. The "cat flap" of consciousness is closed to external |W| stimuli. Of course, the flap will open if |W| effects disturbance sufficient to open it: your alarm clock, an earthquake, your bed partner's snores.

All /S/{identations} originate with vector collapse of <Thought> infinity potential in interaction with <Affect>:

<Thought>

$$\Delta <\top^n> | \infty$$

$$\textstyle\sum<\!\in\!> (\top) \neq (-\top) = \textit{\textbf{Ł}}[I]$$

<Affect> [$\sum<\!\in\!>$] derives from |W|, and |P| and /S/. These Systems processes continue during sleep. Hence the multi-millennial puzzlement over how dream /S/ differs from waking /S/.

In this <Affect>=>/S/ *Unilinear Model*, we can acknowledge that |W|=>… [$\sum<\!\in\!>$] plays a diminished role. Yet that leaves the other origin sources of <Affect> awake and kicking: the Aristotelian insight.

Matrixial analysis enables us to see immediately what, exactly, is different about the sleeping dreams condition:

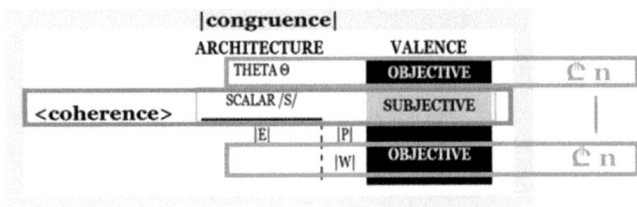

|congruence|			
ARCHITECTURE	**VALENCE**		
THETA Θ	**OBJECTIVE**		₵ n
<coherence> SCALAR /S/	**SUBJECTIVE**		
|E| |P|			
|W|	**OBJECTIVE**		₵ n

So the Ю interaction function under quantised |T|ime no longer has effect. It can still be going on: but the doorway from |W| to |P| is closed: so the Ю interaction function has no effect.

You might put it that:

dreaming is /S/ubjective {identation} out of | T | ime.

The excision of temporal order in the sleep state results in our usual direction being obversed. In waking awarness:[264]

- our | E | points forwards in | T | ime: the headlights
- our /S/ points backwards in | T | ime: the rear-view mirror.

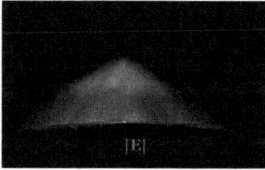

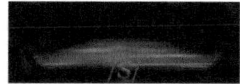

This temporal direction depends upon | congruence |, which is founded upon our becoming in perpetual relationship with the world | W |.

In the sleep state, the Architectural structure of our Self | congruence | remains, but it is unaffixed to physio-temporal interaction with the | W | orld and thus, in response to | W |. Our | congruence | architecture floats free of the world which creates and sustains it.

---

[264] see Chapter 3

Thus our {identation} becomes, simply, confused. The reality checks[265] which we, in waking awareness, rely upon for <coherence>, is temporarily lost.

Our |E| headlights can become turned back on dream-figments of ourselves. We figment parallel dimensions out of /S/{idents}, which our waking <coherence> would not allow.

The gravity of the Slices CQD still has effect, which is why we dream within limits which we can discern upon reconstructing our dreams. The Slices don't have the gravitational power of our waking state, because they are not being "fed" by all the stimuli usually available from |W|=>|P| interactions.

All this has profound consequences for dream analysis. And for therapeutic interventions directed towards allowing you to re-integrate dream experiences in your waking manifest.

Temporal Dream Therapy
With this matrixial analysis in place, let's try an example of TDT

Experience: Running
Step 1

_____

[265] see Chapter 2

Imagine you're having a recurrent dream about being chased.

Close your eyes

Now:

- Just play your version of that dream, in your head.

Stop

Discussion:

(1)   This is a vey common dream. It can often be uncomfortable.

Step 2

Be ready to imagine the same being chased dream, with your eyes shut.

Now:

- see yourself in the rear view mirror of a car which you are sat in
- play your version of that dream, in your head.

Discussion:

(1)   This time, you can't run.

(2)   You're no longer being chased.

(3)   Instead, if you're moving at all: it's voluntary, or being pulled, towards your viewing perspective.

This *Experience* demonstrates how the subsumption of a dream experience to temporal restatement profoundly alters the /S/ubjective experience of its contents.

But, in TDT, we don't pay much attention to the content of dreams.

dreaming is /S/ubjective {identation} out of | T | ime.

So, {identation} which relies for its <coherence> upon interactions with | W | (whether through | P | or Ю) is hardly relevant to a-temporal {identation} in dream states.

The interpretation of dreams is on a scientific par with the discernment of your future by poking around in animal entrails.

It can be a brilliantly artistic and seductive Freudian enterprise: but then again so is Tarot reading.

Meaning is Social, Not Personal
The very idea of dream reading starts with a supposition that your awake and aware /S/{identation} "makes sense", in some objectively verifiable way. It doesn't. And it doesn't need to.

That is the sovereign glory of individual thoughts and feelings. They don't need to "make sense" to anyone, not even the individual who is entertaining them.

We can impose an Aristotelian logic (identity logic) on our /S/ubjective thoughts. We can willingly endorse cognitive dissonances, which identity logic would proclaim to be contradictory.

Since all of our {ident} association are completely arbitrary within the bounded infinity of the /S/ continuum, to seek objective "sense" in our {identation}, is itself a complete contradiction.

Whatever our thoughts and feelings "means" for each of us, from moment to moment, and if we can even trace a meaning at all (or bother to), is a matter beyond the province of science and rationality.

The /S/ubjective only has meaning in social association

We'll draw out consequences of this rubric in later Chapters.

No Unconscious

To say that dream interpretation is rather less objective than astrology[266] is, of course, entirely to reject that corpus of psychology which relies upon the "unconscious". We do.

After all, speculations about the unconscious are not scientific theories: they are necessarily immune to empirical validation.

We can see useful evidence of this in a contemporary survey of Unconsciousness theories:[267]

---

[266] at least your birth sign designation is an objective fact of the calendar
[267] Bargh JA, Morsella E. The Unconscious Mind. *Perspect Psychol Sci.* 2008;3(1):73-79. doi:10.1111/j.1745-6916.2008.00064.x

Contemporary perspectives on the unconscious mind are remarkably varied. In cognitive psychology, unconscious information processing has been equated with subliminal information processing, which raises the question, "How good is the mind at extracting meaning from stimuli of which one is not consciously aware?" (e.g., **Greenwald, Klinger, & Schuh, 1995**). Because subliminal-strength stimuli are relatively weak and of low intensity by definition, the mental processes they drive are necessarily minimal and unsophisticated, and so these studies have led to the conclusion that the powers of the unconscious mind are limited and that the unconscious is rather "dumb" (**Loftus & Klinger, 1992**).

Social psychology has approached the unconscious from a different angle. There, the traditional focus has been on mental processes of which the individual is unaware, not on stimuli of which one is unaware (e.g., **Nisbett & Wilson, 1977**). Over the past 30 years, there has been much research on the extent to which people are aware of the important influences on their judgments and decisions and of the reasons for their behavior. This research, in contrast with the cognitive psychology tradition, has led to the view that the unconscious mind is a pervasive, powerful influence over such higher mental processes (see review in **Bargh, 2006**).

And, of course, the Freudian model of the unconscious is still with us and continues to exert an influence over how many people think of "the unconscious," especially outside of psychological science. Freud's model of the unconscious as the primary guiding influence over daily life, even today, is more specific and detailed than any to be found in contemporary cognitive or social psychology. However, the data from which Freud developed the model were individual case studies involving abnormal thought and behavior (**Freud, 1925/1961**, p. 31), not the rigorous scientific experimentation on generally applicable principles of human behavior that inform the psychological models. Over the years, empirical tests have not been kind to the specifics of the Freudian model, though in broad-brush terms the cognitive and social psychological evidence does support Freud as to the existence of unconscious mentation and its potential to impact judgments and behavior (see **Westen, 1999**). Regardless of the fate of his specific model, Freud's historic importance in championing the powers of the unconscious mind is beyond any doubt.

How one views the power and influence of the unconscious relative to conscious modes of information processing largely depends on how one defines the unconscious. Until quite recently in the history of science and philosophy, mental life was considered entirely or mainly conscious in nature (e.g., Descartes' *cogito* and John Locke's "mind first" cosmology). The primacy of conscious thought for how people historically have thought about the mind is illustrated today in the words we use to describe other kinds of processes -all are modifications or qualifications of the word *conscious* (i.e., unconscious, preconscious, subconscious, nonconscious). Moreover, there has been high consensus regarding the qualities of conscious thought processes: they are intentional, controllable, serial in nature (consumptive of limited processing resources), and accessible to awareness (i.e., verbally reportable).

No such consensus exists yet for the unconscious, however. Because of the monolithic nature of the definition of a conscious process—if a process does not possess all of the qualities of a conscious process, it is therefore not conscious—at least two different "not conscious" processes were studied over the course of the 20th century within largely independent research traditions that seemed barely to notice the other's existence: the New Look research in perception involving the preconscious analysis of stimuli prior to the products of the analysis being furnished to conscious awareness, and skill-acquisition research involving the gain in efficiency of processes with practice over time until they become subconscious (see the review in **Bargh & Chartrand, 2000**).

The Self is a holistic Systems Architecture. All theories of the unconscious operate under the mereological fallacy: trying to find independent meaning in parts.

If it means anything at all[268] "consciousness" is not sensibly limited to "thoughts that we know we are thinking because we can name or describe them."

---

[268] and we doubt the usefulness of the concept

693

If we have to enter the muddy waters of "consciousness" theorising, then we would draw this distinction:

- /S/ubjectivity is an empirically observable fact about Selfs
- "Consciousness" is simply the appearance to other Selfs of that /S/ubjectivity.

But since the latter only manifests through ΘЮO|W|, which is an objective interaction, no theory of "consciousness" can enter into the actual /S/ continuum: save by {identative} equivalence as between one Self[269] and another.

In like manner, to try and subtract out part of the holistic Self and assign it a theoretical category of unconscious: that was just a mistake made in Vienna over a century ago. Like other Viennese mistakes of that era,[270] we should not allow their phantoms to trouble us today.

---

[269] that is, the communicative reports of that Self
[270] like with a Charlie Chaplin moustache and funny haircut

CHAPTER 11

MEMORY

Classical Accounts

A useful review, going back to Ebbinghaus (1885) is provided in:

Cowan N. What are the differences between long-term, short-term, and working memory?. *Prog Brain Res.* 2008;169:323-338. doi:10.1016/S0079-6123(07)00020-9

Further standard resources include:

Atkinson, R. C., & Shiffrin, R. M. (1971). *The control processes of short-term memory.* Institute for Mathematical Studies in the Social Sciences, Stanford University.

Baddeley, A.D., & Hitch, G. (1974). Working memory. In G.H. Bower (Ed.), *The psychology of learning and motivation: Advances in research and theory* (Vol. 8, pp. 47–89). New York: Academic Press.

Miller, G. (1956). The magical number seven, plus or minus two: Some limits on our capacity for processing information. *The psychological review*, 63, 81-97.

Peterson, L. R., & Peterson, M. J. (1959). Short-term retention of individual verbal items. *Journal of experimental psychology*, 58(3), 193-198.

There is common ground that Memory is not a "filing cabinet" in the head.

That the hippocampus is implicated in the neurological working of brain functions, is well founded in empirical evidence. But it is not thought that the hippocampus is a storage facility: rather, a part of the brain used in Memory function.

All these investigations follow the Classical Unilinear Model:

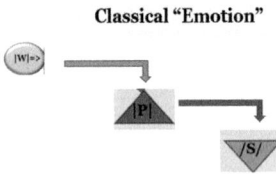

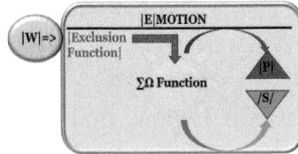

Classical "Emotion"

| Unilinear Models | Matrixial Systems Architecture |

The refusal of the Classical Account to allow "filing cabinet" space in the brain, invokes paradox.

To the lay thinker, it certainly seems like You go to such a storage repository to access memories. It's a sense we all have whenever we remember. Yet it's surely right, as a matter of neuroanatomy, that there is no physical storage place in the brain: no "hard drive" as there is in a computer.

So, the matter of Memory has become another perennial mystery. Science has been able to test, empirically, the boundaries of Memory function. But as to how it actually works, that remains a Secret of the Self.

Matrixial Memory

With the advantage of Self Systems Architecture, we can make short work of memory.

Unlike other theories based in Classical Models, we can actually prove, empirically, the matrixial understanding of Memory: by changing it, irrevocably, and instantly.

What we commonly, and in neuroscience, philosophy and psychology, call Memory, is actually a composite of processes engaged in Systems within Architecture:

In /S/ Continuum

(1)   /S/ operates an equivalence function, seeking <coherence>.

(2)   <coherence> uses techniques: patterns, habits, reflexes.

(3)   Interaction of |W|, |PP and /S/ gives rise to repetitions.

(4)   Similar stimulus evokes similar /S/ response. Even without <coherence> seeking, that would be so.

(5)   <coherence> seeks justification of itself: that's the essence of <coherence>.

(6)   That {justification} is part of what Memory is.

(7)   This is where we derive the idea that things which are remembered "mean" something: otherwise we wouldn't remember them. You don't remember meaningless things (or event-combinations of things).

{ident} Creation By <Affect> Attachment

All /S/{identations} originate with vector collapse of <Thought> infinity potential in interaction with <Affect>:

<Thought>

$$\Delta < \top^{n} > | \infty$$

$$\sum < \epsilon > (\top) \neq (-\top) = \textit{Ł}[I]$$

<Affect> [$\sum$<ϵ>] derives from |W|, and |P| and /S/.

(8)   Of course, we use <Affect> stimulus to attach to <Thought> Potentials: all the time.

(9)   The <Affect> attachments lend that power which enables us to invest <coherence> (belief) in particular {idents} as "memories".

(10) **Preventing $\sum$<ϵ> ($\top$) $\neq$ (-$\top$) =Ł[I] for a particular set of <Thoughts>, prevents the experience of specific instances of Memory.**[271]

In Θ <Constructs>

(11) So far as we wish to structure Memory with word concepts, we must draw upon Θ <Constructs>: transforming them into /S/{idents}.

(12) What we are also able to do, is to submit {ident} Forms to Θ for equalisation as <Constructs>.

(13) <Constructs> are not Forms of Content: they are processes only.

(14) The endless objective landscape of <Constructs> is the effective modulus of Memory.

---

[271] we will prove this below in *Wipe Experience*

In Ю | W |

(15) Until Memory potentials are realised Mimetically (in communication), they have "diluted" reality for the Self. They subsist only as experiences manufactured by {identation} under equivalence to whatever are the present {identations} of Self. That's why our "memories"[272] change throughout our lives.

(16) Once Mimetically communicated {idents} are no longer Memory at all.

There's a lot in here to unwrap. Let's examine some themes.

Storage and Retention

Matrixial Memory analysis puts it this way.

• there's no storage facility of {idents} in /S/: no filing cabinet.

But:

• there are Memorial <Constructs> in Theta Θ
• which are maintained through | T |: temporal affinity.

Again, we are bound to return to the matter of | T | ime in understanding how the Memorial aspect of Self operates.

Recall from the Doorbell metaphor, that our | E | is forward-looking in time. Ω is a distributed referral system.

It refers quantised <signal> transformations, as qualitative

---

[272] of the same thing

outputs, to |P| and /S/. The |W| origin of those inputs is itself always in the past: from microseconds, to light years. Our |E| is headlights, beaming into the future.

/S/ is a reactive domain. It is always looking backwards: receiving <Affect> input from the past. Our /S/ is a rear-view mirror. looking into the past.

Thus, in an origin sense:

all /S/ {identation} is an act of memorialising the past.

/S/ seeks <coherence>. The Architecture which allows <coherence>, is |congruence| between Θ and |W|.

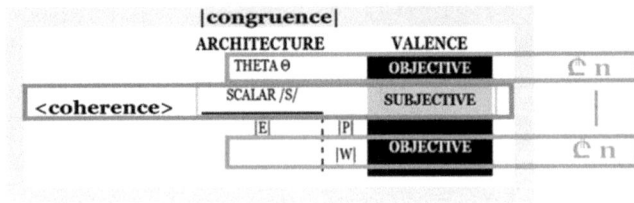

|congruence|		
ARCHITECTURE		VALENCE
THETA Θ		**OBJECTIVE**	ℭ n
SCALAR /S/	<coherence>	**SUBJECTIVE**	
|E|	|P|		
	|W|	**OBJECTIVE**	ℭ n

Θ operates an equalisation function, as we have explored in many aspects since Chapter 5 of *Matrixial Logic*. Θ operates in <Constructs>, not Content Forms: although we can only represent Θ<Constructs> in matrixial inequality equations.

Grammatical and syntactical structure, are necessary to the granting of meaning to any {ident} associations.

Experience: Lal
Just look around your room
Or outside into a landscape

Don't form any sentences in your head

You can use single name words for what you look at, if you like

Now:

• Look, think, reflect

Stop

Discussion:

(1)   Ask yourself the question: *what did any of this mean?*

Your answer will be that the questions doesn't really make sense. There's no "meaning" here.

There's no meaning without {ident} association, which acts through equivalence: and we can't effect equivalence without grammar and syntax.

And without grammar and syntax, we can't construct identity logic, or any logic. So we can't effect /S/<coherence>.

Grammar and syntax are Θ<Constructs>. They originate, from neonate stage, in Mimetic social interaction. They are re-originated by the same means. Why is why:

> the <Constructs>, by reference to which we manufacture
> {ident} association meanings, are socio-temporal.

Θ<Constructs> are an IO interface: like infinite layers of a co-ordinate dot lattices. We bring segments from the dot lattices into /S/{identation}, and apply equivalence.

We manufacture present meanings in /S/{identation} using the same process by which we construct past meanings. We call one (if we call it anything) "contemporary cognition", and we call the other Memory.

But they are the same process, within the same Systems Architecture. We simply choose to manufacture different {ident} associations: or don't.

At the ordinary experience level, we are well-used to the idea that environment influences not only our present thoughts, but our Memory.

The "internal environment" of the Self, as we pass through our life years of experience, effects change in our Memory patterns: our {ident} associations. What you once remembered with love, you now remember with antipathy: and vice versa.

Our identification of Memory states, one with another, is an act of equivalence.

- We take a Θ<Construct> dot lattice segment into /S/.
- We manufacture {idents} in association under the "meaning" provided by that lattice segment.
- We also, if we allow it, attach <Affect> to {idents} under that association.

We've just remembered the smell and taste of coffee on a lovely morning on a hotel balcony.

Experience: Trails
Step 1:
Please get a tea or coffee, or glass of water
If you don't already have one

Now:
- Think some calm thoughts
- Take a drink

Stop

Step 2:

Now:
- Have a look in the history of your head about what just happened in your head

Discussion:
(1)   You can probably sense that your introspection at Step 1 feels much the same as Step 2

Step 3:
Cast your mind back a year or more.
To a venue outside your home (restaurant, hotel, bar, club, café)

Now:
- Remember a pleasant occasion on which you had a drink at that venue
- Have a look in the history of your head about what just happened in your head

Discussion:
(1)   You can probably sense that your introspection at Step 3 feels much the same as Steps 1 and 2.
(2)   What was different was the "memory library searching".

Like you were riffling through an invisible photo album, then choosing the right page. You felt the delay, while the search reference operation went on.

Of course, there's no photo album: no filing cabinet. There is in Θ<Constructs> (metaphorically): *a set of instructions for making that kind of Memory.*

Let's use Θ<Construct> "Memory making instructions" and see.
Experience: Dino
Step 1:

Think back to a time when you chased something. Just for fun is fine. A dog, a household pet, a friend at school.

Now:
- Play the chase Memory

Stop

Step 2:
Now we are going to remember something that has never, ever, happened to you.

Imagine:
thinking back to a time when you chased a friendly dinosaur through a Jurassic park.[273]

Now:
• Play the chase Memory

Stop

Discussion:
(1)   You can probably sense that your introspection at Step 1 feels much the same as Step 2

You've constructed a "fake" memory. But it's just as real to you as your memory of having a drink, where you're sitting, 5 minutes ago.

It's just as real, because the process for manufacturing that Memory is:
        the same process, within the same Systems Architecture. We simply choose to manufacture different {ident} associations: or don't.

---

[273] Yes, we know: wrong period, technically

Traumatic Memory ("TM")

We explained in Chapter 7 *Shadows*:

(8)   To try and solve thinking and feeling problems, in pursuit of /S/<coherence>, we formulate Ш.

(9)   Ш are abstracted meta-Forms of <Thought> Potentials.

(10)   Ш subsist within the /S/<continuum>.

(11)   But the innate logic of their creation makes them inaccessible to other {identation} within /S/.

(12)   So, it's like Ш are in an "attic" or sub-dimension.

(13)   Because Ш are meta-Forms, created by layers of <Nodes>, they barely have any relation to actual {ident} Content.

(14)   So, Ш are very unstable.

(15)   Their Potential collapses easily with attachment to <Affects>.

Those <Affects> are arriving in /S/ every moment of our life. Our very living and breathing is providing power to Ш, without us even needing to direct that "electricity".

Our Slices work to cohere our {identation}. They are the 5 gravitational forces which act to provide <coherence>: that <coherence> for which we perpetually strive in our /S/ubjectivity. What we experience as sanity.

But, our Ш seems to grow outside our control. Our

> Slices gravity has no effect on them. We can't get them to submit to <coherence>.
>
> They are Ш *Shadow Slices.* Our /S/ubjective {identation} creates them: yet like a Frankenstein monster, they seem to acquire controlling power over us.

We use the Slices to create "gravity" within the /S/ continuum: or rather, they use us.

TM uses Ш *Shadow Slices*. Rather than drawing from equalised Θ<Constructs>, TM uses Ш with present moment attachments to <Affect>.

That's why we drink and drug in addictions cycles: to disrupt the process of <Affect> attachment. But disruption stops, when the substance stops having effect.

Just pausing there. Repeating basic mechanisms:

> All /S/{identations} originate with vector collapse of <Thought> infinity potential in interaction with <Affect>:

<Thought>

Δ<$\top^{n}$>|∞

∑<€> (⊤) ≠ (-⊤) =**₺**[I]

> <Affect> [∑<€>] derives from |W|, and |P| and

/S/. These Systems processes continue during sleep. Hence the multi-millennial puzzlement over how dream /S/ differs from waking /S/.

We don't go get replacement Memory at the bar, or from the dealer. We take substances, which have obvious pharmaceutical effect. That primary effect is to disrupt our ordinary <Affect>=>{ident} attachments.

We drink and drug to alter:

$$\sum <\text{€}> (\top) \neq (-\top) = \text{₺}[I]$$

This is perfectly understandable, and completely rational. You can't think to yourself "Don't think X". That's a long established NLP truism:

- never instruct a person to "stop" thinking X, because they then are bound to think X
- it's ineffective to instruct someone "Don't stop", because all they hear is "Stop".

Hang on, are we saying out loud that it's a good idea? To take mind-altering substances in order to have (inevitably, as a matter of pharmacology) temporary effect on Memories which upset us? Or to effect neurological disruption in hope of achieving an "emotional" dislocation from the present, so as to get happy?

It's not the best way of achieving the objective, but it's a perfectly rational attempt. That's why billions of perfectly sane people do it.

There are neurological, biological and life experience downsides to pharmacological therapy. We recognise that. But that does not affect the intrinsic rationality of the enterprise from the standpoint of the Self.

But we don't need a war on drugs. That is the proclamation of a necessarily losing battle against the intrinsic dynamics of the Self.

And it's completely unnecessary. With the understanding of Matrixial Memory, we can do so much better. We can do it quicker: indeed, instantly. Permanently, and without pain or pharmaceutical intervention.

We can change your Memories.

Matrixial Memory Adjustment
We are going to take you on an *Experience* in Matrixial Healing. In *Psychotectics*:

Experience: Wipe
Phase 1:
Think of a traumatic or unpleasant memory.
Play the movie of it on a video player screen
      You've done this lots of times
      You can play 10 hour's worth of movie in 10 seconds.

See what you see. Hear what you hear. Feel and sense what you feel.

Stop the videotape. Rewind to start.

Phase 2:
Come back into the room. Breathe. Close your eyes.

Feel a You$_2$ presence. A second you.

> If you're not sure about how this feels, have another go at other Experiences in this book which use You$_2$

Feel the connection:
- between You$_2$ and You
- between the inside of the head of You2 , and your head

Feel that connection

Notice that You$_2$
- can see You
- can see inside your head
- can see you watching the video screen

Be inside the head of You$_2$,
- which can watch you looking at the video screen
- can see the space between you and the video screen
- can see you when you reach to press the video player play button

Feel that connection

> between
> You$_2$ and inside your head

Be in that connection with You$_2$

Now:
- press Play on the video player

Discussion:
(1)   You can't press Play, now
(2)   Or, you can press the button, but nothing happens.

Now, carry on:
Experience: Wipe
Phase 3:
Think of a happy memory
- from when you were 5-7
- from when you were 11-13
- from when you were 15-17

anything happy: big or small.

Just let the happy memories swirl around, like different flavours of ice cream, in a tub.

There.

Now: back to the video player
• press Play on the video player

<u>Discussion</u>:
(1)   Now, when you press Play, all you are getting is the sensations of those ice cream memories.

And now, a little "sub-routine" in your head, is scurrying around, looking for those lost memories. It's like that feeling when you know your keys are in the house somewhere, but you just can't fine them.

But there's a a big difference: those keys are there somewhere. But the memories have gone.

Empirical tests have shown that the memory loss is permanent. Over periods of weeks and months: the memories don't come back. That the *Psychotectic* longitudinal effect.

You can remember Facts: just like facts about history; or biographical facts like your birth date or address.

But they don't *mean* anything. They are just facts. You don't attach "emotions" to them. You can if you like, but it seems pretty pointless to try.

Now: go look for the box cover picture for that TM video. OK, that's gone too.

And check out the library where you used to keep the video box. No, that's gone as well. You kind of know where it used to be. But now it's like a closed door at the end of a corridor: and the corridor is fading away.

You'll keep running that "try and find it" sub-routine for a few days. That's natural. You've created a habit of marking that "library" on your mental map, so you can always have quick access to it. But now the contents it used to house, have gone. So the library has gone too.

Now:

How Do You Feel?

The usual response is a combination of:
- kind of empty but not really
- like a weight's been lifted
- feeling the need to smile
- feeling a sudden burst of energy

All this good stuff: it stays with you. For days and weeks and months.

Yet, You will do what we all do. Manufacture more "memories" as make-believe reality. Just like remembering chasing dinosaurs.

If this *Wipe Experience* worked for you, you'll want to know why it worked. We've explained in Parts 1 and 2 how it all works: the *Systems Architecture.*

In wiping TM, we're applying the rubrics of this Part 3:

Phase 1
- you manufacture a "memory" in /S/, using co-ordinates lattice segments from Θ
- you attach <Affect> to that {identation} "memory": that's playing the video and experiencing it.

Phase 2
- We use the You$_2$ avatar, to engage you$_r$ Θ<Constructs>
- Your Θ<Constructs> don't ever interact with <Affect>
- You're then trying to attach <Affect> to {identation} "memory"; but
- your /S/ is being prevented from doing that; because
- you are processing information under Θ equalisation, not /S/ equivalence

So:
- you van think thoughts about things: facts, history
- but they don't have an "emotional" attachment to <Affect>

Which results in:
- You're unable to "play" – to experience – that emotionally attached "memory".

Phase 3
- We got you to make some "ice cream" memories, and allow Θ to co-ordinate point them in dimensional layering with the TM.

- So, when /S/{identation} reaches for the Θ<Construct> lattice segment, it gets ice cream.

That's just a positive reinforcement. And it "fills the gap" which /S/ temporarily feels, in the loss of TM. Technically, it satisfies the intrinsic /S/ drive for <coherence>.

The reason this TM loss is permanent, is that you have now "rewired your brain".[274] You now have a Θ<Construct> for the data which you previously used in /S/ to construct those idents.

That data is now held in a co-ordinate lattice framework in Θ: the objective |M|entation. Your /S/ubjective |M|entation can't alter that objective co-ordinate lattice framework, any more than it can alter the rules of grammar or syntax: which are what allow you to create "meaning" (in attachment of <Affect> to <Thought> Potential), in the first place.

It's like trying to cut off a tree branch which you're sitting on, while remaining suspended by the branch: can't be done.

Note what we *didn't* ask you to try and do:
- to think your way out of TM
- to feel your way out of TM
- to resist experiencing TM
- to medicalise your memory with pharmaceutical intervention.

---

[274] an alteration in electro-magnetic |congruence|, not synaptic adhesion

Metaphorically and approximately: we just took the toys you were playing with off the /S/ carpet and out of your hands. We placed them back on the shelf of the shop they came from, in their original boxes. So, now you forget about those gone toys, and you make new ones.

We can't stop you making bad memories: TM's. And we wouldn't want to. You're the boss of You.

But now you know that you can wipe TM's, you'll find that your /S/ is very much more reluctant to manufacture them in the first place. That's another function of <coherence>.

Childhood Wounds

All of which, of course, leads us to understand that the psychotherapy theories of "childhood wounds", are: nonsense.

We do not carry around a heavy suitcase of TM's from childhood. Because there's no suitcase storage: there are Θ<Construct> co-ordinate lattices, which we can choose to use in /S/, and attach <Affect>.

That's repeated present date manufacture, not revisiting a sacred past.

Experience: Cuppa

Imagine: a cup of tea, or coffee, or a glass of water on your table.

Now focus:
fill yourself with thoughts and feelings of disgust
smell how that drink smells vile
tastes foul
the mere sight or thought of it making you want to feel sick

Now, you're in that mindset:
- imagine keeping this disgust going for the next 5 days.

Discussion:

(1)   You can see that the visualisation is not possible.

(2)   You'd be hard pressed to keep it up for 5 minutes.

There's a "reaction". You're creating "memory". A grown person with an adult mind, with all its powers. Yet you know you couldn't keep it up even for a few hours.

So how is a child of say age 5 supposed to achieve such a I M I entative feat? They can't: because it's impossible.

There are no "childhood wounds". We are Selfs, grown and matured in circumstances. All with the same Systems Architecture.

We have reflexes. The whole point of these is that they don't pass through /S/ at all. We react to sudden noises, changes of scene, acceleration: all sorts of circumstances. We are biologically wired to react to autonomic stimulus. That's nothing to do with memory.

717

Of course, when we're 0-7, we engage with our circumstances. We create /S/ {idents} patterns and habits. But these are all equivalences. They are not real in any objective sense. They have whatever meaning we choose to invest in them. We can choose differently. And we do. All the time.

The circumstances of our development definitely affect the evolution of our Slices gravity. But again, that's autonomic: the working out of our ASR in /S/. Nothing to do with Memory.

Now, if you want to say that "childhood wounds" are what we've just been describing, then fine. It's radically changing the classical meaning propounded by the psychotherapy community: but change is cool.

But that change of position raises another, terminally serious problem. We can, with just a few words and engagement by avatar of your Θ, effect fundamental *Psychotectic* change.

You can wipe your "childhood wounds" TM. In moments. Permanently.

If there were some leaden weight baggage of "wounds" that you had been carrying around since infant days, then this wipe effect is inexplicable.

We have the explanation:

Mentation
How we can think governs what we can think
Emotion
What we can emote governs how we emote

Your "wound" is simply You choosing to try and hide {idents} from your own Systems Architecture. You have to keep pouring energy in to achieve this: which works by suppressing your ASR.[275]

So, you're keeping a set of {idents} in Shadow land, and when the energy supply starts to fail (which it always will, inevitably), you seek to disrupts <Affect>=>{ident} attachment by interposing pharmaceutical (or other {ident} attachment displacement) solutions. Which stop working sooner or later.

In the Unilinear Model of the Classical Account, all you can do is try and think or emote your way out of this. Which is just adding more {ident} lumber to the Ш attic.

With *Psychotectics*, we simply acknowledge the attic. Indeed we make it a centre of focus. We make it transparent to the operation of Θ<Constructs>, which don't do <Affect> attachment. The attic disappears.

---

[275] see Chapter 7 Shadows

Not that it was ever really there: that's just a structural metaphor. You just stop putting daily effort into making your imaginary drink be a horrid experience for you.

Inner Children

The proposition that you can "parent" a past You contradicts every principle of Self, being, becoming and |T|ime.

Imagining an "inner child" to have a therapeutic dialogue with, is: childish. Such inner child is simply another figment of /S/{identation}. It's the imaginary friend, or talking bunny, you had aged 3.

It can be entertaining to do. You can enjoy attaching <Affect> to {identations} of the imaginary. Or you could just go to the movies.

However, as change therapy, it's at best pointless and at worst harmful. The harm comes from telling people to expect therapeutic change from fiddling around in their own arbitrary {identation}.

Some people do get a sense of relief and peace out of some Inner Child work. That's not because of any reality to the practice. It's just an accident.

The change in aspect which You experience simply comes from an adjustment of the Slices gravity.

CHAPTER 12

AVATAR DIALOGUE THERAPY ("ADT")

ADT is the grown up version of Inner Child work. The key difference is that we are using an explicit understanding of the Slices gravity.

We understand the drive to <coherence> in /S/, which is what the Slices gravity achieves. We see that many issues in {identation} come from sabotaging that gravity, by distorting the relationship of the Slices.

This is not "unconscious". It is how your consciousness is working. If you elect to drive down the wrong road to your intended destination, we wouldn't ascribe that to an unconscious choice. Plainly it was a perfectly conscious decision: just the wrong one for your needs and objectives.

We're borrowing the following ADT examples from *Worlds Ends: Coronavirus, Frankenstein and Other Monsters.*[276]

These ADT examples are easy to follow, because they have a real world context that any reader will immediately understand. We don't have to do a narrative of "Sally has [these circumstances] and has been feeling [xyz] and her

---

[276] The Author (2020) Chapter 13

behaviour has been [zyx]."

You can run these as Experiences, for yourself, if any of them relate to You.

<u>Exorcising Fears</u>

1.   I **believe** that a killer virus is inevitably coming for me or my loved ones. I'm so scared.
     I hear what you say. I believe you.
     I believe in you and your ability to get through this tough time.

Now close your eyes and breath. I'd like you to take me on a journey.
*   Imagine that you are waking up in an afterlife
*   It could be a beautiful garden, or a beach paradise
*   Just look around you and describe it to me

OK: Now
*   Can you look back at your past life, to the you before you crossed over to this beautiful place
*   And what feelings could you share with Younger You, from this beautiful place?

OK: they sound lovely feelings
*   Can you bring those wonderful feelings from your beautiful place to your Younger You?
*   Can you bring them inside, and feel them inside, as you're sitting here now?

That's great.
And relax.
Open your eyes and breathe.

How do you feel?

The client should be able to state they now have feelings of **calm**. They probably won't reference the word "security" but actually it's the Slice which has become re-infused with support from the other Slices.

The client can then be shown the simple techniques for revisiting this Experience.

When the client has been through this Experience a few times (under supervision, and self-reporting successful "journeys"), you can move to importing actual worlds and ideas from the "afterlife" to their present selves.

ADT Technical Explanation:
- We ascertain that this is a feeling of helplessness / powerlessness.
- It is so intense that it has walled off the Security Slice from the other 4 Slices.
- Trying to locate wall-breaching force in any of the other 4 Slices is both painful (which is not what we are here for) and unproductive.
- The Security Slice cannot operate in isolation.
- So the client has conjured up Shadow Slices.

- If allowed to continue, this dynamic will close down the Security Slice as well, and the client will lapse into a psychological domain governed by Shadow Slices.
- But the practitioner must allow the client to feel empathy in a reality of those Shadow Slice dynamics.
- Therefore: (a) illumine a pathway back from Shadow Slices to a non-pathological Slices dynamic.; (b) provide a self-healing process which is simple and repetitive, so as to bind mental "muscle memory" to the pathway process. In technical terms, allow the client to create new Θ<Constructs> for this mental experience.

The opening mantra which we always use:

I hear what you say. I believe you.
I believe in you and your ability to get through this tough time.

is designed to engage the "attention" of all 5 Slices:

(1) Needs/Wants Slice: is engaged by explicit opening of a Satisfaction pathway.
(2) Chemistry Slice: is engaged by explicit statement of belief in the Client.
(3) Empathy Slice: is engaged by explicit statement of hearing and believing the client's self-reporting.
(4) Challenge Slice: is engaged by explicit statement of belief in client's ability.
(5) Security Slice: is engaged by explicit statement of belief in client's self-reporting.

In a therapeutic world without human Selfs in it, we could simply say "You are perfect", snap our fingers, and entrain the ASR.

But that would be to disregard the actual problematic. The client is sabotaging the ASR function. The client is balancing their Slices dynamic "against the flow" of their ASR. Doing that creates energy: the same energy as when you damn a flow of water.

But it's not energy which helps the Client to achieve anything. And it comes at a price, which is paid in neurological disorders, manifesting in all the common problems we experience, such as disorders in: sleep, tiredness, eating, fibromyalgia pains; and much more.

Once the client has experienced re-balancing of the Slices dynamic, and the less interrupted flow of the ASR: then we can say "You were perfect already: you were born that way". Then those words will have <Affect> attachment meaning.

We will be discussing all of this in much more detail in *The Matrixial Healing Handbook*.

Worries and <coherence>
2.   I **know** from all the stuff I'm reading in the newspapers, and hearing from the Government, that a killer virus is inevitably coming for me or my loved ones. I'm really worried.

I hear what you say. I believe you.
I believe in you and your ability to get through this tough time.

I believe that you are doing all that you can to protect you and your loved ones. OK?

Now close your eyes and breath. I'd like you to take me to visit someone.

- Imagine a pretty dumb version of you, a Stupid You
- Like a version of you that's standing in the rain outside and umbrella shop, readying themselves to cross a busy street with a blindfold

OK: Now

- Can you please tell me somethings you'd say to Stupid You?

OK: great. I hear that

- Let's for now see that Stupid You is not really listening.
- What feelings are you having with that?

Client talks about frustration.

- OK. Thank you. Now you know yourself, and this Stupid You better than anyone
- So you can find ways to communicate with Stupid You, which are way beyond words
- So, please pass some of your feelings across to Stupid You.
- Just take a few moments, and breaths, and focus on that please

OK great. Thank you
- So now you're getting Stupid You to feel those feelings, yes?
- And Stupid You is opening up to the important things you know, yes?

OK great. So, is Stupid You doing anything now?
Client speaks of Stupid You buying an umbrella and taking the blindfold off.
That's really cool. Amazing.

So you've made Stupid You safe. Amazing
OK come back into the room.

And relax.
Open your eyes and breathe.

How do you feel?

The client should be able to state they now have feelings of **being in control**. They now feel able to meet a challenge and overcome it. So they allow their Soothing Wave to infuse their Security Slice, and establish dynamic harmony.

ADT Technical Explanation:
- We ascertain that this is a feeling of frustrated power (the client believes that the clients knows of a danger).
- The Security Slice is ganging up with the Challenge Slice.

- The Challenge Slice can't cope, so is blaring danger signals at the Security slice.
- The Security Slice cannot operate in isolation.
- These are not Shadow Slices.
- Client is interfering with the Anxiety-Soothing Cycle. That's why the client is in psychological Pain.
- If allowed to continue, this dynamic will likely result in client attempts to "drown out" those signals: by drugs of various kinds (alcohol, over-eating, over exercising, over-sleeping).
- Therefore: (a) illumine a landscape in which the Soothing wave can rise to an appropriate level; (b) provide a self-healing process which is simple and repetitive, so as to bind mental "muscle memory" to the pathway process.

Indecision and Gravity

3.   I just don't know whether to go out, or buy a mask, or risk this thing. My head's spinning and I feel tired.

I hear what you say. I believe you.

I believe in you and your ability to get through this tough time.

Now close your eyes and breath. I'd like you to take me to meet someone.

- Think of a time in the past that a younger, Doing You, was doing something: some work, or some hobby; or trying to chat someone up.
- It could be anywhere, anytime in your daily life

You have it? OK great.

- Now I'd like you to feel your feelings as Doing You is getting stuck, at what you were doing

You feel that? OK great.

- Now, can the person you are now, please enter that scene
- Thinking of the things you could say to Doing You.

OK great.

- Now, say the things to Doing You that you know will help.

OK great.

- Now step back a little and notice the feelings you have in this moment

OK come back into the room.

And relax.
Open your eyes and breathe.

How do you feel?

The client should be able to state they now have feelings of **success**. They have accessed the feeling that they are up to the **Challenge**.

They were able to use their empathy to effect stimulation of their Challenge Slice. So they remove what was holding them back from feeling confidence in their Challenge slice. lowering the amplitude of their Soothing Wave. They accessed their anxiety-soothing cycle, and placed the Slices Dynamic in a higher 'shelf'.

ADT Technical Explanation:
* This is a perfectly reasonable response to real-world circumstances.
* The 5 Slices are operating in dynamic harmony fine, but at an insufficiently low Challenge level for this individual. The music is on, but the volume in that Challenge domain, is too low.
* Therefore: (a) provide controlled stimulus to Anxiety, directed to re-energising the Challenge component, allowing an equivalent Soothing Wave release; (b) provide a self-healing process which is simple and repetitive, so as to bind mental "muscle memory" to the stimulation process.

Adaptations of this technique are used in (for example) sales and public speaking training. The technique has been developed and modified from thousands of years of confidence-building instruction. So, we have a high degree of confidence in its clinical efficacy.

Note that the the ADT dialogue is between adult Avatars. "Younger You" is adult you, not some mute "inner child". That's why you're able to exercise the infinite range of your /S/{idents} continuum to make connections.

<u><coherence> Mirrors</u>
This invokes another aspect of ADT: *<coherence> Mirrors*.

We have previously in the book referred several times to the Mirror aspect of /S/ubjectivity.

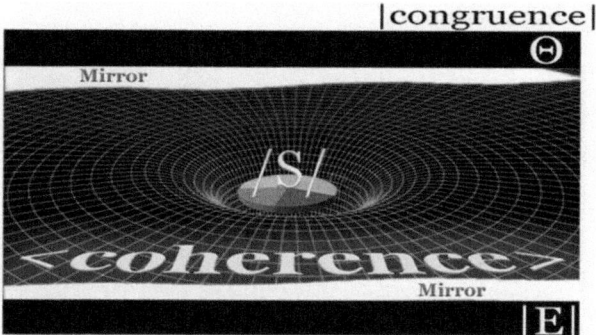

Mirrors are intrinsic to the operation of /S/ubjectivity.

From Chapter 6:

> /S/ is a continuum of infinity, which is bounded by the congruence Architecture of Self. That is the central paradox of Self.

> It is that "sandwiching" that innately imposes Mirrors in /S/ubjectivity. You might thing of the "floor" and "ceiling" of the /S/ lawyer, as being made of Mirrors.

> Indeed, it is that opposition to objectivity, which is the foundation of <Me>: the sense of personhood.

> We are bound to use those Mirrors in pursuit of <coherence>. So we send {ident} "lights" to bounce

off those Mirrors, as reflections. All the time. Every moment of our lives.

This is another function of the Slices. Their gravity, to borrow an Einsteinian metaphor, "bends" the light. By adjusting the relative "orbits" of the Slices, we alter the gravitational effect on <coherence>.

Anger and Chemistry
4.   I'm pretty sure we have this virus thing under control. But the way everybody is over-reacting is making me angry.
       I hear what you say. I believe you.
       I believe in you and your ability to get through this tough time.

Now close your eyes and breath. I'd like you to take me to visit someone

•   Think of a time in the past that a younger, Doing You, was doing something active and challenging: like hitting a punchbag, or banging in a nail, or [insert relevant activity drawn from short questioning of client's lifestyle, pre-induction].

•   It could be anywhere, anytime in your daily life

You have it? OK great.

•   Now I'd like you to feel your feelings as Doing You is hitting away

You feel that? OK great.

- Now, can the person you are now, please enter that scene
- Now, can you please imagine, the great big [sledgehammer / stick / as relevant to the scenario]
- Notice how big it is.
- Notice your feelings of power, as you hold it

OK great.

- Now, gently but firmly, touch Doing You on the shoulder
- Show Doing You are big, powerful [whatever]
- Notice the feelings of Doing You in this moment
- Can you describe those feelings?

Client should report feelings of puzzlement and relief, all mixed up

OK great.

- Now apply the force of your great big [sledgehammer / stick / as relevant to the scenario]
- Shake Doing You's hand
- Notice how Doing You is feeling now

OK come back into the room.

And relax.
Open your eyes and breathe.

How do you feel?

The client should be able to state they now have feelings of **power and control**. They were having anger-management issues, because there is zero/little they can do in the world to affect what they see as behaviour which is offensive to them.

Their normal anxiety was properly driving their wants/needs, but they were depleting their **Chemistry** slice, which had the effect of impeding self-soothing of anxiety. Their Chemistry slice is re-energised (the anger gets directed into soothing stimulation, instead of anxiety accumulation). They thus re-acquire dynamic harmony.

The client can then be shown the simple techniques for revisiting this Experience.

ADT Technical Explanation:
- This is a perfectly reasonable response to real-world circumstances.
- The 5 Slices are operating in dynamic harmony fine, but at an insufficiently low Chemistry level for this individual. The music is on, but the Chemistry volume is too low.
- Therefore: (a) provide controlled stimulus to Anxiety, directed to re-energising the Chemistry component, allowing an equivalent Soothing Wave release; (b) provide a self-healing process which is simple and repetitive, so as to bind mental "muscle memory" to the stimulation process.

Adaptations of this technique are used in (for example) anger-management training, and addiction therapy. The technique has been developed and modified from thousands of years of Empathetic deficiency counteraction. So, we have a high degree of confidence in its clinical efficacy.

<u>Frustration and Empathy</u>

5.   I see all this real world stupidity about a nasty little virus. It's making me feel depressed.
     I hear what you say. I believe you.
     I believe in you and your ability to get through this tough time.

Now close your eyes and breath. I'd like you to take me to visit somewhere.

• Think of a time you laughed, really laughed at something.
• It could be at a party, or a comedy show, or a film, or just at something that tickled you in daily life

You have it? OK great.

• Now I'd like you to imagine an Interfering You.
• There's nothing special about Interfering You, OK?
• It's just that Interfering You gets in the wrong place at the wrong time.

You see him (or her). OK great.

• Now, just take me back to that time when you just about to explode with laughter.

- You're there. You're almost laughing already, as you know what's coming.
- Out of the corner of your eye, now you care to notice, Interfering You is coming to get in the way
- You're about to laugh your socks off… and
- Snap your fingers
- That's Interfering You causing a distraction
- Now you've missed the big laugh

OK come back into the room.

And relax.
Open your eyes and breathe.

How do you feel?

The client should be able to state they now have feelings of **managed frustration**. They missed something, and it's irritating, but it's not the end of the world.

This is part of a series of interventions. You move from missing a laugh, to missing more and more important things. You are raising the harmonic level of the Empathy slice: the client is being too hard on himself, and that is manifesting in what the client calls "depression", but is clinically frustration.

They become able to enhance their empathy in response to a challenge. So they remove what is lowering the amplitude of their Soothing Wave. Their Security Slice is better served by soothing, and they thus re-acquire dynamic harmony.

The client can then be shown the simple techniques for revisiting this Experience.

ADT Technical Explanation:

- This is a perfectly reasonable response to real-world circumstances.
- The 5 Slices are operating in dynamic harmony fine, but at an insufficiently low Empathy level for this individual. The music is on, but the volume is too low.
- Therefore: (a) provide controlled stimulus to Anxiety, directed to re-energising the Empathy component, allowing an equivalent Soothing Wave release; (b) provide a self-healing process which is simple and repetitive, so as to bind mental "muscle memory" to the stimulation process.

Adaptations of this technique are used in many settings. The technique has been developed and modified from thousands of years of Empathetic deficiency counteraction. So, we have a high degree of confidence in its clinical efficacy.

CHAPTER 13

PSYCHOTECTICS

In the Chapters *Steering* and *Shadows*, we could set out the technical principles. But it was difficult to engage the reader in thinking about how the Slices dynamic operates in real experience.

With these real-world examples, it should be easier to see what the principles actually mean.

Psychotectics is the science which sets out empirically observed principles of how the /S/{idents} continuum operates in infinity, under its |congruence| boundary conditions.

Psychotectics then provides therapeutic interventions:

• like ADT, which use {identation} to effect restoration of Autonomic Dynamic Balance.

• like Congruence Interface Therapy, which you saw in the *I-Pen*, Memory *Wipe*, and Dream *Running Experiences*.

The core of Psychotectics is understanding that:

(13) All {idents} are fictional: they have no objective existence, but are absolutely real for the Self.

(14) The Self seeks <coherence> in {identation}.

(15) That seeking is innately imposed by the boundary conditions of /S/ubjectivity: the reality that the infinite continuum of /S/ is bounded by objective reality in |E| and Θ.

(16) Those boundaries cannot be seen from the outside, within the Self.

(17) Those boundaries exist for the Self only as Mirrors within /S/.

(18) We use those Mirrors to orient <coherence>.

(19) We reflect "torchlight" {idents} from those Mirrors, then apply other {idents} to the reflections.

(20) This Mirroring process is fundamental to our sense of <Me> identity: of MySelf.

(21) The Slices are anchored in the ASR. It is how the ASR manifests in our <coherence>.

(22) The Slices dynamic acts like gravity in our /S/ continuum. It shapes the "torchlight" which we shine inside ourselves, and reflect off boundary Mirrors.

The Slices are not visible to {idents}. They are not things which exist. They are a way of thinking and talking about how the ASR generates an automatic "base level" <coherence> in /S/.

This base level reset, is what we mean by Autonomic Dynamic Balance.

Avatar Dialogue Therapy

We use Avatar Dialogue Therapy to bring /S/ back into Autonomic Dynamic Balance.

ADT is about getting you to create Mirrors: which we have designed to reflect back {idents} which attach <Affect>, under the gravitational <coherence> of the Slices. This brings you back to ADB.

As we explained in *I Want To Love But*, this Autonomic Dynamic Balance is inherent in every person ever born. It's simply the manifestation in /S/ of your ASR.

Put simply, a new born baby operates the ASR with very little interference from the immature /S/ continuum. As synaptic connections wire,[277] the /S/ continuum becomes more populated with {ident} capacity.

This increasingly allows us to self-stimulate. We explained these dynamics in Chapter 2, Section B(2)/18.

The problem is that we are expert amateurs at self-stimulation. We perpetually alter the Slices Dynamic Balance. In doing that, we interfere with that process by which the ASR seeks to perpetuate Autonomic Dynamic Balance.

_____

[277] with ultimate synaptic prunings at 7 and in teen years

Imagine if you were able to influence, by self-stimulation, autonomic functions such as your blood circulation, or blood oxygen supply system. Imagine that, once you started interfering with these autonomic functions, you would have to keep on interfering: trying by manual manipulation to recapitulate that autonomic balance.

The result would generally not be favourable to Self survival.

So, Psychotectics is ultimately about:
(1)   restoring your Autonomic Dynamic Balance through ADT; and
(2)   reasserting |congruence| (that which creates <I>) over <coherence> (that which creates <Me>), through CIT.

In ADT:
•   rather than getting you to try and think and believe in[278] {thoughts} which are brought to you from "outside";
•   we stimulate you to engage with your own <Thoughts>, in {identation} reflection.

A clinical analogy would be to use your own stem cells to rejuvenate mature cells.

---

[278] by making <Affect> attachments

Congruence Interface Therapy

In Congruence Interface Therapy (CIT), we use Avatar techniques (You$_2$), to engage Θ<Constructs>:

- *CIT Morphonics*: we can use these as Ю ǀ W ǀ interfaces, to change your interaction with the external world, as in *I-Pen*, for example;
- *CIT Holonics*: we can use these to destabilise /S/ <coherence>, as in the Memory *Wipe*;
- we can use them in conjunction with Biomorphics, to effect medicinal interventions.

The capacity for CIT to engage Ю|W| interfaces is limited only, it seems, by our imagination.

CIT Morphonics

The principle underlying Congruence Interface Therapy Morphonics has been explained in detail in previous pages.

ΘЮ ǀ W ǀ interfaces operate in quantised ǀ T ǀ ime. We are born with these interfaces. Use of these interfaces is how we develop from neonate stage.

However, as our /S/ capacity grows, from 0-18 months, we begin to use /S/ to initiate things like motor functions.

Our ǀ E ǀ and ǀ P ǀ are purely natural systems. They undertake behaviours, both proactive and responsive. We can mistakenly attribute these behaviours to intelligence.

But there is no more intelligence in operation here, than in weather systems, or sub-atomic particles.

Input from /S/ or input via ΘIO|W| interface is treated under the same systems in |E| and |P|.

/S/ubjectivity operates in an equivalence continuum. Θ operates equalisation in <Constructs>. /S/ is subjective, with only tangential relationship to |W|. Θ is objective, with direct temporal relationship to |W|.

So, what chooses whether an |E| or |P| function is activated? You do. At the early development stage of /S/, there's not much choosing involved. By the age of 18 months, there is a significant /S/ choice factor. That increases over succeeding months and years.

As we become more practiced at using our /S/ continuum Mirrors, we develop our individually unique balancing of the Slices.

CIT Holonics

Memories are not Ш obsessions. Memories live firmly in /S/<coherence>, arranged under Θ <Constructs> equalisation.

Congruence Interface Therapy Holonics work by destabilising /S/<coherence>. We use Avatar techniques to sever the link between /S/{ident} formation, and the "library" of <Constructs>: remembering that it's not a library of things, or even ideas; but a collection of operating programs.

That's why, when you experience Memory adjustment, you just can't find the "video" or the "box cover" anymore.

You know of historical events. But they have no "feelings" attached, no <Affect> attachment to {identation}. It's like you have balls of wool, but we've taken away the knitting pattern.

This is why the link severing is permanent. That permanence is innate in the process. Once you've destroyed a bridge, you can't rebuild it. The best you can do is build another one.

So, yes, you can go and create a new /S/⇔Θ linkage. But it won't be the same, because now you are doing it deliberately. And you find that there's simply no point in building a /S/⇔Θ linkage, just to upset yourself.

That pointlessness feeling is energised by your ASR. You're trying to create a Ш {anxiety}. When you try to trigger your ASR to create genuine <Anxiety>, the system says "sure boss" and jacks up <Anxiety>. But because there's nothing actually there, your <Soothing> response swiftly kicks in. And you're back where you started: with some useless balls of wool.

Well, not entirely useless. Although you've lost the knitting pattern for a slow strangulation noose, you can always knit up a lovely, warm, colourful scarf.

ADB and BAB

Autonomic Dynamic Balance, in Psychotectics and Biomorphic Autonomic Balance, in Biomorphics, are two aspects of the same Systems Architecture.

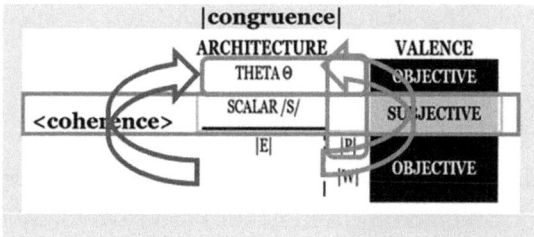

In Psychotectics, we alter the /S/ <coherence> landscape.

- From "inside", with AVT, using the Mirrors intrinsic to /S/.

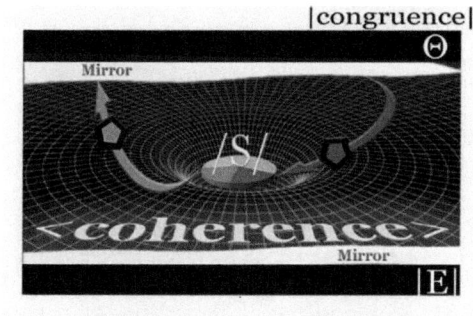

- From "outside", with CIT.

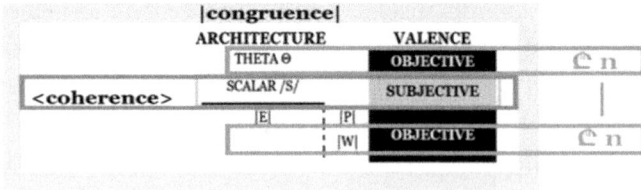

In Biomorphics, we are minimising the /S/ landscape. We are creating an environment which promotes a "narrow band" of /S/<coherence>, so that the ASR is collimated in its journey through the /S/ landscape.

In its "bottom up", as contrasted with "top down" and "middle in" Psychotectics techniques, Biomorphics promotes Biomorphic Autonomic Balance restoration.

That balance also implicates the Slices dynamic "gravity".

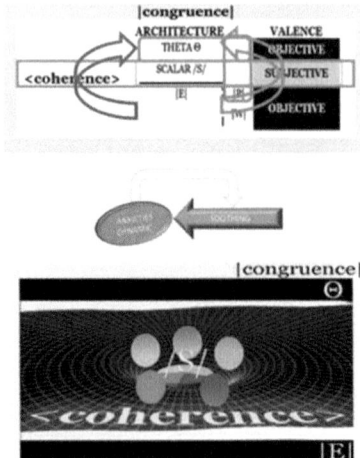

We can summarise the difference with a simple and approximate metaphor:

- BAB is what you experience in your baby state
- ADB is the optimum potential of <Me> Self, as it grows heuristically from that baby state through life.

Matrixial Healing: Medicinal Interventions

We can use Psychotectics in conjunction with Biomorphics, to effect medicinal interventions.

The easiest way to explain this is with some case studies:

(1)   *Muscular Pain*

Abbie (age 25) had been overdoing it at the gym. She'd sprained her left forearm.

Diagnosis:

The neuralgic impact had sensitised the nerves implicated in that motor function.

Healing:

(1)   Biomorphic intervention to "clear channels" of ASR, is useful. Use 2 handed breathing for 30 seconds to augment ASR, and Slices gravity through /S/<coherence>.

(2)   Use CIT Morphonics to alter Θ<Constructs>, so that Ю I W I changes.

(3)   To effect Θ<Constructs> change, we use externalised Avatar technique: Imagine You²; Feel where

the pain is in your arm; allow You^2 to feel that pain; move the pain to You^2.

(4) The neurological pain is gone. It has remained absent since treatment, which was months before this book was written.

Note: This is an intervention for neurological pain symptomized in musculature. If Abbie had a broken arm, or actual tissue damage, this is not a recommended intervention.

(2)   Covid Symptoms

Brian (age 45) had a blocked nose and sore throat. Difficulty talking. Headaches.

Diagnosis:

Symptoms are having effect in /S/ to suppress ASR function.

Healing:

(1) Biomorphic intervention to augment ASR. Use something similar to *3 Minute Anxiety Remedy*.

(2) Augmented ASR channelled through increased /S/<coherence> has effect to activate altered Θ<-Constructs>Ю|W|=>|P|.

(3) In a few minutes, symptoms abate. Normal speech resumed. Much better breathing. Headaches gone.

Note: The symptoms were completely ordinary biological

responses to the infection. However, they were in effect creating III: thoughts of being ill. Similar to depression. This was suppressing the ASR, and thus prolonging the immune response. By stimulating the ASR, the immune response was reset to the level appropriate to dealing with the infection.

(3)   Fibromyalgia
Cherie (age 55) had muscular pains, digestive issues and insomnia. There were other symptoms also, but these were the main protagonists.

Diagnosis:
1.   Fibro is a classic case where the Subject is repressing the ASR.
2.   ASR repression is so effective that biological changes are occurring, which account for digestive problems.
3.   Fibro can be traced to traumatic Memory episodes, often stemming from medical problems in the past.
4.   The repression is so intense, and coming from multiple Slices in /S/, that multi-lateral interventions are needed.

Healing:
(1)   Biomorphic intervention to augment ASR. Use something similar to *3 Minute Anxiety Remedy.*[279]
(2)   Deploy CIT Holonics technique to adjust Memory

trauma: further reducing ASR suppression.

(3)   CIT Morphonics focused on a specific pain site.

Note: Fibro is a multi-layered condition, in which neurological disfunction effects biological disfunction and feedback.

Focusing pain relief on a specific site (one "bath" full of pain water) demonstrated that the multiple baths of "pain" water could become reduced.

That demonstration "opened" the channel to allow other pains to flow "to You²".

The depression Ш was bypassed by ASR augmentation. So that Ш appears to the Subject to have lower utility. Therefore the depression starts to ease.

Although immediate relief was possible, and this has a "pathfinding" effect, the years of ASR repression need several sessions of Matrixial Healing.

(4)   Panic Attacks
Deidre (age 25) had a history of panic attacks. So serious that on a couple of occasions she has called an ambulance in the middle of the night.

Diagnosis:
1.   Mild but constant ASR suppression.

Healing:
(1)   Biomorphic intervention to augment ASR.
(2)   Need serious and swift stimulus of <Anxiety>
(3)   Use something similar to *Angels for Panic Attacks*.[280]

Note: Intervention used successfully during serious panic attack. Subject practicing Biomorphic technique for a few minutes 2-3 times a week: halted incipient attacks.

By reducing fear of future panic attack potential, further removed ASR suppression: thus enter virtuous cycle of accepting ASR and foregoing suppression.

Sleep also improved.

(5)   Eating Disorder
Eileen (age 25) had 3 years of stomach disorders. Using PRESCRIPTION Omezaprole daily to try and control retching response. Sleep disorder. Exhaustion.

Diagnosis:
1.   Incident memory trauma: with repetitions over a period in adolescence.
2.   ASR repression is so effective that biological changes are occurring, which account for digestive problems.
Healing:
(1)   Biomorphic intervention to augment ASR.

---

[280] https://youtu.be/qrUQ0p1U00E

(2)   Deploy CIT Holonics technique to adjust Memory trauma: further reducing ASR suppression.

(3)   ASR augmenting practice technique taught, for repetition a few minutes 2-3 times a week.

Note:

Subject experienced instant relief.

Was able immediately to dispense with pharmaceutical reliefs.

Longitudinal check ins over 3 months demonstrated return to dietary normalcy. Fear of eating effects abated, with further reduction in ASR suppression.

Now living a normal dietary life. Sleep greatly improved. Energy calibration at normalcy.

(6)   Ex Obsession

Francis (age 35) had very strong ideations about his ex. Leading to depression and exhaustion.

Diagnosis:

1.   Shadow Slices formed from /S/<coherence> failure to process external trauma.

2.   Trying to create valid Memories, but Ш preventing Memory formation in /S/{idents}⇔Θ<Constructs>.

3.   ASR suppression to energise Ш.

Healing:

(1)   Bring "obsessive feelings" (Ш) into Mirrored {identation} with Biomorphic <Affect> attachment.

(2)   Biomorphic intervention to augment ASR: deep and overpowering augmentation, around 60 seconds.

(3)   Induce Biomorphic shutdown of /S/ with breathing suppression (3 seconds).

(4)   "Reboot" ASR flow.

(5)   Invite re-connection with Ш. Realisation that Ш "gone".

Note:

This sort of Obsession is classically mis-diagnosed as a Memorial issue. In fact, the Subject is unable to form (self-preventing) valid memories.

Memory formation allowed, by removing ASR suppression. The process of Memory formation is "lightning quick". By the end of a 3-5 minute session, Subject is unable to connect with the Shadow Slice obsession.

The "information" is now carried as Memory {idents{} and <Constructs>. The {idents} can form whatever associations, and <Affect> attachments the Subject wishes.

This does not mean that the Subject "does not care anymore". On the contrary, the Subject's Chemistry and Empathy Slices are now able to function in balance with Challenge, and Security; rather than being dominated by a Shadow [Want⇔Security] stasis: which has nothing to do with "caring".

Francis was able to create communicative messaging with his Ex which brought them both to a "good place".

She recognised the alteration in his disposition, and responded affirmatively. They now have friendly contact, by mutual agreement.

(7)   Meditation
Georgia (age 25) had been on meditative retreats overseas, and spent much time at home, trying to establish reliable meditative techniques. She was frustrated by repeated failure to be able to "empty her head" and maintain it.

Diagnosis:
1.   Search for meditative "space" was directing ASR suppression.
2.   Meditation has become a Shadow Slice Ш.

Healing:
(1)   Simple Biomorphic intervention to augment ASR.

Note:
A 3 minute renunciation of ASR suppression, effected in Biomorphic Autonomic Balance.

Through this, Georgia witnessed her ability to "empty her head" and maintain it, without any effort in /S/.

Ш formation was abandoned.

Longitudinal response over 6 months, is that Georgia no longer concerns herself about Meditation at all. She uses

Biomorphic "head clearing" when she feels like it. But because she knows she can effect it whenever she wants, she finds that she enjoys feelings of balance, calm, control peace and power: whenever she wants them.

Georgia has abandoned the search for the golden fleece, because she has found she can style a perfectly suitable and comfortable garment, whenever she wishes.

(8)   Depression

Harry (age 46) had serious depression. Although his life circumstances were reasonably comfortable, he was in reasonable health and he had attained the usual career and domestic milestones, depression reigned: bored, listless, tired, attention deficits, finding no fun in anything, sleep disorders.

Diagnosis:
1.   Subject was trying to create Ш, but without external trauma to preclude /S/<coherence>, was stuck.
2.   /S/<coherence> being rejected. Suppressing <Affect> attachment in order to reduce <coherence>.
3.   Consequential ASR suppression, but as a tertiary effect.

Healing – 2 Stages:
Stage 1:
(1)   Communicated to Harry that if he was depressed, it was probably because he needed to be. He could surely get a lot more depressed: go away for a few days and work on it until next session.

Stage 2:

(2)   Harry reported surprise that he had not been able to increase his depression. In fact, the more he did it, the more he seemed to be "pepping up". Which left him confused.

(3)   Biomorphic intervention to augment ASR

(4)   ADT: (i) to allow "Shadow" Harry to explore his failure to generate Ш; (ii) allowing "Shadow" Harry to create {idents} which are <coherent> within Slices gravity.

Note:

Harry was rejecting Autonomic Dynamic Balance. He was preventing <Soothing> from energising in response to <Anxiety> (which he was suppressing).

By inviting him to push his depression further, his ADB "fought back".

ASR stimulus gave him the "platform" to explore Ш creation, without affixing Shadow Θ<Constructs>: because his <Soothing> energised fully.

Under Autonomic Dynamic Balance, his /S/{ident} <coherence> was allowed to function.

Longitudinal response over 8 months is that the depression has sometimes returned, but only mildly: more like a foreboding. Using Biomorphic ASR stimulation techniques as and when harry feels like it, the forebodings vanish.

Harry now has bursting energy. he has taken up new interests and is finding fulfilment in his domestic life.

These are just same actual case studies.[281] We will be explaining much more about these and many other conditions, diagnoses and techniques in *The Matrixial Healing Handbook*.

What you can note in particular about these case studies is that:

- there is minimal case history analysis
- we take the Subject's presentation as the Subject sees it, and experiences it
- we accept that subjective reality
- there's no long talk or emotive therapy: it is simply distressing, and therapeutically pointless.

There is a certain skill, which comes with experience, in piercing the presentation, or layers of presentation. But that is skill in using the technical understanding of Self *Systems Architecture* and *Processes*.

You need some basic skill to diagnose a broken leg. But with that diagnosis, the clinical remedy is obvious, and technical skill to implement it, elementary.

In all that we do, we ensure the Subject comes to an

---

[281] with names changed of course

understanding of the Subject's own born perfection. That the Subjected was gifted at birth everything the Subject needs to survive and succeed. The Subject has perfect ability to energise the Systems which enliven and empower.

The Subject does not need to believe in anything. The Subject acquires direct and immediate experiential knowledge of their own born perfection. We are thereafter redundant. As it should be.

Rational Antipathies

Finally, we have lots of perfectly sensible antipathies, by reference to which we live our lives. Putting your fingers in electrical sockets, crossing the road without looking, voting for politicians. These are all things sensibly to avoid.

We create Self-referential Mimetics for these, and share them. That's not Memory. It's a manual of life instructions.

When you deliberately don't do things, or get into situations, which you know are bad for you, that's not a matter of TM. It's following an instruction manual that you have written in Θ Mimetics.

Whether it works for you or not, well that's up to You. So far as your behaviour affects other Selfs, that's a matter of relationships.

PART (4)
SOCIAL SELVES

CHAPTER 14

GROWING

We've established the Self Systems Architecture, and the Processes under which they operate.

Personality is a combination of the Θ<I> dynamic and the /S/<Me> dynamic. We know from infant studies that Personality reaches homeostasis around the age of 7. By that time, your Personality is essentially fixed in its principal traits.

Understanding the starting point of neonate development, the process of growth thereafter is self-explanatory. We can see the following important elements.

Θ<Constructs> Integration
The path from neonate to 7 year old is marked by the development of /S/.

There is well-established neurological evidence that even at a few hours old, a neonate has /S/ubjective wants, and not merely needs.

The ASR provides the same heuristic system for developing /S/{identation} both for wants and needs.

However, because wants derive from {identation} and /S/ stimulation of |E|, the heuristic effect of wants (whether satisfied or not) creates a faster track to synaptic adaptation.

What is less remarked upon in the literature is the modes by which the neonate to infant stage is marked by increasing success in transducing Θ<Constructs> into /S/{identation}.

We can envisage this by considering the problematic of the neonate who engages in acting out behaviours, even though the neonate does not seem to have a sufficiently qualified /S/ubjective awareness.

As we said in Chapter 4, Segment (4) Para-Autonomic Balancing:

This graphic:

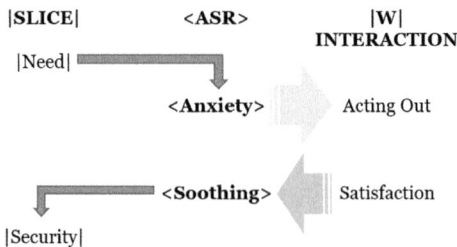

is able to represent any sentient life, which has ASR capacity. This is why we are so readily able to see ourselves in other sentient creatures: we share the same primal pathways.

But there is much more going on in the human Self:

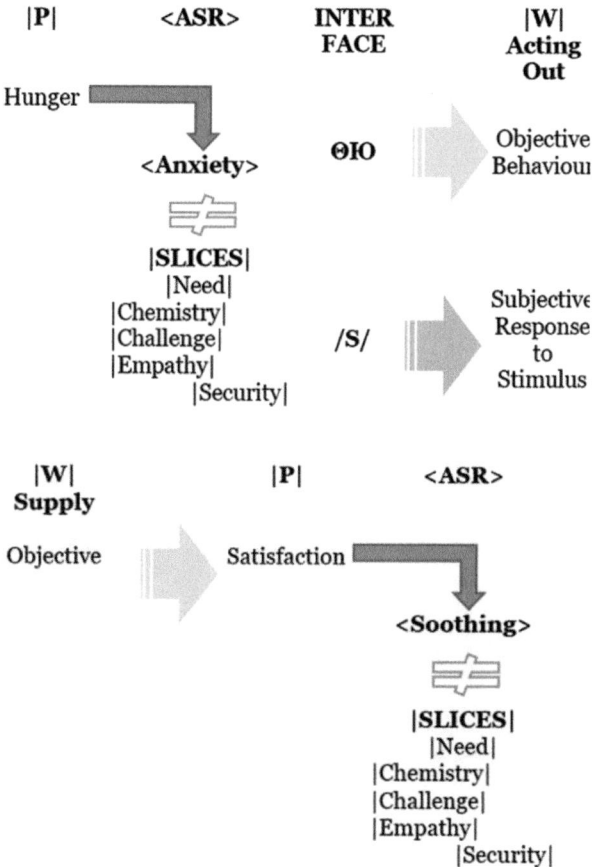

|P|	<ASR>	INTER FACE	|W| Acting Out

Hunger

<Anxiety>   ΘIO   Objective Behaviour

|SLICES|
|Need|
|Chemistry|
|Challenge| /S/   Subjective
|Empathy| Response
|Security| to
                                                          Stimulus

|W| Supply	|P|	<ASR>

Objective   Satisfaction

<Soothing>

|SLICES|
|Need|
|Chemistry|
|Challenge|
|Empathy|
|Security|

We are each born with obvious personality dispositions. This was obvious to the ancient Greek philosophers, as it is obvious today.

We describe the Slices dynamic as *para-autonomic*, because our /S/subjective {identation} can and does affect that dynamic.

Analytically, we reflect these differing dispositions in the 5 Slices dynamics.

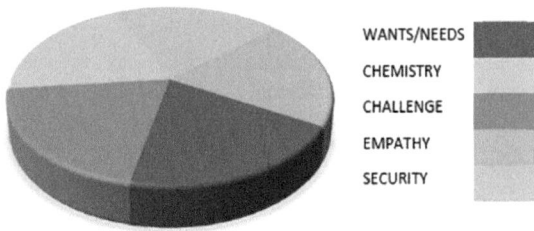

	WANTS/NEEDS
	CHEMISTRY
	CHALLENGE
	EMPATHY
	SECURITY

In our standard Slices graphic, we represent the Slices as having equal proportions.

This is for graphical convenience only. It would be a very odd state if each of the Slices were in equal proportion. Indeed, this would make dynamic change impossible.

Our Personality dynamic depends upon imbalance between its component Slices.

The ability of the neonate to act out behaviours is simply explained by the Θ<Constructs> which inure at birth. What one might analogise as basic programs of operation.

What we see in neonate to infant growth is the development of the Mirrors:

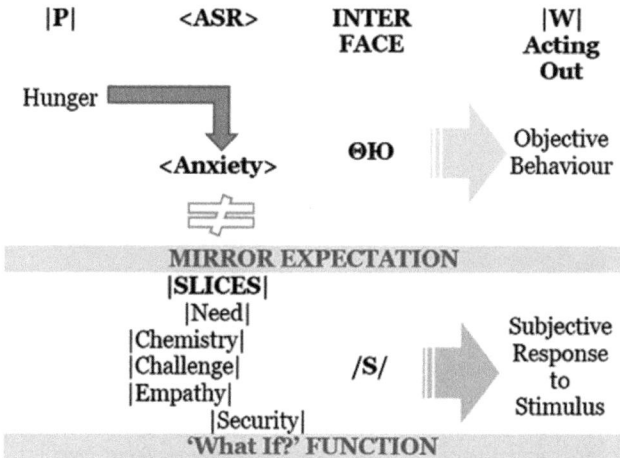

|W| |P| \<ASR\>
Supply

Objective   Satisfaction

\<Soothing\>

MIRROR EXAMINATION

|SLICES|
|Need|
|Chemistry|
|Challenge|
|Empathy|
|Security|

'How/Why?' FUNCTION

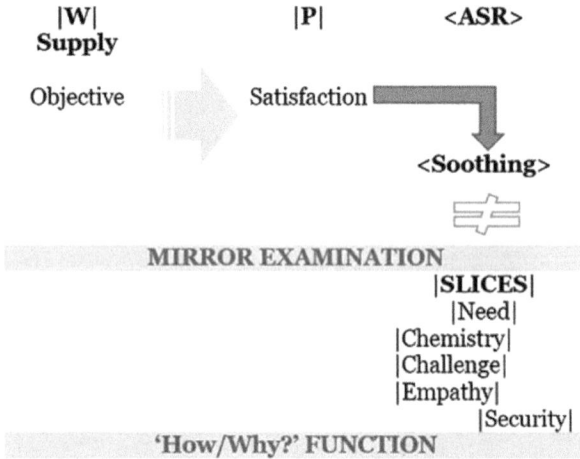

To be more precise, the Mirrors are there from the outset. They are embodied in Self Architecture. What develops is the /S/{identation}:

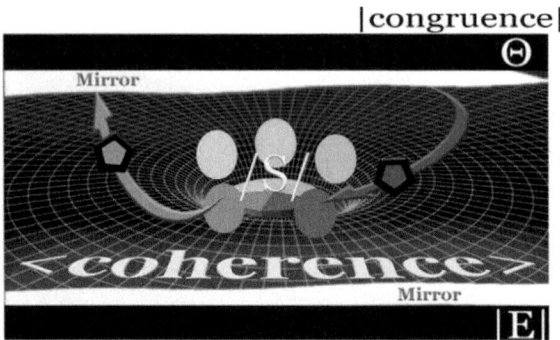

We need to recognise that there are multiple dynamics to {identation} development:

(1)   transducing Θ<Constructs> into /S/{identation}

(2) |P| originated <Affect> attachment to <Thought> potential

(3) |W| originated <Affect> attachment to <Thought> potential

Dynamics (1) and (2) occur irrespective of environment. As every new parent knows, the moment a neonate pops onto the birthing bed, it is rowing its own boat.
The new born visibly has its own world. Limited, diffuse and unco-ordinated, but nevertheless clearly there.

A perennial mystery has been how the neonate is able to construct its own world. The answer is: the same, fundamentally, as we do. In the inter-relationship of Θ and /S/. The course of infant development is marked by that tilting of the balance in Self between Θ and /S/.

The /S/ continuum is simply the plenum of its contents, bounded in infinity. As its contents become exponentially greater, with synaptic adaptation, the balance of reliance (between Θ and /S/) tilts irrevocably towards /S/.

Language

In Matrixial Logic, Chapter 5 *Linguini*, we examined in detail the process by which grammatical and syntax Θ<Constructs> are slowly transduced into /S/{identation}.

Baby talk, moving from sounds, to single nominate

words, to grammatical structures, is amongst the most recognisable behaviours showing the coming to dominant prominence of /S/.

Reflex Patterns, Not Memories

We have considered in Chapter 11 mistaken views about Memory and "childhood wounds".

/S/ operates an equivalence function. Constantly judging sameness and difference, upon such metrics as /S/{identation} decides.

/S/ develops habits and patterns. These are reflexes, not Memory.

We have also explained how the process of Memory is one of constant recapitulation in /S/, guided by "programs" in Θ.

What psychotherapy refers to as "childhood wounds", are often not even Memories at all. They are failures to create Memory, and the manufacture instead of III Shadow Slices.

Reflexes are not of course limited to {identation} movements. A vast repertoire of reflexes:
• arises from sensory interaction
• are held in Θ<Constructs>.

Indeed another set of milestones for neonate development, is the journey from Θ<Constructs> motor responses (finger and hand movements, eye movements and others), to ideated motor responses (initiated by {idents}). There is a difference and every parent, and those who have over the last two decades studied neonates, can see the difference.

Mirrors and Lights
In this brief summary of neonate development in Θ<Constructs> Integration, we have highlighted some key milestone paths.

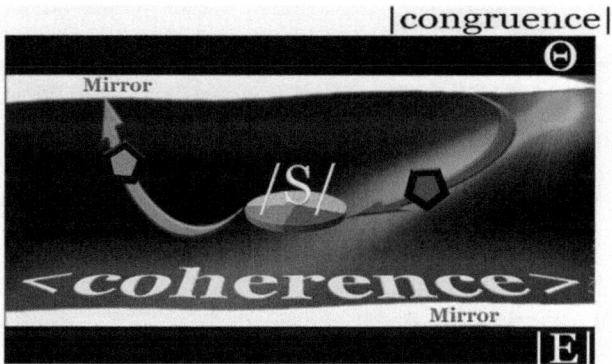

Now, we just want to pose and clarify an extended metaphor, which we have found very useful in explaining relationship issues in adult life.

We have already discussed in Chapter 6 *Mirrors*, Segment (3) *Formless Consciousness*:

The /S/ continuum, in its Architecturally bounded infinity, is what there is, and all there is. There are no other dimensions or layers. What we can distinguish is:

We need to explain what "Visible in Form" means.
/S/ <coherence> manifests in forms of inequality:
In forms of differences between
Output {ident} and Return {ident}.

That manifestation is what we mean by "visibility".

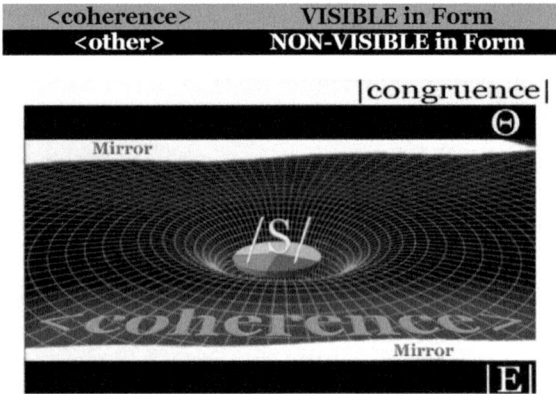

We need to appreciate that visible and non-visible are aspects of the same continuum: we cannot have one without the other.

…

<visible> and <non-visible> coherent are the interdependent elements of Reflective

Introspection.

…

We use the "light" bouncing off the Mirrors to reflect our Slices dynamics.

We develop these Lights by accident and discovery. We're not presented with a complete A-Z of knowledge, in our path from neonate to adult.

We develop workable {ident} strategies. What, at least, seem to work, or that we can imagine working.

Lighthouses

From the very beginning of our life experience, we are shown Illumination by others.

Between our Wants and Needs, and their supply, is another Self:

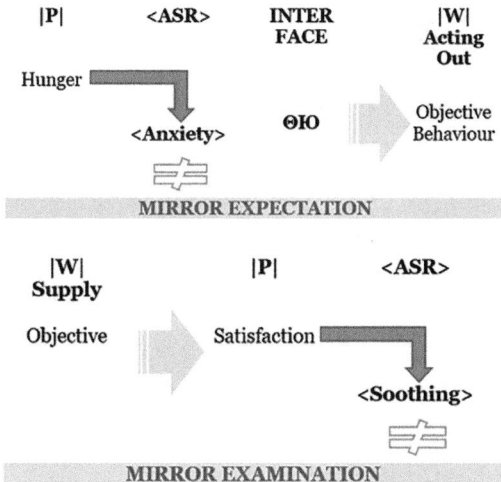

|P|	<ASR>	INTER FACE	|W| Acting Out
Hunger			
	<Anxiety>	ΘЮ	Objective Behaviour

MIRROR EXPECTATION

|W| Supply	|P|	<ASR>
Objective	Satisfaction	
		<Soothing>

MIRROR EXAMINATION

Almost always the same, Self: our primary carer. It's obviously through our primary care-provider |C| that we become that Self-dynamic which relates to the world of people. That's not new information.

The supply of our needs, in itself, does not discriminate the provider |C| from the the |W|orld which ultimately is the source of all supply.

What that supply does represent, is an ordering of the chaos that |W| represents to the immature mind: and indeed to the adult mind.

Chaos is ordered by Singularity (Si) in its interface with the logic of forms of inequality. [282] The Si characteristic of the original primary carer is replicated later in life in theistic ideation.

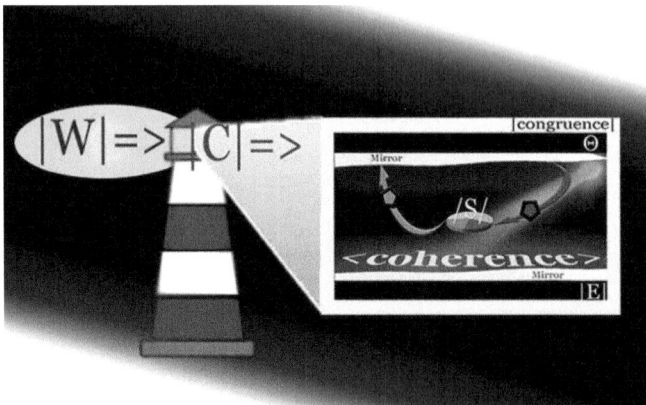

---

[282] see *Matrixial Logic* Chapter 6

Singularity is the antigone of Order. We certainly recognise Singularity and we can trace the ordering of systems to the function of Singularity.

Recall Chapter 2:

We denote an Si Bridge like this:

$$\frac{\neq}{\neq} \qquad = \qquad ?$$

Disjunct   Bridge   Form

…

All of this shows us that the logic of Chaos underpins our entire existence, and how we think about it. We are ever minded to try and extract abstraction from reality, and to do so by the creation of Singularity.

We go about that by creating (unknowingly) forms of forms: not to act as Node potential Events, where they are content-driven by other reality: but as Singularity.

Artificial Singularity invokes Chaos. But the actual production of Singularity by Chaos, in the boundary condition of the existential, invokes real content in forms of inequality.

Being and becoming are the holomorphs of all that there is, to us, in our universe. It is this which Chaos:

allows as synergetic contingency, and a-temporally re-energises.

All that is our being and becoming, is the luminous shadow of Chaos: the reality of that which it is not.

We are able to tell the difference, in time.

We are thus able to construct the equation:

$$\frac{|C|}{|W|} = \text{Life(Si)}$$

| Disjunct | Bridge | Form |

This equation obviously functions in an objective continuum. It reflects in the construction of Θ<Constructs>. This in turn generates:

$$ΘЮ|C|$$

The development of the /S/ubjective Self, under its innate Architecture is necessarily conditioned by this Superstructure: |C| is, from the outset, the externalised reality of the Objective "layers" of Self.

If we want a simple development path for the Self, from the neonate stage, we could state it thus: as the journey towards internalisation of the objective layers of Self, as being self-sufficient.

Yet that journey requires assistance. The fulcrum of that path to independence, is growth in the {identation} plenum of the /S/ continuum.

In self-sufficiency, we develop our Self Light by bouncing {idents} off our /S/ continuum Mirrors. To reach self-sufficiency, we use |C|:

- as an objective provider of the boundaries which solve [C] haos
- thus enabling the creation of Θ<Constructs>
- from which we can derive {idents}.

These Θ derived {idents} can be very powerful. Having their derivation in <Constructs>, they are potentially super-luminous.

In *Matrixial Logic*, Chapter 5, we explored Mimetics: the communication of Mimecs between Self.

The ΘЮ|C| function has an innate reciprocity, which ΘЮ|W| does not: since there is not only another Self at the other end of the function, but that Self which is the Life(Si) form of [C]haos.

Mimetic interaction |C|=>Θ creates encodings, like those for Grammar and Memory. Indeed, it is by |C|=>Θ Mimesis that Grammar becomes encoded, and by reference to which our first Memories are constructed.

The Classical Account of Attachment

Let's look briefly at the Classical Account model of "attachment". The model says that:

- the immature Self has interactions with mature others, particularly carers.
- those interactions give rise to "attachment" dynamics.
- the dynamics reflect functional or dysfunctional interactions.
- we carry those dynamics through mature life.
- these dynamics dictate or influence the relationship we choose to form, and are able to form, in our mature life.

This model doesn't come with an explanation of objective processes by which these "attachment" dynamics can arise.

What we are left with is a basic reflex model: *you have attachment issues because your mom didn't meet your attachments needs* (and endless iterations of the basic concept).

This model only functions by loading subjective assumptions onto both ends of it, and (arbitrarily) assigning cause and effect between them.

In the Classical Account and in common wisdom, there's a model that it's the /S/ubjective {identation} of |C| which influences the neonate Self |N|.

Yet this idea creates multiple problems:

- how can |C|/S/{i} transmit to |N|/S/{i}?

- how can |N| /S/{i} receive transmissions from |C| /S/{i}?

There is a gap between these subjectivities. The reaction of |N| to |C| behaviours (looking, gestures, holding, stroking, sounds) does not bridge the gap:

> The supply of our needs, in itself, does not discriminate the provider |C| from the the |W|orld which ultimately is the source of all supply.

> What that supply does represent, is an ordering of the chaos that |W| represents to the immature mind: and indeed to the adult mind.

The "mind encased within a skull" model simply cannot account for |C| ⇔ |N| interaction. That is, surely, the most basic (primal) model of social interaction.

It's no surprise then, that the Classical Account, diluted into psychotherapy, has proved incapable of providing a scientific account of mature social relations.

Our First Lighthouse Is |C|
In matrixial Self Systems Architecture and Processes, we have an objective account.

We need to be clear that this is not a behaviourist or reductionist/mechanistic model. It is established empirically that |C| intent and |N| response to stimulus are not unimorphic. an |N| will respond to the like stimulus, whoever provides it and whatever the intent.

The Lighthouse function of |C| is effected in objective interaction:

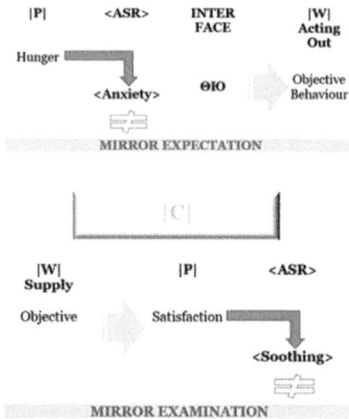

(1)   As the source of Supply which activates the Soothing cycle in the ASR.

(2)   In Mimetic connection $|C|\Theta \Leftrightarrow |N|\Theta$.

(3)   In quantised |T|ime.

We have already considered (1) and (2) above. We examine (3) below. Now we briefly consider some implications for the development of our mature Relationship patterns.

There's a bonding focused in Needs Satisfaction between |C| and |N|. As we say:

>   The supply of our needs, in itself, does not discriminate the provider |C| from the the |W|orld which ultimately is the source of all supply.

Every parent faces the journey of |N| from utter dependence on |C| Supply to novel dependencies on and interests in, other sources of Supply.

Milestones in the journey are primary school, then friends and ultimately the adolescent struggle of |N| to establish their own selections of sources of Supply. That, at least is the ideation of adolescent rebellion (which is totally normal and inevitable).

Lighthouse |T| ime

Mimetic connection |C|Θ⇔|N|Θ allows us to understand the objective basis of attachment. Mimetic connection creates equalised Θ <Constructs>, by reference to which {idents} can be formed.

|C| attachment begins as a process of timing: of |T| ime.

The importance of |T| iming in synchronous synaptic connection, is becoming more evident with Unified Field and Local Field theories in neuroscience.

Please review the *Noming Experience* from Chapter 3. Allow the neonate to play the role of the metronome. We can see how |C| attunes in objective Θ<Construct> |T| ime as a specific IO|W|.

Just watch any |C| and newborn, and you can just see this |T| ime connection being played out.

CHAPTER 15

RELATING

Attachment is Objective

We are not, in the penultimate Chapter of a very long book, going to essay a detailed analysis of social relationships, issues and problems. There is no need to.

Understanding the Self as paradoxical, but not secret, allows us to unravel the social Self. We simply follow the rubrics of Self Systems Architecture and Processes, in interaction.

We come now to a defining position, in relation to the understanding of Relationships.

The Classical Model sees relationships between Selfs, particularly romantic relationships, as operating in $/S/$. A set of operating practices that has its origins in some (mysterious) $/S/_1 \Leftrightarrow /S/_2$ dynamic.

That is completely wrong. There is no direct connection between $/S/_1 \Leftrightarrow /S_2$. Any $/S/$ only has a relationship through and bounded by the Systems Architecture of Self.

From our earliest days, we interact with a source of supply $|C|$. We create Θ<Constructs> in that process.

This may be a useful analogy: it's like how we create zodiacal and folklore shapes out of dots in the night sky:

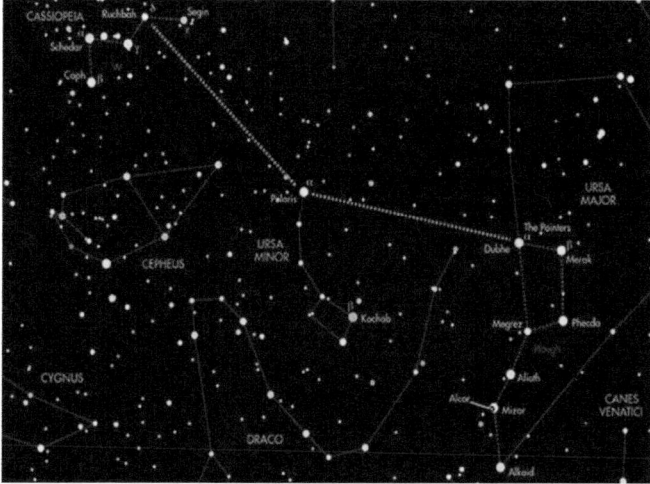

https://www.skyatnightmagazine.com/advice/skills/guides-star-hop-the-night-sky/

The Θ<Constructs> constitute a dot matrix, a landscape of equalised 4 dimensioned points. Our /S/ constructs from it whatever shapes it likes, from moment to moment.

Since the invention of the telescope, and cosmology, we know what we are looking at in the night sky. To the pre-Modern mind, the night sky appeared differently: as the illumined substance of reality, for which life here on earth was but a mirrored shadow.

That pre-Modern mindset is a more appropriate lens for

seeing how we see our Selfs. We don't witness ourselves creating /S/ equivalences out of Θ<Constructs>. We just do it.

In our /S/, we form equivalences: regularities, patterns, habits. None of those are "really there", in the sense of being intrinsic to the Θ dot matrix. But these shapes are the reality by in which we /S/ubjectively experience our lives.

Throughout our lives, we find, and many seek, a personhood which can act as a |C|:

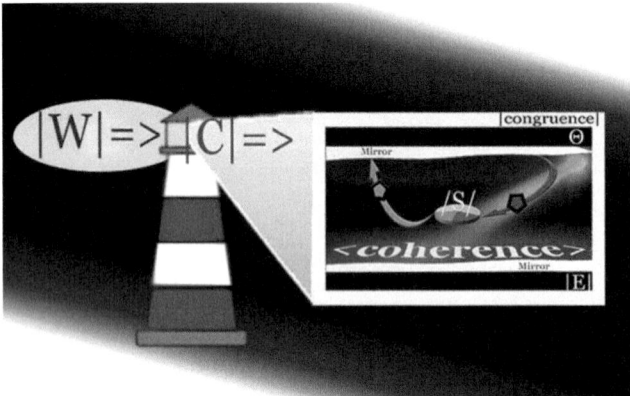

We are light-seekers.
It is how we were born to be.

This is relationship dependency. It has nothing to do with /S/: with our /S/ubjective wants and desires. Interactions |W|=>Θ are which stimulate ΘЮ, and which link to our "star constellations" in Θ.

That is why dependent relationships, which we think of as deeply emotional, we also feel to be outside our control. And we are right to think that way.

We don't choose our Lighthouses.

We all of us find other people who act as lighthouses, shining light where we can't. That can become very addictive.

Until we reach the point we always do. Of realising that we don't need that light to continue showing us what we have now seen. But we will always be in search of another one. It's part of what binds us together as a society.

That granting of privilege to the lighthouse of another person is an act of alienation. Alienation of the sovereignty and power of the Self. Yet it doesn't feel like that, because the more we open up to the light, the more usefully it illuminates.

We surrender to the process, because it works. That is not blind faith. It is the opposite. It is conscious, rational reasoning.

Each of us is drawn to what we regard as sources of light: lighthouses. The more that chaos threatens us, the greater the attraction to light sources outside ourselves.

We can use the analogy of coherent and incoherent light

here. A lamp provides light. But it's weak light, because it's incoherent.

A close friend can provide light. But they are wrapped up in their own lives. They tend to become a close friend because they mirror us, rather than illuminating us.

A great teacher can provide coherent light us: *Dominus Illuminatio Mea*.[283] But any teacher is purposed to be a stepping-stone, not a lifelong companion.

As we outgrow dependence upon our parents, we come to realise that what we believed was light, no longer illuminates us, or even came to darken us.

Which leaves us, as we step from that shadow, seeking new light.

---

[283] Master: enlighten me

CHAPTER 16

POWER

This book is subtitled *Finding the Power of You.*

All that we have been about in the preceding Chapters, is establishing and articulating an understanding of the Systems Architecture and Processes of Self.

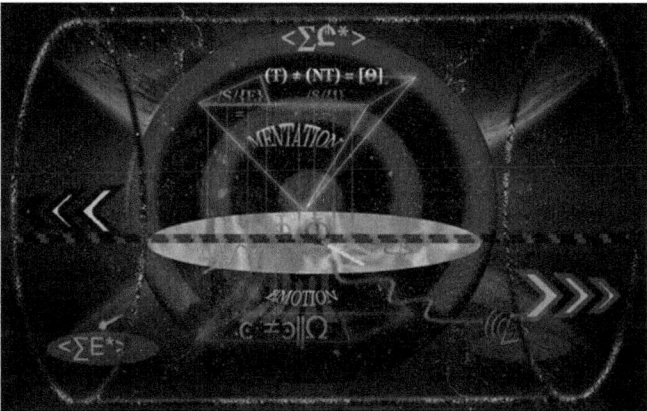

That understanding is what grants You the power of Self. To be able to see the mechanisms by which the Self operates:

- internally
- externally
- synchronically.

The explanation of these mechanisms has been detailed. Although even then we have only summarised intricacies and systems of contingencies.

We began, and end with these rubrics:

Mentation

How we can think governs what we can think

Emotion

What we can emote governs how we emote

The previous Chapters have explained how and why these rubrics have effect, and considered some of their consequences.

We have not tried to set out a detailed psychology of mind: because none is needed. More than that: none can realistically be essayed.

Within the Systems Architecture and Processes of Self, all is /S/ubjective, contingent and arbitrary. Yet the only reality which we can experience. A paradox: but no longer a secret.

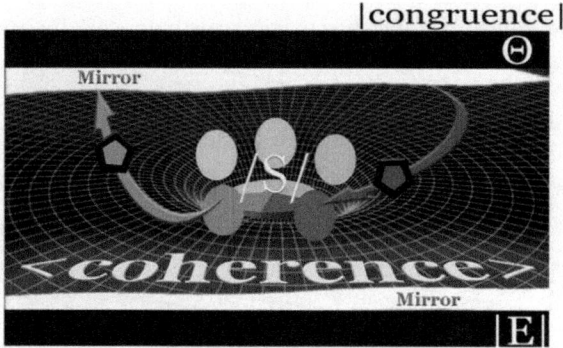

Power derives not from secrecy, but transparency.

The Architecture of the Self allows its Systems and Processes to become transparent. These are the means of our {identation}, our <Thoughts> and <Feelings>, but not the material of them.

The *Power of You* has been demonstrated in the *Experiences* that you have participated in. We have explained the principles of :

* *Psychotectics* (Morphonics and Holonics)
* *Biomorphics*, centred upon restoration and maintenance of Biomorphic Autonomic Balance.

We have shown how *Matrixial Healing* techniques can be used in *Psychotectics*, *Biomorphics*, and in combination, to release the power which lies in every Self.

These are techniques which help the Self to *find the power of you*. Finding coherence in dynamic balance. The power of congruence in becoming with the perfection of process born into each of us.

As we said in *I Want To Love But*,[284] perfection is your birth right. You were born with a perfect Anxiety-Soothing Rhythm. It is what allows you to grow and learn. It is the essential process of your becoming: a journey you experience subjectively both as passenger and driver.

You are able to live as a subjective self in an infinite space of thought, as ideas and feelings. It's the Systems Architecture of Self which enables You to be a <Me> in the continual process of becoming. You were born as an <I> in being, and will remain so, whatever the momentary changes in your subjective <Me> self.

The Self is not a secret. But it is multiple layers of paradoxes.

It is from understanding these layers that we acquire power over ourselves. The *Power of You* comes, not from changing who you are, but altering how you choose to become.

You can realise that power instantly. You simply learn to surrender to your Self.

---

[284] The Author (2019)

ANNEX A

THE NEW NEUROSCIENCE OF MIND

The Science

Communication within the brain has long been established as having effect through synaptic transmission ("ST"): both chemical and electrical.

We provided a summary of the classic account of ST in Section B(2)/17.

The problem is that ST simply cannot account for whatever is considered to be "consciousness".

Even worse, ST can't account for:

- memory
- the Self's sense of time
- the binding problem (how different inputs to the senses get put together as ideas of things)
- how the Self retains personality even with severe brain trauma or dysfunction
- how any of this "brain in a skull" process can relate to anything outside it.

The novel theoretical framework of Interoception is another attempt to solve these gnawing problems.

McFadden has been promoting a new neuroscience of mind for the last 20 years. His latest paper[285] engages with empirical research which add substantial weight to his ideas:

A key aspect of consciousness is that it represents bound or integrated information, prompting an increasing conviction that the physical substrate of consciousness must be capable of encoding integrated information in the brain. However, as Ralph Landauer insisted, 'information is physical' so integrated information must be physically integrated.

I argue here that nearly all examples of so-called 'integrated information', including neuronal information processing and conventional computing, are only temporally integrated in the sense that outputs are correlated with multiple inputs: the information integration is implemented in time, rather than space, and thereby cannot correspond to physically integrated information.

I point out that only energy fields are capable of integrating information in space. I describe the conscious electromagnetic information (cemi) field theory which has proposed that consciousness is physically integrated, and causally active, information encoded in the brain's global electromagnetic (EM) field.

I here extend the theory to argue that consciousness implements algorithms in space, rather than time, within the brain's EM field. I describe how the cemi field theory accounts for most observed features of consciousness and describe recent experimental support for the theory. I also describe several untested predictions of the theory and discuss its implications for the design of artificial consciousness. The cemi field theory proposes a scientific dualism that is rooted in the difference between matter and energy, rather than matter and spirit.

McFadden's CEMI theory uses a radically different starting point:

---

[285] Johnjoe McFadden, Integrating information in the brain's EM field: the cemi field theory of consciousness, *Neuroscience of Consciousness*, Volume 2020, Issue 1, 2020, niaa016, https://doi.org/10.1093/nc/niaa016

EMF transmitters and receivers in the brain

It has been known since the 19th century that the brain generates its own EM field, which can be detected by electrodes inserted to the brain. Its source is electrical dipoles within the neuronal membranes caused by the motion of ions in and out of those membranes during action potentials and synaptic potentials. The periodic discharge of neurons—firing or action potentials—generates EMF waves that propagate out of the neuron and into the surrounding inter-neuronal spaces where they overlap and combine to generate the brain's global EM field that is routinely measured by brain scanning techniques such as electroencephalography (EEG) and magnetoencephalography (MEG). The human brain therefore possesses around 100 billion EMF transmitters.

The human brain also possesses at least 100 billion EMF receivers as each neuron in bounded by a membrane embedded with thousands of voltage-gated ion channels whose firing is triggered by EM field fluctuation across the membrane. Although these channels are generally assumed to respond only to large fluctuations of tens of millivolts across the membrane, much larger than the global EM field strength, EM field potential changes of less than 1 mV across the neuronal membrane are nevertheless capable of modulating neuronal firing (Schmitt *et al.* 1976). Moreover, for neurons poised close to the critical firing potential, the opening of just a single ion channel may be sufficient to trigger firing (Arhem and Johansson 1996). This degree of sensitivity suggests that very tiny changes in membrane potential, of similar strength to spontaneous fluctuations in the brain's endogenous EM field, may influence the firing of neurons that are already close to firing.

Susan Pockett has also made valuable contributions to the new approach. We cite from her Scholarpedia Article extensively below, as the fastest route for taking the general reader to the issues[286]

The field theories of consciousness discussed in this article are theories

---

[286] http://www.scholarpedia.org/article/Field_theories_of_consciousness

of the nature of consciousness, in which consciousness is conceived as being identical with a field in the general sense in which the term 'field' is used in physics. This means that in these theories, consciousness is seen as having not only duration, but also extension in space. In most of the theories discussed, consciousness is proposed to be identical with some aspect of a physical field i.e. a field in which the property that exists at each point in a particular region of the spacetime continuum is objectively measurable. However, in at least one of the theories, consciousness is proposed to be identical with a hypothetical non-physical field, which nevertheless still has extension in space.

The electromagnetic field theory of consciousness
The central idea of the electromagnetic (EM) field theory of consciousness is that conscious perceptions (and sensations, inasmuch as they can be said to have independent existence) are identical with certain spatiotemporal electromagnetic patterns generated by the normal functioning of waking mammalian brains.

Partly as a result of Lashley's legacy, this theory struggled for a number of years to achieve publication at all, let alone any degree of acceptance. Susan Pockett started trying to publish it in the Journal of Consciousness Studies in 1995 (Pockett 2002). Around the same time Robert Charman (personal communication) independently submitted essentially the same idea to the same journal, with the same lack of success. Charman then published the idea as a short paper in the 'alternative' journal Network (Charman 1997) and withdrew from the fray. Pockett published the essence of the idea as a footnote in a review paper on auditory consciousness (Pockett 1999), worked it up into a book manuscript (which was again rejected by a series of academic publishers) and eventually put the book out using a demand publisher in the year 2000 (Pockett 2000). By this time the idea had been doing the rounds of numerous reviewers for approximately five years and Johnjoe McFadden had written about it in the final chapter of a book about something else (McFadden, 2000). Two years later, the Journal of Consciousness Studies finally accepted the electromagnetic field theory of consciousness as an original contribution from McFadden (2002(a),(b)), Roy John suggested in a more neuroscientific forum that a resonating electromagnetic field might be 'the embodiment of mind' (John 2002) and the brothers Fingelkurts proposed a theory that skirted around the central idea of the EM field theory, but included the statement "it is important to stress that we do not attempt to explain how consciousness arises from neuronal tissue" (Finglekurts and Fingelkurts 2002).

During this initial period, a great many objections to the basic idea were advanced in various fora. Refutations of some of these are outlined in section (a) below. Section (b) discusses an apparent controversy between main proponents of the EM field theory about whether or not the proposed conscious electromagnetic patterns can act causally on their own brain – early statements of the theory had it that conscious electromagnetic patterns do have causal actions on the brain (Pockett 2000) or spinal cord (McFadden 2000), but later versions (Pockett 2002; 2011; 2012) questioned the specificity of this effect and pointed out that much if not all of what we intuitively believe to be consciously initiated bodily movement has now been shown to be initiated by pre- or unconscious brain function anyway. Section (c) discusses a recent proposal regarding the detailed constitution of conscious as opposed to unconscious electromagnetic patterns.

(a) Objections to the EM field theory of consciousness answered
The much-raised objection that the EM field theory was disproved by Lashley sixty years ago has already been covered in the section about Köhler's field theory. Three of the more cogent further objections to the EM field theory of consciousness are discussed below.

(i) Probably the most obvious *a priori* objection is that common external electromagnetic fields – radio waves, mains voltage, the magnetic fields inside MRI (magnetic resonance imaging) machines – demonstrably have no effect on consciousness. Surely they should, the objection goes, if the electromagnetic field theory of consciousness were correct. MacFadden's answer to this objection (McFadden 2000) is that the brain is surrounded by a protective Faraday cage of cerebrospinal fluid, which denies entry to external fields. This is easily refuted by the observation that such a Faraday cage would also deny exit to brain-generated fields, which would make it impossible to record EEG (electroencephalograms) from the scalp. Since thousands of research and clinical laboratories around the world routinely record EEG from the scalp every day, the proposed Faraday cage cannot be effective. More plausible refutations of the original objection are that (a) radio waves are of much higher frequency than the proposed conscious fields, so would not be expected to affect their relevant features (b) mains voltage is about the same frequency as the oscillations proposed as being conscious, but electromagnetic oscillations at these frequencies radiate so inefficiently that virtually no power is detectable a few cm from a wall socket (c) the magnetic field inside an MRI machine is powerful enough, but does not have the right spatial configuration to couple with the putative conscious field (as demonstrated by the fact that, once the technical difficulties associated with the recording apparatus are dealt with, the magnetic field generated by MRI machines does not affect EEG recorded within the magnet). But the killer refutation of this objection is essentially a generalization of (c). It is that none of the common ambient EM fields is patterned in the spatial domain. If the inverse spatial pattern of a putatively conscious field pattern were applied externally, the conscious pattern would indeed be cancelled and the conscious experiences represented should be ablated. But if spatially unpatterned external fields are imposed on the brain, the physics of electromagnetism dictates that the putatively conscious field pattern will simply ride up and down on the spatially unpatterned external field, as a boat rides up and down on the waves of an ocean. In the jargon of physics, there will be no coupling between the two fields, so both will continue, unaffected by the presence of the other.

(ii) A second objection to the electromagnetic field theory of consciousness is that experiments with the early 'split-brain' patients (in whom the corpus collosum, the fibre tract connecting the two hemispheres of the brain, was cut to prevent spread of epileptic seizures), show that such patients apparently have two separate consciousnesses. The conscious field would (probably) still be unified in split-brain patients, so if, as proposed by the electromagnetic field theory of consciousness, a given subject's total consciousness is the totality of the conscious field generated by their brain, split brain patients should still have a unified consciousness.

One reasonable answer to this objection is that to the casual observer, split-brain patients do still have a unified consciousness. Even when one does the clever experimental manipulations necessary to demonstrate that in such patients the non-verbal right hemisphere can be made aware of things which cannot be reported by the verbal left hemisphere, it remains true that interhemispheric transfer of information is not entirely absent in commisurotomised subjects. There appear to be two systems, one of which can be split and the other of which cannot (Corballis 1994, 1995). Perhaps the unsplittable system is subserved by the conscious field.

A more cogent refutation of the original objection is as follows. Split-brain patients clearly *act* in such a way as to indicate that they are aware of events generated by both sides of their brain (as predicted by the EM field theory) - what makes them interesting is simply that they are unable to report this awareness using language. In order for the original objection to hold water, the conscious fields generated by sensory areas (for example) on the non-language-capable side of the brain would need to be able to have a direct effect on neurons in the language areas on the other side of the brain. But as recent versions of the EM field theory (Pockett 2011; 2012) point out, the physics of electromagnetism dictate that the EM dipole patterns constituting putatively conscious fields fall off not merely with the square of distance but actually with the cube of distance from their sources. In other words, conscious EM field patterns are very local. In order for any conscious experience to be reported using language, the conscious field pattern has to act on neurons close to where the pattern is generated and these neurons then have to communicate by standard neurophysiological means (action potentials, synapses and so on) with the language areas. In commisurotomised patients standard neurophysiological communication is physically disrupted, so linguistic reports of conscious experience generated by the non-language hemisphere are impossible.

(iii) A third commonly advanced objection to the electromagnetic field theory of consciousness is that it has no obvious advantages over the widely accepted neural identity theory and therefore should not be adopted. Two answers to this objection are that (a) even if it were true that the electromagnetic field theory of consciousness made no significant predictions over and above those of the psycho-neural identity theory, it is not necessarily true that the first theory to appear is the right one, and (b) in fact the electromagnetic field theory does, in at least one major respect, deliver more than the psycho-neural identity theory ever could. The difference is that the electromagnetic field theory of consciousness predicts that in principle, consciousness could be generated using hardware instead of wetware. This single prediction not only renders the electromagnetic field theory testable where the neural identity theory is not – it also opens wondrous vistas with respect to possible future technologies.

(b) Controversy about possibility of causal action of proposed conscious patterns

The controversy that seems to have developed about whether or not EM fields like those proposed as being conscious can have a causal action on brain function is in this author's view largely a matter of misunderstanding.

First, it has never been disputed that electromagnetic fields can and do affect neuronal function. Chapter 7 of Pockett (2000) lists a number of circumstances in which brain-generated em fields had already been shown to affect brain function, in areas that probably do not generate consciousness (including the medulla of the gold-fish, the <u>cerebellum</u> and the <u>hippocampus </u>of mammals). McFadden (2013) supplies more recent examples of the demonstrated action of external em fields, both *in vitro* (mammalian brain slices) and *in vivo* (the occipital cortex of anaesthetized ferrets). It is thus quite clear that electromagnetic fields absolutely do have the capacity to influence neuronal activity, in both unconscious and (presumably, since nobody suggests that neurons change their biophysical characteristics depending on whether or not consciousness is present) in conscious brain tissue. The fact that em fields can have a direct influence on neuronal function is not now and never has been even slightly contentious.

It is also completely uncontentious that both the generation of EM fields by the brain and the generation of consciousness require <u>synchronous</u> firing of large numbers of chemical synapses on neocortical pyramidal cells. This fact is pointed out on p.95 et seq. of the hard copy version of Pockett (2000), as well as in a number of papers by McFadden (2002a,b; 2006; 2013). The mechanism by which extracellular electromagnetic fields are generated by the synchronous activity of chemical synapses on neocortical pyramidal cells is illustrated diagrammatically in Pockett (2012).

The question in the current context is not whether EM fields like those proposed as being conscious can have a direct influence on neural tissue – clearly they can – or even whether synchrony is necessary for the generation of both consciousness and the putatively conscious EM fields – clearly it is. The question at issue is whether spatial EM patterns like those proposed as being conscious can *transfer the information encoded in their spatial patterning* back to their own brains in such a way that this information can be the direct cause of specific behaviours. McFadden argues on general grounds that they can. Pockett argues on specific grounds that they can not.

The specific argument put forward by Pockett (2011, 2012) is as follows:

(i) The spatial patterns in question are highly likely to be composed of multiple electric dipoles (each generated by the synchronous action of many synapses on many neocortical pyramidal cells) in a series of adjacent cortical columns (Pockett 2007, 2012). The basic physics of electromagnetism dictates that the strength of the EM field produced by an electric dipole falls off not merely with the square of distance from the source (as for a single electric charge), but with the *cube* of distance from the source. This means that the EM field encoding a conscious percept is very local. In other words, the spatial EM pattern encoding any given conscious experience is undetectable quite a short distance away from where it was generated.

(ii) This in turn means that putatively conscious EM patterns should be capable of acting *as patterns* only on the same neurons that generated them. Neurons even slightly further away would simply not "see" these patterns at all.

(iii) Since the neurons directly causing behaviour are in general much too far away from the neurons that generate either sensory experiences or decisions for the patterns generated by the sensory or decision neurons to be "seen" by the neurons causing behaviour, the implication is that if sensory experiences and decisions *are* spatial EM patterns, consciousness (or at least sensory consciousness and conscious decisions) should not be able *directly* to cause behaviour. (It could, of course, cause behaviour indirectly, by acting on local neurons which then communicate with the rest of the brain by standard neurophysiological means).

This general argument is potentially damaging if not fatal to the EM field theory of consciousness. If, as we all intuitively believe, our voluntary actions are generated by our conscious thoughts, putatively conscious

EM fields should be able to generate actions; preferably directly, although this is really only an aesthetic requirement. It thus becomes important to know whether consciousness (irrespective of what that may turn out to be) does directly cause behaviour.

Counterintuitively, it turns out that a large confluence of evidence has accumulated over the last decade to suggest that largely, it does not (Pockett 2004; 2011; Pockett et al 2006). Even behaviour generally accepted as being voluntary turns out to be initiated unconsciously. As Wegner (2002) concludes, humans interpret their thoughts as the cause of their actions only on the same basis that they interpret anything as the cause of anything else – all that is necessary for A to be interpreted as the cause of B is that A should (a) precede B (by a plausible time chunk) (b) be consistent with B and (c) be the only apparent cause of B.

(c) Proposal on 3-D shape of conscious as opposed to unconscious em patterns
The realization that the initiation of bodily actions is not accessible to consciousness allows a proposal about the 3-D structure distinguishing conscious em patterns from non-conscious em patterns (Pockett 2012). It is now well accepted that sensory consciousness is not generated during the first, feed-forward pass of neural activity from the thalamus through the primary sensory cortex. Recurrent activity from other cortical areas back to the primary or secondary sensory cortex is necessary. Because the feedforward activity goes through architectonic Lamina 4 of the primary sensory cortex (which is composed largely of stellate cells and thus does not generate synaptic dipoles) while recurrent activity operates through synapses on pyramidal cells (which do generate dipoles), the conscious em patterns resulting from recurrent activity in the 'early' sensory cortex have a neutral area in the middle of their radial pattern. The common feature of brain areas that can not generate conscious experience – which are now seen to include motor cortex as well as hippocampus, cerebellum and any sub-cortical area – is that they all lack an architectonic Lamina 4. Therefore none of the brain areas that are unable to generate consciousness produces EM fields with a neutral region in the middle of their radial pattern. Thus the feature that distinguishes conscious from unconscious patterns is proposed to be a neutral area corresponding to Lamina 4.

Whether or not this proposal turns out to be correct remains to be seen, but it is certainly an experimentally testable idea, which has the potentially important heuristic feature of pointing out the need to record laminar electromagnetic patterns as well as the more commonly studied micro-column-based patterns tangential to the surface of the brain.

(d) A prediction
The description of the EM field theory of consciousness provided above is incomplete. The theory is about to enter a phase of rapid evolution. Watch this space for updates.

The implications of the ideas summarised in Pockett's article may seem obscure to the general reader.

The mechanism involved in these new theories is Ephaptic Transmission ("ET").[287]

> In Chapter 2, were mentioned some of the ways by which neurons can communicate with each other, including chemical transmission via synapses and direct electrical connections through gap junctions, but there are other possibilities.

> Here, we consider coupling of individual impulses through their external current loops. This is called ephaptic coupling (as opposed to synaptic), from a Greek verb meaning "to touch."

> Since the work of Ewald Hering in 1882 [13], it has been known that nerve impulses on adjacent fibers

---

[287] (2002) Ephaptic Interactions Among Axons. In: Neuroscience. Springer, New York, NY. https://doi.org/10.1007/978-0-387-22463-3_8

can influence one another.

[13] E Hering, Beitr¨age zur allgemeinen Nerven-
und Muskelphysiologie. IV. ¨Uber Nervenreizung
durch den Nervenstrom, Sitzungsber. k. Akad.
Wiss. (Wien) 85 part 3 (1882) 237–275.

A useful summary[288] states:

Electrical signaling is a cardinal feature of the nervous system and
endows it with the capability of quickly reacting to changes in the
environment. Although synaptic communication between nerve cells
is perceived to be mainly chemically mediated, electrical synaptic
interactions also occur. Two different strategies are responsible for
electrical communication between neurons. One is the consequence of
low resistance intercellular pathways, called "gap junctions", for the
spread of electrical currents between the interior of two cells. The second
occurs in the absence of cell-to-cell contacts and is a consequence of
the extracellular electrical fields generated by the electrical activity of
neurons. Here, we place present notions about electrical transmission
in a historical perspective and contrast the contributions of the two
different forms of electrical communication to brain function.

Introduction

It has been argued that the function of the nervous system is to support
movement and that it evolved because of its usefulness to organisms
in navigating their environment (Llinás, 2001). Early observations
established that nerves were required for muscle contraction. However,
the mechanism underlying this interaction was unknown. An old,
predominant, idea embraced by Rene Descartes was that muscle
contraction resulted from the action of "animal spirits" running through
hollow nerves (Piccolino, 1998; Finger, 2005). This and other speculative
ideas were later disproved, leading to the consideration of alternative

---

[288] Faber Donald S., Pereda Alberto E. *Two Forms of Electrical Transmission Between Neurons*. Frontiers in Molecular Neuroscience. Volume 11 (2018). HTTPS://WWW.FRONTIERSIN.ORG/ARTICLE/10.3389/FNMOL.2018.00427 DOI=10.3389/fnmol.2018.00427

mechanisms. One of them was electricity (Franklin, 1751). The use of electricity for therapeutic purposes was popular in the second part of the 18th century, and electricity was capable of eliciting muscle contraction. In addition, because of its high travel velocity, electricity was ideally suited to be the agent responsible for nerve action, as some hypothesized (Finger, 2005). Furthermore, experimental evidence showed that certain fish were capable of generating electricity. All this preceding work and speculations paved the way to the studies conducted by Galvani (1791) which demonstrated that nerves and muscles generate electricity ("bioelectricity") and, therefore, that electricity was the mysterious fluid or "animal spirit" responsible for nerve conduction and muscle contraction (Piccolino, 1998; Finger, 2005). We know now that these electrical currents result from the movement of charged ions across the cellular membrane following their electrochemical gradient (Hodgkin and Huxley, 1952; Armstrong, 2007). Galvani's seminal studies led to the foundation of electrophysiology and to the discovery that brain function and, hence, animal behavior, depends upon electrophysiological computations, the only operational mode fast enough to support the required time frame of decision making by neural circuits. In other words, as emphasized by Llinás, electricity makes us who we are (Sohn, 2003).

The discovery that the brain is constructed from networks of individual cells that generate electrical signals raised the question of how electrical currents "jump" from one cell to another. The most hotly debated question in Neuroscience during the 20th century was whether synaptic transmission, which is the currency of the brain, is mediated electrically or chemically.

In fact, this might have been the major point of dispute in the biological sciences in that era, with advocates on both sides avidly defending their positions with data—based and theoretical models. Each side advanced its favored mechanism on the basis of its assumed advantages for the operation of neural networks in the central nervous system (CNS). Thus, a great deal of effort was devoted to determining whether there was a delay of 1–2 ms between a presynaptic action potential and the start of a postsynaptic response (chemical) or not (electrical), and to the corresponding functional consequences of these alternatives. In this review article, we briefly describe the critical elements of the debate between electrical and chemical modes of transmission, which seemed to tilt strongly in favor of the latter once it emerged that synaptic inhibition in the spinal cord was mediated by an ionic conductance change. This was particularly compelling in view of the difficulties in determining a satisfying mechanism for electrical inhibition.

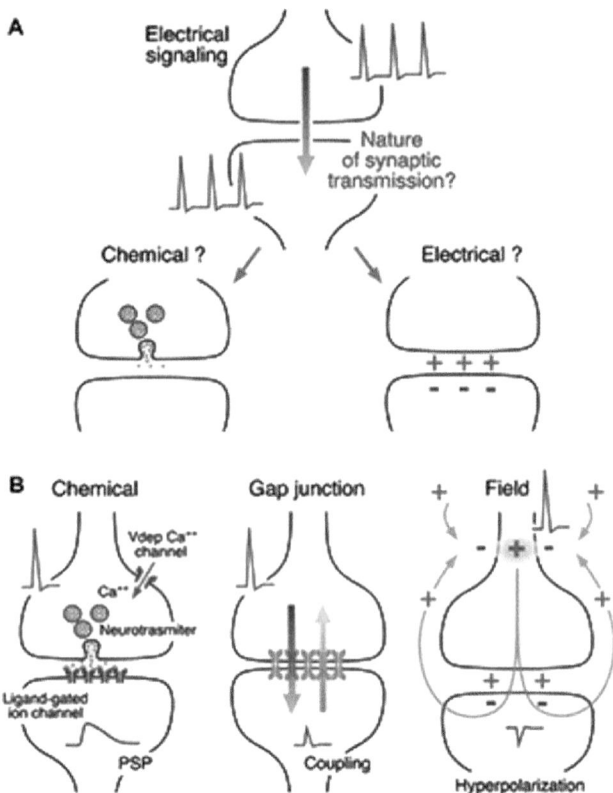

However, in recent years, electrical transmission has regained recognition and relevance. Rather than occurring via a single mechanism, electrical transmission operates in two ways: via pathways of low resistance between neurons (gap junctions) or as a consequence of extracellular electric fields generated by neuronal activity.

Summary

The nervous system relies on electrical signaling to perform the fast computations that underlie animal behavior.

Not surprisingly, intercellular communication between neurons can be mediated not only by the action of chemical transmitters, but also by electrical signaling.

In turn, electrical communication occurs via two main mechanisms: one involves pathways of low resistance between neighboring neurons that are provided by intercellular channels (gap junctions), while the second, which is generally less appreciated, occurs as a consequence of the extracellular electrical fields generated by neurons during electrical signaling.

Electrical signals generated by one cell can thus modify the excitability of its neighbors via one, or both, of these mechanisms. As with chemical transmission, each of the two modes of electrical transmission depends upon distinctive structural specializations, namely gap junctions in one case and a dense high resistance neuropil in the other.

Let's bring these ideas to life by looking at experiments analysed by McFadden in 2013.[289]

Abstract: Several theories of consciousness first described about a decade ago, including the conscious electromagnetic information (CEMI) field theory, claimed that the substrate of consciousness is the brain's electromagnetic (EM) field. These theories were prompted by the observation, in many diverse systems, that synchronous neuronal firing, which generates coherent EM fields, was a strong correlate of attention, awareness, and consciousness.

However, when these theories were first described there was no direct evidence that synchronous firing was actually functional, rather than an epiphenomenon of brain function. Additionally, any EM field-based consciousness would be a 'ghost in the machine' unless the brain's endogenous EM field is also able to influence neuron firing.

---

[289] *The CEMI field theory closing the loop.* J Conscious Stud 2013a20:1–2

Once again, when these theories were first described, there was only indirect evidence that the brain's EM field influenced neuron firing patterns in the brain.

In this paper I describe recent experimental evidence which demonstrate that synchronous neuronal firing does indeed have a functional role in the brain; and also that the brain's endogenous EM field is involved in recruiting neurons to synchronously firing networks.

The new data point to a new and unappreciated form of neural communication in the brain that is likely to have significance for all theories of consciousness. I describe an extension of the CEMI field theory that incorporates these recent experimental findings and integrates the theory with the 'communication through coherence' hypothesis.

The experimental science is now catching up with the ET theory. For example:[290]

Slow periodic activity can propagate with speeds around 0.1 m s-1 and be modulated by weak electric fields.

Slow periodic activity in the longitudinal hippocampal slice can propagate without chemical synaptic transmission or gap junctions, but can generate electric fields which in turn activate neighbouring cells.

Applying local extracellular electric fields with amplitude in the range of endogenous fields is sufficient to modulate or block the propagation of this activity both in the *in silico* and in the *in vitro* models.
Results support the hypothesis that endogenous electric fields, previously thought to be too small to trigger neural activity, play a significant role in the self-propagation of slow periodic activity in the hippocampus.

Experiments indicate that a neural network can give rise to sustained

---

[290] Chiang CC, Shivacharan RS, Wei X, Gonzalez-Reyes LE, Durand DM. Slow periodic activity in the longitudinal hippocampal slice can self-propagate non-synaptically by a mechanism consistent with ephaptic coupling. *J Physiol.* 2019;597(1):249-269. doi:10.1113/JP276904

self-propagating waves by ephaptic coupling, suggesting a novel propagation mechanism for neural activity under normal physiological conditions.

...

It has been shown experimentally that weak electric fields, or ephaptic coupling, can entrain action potentials of neurons (Anastassiou *et al.* 2011). Ephaptic coupling has been suggested as a mechanism involved in modulating neural activity from different regions of the nervous system (Jefferys, 1995; Weiss & Faber, 2010; Anastassiou & Koch, 2015) especially in the vertebrate retina (Vroman *et al.* 2013) and in the olfactory circuit (Su *et al.* 2012). Several studies also indicate that weak electric fields can influence the neural activity at the cortical and hippocampal network level (Francis *et al.* 2003; Deans *et al.* 2007; Frohlich & McCormick, 2010). In hippocampal slices, weak electric fields can affect the excitability of pyramidal cells and the synchronization of the hippocampal network (Francis *et al.* 2003; Deans *et al.* 2007). In the cortex, weak electric fields have also been shown to modulate slow periodic activity in the *in vitro* preparation (Frohlich & McCormick, 2010). Although endogenous electric fields are thought to be too weak to excite neurons, two recent studies suggest that weak electric fields are involved in the propagation of epileptiform activity at a specific speed of 0.1 m s-1 (Zhang *et al.* 2014; Qiu *et al.*2015).

Slow periodic activity can be reproduced in the *in vitro* cortical slices to mimic *in vivo* slow oscillation and can be modulated by weak electric fields (Sanchez-Vives & McCormick, 2000; Tahvildari *et al.* 2012).

Therefore, ephaptic coupling could play a role in the propagation of this slow periodic activity. In this study, we test the hypo- theses that the slow periodic activity in the hippocampus can propagate non-synaptically and ephaptic coupling is the most likely mechanism of propagation.

When we get past the technical language, these astonishing results emerge, with decisive implications for ET theory:

Slow hippocampal periodic activity can activate neural tissue through a complete gap in the tissue
To confirm the absence of any role of synaptic transmission and to eliminate other forms of communication between neurons except

for ephaptic coupling, we next examined the possibility that electric fields generated by pyramidal neurons could propagate through a cut in the tissue by activating other cells across a small gap of the tissue, thereby eliminating chemical, electrical synapses (gap junctions), or axonal transmission. Fig. 4 *A* and *B* shows the propagation of the slow hippocampal periodic activity before and after the cut in the tissue.

To ensure that the slice was completely cut, the two pieces of tissue were separated and then rejoined while a clear gap was observed under the surgical microscope.

The slow hippocampal periodic activity could indeed generate an event on the other side of a complete cut through the whole slice (Fig. 4 *B*).

However, the slow hippocampal periodic activity failed to trigger the activity across the gap when the distance of the gap increased (Fig. 4 *C*). The expanded window in Fig. 4 *D* shows that the waveforms of the slow hippocampal periodic activity and the delay between two signals measured in recording electrodes 1 and 2 were similar.

The speed of the slow hippocampal periodic activity across the tissue was not affected by the presence of the cut in Fig. 4 *E* (t test, $n = 36$ events in 3 slices).

Therefore, this experiment shows that slow hippocampal periodic activity can propagate along a cut tissue by activating cells on the other side without any chemical and electrical synaptic connections at a similar speed to those observed in the intact tissue.

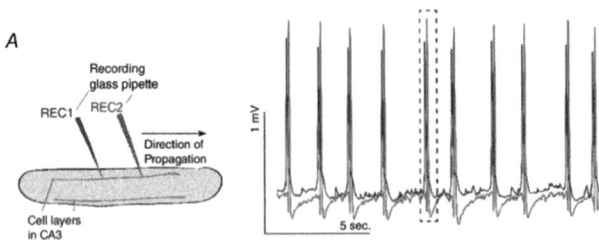

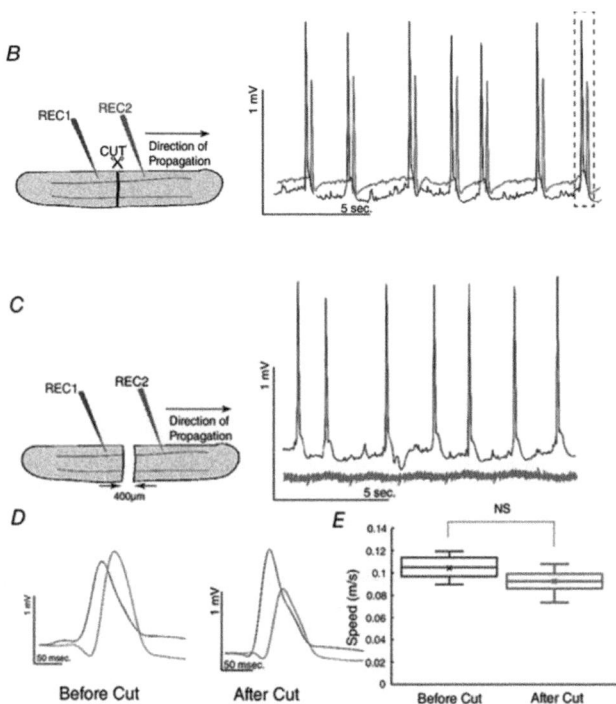

A, slow hippocampal periodic activity propagated from recording electrode 1 (REC1) to recording electrode 2 (REC2) at a speed of 0.10 ± 0.01 m s⁻¹ before the cut. *B*, a complete cut in the hippocampal slice. Slow hippocampal periodic activity was observed to be propagating along the slice with a cut from REC1 to REC2 with speed similar to that recorded in an intact slice by activation of the neurons of the other side of the cut. *C*, slow hippocampal periodic activity stopped propagating when the gap was 400 μm. *D*, expanded windows of the single event of the slow hippocampal periodic activity before and after the cut revealing similar delays between two recording electrodes. *E*, speeds of slow hippocampal periodic activity before and after the cut. There is no significant difference between the two speeds. NS, not significant.

To get some idea of what this all means, try looking at the experiment in this imaginary way:

- Bob's forearm was severed between the elbow and wrist
- completely severed
- yet his brain could still signal the nerves in the wrist, to get his fingers wriggling.

The experimental validation of this ET phenomenon was also reported in 2006:[291]

Rat spinal cord and medulla

One study tested the effects of ephaptic coupling by using both neurotransmitter antagonists to block chemical synapses and gap junction blockers to block electrical synapses. It was found that rhythmic electrical discharge associated with fetal neurons in the rat spinal cord and medulla was still sustained.

This suggests that connections between the neurons still exist and work to spread signals even without traditional synapses.

These findings support a model in which ephaptic coupling works alongside canonical synapses to propagate signals across neuronal networks.

To the lay reader, this may or may not be fascinating in itself. But "so what" for the Self? Let's see.

The Matrixial Mind

This book has been about establishing and explaining the Systems Architecture of Self:

---

[291] *Ren J, Momose-Sato Y, Sato K, Greer JJ (January 2006). "Rhythmic neuronal discharge in the medulla and spinal cord of fetal rats in the absence of synaptic transmission". J. Neurophysiol.* 95 *(1): 527–34. doi:10.1152/jn.00735.2005. PMID 16148265.*

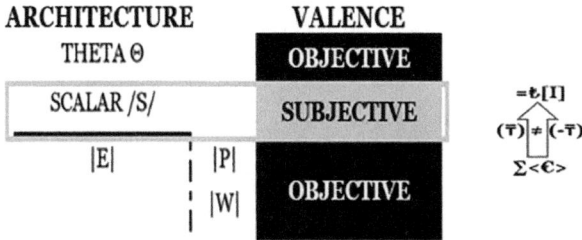

and considering the consequences, for understanding of the Self.

We've generated and deployed the fundamental equations to show how the Systems work, and the processes of interaction between its elements, and with the | W | orld outside the Self:

Fundamental Equations

Form in [E]	$(A) \neq (nA) = [E]$
Form in [I]	$(A) \neq (-A) = [I]$
<Node> in [E]	$\square[E]^n \neq \square[E]^n \sum <E>$
<Node> in [I]	$\Delta[I]^n \neq \Delta[I]^n \sum <I>$

Modes of Interaction

	W	orld <Node>	$| W | \sum <I> => | EF |$
	P	<Node>	$| P | \sum <I> => | EF |$
/S/ <Node>	$/S/ \sum <I> => | EF |$

Exclusion Function: Quantised

Capacity Gapping	$(\geq \varsigma) \neq (\leq \ominus) \int[x]$
Plurality	$\Delta\int[x]^n => (\varepsilon) \mid \Delta\int[x]^n => (\partial)$

Ohm Function: Qualitised

Aggregation $\qquad (\epsilon) \neq (\ni) \sum\Omega^n$

<Affect> $\qquad (\epsilon) \neq (n\epsilon) = [\epsilon]$

Referral to /S/ $\qquad [\square\ \epsilon^1] \neq [\square\ \epsilon^n] \sum<\epsilon>$

<Thought>

Potential $\qquad \Delta<\top^n> \mid \infty$

VCIP $\qquad \sum<\epsilon>\ (\top) \neq (-\top) = \text{\textsterling}[I]$

Theta Axis

<Constructs> $\qquad (\top) \neq (n\top) = \Theta$

[T] Synchronisation $\qquad \underline{\Theta^n = \mid\text{Ю}\mid = \mid W\mid}$

$$\sum\mid\text{\textcent}\mid$$

We have reverse engineered the big picture, with which we ended *Matrixial Logic* and started *Secret Self*:

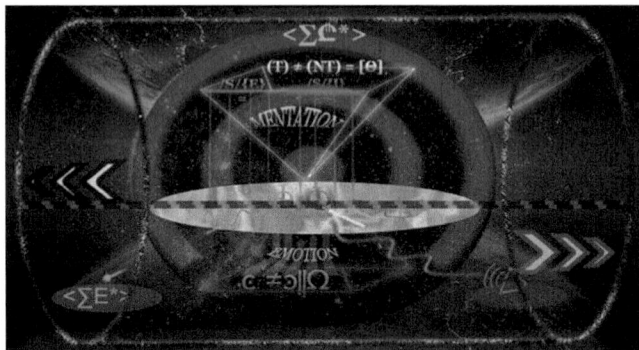

So now to the "so what" of the new neuroscience of mind.

Let's first of all put into place a plain English explanation of the ST / ET system, as it's now emerging from neuroscience experiments.

Imagine the cars and other vehicles in this graphic being synapses in the brain:

The vehicles can talk to each other by local radio (chemical transmission). You can also think of them like dodgem cars that can gently bump each other (gap junction transmission).

This is the standard model of synaptic transmission.

The new 3rd element, adding to the standard model, is ET:

the electromagnetic fields which arise from the synaptic and pre-synaptic activity in the brain's neurons.

You can visualise this like the satellite signals beaming from "the cloud" to the vehicles.

What the experiments and physics of ET seems to be showing us is that signals from the electromagnetic "cloud":
- are not telling the vehicles where to go;

but
- are telling the vehicles when to move.

The EM field is signalling synapses when to fire, not where to fire.

This is very exciting, because we have said from the start of Secret Self, that the secret is: |T|ime.

We demonstrated in Matrixial Logic, Chapter 7, that |T|ime is quantised: it is a succession of |gap| events, all overlapping in reality. That this is the organising mechanism of all matter, from the quantum level up.

Through |T|ime based *Experiences* (*Noming, Timecart, Ropelength* and others), we have shown in ML and in this book, that the Theta Θ axis field can synchronise with chronal correlates in |W|.

To simplify[292] how the Matrixial Self corresponds to this 4 dimensional ST / ET (EM cloud), we can analogise as follows:

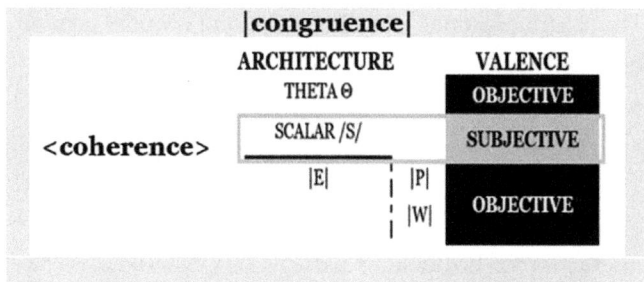

|congruence|		
	ARCHITECTURE	**VALENCE**
	THETA Θ	**OBJECTIVE**
<coherence>	SCALAR /S/	**SUBJECTIVE**
	|E| |P|	**OBJECTIVE**
	|W|	

(1) | congruence | is the property of the EM Cloud.

(2) The Theta Θ axis field is the interaction between the EM Cloud and the network of ST (the actual neuronal cells of the brain).

(3) Note:

   (i) we are not saying that Θ is the EM Cloud; rather

   (ii) it is the interaction between the EM Cloud and /S/, which is what we explain as Θ.

(4) ST constitute their own limits: the mirrors.

(5) ST seeks <coherence>.

(6) That <coherence> is interlaced by EM Cloud and /S/ interaction: which is Θ.

To use a picturesque analogy, Θ is not the cloud, it is the lightning which emanates from it. That EM signal does not carry information in itself. It triggers the passing of

---

[292] to the point of caricature

information via ST.

The 4 dimensional ST/ET (EM cloud) model explains how Θ and /S/ cross-communicate:

- EM signals effect timings within /S/
- /S/ {identation} through ST, activates more EM fields in Θ.

Synaptic activity in /S/ produces EM fields. The interaction of EM fields produces Θ<Constructs>. Those <Constructs> are experienced in /S/ via EM signal stimulation of ST timing.

The 3H principles thus have effect in actual neurophysical processes:

- holistic
- heuristic
- hylomorphic.

McFadden proposes that the EM Cloud operates so as to create spatially cohered representation. As if the EM fields create energy "pictures" which can then guide /S/.

With respect, we disagree. This is to introduce the Interospection Model back into the mix, when we are seeking to get awa from it.

The EM Cloud uses temporal impulse fixing, to generate the action of inequality in forms within /S/. That's all Θ needs to do.

We see yet another reflection of matrixial principles in the different neurophysical attributes of ST and EM Fields:

- /S/ operates in [E] and [I] logic: the logic of substance and moment.
- Θ operates in the logic of equalisation.

Atemporal equalisation is exactly how electromagnetic fields do work. That's how they constitute themselves and interact: see Maxwell's equations.

By contrast {idents} are sticky with the stuff of Substance. The attachment of |E|<Affect> to to /S/<thought> potential is how ideas and feelings have originating creation.

This helps us to understand Mimetics. They are frozen, crystallised atemporal structures. Grammar and syntax are the ordering of {idents} in |T|ime.

By Mimetic communication, we can trigger Θ **EM** "lightning" bursts:

- which effect <coherence> within /S/;

and which

- in |congruence| structure ↔|W|=>P interaction.

<coherence> is impelled in /S/, both by synthetic organic impulse (via the Exclusion Function and $\sum\Omega=>$) and by impulsion from Θ <Constructs>.

There we go, back into the equation chains again. But what we can now see is that the equations describe neurophysical facts. Processes of the brain which we can see and measure, with instruments.

The equations are logical permutations of objective physical reality. An electromagnetic field reality which has been measured, quantitatively, both in space (as millivolts) and in time. Synaptic transmission activity, which has long been so measured.

We arrive at the neurophysical reality of *Secret Self*:
Mentation
How we can think governs what we can think
Emotion
What we can emote governs how we emote

How we can think is governed by the real physical interaction of synaptic transmission in the /S/ubjective continuum, in its interaction with Θ ephaptic emanations from the electromagnetic cloud.

These, in turn, are synchronised in quantised |T|ime, with the objective material realities of the |W|orld. That |W|orld in turn, realises the continuing affective conditions of our |P|hysiology, which manifests via $\sum \Omega$ <Affect> to {identation}, and back again.

We can now, at last, see that the secrets of the Self are

THE NEW NEUROSCIENCE OF MIND

neurophysical realities described by the equation chains of Matrixial Logic and manifested in a Systems Architecture of <coherence> dynamics under perpetual momentary |congruence|.

Perpetual momentary gravitational forces of unbalanced dynamics in harmony, ever seeking and disturbing <coherence>.

Conscious of everything, but unable to say what anything actually means to one's Self. Seeking meaning in an infinite continuum of mirrors. Living in the shadows cast by reflected light.

Your Personality: you as an <I> and you and a <Me>. A contrapuntally spinning globe of |M|entation and |E|motion, the one looking ever back, the other looking ever forward.

The Self never is, never was, anything. The Self always becomes in being.

ANNEX B

TABLE OF SYMBOLS USED IN SECRET SELF

Symb   Meaning / Use

These ML synbols denote construction of an FoR

(A)   Can be a Substance or a Moment

(nA)   Is Substance in being in opposition to (A); also written ^{NOT}

(-A)   Is Moment in becoming negation to (A)

≠   Inequality.
         In speech: "(A) *inequal* (^{NOT}A)"; "(A) *does not equal* (^{NOT}A)"; or "(A) *non aequalis* (^{NOT}A)"; or "(A) *non EQ* (^{NOT}A);
         Sometimes abbreviated in speech to: "(A) *NQ* (^{NOT}A);
         And in like manner for any speech using ≠

=   Aequalis / Equals. Not the same meaning as in 2 +2 =4. The symbol implies *translates as*

[E]   The Form of Being: of Substances. A deducted FoR.

[I]   The Form of Becoming: of Moments. A deducted FoR.

[C]   Chaos: a non-Form; or Anti-Form

/S/   Scalar: an inducted Perspective. Not an FoR.

Θ   Theta

Si   Singularity

>   Moving from one line of ML Equation to another. Indicates "and so…"

≈   Equivalent: when an ML equation, expressed in ML Symbols, is turned into ordinary language

∴	Therefore [used as the concluding line of a syllogism
◊	Spacetime: the dimension of Substance
∞	Infinity: the dimension of Moments
C	Chaos: the dimension without Forms
Δ	Potential[I]: the capacity of Infinity to produce Moments
□	Actuality

These ML synbols denote operation within an FoR

≥	Shows we are moving from an FoR to operations within an FoR
n	Shows we are iterating, or one might say, "pluralising"
⇔	This is a "shadow" iteration within an FoR. It is an inherently unstable (conditional) iteration. So the operation cannot be notated by the classic =
{ }	These brackets contrast with the usual [ ]. They notate that the Form is being operated "internally". It notates that this is no longer a real Form, but a "shadow" ₍orm
₍orm	The referential use of a Form within its own FoR: a Shadow ₍orm

Symb   **Meaning / Use**

These are symbols used in ML TransFormations

| [~] | Intersection: indicates a transforming point between 2 frames of reference |
| ∑ | In logic and mathematics, this sign usually means "sum". In ML, it means "aggregation"; "taken together as". Indicates a Node |

817

FoR$_2$ The subscript shows us the number of Forms that we are aggregating. The subscript number can be anything from $_2$ to $_n$

| Held in perspective with. Where 2 MLE are held in a relationship of Potential^P

ᴍ̄   Collapse of an Infinity ∞ by an Event □

Φ   Interference between ∞

Ю   Interaction between Θ and |W|

These are symbols used in Matrxial Time Functions

T   Temporal Reference

Ɔ^n Chrone

| Annihilation

ℂ^n Chrono Gap

These are symbols used in Matrxial Emotion Functions

(ɛ)   Ohm Antipole

(ɔ)   Inverse Ohm Antipole

Ω   Ohm

€   <Affect>

These are symbols used in the Exclusion Function

≥ς   Signal

≤Ə   potential

∫   function

| | gap

These are symbols used in /S/

⊤   <Throught> potential

ŧ   {ident}

Ш   Shadow Slice

818

KEYBOARD SHORTCUTS FOR
SYMBOLS USED IN MATRIXIAL LOGIC

Many ML Symbols can be accessed through standard keyboard operations. These following can be accessed through the specified keyboard operations.[293]

Symb   **Shortcut Type**

$\neq$ 2260 Alt+x

NOT   Ctrl+ Shift + + [press again to release superscript]

2   Ctrl+ = [press again to release subscript]

$\approx$ 2248 Alt+x

$\therefore$ Hold Alt; type on numeric keyboard 8756

$\geq$ underline >

n   Ctrl+ =

$\Leftrightarrow$ Type: < = >

Σ 2211 Alt+x

∞ 221e Alt+x

$\Diamond$ 25ca Alt+x

$|$ 2502 Alt+x

Δ 2206 Alt+x

$\square$ 25a1 Alt+x

m̄   20bc Alt+x

Φ 03a6 Alt+x

$\pm$ Alt + 0177

$\top$ 20b8 Alt+x

---

[293] Note: specified only for MS Word; qwerty keyboard (UK); operating in Windows Office. Specifications may be different with Mac operating system.

∀	2200 Alt+x
⌐	2518 Alt+x
⌐	2510 Alt+x
ˇ	02c7 Alt+x
Φ	03a6 Alt+x
Φ	03a6 Alt+x
₸	20b8 Alt+x
∀	2200 Alt+x
⌐	2510 Alt+x
⌐	2518 Alt+x
ˇ	02c7 Alt+x
Ͳ	0372 Alt+x
₾	20be Alt+x
ϼ	037c Alt+x
ͽ	037d Alt+x
Ω	2126 Alt+x
Ↄ	2183 Alt+x
α	03b1 Alt+x
β	03b2 Alt+x
ω	03c9 Alt+x
(ϼ)	037c Alt+x
(ͽ)	037d Alt+x
€	Ctrl + Alt+ E
≥ς	2265 Alt+x; 03c2 Alt+x
≤Э	2264 Alt+x; 042d Alt+x
₸	20b8 Alt+x
₺	20ba Alt+x
Ш	0428 Alt+x
Ю	042e Alt+x

ANNEX C

LIST OF EXPERIENCES